THE NEW DEAL

The
NEW DEAL
Conflicting Interpretations and Shifting Perspectives

EDITED BY

Melvyn Dubofsky

Department of History
State University of New York at Binghamton

GARLAND PUBLISHING, INC.
New York & London
1992

All essays are reprinted by permission of the original publishers.

Library of Congress Cataloging-in-Publication Data

The New Deal : conflicting interpretations and shifting perspectives /
edited by Melvyn Dubofsky.
      p. cm.
Includes bibliographical references and index.
ISBN 0-8153-0765-9
1. New Deal, 1933–1939. 2. United States—History—1933–1945. I.
Dubofsky, Melvyn, 1934– .
E806.N4147 1992   91–42818
973.917–dc20   CIP

Printed on acid-free, 250-year-life paper
Manufactured in the United States of America

CONTENTS

EDITOR'S INTRODUCTION

The Great Depression and the New Deal of the 1930s represented an extraordinary watershed in twentieth-century United States history. Domestic economic catastrophe and the New Deal response to it left no aspect of American society, economics, politics, and culture untouched. Out of economic misery and the efforts to cure it emerged the modern American leviathan state; the New Deal Democratic party as the dominant national political organization and exemplar of "American pluralism," enrolling in its ranks citizens of nearly every nationality, religion, and race; and the American nation as an active player in the affairs of the world. What the chief executive officer of the United States Steel Company, Myron Taylor, characterized as the "turbulent years" set the stage for the emergence of the United States as a hegemonic global power in the decades following World War II.

From the Great Depression to the 1980s, the New Deal set the agenda for American history. Whether embellished in Harry S Truman's Fair Deal or John F. Kennedy's New Frontier, or Lyndon B. Johnson's Great Society, Democratic Presidents promised to expand the rudimentary social welfare state initially created by the New Deal of Franklin D. Roosevelt. Even such Republican chief executives as Dwight D. Eisenhower and Richard M. Nixon either legitimated the basic reforms implemented by the New Deal or, in the case of the latter, widened them at the margin. And from Truman to Nixon, the Democratic party remained the majority party nationally in terms of voter identification as well as political home for a diverse coalition of citizens. During the 1980s, however, what had been taken for granted for nearly half a century came to an end, so much so that two younger scholars in their introduction to a collection of essays that they edited in 1989 proclaimed bluntly that "The New Deal order is dead."[1]

Not only is the New Deal now truly a part of the past rather than the present, but it is also the subject of an ever-growing corpus of historical literature. Since the 1930s the scholarship published on the Great Depression and the New Deal has multiplied geometrically. Not only have histories of the subject proliferated over six decades, but fashions in interpreting the New Deal have shifted as well. At first historians and other scholars acted the role of judges. They tended to condemn businesspeople and Republicans for subjecting the masses of American people to the sufferings of the Great Depression. By contrast, most early interpreters of the New Deal esteemed Franklin D. Roosevelt, his advisers, and the Democratic party as the saviors of the American nation and its people. To such historians as Arthur M. Schlesinger, Jr., Eric Goldman, James MacGregor Burns, and others, Roosevelt and his administration not only lifted the United States from the depths of depression, but they also provided an alternative to the totalitarianism of Adolf Hitler, Benito Mussolini, and Josef Stalin. For such scholars, the New Deal culminated more than a century of American reform, which swept from the Jeffersonians through the Jacksonians, Populists, and Progressives, and in which the people triumphed over the interests, the commonweal over business cupidity.[2] Summing up what had by the early 1960s become the conventional wisdom in a book that took a more dispassionate view of the New Deal and that tried to be as critical as it was laudatory, the historian William Leuchtenburg concluded that Roosevelt and his associates "fashioned a government which sought to make the industrial system more humane. . . . Heirs of the Enlightenment, they felt themselves part of a broadly humanistic movement to make man's life on earth more tolerable, a movement that might someday even achieve a co-operative commonwealth."[3]

Almost as soon as Leuchtenburg wrote those words, a reaction erupted among a younger generation of scholars who saw far less to praise in Roosevelt and his New Deal. Often themselves active participants in the upheavals of another turbulent decade, the 1960s, these "revisionist" scholars charged the New Dealers with failing to alleviate the impact of economic depression; with leaving the rich and powerful, whose policies and selfishness had produced the Great Depression, with as much wealth and power as they had enjoyed before the economic collapse; with creating an all-powerful central state that limited the liberties of its citizens without eradicating the legacy of poverty, racism, and sexism; and, finally, with bequeathing the nation an economy as capitalistic and inegalitarian as it had been during the heyday of the Roaring Twenties. Barton Bernstein's essay, "The New Deal: The Conservative Achievements of Liberal Reform," reprinted in this volume, represents perhaps the most succinct yet fullest indictment of the New Deal by the revisionists.[4]

Since the late 1960s and early 1970s, scholarship about the Great Depression and the New Deal has grown more subtle, sophisticated, and international in scope. Instead of searching for villains or heroes (Herbert Hoover and the plutocrats vs. Roosevelt and the masses), scholars now seek instead to understand better the factors that precipitated depression and the substantial changes wrought in the American nation by the New Deal. They are equally interested in exposing the structural and cultural obstacles to reform during the 1930s. Borrowing heavily from the more theoretical work of political scientists and sociologists, historians shifted their attention away from great leaders and Presidents to the deeper, more perdurable long-term structural factors at work in the national society, economy, polity, and culture. Historians, however, unlike the more theoretically inclined social scientists, stressed the complexity of human experience and the power of historical contingency. Part of this shift in interpretation was prefigured as early as 1964 in Leuchtenburg's essay "The New Deal and the Analogue of War" in which he suggested how the experiences of key New Dealers during the era of World War I simultaneously shaped their response to economic catastrophe and circumscribed their ability to lift the economy from depression. Two years later, in 1966, Ellis Hawley showed how the heavy hand of the past limited the ability of New Dealers to regulate giant enterprises in the public interest.[5]

More recently, however, political scientists, sociologists, and even historians have constructed a far more sophisticated conceptualization of the relationship between the state and society in the twentieth-century United States, especially for the years during and since the New Deal. No single approach or theory unites these scholars who have altered our understanding of the New Deal experience, yet certain common threads of interpretation can be discerned. For one thing, contemporary scholarship examines groups more than individuals. Students of voting behavior, for example, trace how class, ethnicity, race, and religion as well as region affect political choices in the polling place. For the era of the New Deal they have stressed how an amalgam of white and nonwhite, old-stock, old-immigrant and new immigrant (or ethnic), Protestant, Catholic, and Jewish, urban and rural elements combined to create the Democratic party coalition.[6] Scholars of business and the economy examine how functional groups have organized themselves and through organization influenced the state to serve private interests. They have developed an interpretation of the New Deal that stresses "corporatism," that is, how functionally related groups seek to amass for themselves the power of self-regulation, and how such groups harnessed the authority of the government to advance private interests through a broker state that showered its favors on organized groups with the greatest political power.[7]

Thomas Ferguson's essay, "Industrial Conflict and the Coming of the New Deal," offers an excellent example of this new approach. Ferguson attempts to prove that capital-intensive, mass-consumption, multinational enterprises linked to major investment banking houses and mass-market retail establishments sponsored the most innovative of New Deal reforms in order to serve their own special economic needs. Ferguson, indeed, comes close to an interpretation of the New Deal that may be characterized as neo-Marxist. The American neo-Marxists, whose work relies heavily on a group of French theorists of capitalism and "Fordism," argue that a relatively autonomous state acts to save capitalism as a system in the long run by opposing the short-term interests of individual capitalists, who lack the foresight to deal with economic crisis. State managers intervene to protect businesspeople from themselves by modifying and reforming capitalism in a manner that preserves its viability. In interpreting the New Deal, neo-Marxists thus have a ready explanation for why the Roosevelt administration enacted the social security system and promoted trade unionism and collective bargaining in the face of vigorous opposition from the business community.[8]

Theda Skocpol's essay, "Political Response to Capitalist Crisis," provides a particularly fine example of a neo-Marxist interpretation of the New Deal. Skocpol clearly outlines conflicting interpretations of the New Deal and through an examination of labor law reform (the Wagner Act) explains why her conceptualization of state managers as relatively autonomous political actors proves superior to that of traditional Marxists, who view the state as an instrumental slugging agency for the capitalist class, and of corporatists and pluralists who see the state as a broker among competing private interest groups.

While sociologists and political scientists have done a great deal to clarify aspects of the New Deal experience, much of the more recent historical scholarship on the subject has exposed the contradictions and contingencies that hampered the efforts of reformers to combat economic catastrophe. Without doubt, large numbers of working people, farm folk, women, and nonwhites, especially African-Americans, felt deeply grateful to Roosevelt and the Democratic party. They credited the New Dealers with saving them from starvation, providing millions of workers with alternative forms of public employment, protecting private homes and farms from the mortgage hammer, promoting the cause of trade unionism, demonstrating special solicitude for nonwhites, and offering women influential roles in the administration. In return, workers, farmers, women reformers, and African-Americans gave their loyalty and votes to the Democratic party. Yet, for most of these people and groups, the New Deal's promises remained only partly redeemed on the eve of World War II.[9]

Among all Americans the Great Depression and the New Deal had the greatest single impact upon the lives of working people. The Depression cut like a giant scythe through the ranks of workers, leaving nearly a third of the labor force without jobs and income at the depth of the economic contraction in the winter of 1932–1933. Despite sometimes dramatic improvements in the level of employment during the next six years, mass joblessness remained the reality for working people until the outbreak of World War II. As a consequence of unemployment, millions of Americans lost their homes, automobiles, and dreams of a better future. For the first time in American history, new entrants to the labor force could not expect to improve on the situation of their parents and elders. John Garraty's essay suggests how devastating was the joblessness associated with depression, the global character of the phenomenon of unemployment, and also how powerful political and cultural traditions limited the ability of public officials to reduce joblessness.[10] And William Bremer's article on the New Deal's efforts to aid the unemployed illustrates that, although the federal government provided jobs and incomes for millions of workers, the program, in Bremer's words, "remained more relief than work, more charity than employment."

The reforms associated with the New Deal, however, prompted workers to act forcefully in order to transform disillusionment into hope, frustration into achievement, and failure into success. From 1933 through 1937, workers rebelled against the circumstances of their lives and sought to grasp a share of power from those who had heretofore dominated them. Massive waves of strikes flowed across the country in its major industries in the years 1934 and 1937. A labor movement that had fallen on hard times between 1922 and 1929 and then nearly expired in the early years of the Depression rejuvenated itself. Part of the labor militancy had been generated by what the historian Irving Bernstein and others have character- ized as the New Deal revolution in labor law. Another part of the militancy cascaded directly from the activities of workers who were no longer willing to subjugate their needs and desires to the whims of others with more power. Whatever the source of the new labor militancy, masses of American workers acted to transform every- day work practices on the factory floor, the distribution of power between employers and employees, and the structure of national political parties. For the first time in United States history, trade unions wrested recognition and collective bargaining agreements from such corporate giants as General Motors, U.S. Steel, General Electric, and Westinghouse. The number of union members soared from under 3 million in early 1933 to more than 8 million by 1939. Along with the resurgence of trade unionism came a political reawakening among workers. In many industrial centers, workers built their own political organizations and grasped for a full share of local power. More often than not, however, the political reawakening made itself felt within the Democratic party. In the words of the historian Lizabeth Cohen, "workers made their own New Deal."[11]

Two of the essays in this collection stress the persistence of older patterns in the labor history of the 1930s. My essay, for example, concedes that the years of the Great Depression were a turbulent decade for workers during which the labor movement transformed itself, and workers awakened politically. Yet it also seeks to suggest how cultural traditions and ethnoracial influences shaped the labor militancy in a manner that limited its transforma- tive impact. Christopher Tomlins's article reminds readers that, although much of the labor history of the 1930s revolved around the efforts of mass-production workers to form new unions and the role of the Congress of Industrial Organizations (CIO) in that process, the more traditional craft and quasi-industrial unions in the established American Federation of Labor (AFL) proved far more successful than the new unions in recruiting members and benefitting from the reforms of the New Deal.[12]

Closely associated with the militancy of workers and the transformation of industrial relations was the so-called New Deal legal revolution. During the first years of the New Deal, the federal judiciary, especially the Supreme Court, stood as a conservative bulwark against the more far-reaching reforms of the Roosevelt administration. As a result, the President decided in 1937 to declare political war against the Supreme Court by proposing a plan to increase the number of sitting justices, a proposal condemned by its critics as "court packing." Although Roosevelt lost, and lost badly, in his attempt to restructure the Supreme Court, he achieved his larger goals. In a series of rulings beginning in the spring and summer of 1937, many of which concerned aspects of New Deal labor policy, the Supreme Court reversed precedents that had limited the federal government's power to regulate industry, labor relations, wages, and working conditions. By the end of the 1930s, new appointments to the Supreme Court and to lesser federal courts produced what many scholars referred to as a revolution in constitutional law. New Deal judges simultaneously implemented and reinterpreted basic aspects of labor and property law, giving them more liberal and sometimes radical twists. They also extended more widely than ever before in U.S. history the civil liberties of American citizens, making the Bill of Rights and the Fourteenth Amendment apply more broadly across the board. In the words of one federal circuit court judge, "Perhaps the cackle of the farmer's hen as she announces the completion of her daily chore, or the squeal of the pig in its struggle to become a porker, are beyond the boundary line [federal power under the commerce clause], but of this we give no assurance."[13] Yet, as with so many other aspects of the New Deal experience, the revolution in law imprisoned people and institutions as it liberated them. Christopher Tomlins's essay on New Deal labor law and industrial pluralism hints at the price that workers and their unions paid for the new legal rights that they obtained from New Deal reforms in industrial relations.[14]

A similar story repeated itself in New Deal relations with African-Americans. Black Americans were among the primary beneficiaries of New Deal reforms that provided public employment for the jobless, minimum wages and maximum hours of work, and public housing for the urban working class. In gratitude for such material benefits, African-Americans switched their political loyalties from the party of Abraham Lincoln to that of Roosevelt, for, as

Harvard Sitkoff's work has shown, the New Deal was indeed just that for them. Yet the Democratic party also still relied on votes from the lily-white South whose politicians dominated many of the most vital congressional committees. Southern white influence in Congress largely explained why southern black tenant farmers and sharecroppers found themselves forced off the land as a result of New Deal agricultural reforms, and why in cities, such as Cleveland, the subject of Christopher Wye's article, African-Americans simultaneously benefitted from public employment and public housing but suffered from persistent racial segregation and exclusion.[15]

Women, too, experienced the New Deal in a contradictory fashion. Women were a major beneficiary of the New Deal's efforts to create a modern welfare state. The New Deal also offered many women an opportunity to prove how much they had to offer public life as reformers and administrators. Yet the New Deal persisted in treating most women primarily as potential wives-mothers and future homemakers of America. For many federal reformers, welfare reforms amounted to a form of natalism intended to protect women's biologically determined destiny as mothers of the race.[16]

No sector of the American economy suffered more from the Great Depression than agriculture, and fewer people endured more misery than small farmers, especially the tenants and sharecroppers among them. Farmers, moreover, had never fully recovered economically from the post–World War I depression of 1920–1921. Already in parlous economic condition, many farmers were devastated by the Great Depression of the 1930s. These were the rural folk symbolized, some might say mythologized, in John Steinbeck's novel *The Grapes of Wrath*. The displaced and wandering Okies, portrayed so empathetically by Steinbeck, were, however, only one element among the afflicted agrarian poor folk. African-Americans in the South and Chicanos in the Southwest suffered greater displacement from the land, deeper deprivation, and fewer opportunities than Steinbeck's poor white folk.

Although the New Deal did much to revitalize and improve rural life in the United States, it lavished its benefits most generously on the larger, more commercialized farmers. True, the New Deal brought electricity to rural areas, tamed wild rivers through flood-control projects, and encouraged new and better forms of soil conservation. Few of those benefits, however, touched the poorest farmers and especially those who worked the land without owning it. Indeed, the New Deal agricultural reforms hastened the process that for decades had pushed marginal rural people from the countryside to the city, while laying the foundation for the post–World War II system of large-scale, heavily capitalized, hyper-productive, and world-market dependent American agriculture. As the twentieth century drew to its end, the United States still felt the impact of New Deal agricultural reforms in its cities as well as the countryside. As Theodore Saloutos writes in the article reprinted in this collection, "The New Deal with all its limitations and frustrations . . . constituted the greatest innovative epoch in the history of American agriculture." Saloutos's article provides readers with a full overview of New Deal agricultural policy, one that treats its deficiencies as well as its strengths.[17]

Like all collections of essays and articles, this one unfortunately cannot offer its readers perspectives on all aspects of its subject. I feel especially displeased that the demands of economics and space rendered it impossible to include more material concerning the New Deal's impact on thought and culture or to illustrate the enormous interest that foreign scholars have shown about the Roosevelt years. That being admitted, I trust that this collection enables readers to see and to appreciate the New Deal in all its complexity and contradictions and to understand how and why it shaped the next five decades of U.S. history.[18] If the New Deal order is truly dead, as Fraser and Gerstle have written, we may now ask, what will come to replace it?

NOTES

1. Steve Fraser and Gary Gerstle, eds., *The Rise and Fall of the New Deal Order, 1930–1980* (Princeton, 1989), xxiv.

2. Arthur M. Schlesinger, Jr., *The Age of Roosevelt*, 3 vols. (Boston, 1957–60); Eric F. Goldman, *Rendezvous with Destiny: A History of Modern American Reform* (New York, 1952); James MacGregor Burns, *Roosevelt: The Lion and the Fox* (New York, 1956).

3. William E. Leuchtenburg, *Franklin D. Roosevelt and the New Deal, 1932–1940* (New York, 1963), pp. 345–346.

4. For an equally condemnatory and fine example of such historical scholarship see Ronald Radosh, "The Myth of the New Deal," in R. Radosh and Murray Rothbard, eds., *A New History of Leviathan: Essays on the Rise of the American Corporate State* (New York, 1972), pp. 146–187.

5. E. Hawley, "The New Deal and the Analogue of War," in John Braeman, John Bremner, and Raymond Walters, eds., *Change and*

Continuity in Twentieth-Century America (Columbus, OH, 1964), pp. 81–143; E. Hawley, *The New Deal and the Problem of Monopoly: A Study in Economic Ambivalence* (Princeton, 1966).

6. Kristi Andersen, *The Creation of a Democratic Majority, 1928–1936* (Chicago, 1979); Gerald H. Gamm, *The Making of New Deal Democrats: Voting Behavior and Realignment in Boston, 1920–1940* (Chicago, 1989); Samuel Lubell, *The Future of American Politics* (New York, 1965 ed.), *passim*, esp. pp. 179–182.

7. One of the key texts concerning the broker state and the privatization of public power is Theodore J. Lowi, *The End of Liberalism: Ideology Policy, and the Crisis of Public Authority* (New York, 1969); for general statements of the theme of corporatism, see Ellis W. Hawley, "The Discovery and Study of 'Corporate Liberalism,'" *Business History Review*, 52 (Autumn 1978), 309–320, and Louis Galambos, "Technology, Political Economy, and Professionalization: Central Themes of the Organization Synthesis," *Business History Review*, 57 (Winter 1983), 471–493; for the corporatist interpretation as applied by a student of labor history see Steven Fraser, *Labor Will Rule: Sidney Hillman and the Rise of American Labor* (New York, 1991); and for an overview of the economy during the Depression that examines stagnation and growth in sectoral terms see Michael Bernstein, *The Great Depression: Delayed Recovery and Economic Change in America, 1929–1939* (New York, 1987).

8. Nicos Poulantzas, *Political Power and Social Classes* (London, 1973); Michel Aglietta, *A Theory of Capitalist Regulation: The U.S. Experience* (London, 1979); and Alan Lipietz, "New Tendencies in the International Division of Labor: Regimes of Accumulation and Modes of Regulation," in Allen J. Scott and Michael Storpor, eds., *Production, Work, Territory: The Geographical Anatomy of Industrial Capitalism* (Boston, 1986), and "Rebel Sons: The Regulation School," *French Politics and Society*, 5 (Sept. 1987) for French theories. For U.S. theoreticians of the state and society see Fred Block, "The Ruling Class Does Not Rule: Notes on the Marxist Theory of the State," *Socialist Revolution*, 33 (May–June 1977), 6–28, and "Beyond Relative Autonomy," in Ralph Miliband and John Saville, eds., *The Socialist Register 1980* (London, 1980) pp. 227–242; Margaret Weir and Theda Skocpol, "State Structures and the Possibilities for 'Keynesian' Responses to the Great Depression in Sweden, Britain, and the United States," in Peter B. Evans, et al., eds., *Bringing the State Back In* (New York, 1985), pp. 107–163; and Margaret Weir, Ann Shola Orloff, and Theda Skocpol, eds., *The Politics of Social Policy in the United States* (Princeton, 1988) for a collection of essays that analyzes the American welfare state from a neo-Marxist perspective.

9. For a recent review-essay that stresses the contingent character and limited impact of New Deal reforms see John Braeman, "The New Deal: The Collapse of the Liberal Consensus," *The Canadian Review of American Studies*, 19 (July 1989), 41–80.

10. For an especially fine survey of the history of unemployment in the United States from the late nineteenth century to the Great

Depression, see Alexander Keyssar, *Out of Work: The First Century of Unemployment in Massachusetts* (New York, 1986).

11. Many books and articles stress the labor upheaval associated with the New Deal and the aroused militancy among working people. The classic study remains Irving Bernstein, *Turbulent Years: A History of the American Worker, 1933–1941* (Boston, 1970). Other more recent books, which stress the left-wing origins of the labor upheaval, include Bruce Nelson, *Workers on the Waterfront: Seamen, Longshoremen, and Unionism in the 1930s* (Urbana, IL, 1988); Joshua Freeman, *In Transit: The Transport Workers in New York City, 1933–1966* (New York, 1989), Chs. 3–9; and Gary Gerstle, *Working-Class Americanism: The Politics of Labor in a Textile City, 1914–1960* (New York, 1989), Chs. 3–7. For a somewhat different perspective on the same process, see Lizabeth Cohen, *Making a New Deal: Industrial Workers in Chicago, 1919– 1939* (New York, 1990), Chs. 5–8. Two excellent essays along the same line are James R. Green, "Working Class Militancy in the Depression," *Radical America*, 6 (Nov.–Dec. 1972), 1–35, and Bruce Nelson, "'Pentecost' on the Pacific: Maritime Workers and Working-Class Consciousness in the 1930s," *Political Power and Social Research: A Research Annual*, 4 (1984), 141–182.

12. For other writings that suggest a similar version of working-class reality during the 1930s, see, for example, David Brody, "Labor and the Great Depression: The Interpretive Prospects," *Labor History*, XIII (Spring 1972), 231–244; Daniel Nelson, *American Rubber Workers and Organized Labor, 1900–1941* (Princeton, 1989), Chs. 5–11, and "The CIO at Bay: Labor Militancy and Politics in Akron, 1936–1938, " *Journal of American History*, 71 (Dec. 1984), 565–586; Steven Fraser, *Labor Will Rule*, Chs. 10–14; and Robert Zieger, *Rebuilding the Pulp and Paper Workers' Union* (Knoxville, TN, 1984). For two excellent contributions that apply more theoretical and social scientific perspectives to the subject, see Stanley Vittoz, *New Deal Labor Policy and the American Industrial Economy* (Chapel Hill, NC, 1987) and David Plotke, "The Wagner Act, Again: Politics and Labor, 1935–37, " *Studies in American Political Development*, 3 (1989), 105–156.

13. Cited in Charles Fahy, "The NLRB and the Courts," in Louis G. Silverberg, ed., *The Wagner Act: After Ten Years* (Washington, 1945), p. 49.

14. For similar interpretations of the impact of the judicial revolution on workers and unions see, Karl Klare, "Judicial Deradicalization of the Wagner Act and the Origins of Modern Legal Consciousness, 1937–1941," *Minnesota Law Review*, 62 (March 1978), 265–339; Katherine Stone, "The Post-War Paradigm in American Labor Law," *Yale Law Journal*, 90 (June 1981), 1509–1580; and James Atleson, *Values and Assumptions in American Labor Law* (Amherst, MA, 1983).

15. Harvard Sitkoff, *A New Deal for Blacks: The Emergence of Civil Rights as National Issue* (New York, 1978); Nancy Weiss, *Farewell to the Party of Lincoln: Black Politics in the Age of FDR* (Princeton, 1983).

16. For fuller treatments of these themes see Susan Ware, *Beyond*

Suffrage: Women in the New Deal (Boston, 1982); Lois Scharf, *To Work and to Wed: Female Employment, Feminism. and the Great Depression* (Westport, CT, 1980); and Winifred Wandersee, *Women's Work and Family Values, 1920–1940* (Cambridge, MA, 1981). On the connection between the welfare state and natalism see Sonya Michel and Seth Koven, "Womanly Duties: Maternalist Politics and the Origins of the Welfare State in France, Germany, Great Britain, and the United States, 1880–1920," *American Historical Review*, 95 (Oct. 1990), 1076–1108.

17. For other perspectives on New Deal agricultural reforms and the costs it exacted among poorer farmers and agricultural workers see David Conrad, *The Forgotten Farmers: The Story of Sharecroppers in the New Deal* (Urbana, IL, 1965); Cletus Daniel, *Bitter Harvest: A History of California Farm Workers, 1870–1941* (Berkeley, 1981), Chs. 6–8; James N. Gregory, *American Exodus: The Dust Bowl Migration and Okie Culture in California* (New York, 1989).

18. For a collection of essays by foreign scholars that stresses the cultural aspects of the New Deal see Maurizio Vaudagna, ed., *L'Estetica Della Politica Europa e America Negli Anni Trenti* (Turin, Italy, 1988). For the impact of the New Deal on thought and culture see Richard Pells, *Radical Visions and American Dreams: Culture and Thought in the Depression Years* (New York, 1973); L. Cohen, *Making a New Deal*, Ch. 8; G. Gerstle, *Working-Class Americanism*, Chs. 5–8; and Warren Susman, *Culture as History: The Transformation of American Society in the Twentieth Century* (New York, 1984).

SOURCE LIST

Bernstein, Barton J.
> "The New Deal: The Conservative Achievements of Liberal Reform," in Barton Bernstein, ed., *Towards a New Past: Dissenting Essays in American History* (Pantheon Books, 1968), pp. 263–268.

Ferguson, Thomas.
> "Industrial Conflict and the Coming of the New Deal: The Triumph of Multinational Liberalism in America," in Fraser and Gerstle, *The Rise and Fall of the New Deal Order, 1930–1980* (Princeton: Princeton Univ. Press, 1989), 3–31.

Skocpol, Theda.
> "Political Response to Capitalist Crisis: Neo-Marxist Theories of the State and the Case of the New Deal, *Politics and Society* 10 (1980), 155–201.

Zieger, Robert H.
> "Herbert Hoover: A Reinterpretation," *American Historical Review* 81 (1976), 800–810.

Dubofsky, Melvyn.
> "Not So 'Turbulent Years': Another Look at the American 1930s," *Amerikastudien/American Studies* 24 (1979), 5–20. Reprinted with the permission of the Institut für Englische Philologie.

Tomlins, Christopher L.
> "AFL Unions in the 1930s: Their Performance in Historical Perspective," *Journal of American History* 65 (1979), 1021–1042.

Garraty, John A.
> "Unemployment During the Great Depression," *Labor History* 17 (1976), 133–159.

Bremer, William W.
> "Along the 'American Way': The New Deal's Work Relief Programs for the Unemployed," *Journal of American History* 62 (1975), 636–652.

Saloutos, Theodore.
> "New Deal Agricultural Policy: An Evaluation," *Journal of American History* 61 (1974), 394–416.

Wye, Christopher G.

"The New Deal and the Negro Community: Toward a Broader Conceptualization," *Journal of American History* 5-9 (1972), 621–639.

Leuchtenburg, William E.

"Franklin D. Roosevelt's Supreme Court 'Packing' Plan," in Hollingworth & Holmes, eds., *Essays on the New Deal* (Austin: Texas Univ. Press, 1969), 69–115. Used by permission of the Walter Prescott Webb Memorial Lecture Committee, The University of Texas at Arlington.

Tomlins, Christopher L.

"The New Deal, Collective Bargaining, and the Triumph of Industrial Pluralism," *Industrial and Labor Relations Review* 39 (1985), 19–34.

THE NEW DEAL: THE CONSERVATIVE ACHIEVEMENTS OF LIBERAL REFORM

Barton J. Bernstein

Writing from a liberal democratic consensus, many American historians in the past two decades have praised the Roosevelt administration for its nonideological flexibility and for its far-ranging reforms. To many historians, particularly those who reached intellectual maturity during the depression,[1] the government's accomplishments, as well as the drama and passion, marked the decade as a watershed, as a dividing line in the American past.

Enamored of Franklin D. Roosevelt and recalling the bitter opposition to welfare measures and restraints upon business, many liberal historians have emphasized the New Deal's discontinuity with the immediate past. For them there was a "Roosevelt Revolution," or at the very least a dramatic achievement of a beneficent liberalism which had developed in fits and spurts during the preceding three decades.[2] Rejecting earlier interpretations which viewed the New Deal as socialism[3] or state capitalism,[4] they have also disregarded theories of syndicalism[5] or of corporate liberalism.[6] The New Deal has generally commanded their approval for such laws or institutions as minimum wages, public housing, farm assistance, the Tennessee Valley Authority, the Wagner Act, more progressive taxation, and social security. For most liberal historians the New Deal means the replenishment of democracy, the rescuing of the federal government from the clutches of big business, the significant redistribution of political power. Breaking with laissez faire, the new administration, according to these interpretations, marked the end of the passive or impartial state and the beginning of positive government, of the interventionist state acting to offset concentrations of private power, and affirming the rights and responding to the needs of the underprivileged.

From the perspective of the late 1960s these themes no longer seem adequate to characterize the New Deal. The liberal reforms of the New Deal did not transform the American system; they conserved and protected American corporate capitalism, occasionally by absorbing parts of threatening programs. There was no significant redistribution of power in American society, only lim-ited recognition of other organized groups, seldom of unorganized peoples. Neither the bolder programs advanced by New Dealers nor the final legislation greatly extended the beneficence of gov-ernment beyond the middle classes or drew upon the wealth of the few for the needs of the many. Designed to maintain the American system, liberal activity was directed toward essentially conservative goals. Experimentalism was most frequently limited to means; sel-dom did it extend to ends. Never questioning private enterprise, it operated within safe channels, far short of Marxism or even of native American radicalisms that offered structural critiques and structural solutions.

All of this is not to deny the changes wrought by the New Deal—the extension of welfare programs, the growth of federal power, the strengthening of the executive, even the narrowing of property rights. But it is to assert that the elements of continuity are stronger, that the magnitude of change has been exaggerated. The New Deal failed to solve the problem of depression, it failed to raise the impoverished, it failed to redistribute income, it failed to extend equality and generally countenanced racial discrimination and segregation. It failed generally to make business more respon-sible to the social welfare or to threaten business's pre-eminent political power. In this sense, the New Deal, despite the shifts in tone and spirit from the earlier decade, was profoundly conserva-tive and continuous with the 1920s.

I

Rather than understanding the 1920s as a "return to normalcy," the period is more properly interpreted by focusing on the con-tinuation of progressive impulses, demands often frustrated by the rivalry of interest groups, sometimes blocked by the resistance of Harding and Coolidge, and occasionally by Hoover.[7] Through these years while agriculture and labor struggled to secure advan-tages from the federal government, big business flourished. Praised for creating American prosperity, business leaders easily convinced the nation that they were socially responsible, that they were ful-filling the needs of the public.[8] Benefitting from earlier legislation that had promoted economic rationalization and stability, they were opponents of federal benefits to other groups but seldom propo-nents of laissez faire.[9]

In no way did the election of Herbert Hoover in 1928 seem to challenge the New Era. An heir of Wilson, Hoover promised an even closer relationship with big business and moved beyond Harding and Coolidge by affirming federal responsibility for prosperity. As Secretary of Commerce, Hoover had opposed unbridled competition and had transformed his department into a vigorous friend of business. Sponsoring trade associations, he promoted industrial self-regulation and the increased rationalization of business. He had also expanded foreign trade, endorsed the regulation of new forms of communications, encouraged relief in disasters, and recommended public works to offset economic declines.[10]

By training and experience, few men in American political life seemed better prepared than Hoover to cope with the depression. Responding promptly to the crisis, he acted to stabilize the economy and secured the agreement of businessmen to maintain production and wage rates. Unwilling to let the economy "go through the wringer," the President requested easier money, self-liquidating public works, lower personal and corporate income taxes, and stronger commodity stabilization corporations.[11] In reviewing these unprecedented actions, Walter Lippmann wrote, "The national government undertook to make the whole economic order operate prosperously."[12]

But these efforts proved inadequate. The tax cut benefitted the wealthy and failed to raise effective demand. The public works were insufficient. The commodity stabilization corporations soon ran out of funds, and agricultural prices kept plummeting. Businessmen cut back production, dismissed employees, and finally cut wages. As unemployment grew, Hoover struggled to inspire confidence, but his words seemed hollow and his understanding of the depression limited. Blaming the collapse on European failures, he could not admit that American capitalism had failed. When prodded by Congress to increase public works, to provide direct relief, and to further unbalance the budget, he doggedly resisted. Additional deficits would destroy business confidence, he feared, and relief would erode the principles of individual and local responsibility.[13] Clinging to faith in voluntarism, Hoover also briefly rebuffed the efforts by financiers to secure the Reconstruction Finance Corporation (RFC). Finally endorsing the RFC,[14] he also supported expanded lending by Federal Land Banks, recommended home-loan banks, and even approved small federal loans (usually inadequate) to states needing funds for relief. In this burst of activity, the President had moved to the very limits of his ideology.

Restricted by his progressive background and insensitive to politics and public opinion, he stopped far short of the state corporatism urged by some businessmen and politicians. With capitalism crumbling he had acted vigorously to save it, but he would not yield to the representatives of business or disadvantaged groups who wished to alter the government.[15] He was reluctant to use the federal power to achieve through compulsion what could not be realized through voluntary means. Proclaiming a false independence, he did not understand that his government already represented business interests; hence, he rejected policies that would openly place the power of the state in the hands of business or that would permit the formation of a syndicalist state in which power might be exercised (in the words of William Appleman Williams) "by a relatively few leaders of each functional bloc formed and operating as an oligarchy."[16]

Even though constitutional scruples restricted his efforts, Hoover did more than any previous American president to combat depression. He "abandoned the principles of laissez faire in relation to the business cycle, established the conviction that prosperity and depression can be publicly controlled by political action, and drove out of the public consciousness the old idea that depressions must be overcome by private adjustment," wrote Walter Lippmann.[17] Rather than the last of the old presidents, Herbert Hoover was the first of the new.

II

A charismatic leader and a brilliant politician, his successor expanded federal activities on the basis of Hoover's efforts. Using the federal government to stabilize the economy and advance the interests of the groups, Franklin D. Roosevelt directed the campaign to save large-scale corporate capitalism. Though recognizing new political interests and extending benefits to them, his New Deal never effectively challenged big business or the organization of the economy. In providing assistance to the needy and by rescuing them from starvation, Roosevelt's humane efforts also protected the established system: he sapped organized radicalism of its waning strength and of its potential constituency among the unorganized and discontented. Sensitive to public opinion and fearful of radicalism, Roosevelt acted from a mixture of motives that rendered his liberalism cautious and limited, his experimentalism narrow. Despite the flurry of activity, his government was more vigorous and flexible about means than goals, and the goals were more conservative than historians usually acknowledge.[18]

Roosevelt's response to the banking crisis emphasizes the conservatism of his administration and its self-conscious avoidance of more radical means that might have transformed American capitalism. Entering the White House when banks were failing and Americans had lost faith in the financial system, the President could have nationalized it—"without a word of protest," judged Senator Bronson Cutting.[19] "If ever there was a moment when things hung in the balance," later wrote Raymond Moley, a member of the original "brain trust," "it was on March 5, 1933—when unorthodoxy would have drained the last remaining strength of the capitalistic system."[20] To save the system, Roosevelt relied upon collaboration between bankers and Hoover's Treasury officials to prepare legislation extending federal assistance to banking. So great was the demand for action that House members, voting even without copies, passed it unanimously, and the Senate, despite objections by a few Progressives, approved it the same evening. "The President," remarked a cynical congressman, "drove the money-changers out of the Capitol on March 4th—and they were all back on the 9th."[21]

Undoubtedly the most dramatic example of Roosevelt's early conservative approach to recovery was the National Recovery Administration (NRA). It was based on the War Industries Board (WIB) which had provided the model for the campaign of Bernard Baruch, General Hugh Johnson, and other former WIB officials during the twenties to limit competition through industrial self-regulation under federal sanction. As trade associations flourished during the decade, the FTC encouraged "codes of fair competition" and some industries even tried to set prices and restrict production. Operating without the force of law, these agreements broke down. When the depression struck, industrial pleas for regulation increased.[22] After the Great Crash, important business leaders including Henry I. Harriman of the Chamber of Commerce and Gerard Swope of General Electric called for suspension of antitrust laws and federal organization of business collaboration.[23] Joining them were labor leaders, particularly those in "sick" industries—John L. Lewis of the United Mine Workers and Sidney Hillman of Amalgamated Clothing Workers.[24]

Designed largely for industrial recovery, the NRA legislation provided for minimum wages and maximum hours. It also made concessions to pro-labor congressmen and labor leaders who demanded some specific benefits for unions—recognition of the worker's right to organization and to collective bargaining. In practice, though, the much-heralded Section 7a was a disappointment to most friends of labor.[25] (For the shrewd Lewis, however, it became a mandate to organize: "The President wants you to join a union.") To many frustrated workers and their disgusted leaders, NRA became "National Run Around." The clause, unionists found (in the words of Brookings economists), "had the practical effect of placing NRA on the side of anti-union employers in their struggle against trade unions. . . . [It] thus threw its weight against labor in the balance of bargaining power."[26] And while some far-sighted industrialists feared radicalism and hoped to forestall it by incorporating unions into the economic system, most preferred to leave their workers unorganized or in company unions. To many businessmen, large and independent unions as such seemed a radical threat to the system of business control.[27]

Not only did the NRA provide fewer advantages than unionists had anticipated, but it also failed as a recovery measure. It probably even retarded recovery by supporting restrictionism and price increases, concluded a Brookings study.[28] Placing effective power for code-writing in big business, NRA injured small businesses and contributed to the concentration of American industry. It was not the government-business partnership as envisaged by Adolf A. Berle, Jr., nor government managed as Rexford Tugwell had hoped, but rather, business managed, as Raymond Moley had desired.[29] Calling NRA "industrial self-government," its director, General Hugh Johnson, had explained that "NRA is exactly what industry organized in trade associations makes it." Despite the arrogance of some big businessmen with Section 7a, the NRA reaffirmed and consolidated their power at a time when the public was critical of industrialists and financiers.

III

Viewing the economy as a "concert of organized interests,"[30] the New Deal also provided benefits for farmers—the Agricultural Adjustment Act. Reflecting the political power of larger commercial farmers and accepting restrictionist economics, the measure assumed that the agricultural problem was overproduction, not underconsumption. Financed by a processing tax designed to raise prices to parity, payments encouraged restricted production and cutbacks in farm labor. With benefits accruing chiefly to the larger owners, they frequently removed from production the lands of sharecroppers and tenant farmers, and "tractored" them and hired hands off the land. In assisting agriculture, the AAA, like the NRA, sacrificed the interests of the marginal and the unrecognized to the welfare of those with greater political and economic power.[31]

In large measure, the early New Deal of the NRA and AAA was a "broker state." Though the government served as a mediator of interests and sometimes imposed its will in divisive situations, it was generally the servant of powerful groups. "Like the mercantilists, the New Dealers protected vested interests with the authority of the state," acknowledges William Leuchtenburg. But it was some improvement over the 1920s when business was the only interest capable of imposing its will on the government.[32] While extending to other groups the benefits of the state, the New Deal, however, continued to recognize the pre-eminence of business interests.

The politics of the broker state also heralded the way of the future—of continued corporate dominance in a political structure where other groups agreed generally on corporate capitalism and squabbled only about the size of the shares. Delighted by this increased participation and the absorption of dissident groups, many liberals did not understand the dangers in the emerging organization of politics. They had too much faith in representative institutions and in associations to foresee the perils—of leaders not representing their constituents, of bureaucracy diffusing responsibility, of officials serving their own interests. Failing to perceive the dangers in the emerging structure, most liberals agreed with Senator Robert Wagner of New York: "In order that the strong may not take advantage of the weak, every group must be equally strong.[33] His advice then seemed appropriate for organizing labor, but it neglected the problems of unrepresentative leadership and of the many millions to be left beyond organization.[34]

In dealing with the organized interests, the President acted frequently as a broker, but his government did not simply express the vectors of external forces.[35] The New Deal state was too complex, too loose, and some of Roosevelt's subordinates were following their own inclinations and pushing the government in directions of their own design.[36] The President would also depart from his role as a broker and act to secure programs he desired. As a skilled politician, he could split coalitions, divert the interests of groups, or place the prestige of his office on the side of desired legislation.

In seeking to protect the stock market, for example, Roosevelt endorsed the Securities and Exchange measure (of 1934), despite opposition of many in the New York financial community. His advisers split the opposition. Rallying to support the administration were the out-of-town exchanges, representatives of the large commission houses, including James Forrestal of Dillon, Read, and Robert Lovett of Brown Brothers, Harriman, and such commission brokers as E. A. Pierce and Paul Shields. Opposed to the Wall Street "old guard" and their companies, this group included those who wished to avoid more radical legislation, as well as others who had wanted earlier to place trading practices under federal legislation which they could influence.[37]

Though the law restored confidence in the securities market and protected capitalism, it alarmed some businessmen and contributed to the false belief that the New Deal was threatening business. But it was not the disaffection of a portion of the business community, nor the creation of the Liberty League, that menaced the broker state.[38] Rather it was the threat of the Left—expressed, for example, in such overwrought statements as Minnesota Governor Floyd Olson's: "I am not a liberal . . . I am a radical. . . . I am not satisfied with hanging a laurel wreath on burglars and thieves . . . and calling them code authorities or something else."[39] While Olson, along with some others who succumbed to the rhetoric of militancy, would back down and soften their meaning, their words dramatized real grievances: the failure of the early New Deal to end misery, to re-create prosperity. The New Deal excluded too many. Its programs were inadequate. While Roosevelt reluctantly endorsed relief and went beyond Hoover in support of public works, he too preferred self-liquidating projects, desired a balanced budget, and resisted spending the huge sums required to lift the nation out of depression.

IV

For millions suffering in a nation wracked by poverty, the promises of the Left seemed attractive. Capitalizing on the misery, Huey Long offered Americans a "Share Our Wealth" program—a welfare state with prosperity, not subsistence, for the disadvantaged, those neglected by most politicians. "Every Man a King": pensions for the elderly, college for the deserving, homes and cars for families—that was the promise of American life. Also proposing minimum wages, increased public works, shorter work weeks, and a generous farm program, he demanded a "soak-the-rich" tax program. Despite the economic defects of his plan, Long was no hayseed, and his forays into the East revealed support far beyond the bayous and hamlets of his native South.[40] In California discontent was so great that Upton Sinclair, food faddist and former socialist, captured the Democratic nomination for governor on a platform of "production-for-use"—factories and farms for the unemployed. "In a cooperative society," promised Sinclair, "every man, woman, and child would have the equivalent of $5,000 a year income from labor of the able-bodied young men for three or four hours per day."[41] More challenging to Roosevelt was Francis Townsend's plan—monthly payments of $200 to those past sixty who retired and promised to spend the stipend within thirty days.[42] Another enemy of the New Deal was Father Coughlin, the popular radio priest, who had broken with Roosevelt and formed a National Union for Social Justice to lead the way to a corporate society beyond capitalism.

To a troubled nation offered "redemption" by the Left, there was also painful evidence that the social fabric was tearing—law was breaking down. When the truckers in Minneapolis struck, the police provoked an incident and shot sixty-seven people, some in the back. Covering the tragedy, Eric Sevareid, then a young reporter, wrote, "I understood deep in my bones and blood what fascism was."[43] In San Francisco union leaders embittered by police brutality led a general strike and aroused national fears of class warfare. Elsewhere, in textile mills from Rhode Island to Georgia, in cities like Des Moines and Toledo, New York and Philadelphia, there were brutality and violence, sometimes bayonets and tear gas.[44]

Challenged by the Left, and with the new Congress more liberal and more willing to spend, Roosevelt turned to disarm the discontent. "Boys—this is our hour," confided Harry Hopkins. "We've got to get everything we want—a works program, social security, wages and hours, everything—now or never. Get your minds to work on developing a complete ticket to provide security for all the folks of this country up and down and across the board."[45] Hopkins and the associates he addressed were not radicals: they did not seek to transform the system, only to make it more humane.

They, too, wished to preserve large-scale corporate capitalism, but unlike Roosevelt or Moley, they were prepared for more vigorous action. Their commitment to reform was greater, their tolerance for injustice far less. Joining them in pushing the New Deal left were the leaders of industrial unions, who, while also not wishing to transform the system, sought for workingmen higher wages, better conditions, stronger and larger unions, and for themselves a place closer to the fulcrum of power.

The problems of organized labor, however, neither aroused Roosevelt's humanitarianism nor suggested possibilities of reshaping the political coalition. When asked during the NRA about employee representation, he had replied that workers could select anyone they wished—the Ahkoond of Swat, a union, even the Royal Geographical Society.[46] As a paternalist, viewing himself (in the words of James MacGregor Burns) as a "partisan and benefactor" of workers, he would not understand the objections to company unions or to multiple unionism under NRA. Nor did he foresee the political dividends that support of independent unions could yield to his party.[47] Though presiding over the reshaping of politics (which would extend the channels of power to some of the discontented and redirect their efforts to competition within a limited framework), he was not its architect, and he was unable clearly to see or understand the unfolding design.

When Senator Wagner submitted his labor relations bills, he received no assistance from the President and even struggled to prevent Roosevelt from joining the opposition. The President "never lifted a finger," recalls Miss Perkins. ("I, myself, had very little sympathy with the bill," she wrote.[48]) But after the measure easily passed the Senate and seemed likely to win the House's endorsement, Roosevelt reversed himself. Three days before the Supreme Court invalidated the NRA, including the legal support for unionization, Roosevelt came out for the bill. Placing it on his "must" list, he may have hoped to influence the final provisions and turn an administration defeat into victory.[49]

Responding to the threat from the left, Roosevelt also moved during the Second Hundred Days to secure laws regulating banking, raising taxes, dissolving utility-holding companies, and creating social security. Building on the efforts of states during the Progressive Era, the Social Security Act marked the movement toward the welfare state, but the core of the measure, the old-age provision, was more important as a landmark than for its substance.

While establishing a federal-state system of unemployment compensation, the government, by making workers contribute to their old-age insurance, denied its financial responsibility for the elderly. The act excluded more than a fifth of the labor force leaving, among others, more than five million farm laborers and domestics without coverage.[50]

Though Roosevelt criticized the tax laws for not preventing "an unjust concentration of wealth and economic power,"[51] his own tax measure would not have significantly redistributed wealth. Yet his message provoked an "amen" from Huey Long and protests from businessmen.[52] Retreating from his promises, Roosevelt failed to support the bill, and it succumbed to conservative forces. They removed the inheritance tax and greatly reduced the proposed corporate and individual levies. The final law did not "soak the rich."[53] But it did engender deep resentment among the wealthy for increasing taxes on gifts and estates, imposing an excess-profits tax (which Roosevelt had not requested), and raising surtaxes. When combined with such regressive levies as social security and local taxes, however, the Wealth Tax of 1935 did not drain wealth from higher-income groups, and the top one percent even increased their shares during the New Deal years.[54]

V

Those historians who have characterized the events of 1935 as the beginning of a second New Deal have imposed a pattern on those years which most participants did not then discern.[55] In moving to social security, guarantees of collective bargaining, utility regulation, and progressive taxation, the government did advance the nation toward greater liberalism, but the shift was exaggerated and most of the measures accomplished far less than either friends or foes suggested. Certainly, despite a mild bill authorizing destruction of utilities-holding companies, there was no effort to atomize business, no real threat to concentration.

Nor were so many powerful businessmen disaffected by the New Deal. Though the smaller businessmen who filled the ranks of the Chamber of Commerce resented the federal bureaucracy and the benefits to labor and thus criticized NRA,[56] representatives of big business found the agency useful and opposed a return to unrestricted competition. In 1935, members of the Business Advisory Council—including Henry Harriman, outgoing president of the Chamber, Thomas Watson of International Business Machines,

Walter Gifford of American Telephone and Telegraph, Gerard Swope of General Electric, Winthrop Aldrich of the Chase National Bank, and W. Averell Harriman of Union Pacific—vigorously endorsed a two-year renewal of NRA.[57]

When the Supreme Court in 1935 declared the "hot" oil clause and then NRA unconstitutional, the administration moved to measures known as the "little NRA." Reestablishing regulations in bituminous coal and oil, the New Deal also checked wholesale price discrimination and legalized "fair trade" practices. Though Roosevelt never acted to revive the NRA, he periodically contemplated its restoration. In the so-called second New Deal, as in the "first," government remained largely the benefactor of big business, and some more advanced businessmen realized this.[58]

Roosevelt could attack the "economic royalists" and endorse the TNEC investigation of economic concentration, but he was unprepared to resist the basic demands of big business. While there was ambiguity in his treatment of oligopoly, it was more the confusion of means than of ends, for his tactics were never likely to impair concentration. Even the antitrust program under Thurman Arnold, concludes Frank Freidel, was "intended less to bust the trusts than to forestall too drastic legislation." Operating through consent degrees and designed to reduce prices to the consumer, the program frequently "allowed industries to function much as they had in NRA days." In effect, then, throughout its variations, the New Deal had sought to cooperate with business.[59]

Though vigorous in rhetoric and experimental in tone, the New Deal was narrow in its goals and wary of bold economic reform. Roosevelt's sense of what was politically desirable was frequently more restricted than others' views of what was possible and necessary. Roosevelt's limits were those of ideology; they were not inherent in experimentalism. For while the President explored the narrow center, and some New Dealers considered bolder possibilities, John Dewey, the philosopher of experimentalism, moved far beyond the New Deal and sought to reshape the system. Liberalism, he warned, "must now become radical. . . . For the gulf between what the actual situation makes possible and the actual state itself is so great that it cannot be bridged by piece-meal policies undertaken *ad hoc.*"[60] The boundaries of New Deal experimentalism, as Howard Zinn has emphasized, could extend far beyond Roosevelt's cautious ventures. Operating within very safe channels, Roosevelt not only avoided Marxism and the socialization of property, but he also stopped far short of other possibilities—communal direction of production or the organized distribution of surplus. The President and many of his associates were doctrinaires of the center, and their maneuvers in social reform were limited to cautious excursions.[61]

VI

Usually opportunistic and frequently shifting, the New Deal was restricted by its ideology. It ran out of fuel not because of the conservative opposition,[62] but because it ran out of ideas.[63] Acknowledging the end in 1939, Roosevelt proclaimed, "We have now passed the period of internal conflict in the launching of our program of social reform. Our full energies may now be released to invigorate the processes of recovery in order to preserve our reforms. . . ."[64]

The sad truth was that the heralded reforms were severely limited, that inequality continued, that efforts at recovery had failed. Millions had come to accept the depression as a way of life. A decade after the Great Crash, when millions were still unemployed, Fiorello LaGuardia recommended that "we accept the inevitable, that we are now in a new normal."[65] "It was reasonable to expect a probable minimum of 4,000,000 to 5,000,000 unemployed," Harry Hopkins had concluded.[66] Even that level was never reached, for business would not spend and Roosevelt refused to countenance the necessary expenditures. "It was in economics that our troubles lay," Tugwell wrote. "For their solution his [Roosevelt's] progressivism, his new deal was pathetically insufficient. . . ."[67]

Clinging to faith in fiscal orthodoxy even when engaged in deficit spending, Roosevelt had been unwilling to greatly unbalance the budget. Having pledged in his first campaign to cut expenditures and to restore the balanced budget, the President had at first adopted recovery programs that would not drain government finances. Despite a burst of activity under the Civil Works Administration during the first winter, public works expenditures were frequently slow and cautious. Shifting from direct relief, which Roosevelt (like Hoover) considered "a narcotic, a subtle destroyer of the human spirit," the government moved to work relief.[68] ("It saves his skill. It gives him a chance to do something socially useful," said Hopkins.[69]) By 1937 the government had poured enough money into the economy to spur production to within 10 percent of 1929 levels, but unemployment still hovered over seven million.

Yet so eager was the President to balance the budget that he cut expenditures for public works and relief, and plunged the economy into a greater depression. While renewing expenditures, Roosevelt remained cautious in his fiscal policy, and the nation still had almost nine million unemployed in 1939. After nearly six years of struggling with the depression, the Roosevelt administration could not lead the nation to recovery, but it had relieved suffering.[70] In most of America, starvation was no longer possible. Perhaps that was the most humane achievement of the New Deal.

Its efforts on behalf of humane *reform* were generally faltering and shallow, of more value to the middle classes, of less value to organized workers, of even less to the marginal men. In conception and in practice, seemingly humane efforts revealed the shortcomings of American liberalism. For example, public housing, praised as evidence of the federal government's concern for the poor, was limited in scope (to 180,000 units) and unfortunate in results.[71] It usually meant the consolidation of ghettos, the robbing of men of their dignity, the treatment of men as wards with few rights. And slum clearance came to mean "Negro clearance" and removal of the other poor. Of much of this liberal reformers were unaware, and some of the problems can be traced to the structure of bureaucracy and to the selection of government personnel and social workers who disliked the poor.[72] But the liberal conceptions, it can be argued, were also flawed for there was no willingness to consult the poor, nor to encourage their participation. Liberalism was elitist. Seeking to build America in their own image, liberals wanted to create an environment which they thought would restructure character and personality more appropriate to white, middle-class America.

While slum dwellers received little besides relief from the New Deal, and their needs were frequently misunderstood, Negroes as a group received even less assistance—less than they needed and sometimes even less than their proportion in the population would have justified. Under the NRA they were frequently dismissed and their wages were sometimes below the legal minimum. The Civilian Conservation Corps left them "forgotten" men— excluded, discriminated against, segregated. In general, what the Negroes gained—relief, WPA jobs, equal pay on some federal projects—was granted them as poor people, not as Negroes.[73] To many black men the distinction was unimportant, for no government had ever given them so much. "My friends, go home and turn

Lincoln's picture to the wall," a Negro publisher told his race. "That debt has been payed in full."[74]

Bestowing recognition on some Negro leaders, the New Deal appointed them to agencies as advisers—the "black cabinet." Probably more dramatic was the advocacy of Negro rights by Eleanor Roosevelt. Some whites like Harold Ickes and Aubrey Williams even struggled cautiously to break down segregation. But segregation did not yield, and Washington itself remained a segregated city. The white South was never challenged, the Fourteenth Amendment never used to assist Negroes. Never would Roosevelt expend political capital in an assault upon the American caste system.[75] Despite the efforts of the NAACP to dramatize the Negroes' plight as second-class citizens, subject to brutality and often without legal protection, Roosevelt would not endorse the anti-lynching bill. ("No government pretending to be civilized can go on condoning such atrocities," H. L. Mencken testified. "Either it must make every possible effort to put them down or it must suffer the scorn and contempt of Christendom."[76]) Unwilling to risk schism with Southerners ruling committees, Roosevelt capitulated to the forces of racism.[77]

Even less bold than in economic reform, the New Deal left intact the race relations of America. Yet its belated and cautious recognition of the black man was great enough to woo Negro leaders and even to court the masses. One of the bitter ironies of these years is that a New Dealer could tell the NAACP in 1936: "Under our new conception of democracy, the Negro will be given the chance to which he is entitled. . . ." But it was true, Ickes emphasized, that "The greatest advance [since Reconstruction] toward assuring the Negro the degree of justice to which he is entitled and that equality of opportunity under the law which is implicit in his American citizenship, has been made since Franklin D. Roosevelt was sworn in as President. . . ."[78]

It was not in the cities and not among the Negroes but in rural America that the Roosevelt administration made its (philosophically) boldest efforts: creation of the Tennessee Valley Authority and the later attempt to construct seven little valley authorities. Though conservation was not a new federal policy and government-owned utilities were sanctioned by municipal experience, federal activity in this area constituted a challenge to corporate enterprise and an expression of concern about the poor. A valuable example of regional planning and a contribution to regional pros-

perity, TVA still fell far short of expectations. The agency soon
retreated from social planning. ("From 1936 on," wrote Tugwell,
"the TVA should have been called the Tennessee Valley Power
Production and Flood Control Corporation.") Fearful of antagonizing the powerful interests, its agricultural program neglected
the tenants and the sharecroppers.[79]

To urban workingmen the New Deal offered some, but limited, material benefits. Though the government had instituted con-
tributory social security and unemployment insurance, its much-
heralded Fair Labor Standards Act, while prohibiting child labor,
was a greater disappointment. It exempted millions from its wages-
and-hours provisions. So unsatisfactory was the measure that one
congressman cynically suggested, "Within 90 days after appointment of the administrator, she should report to Congress whether
anyone is subject to this bill."[80] Requiring a minimum of twenty-
five cents an hour ($11 a week for 44 hours), it raised the wages of
only about a half-million at a time when nearly twelve million
workers in interstate commerce were earning less than forty cents
an hour.[81]

More important than these limited measures was the
administration's support, albeit belated, of the organization of labor and the right of collective bargaining. Slightly increasing organized workers' share of the national income,[82] the new industrial
unions extended job security to millions who were previously subject to the whim of management. Unionization freed them from
the perils of a free market.

By assisting labor, as well as agriculture, the New Deal started
the institutionalization of larger interest groups into a new political
economy. Joining business as tentative junior partners, they shared
the consensus on the value of large-scale corporate capitalism, and
were permitted to participate in the competition for the division of
shares. While failing to redistribute income, the New Deal modified the political structure at the price of excluding many from the
process of decision making. To many what was offered in fact was
symbolic representation, formal representation. It was not the industrial workers necessarily who were recognized, but their unions
and leaders; it was not even the farmers, but their organizations
and leaders. While this was not a conscious design, it was the
predictable result of conscious policies. It could not have been
easily avoided, for it was part of the price paid by a large society

unwilling to consider radical new designs for the distribution of power and wealth.

VII

In the deepest sense, this new form of representation was rooted in the liberal's failure to endorse a meaningful egalitarianism which would provide actual equality of opportunity. It was also the limited concern with equality and justice that accounted for the shallow efforts of the New Deal and left so many Americans behind. The New Deal was neither a "third American Revolution," as Carl Degler suggests, nor even a "half-way revolution," as William Leuchtenburg concludes. Not only was the extension of representation to new groups less than full-fledged partnership, but the New Deal neglected many Americans—sharecroppers, tenant farmers, migratory workers and farm laborers, slum dwellers, unskilled workers, and the unemployed Negroes. They were left outside the new order.[83] As Roosevelt asserted in 1937 (in a classic understatement), one third of the nation was "ill-nourished, ill-clad, ill-housed."[84]

Yet, by the power of rhetoric and through the appeals of political organization, the Roosevelt government managed to win or retain the allegiance of these peoples. Perhaps this is one of the crueller ironies of liberal politics, that the marginal men trapped in hopelessness were seduced by rhetoric, by the style and movement, by the symbolism of efforts seldom reaching beyond words. In acting to protect the institution of private property and in advancing the interests of corporate capitalism, the New Deal assisted the middle and upper sectors of society. It protected them, sometimes, even at the cost of injuring the lower sectors. Seldom did it bestow much of substance upon the lower classes. Never did the New Deal seek to organize these groups into independent political forces. Seldom did it risk antagonizing established interests. For some this would constitute a puzzling defect of liberalism; for some, the failure to achieve true liberalism. To others it would emphasize the inherent shortcomings of American liberal democracy. As the nation prepared for war, liberalism, by accepting private property and federal assistance to corporate capitalism, was not prepared effectively to reduce inequities, to redistribute political power, or to extend equality from promise to reality.

NOTES

1. The outstanding examples are Arthur Schlesinger, Jr., Frank Freidel, Carl Degler, and William Leuchtenburg. Schlesinger, in *The Crisis of the Old Order* (Boston, 1957), emphasized the presence of reform in the twenties but criticized the federal government for its retreat from liberalism and condemned Hoover for his responses to the depression. The next two volumes of his *The Age of Roosevelt, The Coming of the New Deal* (Boston, 1958) and *The Politics of Upheaval* (Boston, 1960), praise the New Deal, but also contain information for a more critical appraisal. His research is quite wide and has often guided my own investigations. For his theory that the New Deal was likely even without the depression, see "Sources of the New Deal: Reflections on the Temper of a Time," *Columbia University Forum*, II (Fall 1959), 4–11. Freidel affirmed that the New Deal was a watershed (American Historical Review, October 1965, p. 329), but in *The New Deal in Historical Perspective* (Washington, 1959), he has suggested the conservatism of the New Deal as a reform movement. Degler, in *Out of Our Past* (New York, 1959), pp. 379–416, extolled the New Deal as a "Third American Revolution." But also see his "The Ordeal of Herbert Hoover," *Yale Review*, LII (Summer 1963), 565–83. Leuchtenburg, *Franklin D. Roosevelt and the New Deal, 1932–1940* (New York, 1963), offers considerable criticism of the New Deal, but finds far more to praise in this "half-way revolution." He cites Degler approvingly but moderates Degler's judgment (pp. 336–47). The book represents years of research and has often guided my own investigations.

2. Eric Goldman, *Rendezvous with Destiny* (New York, 1952); Henry Steele Commager, "Twelve Years of Roosevelt," *American Mercury*, LX (April 1945), 391–401; Arthur Link, *American Epoch* (New York, 1955), pp. 377–440. In his essay on "Franklin D. Roosevelt: The Patrician as Opportunist" in *The American Political Tradition* (New York, 1948), pp. 315–52, Richard Hofstadter was critical of the New Deal's lack of ideology but treated it as a part of the larger reform tradition. In *The Age of Reform* (New York, 1955), however, while chiding the New Deal for opportunism, he emphasized the discontinuity of the New Deal with the reform tradition of Populism and Progressivism.

3. Edgar E. Robinson, *The Roosevelt Leadership, 1933–1945* (Philadelphia, 1955), the work of a conservative constitutionalist, does accuse the administration of having objectives approaching the leveling aims of communism (p. 376).

4. Louis Hacker, *American Problems of Today* (New York, 1938).

5. William Appleman Williams, *The Contours of American History* (Chicago, 1966), pp. 372–488; and his review, "Schlesinger: Right Crisis—Wrong Order," *Nation*, CLXXXIV (March 23, 1957), 257–60. Williams' volume has influenced my own thought.

6. Ronald Radosh, "The Corporate Ideology of American Labor Leaders from Gompers to Hillman," *Studies on the Left*, VI (November–December 1966), 66–68.

7. Arthur Link, "What Happened to the Progressive Movement?" *American Historical Review*, LXIV (July 1959), 833–51.

8. James Prothro, *The Dollar Decade* (Baton Rouge, La., 1954).

9. Louis Galambos, *Competition and Cooperation* (Baltimore, 1966), pp. 55–139; Link, "What Happened to the Progressive Movement?"

10. Joseph Brandes, *Herbert Hoover and Economic Diplomacy* (Pittsburgh, 1962); Hofstadter, *American Political Tradition*, pp. 283–99.

11. William S. Myers, ed., *The State Papers and Other Writings of Herbert Hoover* (New York, 1934), I, 84–88 (easier money), 137, 411, 431–33; II, 202 (public works); I, 142–43, 178–79 (lower taxes). The Commodity Stabilization Corporation was created before the crash.

12. Lippmann, "The Permanent New Deal," *Yale Review*, XXIV (June 1935), 651.

13. Myers, ed., *State Papers*, II, 195–201, 214–15, 224–26, 228–33 (on the budget); II, 405, 496–99, 503–5 (on relief).

14. Gerald Nash, "Herbert Hoover and the Origins of the Reconstruction Finance Corporation," *Mississippi Valley Historical Review*, XLVI (December 1959), 455–68.

15. W. S. Myers and W. H. Newton, eds., *The Hoover Administration: A Documentary History* (New York, 1936), p. 119; "Proceedings of a Conference of Progressives," March 11–12, 1931, Hillman Papers, Amalgamated Clothing Workers (New York).

16. *Contours of American History*, p. 428.

17. Lippmann, "The Permanent New Deal," p. 651.

18. For an excellent statement of this thesis, see Howard Zinn's introduction to his *New Deal Thought* (New York, 1966), pp. xv–xxxvi. So far historians have not adequately explored the thesis that F.D.R. frequently acted as a restraining force on his own government, and that bolder reforms were often thwarted by him and his intimates.

19. Bronson Cutting, "Is Private Banking Doomed?" *Liberty*, XI (March 31, 1934), 10; cf. Raymond Moley, *The First New Deal* (New York, 1966), pp. 177–80.

20. Moley, *After Seven Years* (New York, 1939), p. 155; Arthur Ballantine, "When All the Banks Closed," *Harvard Business Review*, XXVI (March 1948), 129–43.

21. William Lemke, later quoted in Lorena Hickok to Harry Hopkins, November 23, 1933, Hopkins Papers, Franklin D. Roosevelt Library (hereafter called FDRL).

22. Baruch to Samuel Gompers, April 19, 1924, Baruch Papers, Princeton University; Schlesinger, *Coming of the New Deal*, pp. 88–89; Gerald Nash, "Experiments in Industrial Mobilization: WIB and NRA," *Mid-America*, XLV (July 1963), 156–75.

23. Gerard Swope, *The Swope Plan* (New York, 1931); Julius H. Barnes, "Government and Business," *Harvard Business Review*, X

(July 1932), 411–19; Harriman, "The Stabilization of Business and Employment," *American Economic Review*, XXII (March 1932), 63–75; House Committee on Education and Labor, 73rd Cong., 1st Sess., *Thirty-Hour Week Bill, Hearings*, pp. 198–99.

24. *Ibid.*, pp. 884–97; Hillman, "Labor Leads Toward Planning," *Survey Graphic*, LXVI (March 1932), 586–88.

25. Irving Bernstein, *The New Deal Collective Bargaining Policy* (Berkeley, Cal., 1950), pp. 57–63.

26. Quotes from Hofstadter, *American Political Tradition*, p. 336. "It is not the function of NRA to organize . . . labor," asserted General Hugh Johnson. "Automobile Code Provides For Thirty-Five Hour Week," *Iron Age*, CXXXII (August 3, 1933), 380.

27. Richard C. Wilcock, "Industrial Management's Policy Toward Unionism," in Milton Derber and Edwin Young, eds., *Labor and the New Deal* (Madison, Wis., 1957), pp. 278–95.

28. Leverett Lyon, *et al.*, *The National Recovery Administration* (Washington, 1935).

29. The characterization of Berle, Tugwell, and Moley is from Schlesinger, *Coming of the New Deal*, pp. 181–84, and Johnson's address at the NAM is from NRA press release 2126, December 7, 1933, NRA Records, RG 9, National Archives.

30. "Concert of interests" was used by F.D.R. in a speech of April 18, 1932, in Samuel Rosenman, ed., *The Public Papers and Addresses of Franklin D. Roosevelt* (13 vols.; New York, 1938–52), I, 627–39. (Hereafter referred to as *FDR Papers*.)

31. M. S. Venkataramani, "Norman Thomas, Arkansas Sharecroppers, and the Roosevelt Agricultural Policies," *Mississippi Valley Historical Review*, XLVII (September 1960), 225–46; John Hutson, Columbia Oral History Memoir, pp. 114ff.; Mordecai Ezekiel, Columbia Oral History Memoir, pp. 74ff.

32. Quoted from Leuchtenburg, *F.D.R.*, p. 87, and this discussion draws upon pp. 87–90; John Chamberlain, *The American Stakes* (Philadelphia, 1940): James MacGregor Burns, *Roosevelt: The Lion and the Fox* (New York, 1956), pp. 183–202.

33. Quoted from House Committee on Education and Labor, 74th Cong., 1st Sess., *National Labor Relations Board Hearings*, p. 35.

34. For a warning, see Paul Douglas, "Rooseveltian Liberalism," *Nation*, CXXXVI (June 21, 1933), 702–3.

35. Leuchtenburg, *F.D.R.*, p. 88, uses the image of "a parallelogram of pressures."

36. For example, see the Columbia Oral Histories of Louis Bean, Hutson, and Ezekiel.

37. *New York Times*, January 30, 1934; House Interstate and Foreign Commerce Committee, 73rd Cong., 2nd Sess., House Report No. 1383, *Securities Exchange Bill of 1934*, p. 3; "SEC," *Fortune*, XXI (June 1940), 91–92, 120ff.; Ralph DeBedts, *The New Deal's SEC* (New York, 1964), pp. 56–85.

38. Frederick Rudolph, "The American Liberty League, 1934–1940," *American Historical Review*, LVI (October 1950), 19–33; George Wolfskill, *The Revolt of the Conservatives* (Boston, 1962). Emphasizing the Liberty League and focusing upon the rhetoric of business disaffection, historians have often exaggerated the opposition of the business communities. See the correspondence of James Forrestal, PPF 6367, FDRL, and at Princeton; of Russell Leffingwell, PPF 886, FDRL; of Donald Nelson, PPF 8615, FDRL, and at the Huntington Library; and of Thomas Watson, PPF 2489, FDRL. On the steel industry, see *Iron Age*, CXXXV (June 13, 1935), 44. For very early evidence of estrangement, however, see Edgar Mowrer to Frank Knox, November 8, 1933, Knox Papers, Library of Congress.

39. Quoted from Donald McCoy, *Angry Voices: Left of Center Politics in the New Deal Era* (Lawrence, Kan., 1958), p. 55, from *Farmer-Labor Leader*, March 30, 1934.

40. Long, *My First Days in the White House* (Harrisburg, Pa., 1935).

41. Quoted from Sinclair, *The Way Out* (New York, 1933), p. 57. See Sinclair to Roosevelt, October 5 and 18, 1934, OF 1165, FDRL.

42. Nicholas Roosevelt, *The Townsend Plan* (Garden City, N.Y., 1935). Not understanding that the expenditures would increase consumption and probably spur production, critics emphasized that the top 9 percent would have received 50 percent of the income, but they neglected that the top income-tenth had received (before taxes) nearly 40 percent of the national income in 1929. National Industrial Conference Board, *Studies in Enterprise and Social Progress* (New York, 1939), p. 125.

43. Sevareid, *Not So Wild a Dream* (New York, 1946), p. 58.

44. Sidney Lens, *Left, Right and Center* (Hinsdale, Ill., 1949), pp. 280–89.

45. Quoted in Robert Sherwood, *Roosevelt and Hopkins*, rev. ed. (New York, 1950), p. 65.

46. Roosevelt's press conference of June 15, 1934, *FDR Papers*, III, 301; cf., Roosevelt to John L. Lewis, February 25, 1939, Philip Murray Papers, Catholic University.

47. Burns, *The Lion and the Fox*, pp. 217–19; quotation from p. 218.

48. Perkins, Columbia Oral History Memoir, VII, 138, 147, quoted by Leuchtenburg, *F.D.R.*, p. 151.

49. Irving Bernstein, *The New Deal Collective Bargaining Policy*, pp. 100–8; Burns, *The Lion and the Fox*, p. 219.

50. Margaret Grant, *Old Age Security* (Washington, 1939), p. 217. Under social security, payments at sixty-five ranged from $10 a month to $85 a month, depending on earlier earnings.

51. Roosevelt's message to Congress on June 19, 1935, *FDR Papers*, IV, 271.

52. *New York Times*, June 20 and 21, 1935; *Business Week*, June 22, 1935, p. 5.

53. John Morton Blum, *From the Morgenthau Diaries: Years of Crisis, 1928–1938* (Boston, 1959), pp. 302–4.

54. Simon Kuznets, *Shares of Upper Income Groups in Income and Savings*, National Bureau of Economic Research, Occasional Paper 35 (New York, 1950), pp. 32–40.

55. Otis L. Graham, Jr., "Historians and the New Deals: 1944–1960," *Social Studies*, LIV (April 1963), 133–40.

56. *New York Times*, November 19, 1933; May 1, September 30, November 17, December 23, 1934; May 1, 3, 5, 28, 1935; "Chamber to Vote on NIRA," *Nation's Business*, XXII (December 1934), 51; "Business Wants a New NRA," *ibid.*, XXIII (February 1935), 60; "Listening in as Business Speaks," *ibid.*, XXIII (June 1935), 18, 20; William Wilson, "How the Chamber of Commerce Viewed the NRA," *Mid-America*, XLIII (January, 1962), 95–108.

57. *New York Times*, May 3, 4, 12, 1935. On the steel industry see L. W. Moffet, "This Week in Washington," *Iron Age*, CXXXV (March 21, 1935), 41; *ibid.* (April 18, 1935), 49; "NRA Future Not Settled by Senate Committee's Action for Extension," *ibid.* (May 9, 1935), 58.

58. Ellis W. Hawley, *The New Deal and the Problem of Monopoly* (Princeton, 1966), pp. 205–86.

59. Freidel, *The New Deal*, pp. 18–19. On Arnold's efforts, see Wendell Berge Diary, 1938–1939, Berge Papers, Library of Congress; and Gene Gressley, "Thurman Arnold, Antitrust, and the New Deal," *Business History Review*, XXXVIII (Summer 1964), 214–31. For characteristic Roosevelt rhetoric emphasizing the effort of his government to subdue "the forces of selfishness and of lust for power," see his campaign address of October 31, 1936, his press conference of January 4, 1938, and his message of April 29, 1938, in *FDR Papers*, V, 568–69 and VII, 11, 305–32.

60. Dewey, *Liberalism and Social Action* (New York, 1935), p. 62.

61. Howard Zinn, in *New Deal Thought*, pp. xxvi–xxxi, discusses this subject and has influenced my thought. Also consider those whom Zinn cites: Edmund Wilson, "The Myth of Marxist Dialectic," *Partisan Review*, VI (Fall 1938), 66–81; William Ernest Hocking, "The Future of Liberalism," *The Journal of Philosophy*, XXXII (April 25, 1935), 230–47; Stuart Chase, "Eating Without Working: A Moral Disquisition," *Nation*, CXXXVII (July 22, 1933), 93–94.

62. See James T. Patterson, "A Conservative Coalition Forms in Congress, 1933–1939," *Journal of American History*, LII (March 1966), 757–72.

63. Hofstadter, *American Political Tradition*, p. 342; cf., Freidel, *The New Deal*, p. 20.

64. Roosevelt's annual message to the Congress on January 4, 1939, *FDR Papers*, VIII, 7.

65. Fiorello LaGuardia to James Byrnes, April 5, 1939, Box 2584, LaGuardia Papers, Municipal Archives, New York City.

66. Hopkins, "The Future of Relief," *New Republic*, XC (February 10, 1937), 8.

67. Tugwell, *The Stricken Land* (Garden City, N.Y., 1947), p. 681.

68. Roosevelt's speech of January 4, 1935, *FDR Papers*, IV, 19.

69. Hopkins, "Federal Emergency Relief," *Vital Speeches*, I (December 31, 1934), 211.

70. Broadus Mitchell, *Depression Decade: From New Era Through New Deal* (New York, 1947), pp. 37–54.

71. Housing and Home Finance Agency, *First Annual Report* (Washington, 1947), pp. 24–25. Timothy McDonnell, *The Wagner Housing Act* (Chicago, 1957), pp. 53, 186–88, concludes that the Wagner bill would have passed earlier if Roosevelt had supported it.

72. Jane Jacobs, *The Life and Death of Great American Cities* (New York, 1963). Racial policy was locally determined. U.S. Housing Authority, *Bulletin No. 18 on Policy and Procedure* (1938), pp. 7–8; Robert C. Weaver, "The Negro in a Program of Public Housing," *Opportunity*, XVI (July 1938), 1–6. Three fifths of all families, reported Weaver, were earning incomes "below the figure necessary to afford respectable living quarters without undue skimping on other necessities." (p. 4)

73. Allen Kifer, "The Negro Under the New Deal, 1933–1941," (unpublished Ph.D. dissertation, University of Wisconsin, 1961), *passim*. The National Youth Agency was an exception, concludes Kifer, p. 139. For Negro protests about New Deal discrimination, John P. Davis, "What Price National Recovery?," *Crisis*, XL (December 1933), 272; Charles Houston and Davis, "TVA: Lily-White Construction," *Crisis*, XLI (October 1934), 291.

74. Robert Vann of the *Pittsburgh Courier*, quoted in Joseph Alsop and William Kintner, "The Guffey," *Saturday Evening Post*, CCX (March 26, 1938), 6. Vann had offered this advice in 1932.

75. See Eleanor Roosevelt to Walter White, May 2, 29, 1934, April 21, 1938, White Papers, Yale University; Frank Freidel, *F.D.R. and the South* (Baton Rouge, La., 1965), pp. 71–102.

76. Quoted from Senate Judiciary Committee, 74th Cong., 1st Sess., *Punishment for the Crime of Lynching, Hearings*, p. 23. Cf. Harold Ickes, "The Negro as a Citizen," June 29, 1936, Oswald Garrison Villard Papers, Harvard University.

77. Roy Wilkins, Columbia Oral History Memoir, p. 98; Lester Granger, Columbia Oral History Memoir, p. 105, complains that Wagner had refused to include in his labor bill a prohibition against unions excluding workers because of race. When Wagner counseled a delay, Negroes felt, according to Granger, that the New Deal "was concerned with covering up, putting a fine cover over what there was, not bothering with the inequities."

78. Ickes, "The Negro as a Citizen." Ickes had said, "since the Civil War."

79. Schlesinger, *Politics of Upheaval*, pp. 362–80; quotation from Tugwell p. 371.

80. Martin Dies, quoted by Burns, *Congress on Trial* (New York, 1949), p. 77.

81. The law raised standards to thirty cents and forty-two hours in 1939 and forty cents and forty hours in 1945. U.S. Department of Labor, BLS, *Labor Information Bulletin* (April 1939), pp. 1–3.

82. Arthur M. Ross, *Trade Union Wage Policy* (Berkeley, Cal., 1948), pp. 113–28.

83. Leuchtenburg, *F.D.R.*, pp. 346–47. The Bankhead-Jones Farm Tenancy Act of 1937 provided some funds for loans to selected tenants who wished to purchase farms. In 1935, there were 2,865,155 tenants (about 42 percent of all farmers), and by 1941, 20,748 had received loans. *Farm Tenancy: Report of the President's Committee* (Washington, February 1937), Table I, p. 89; *Report of the Administrator of the Farm Security Administration, 1941* (Washington, 1941), p. 17.

84. Roosevelt's Inaugural Address of January 20, 1937, *FDR Papers*, VI, 5.

INDUSTRIAL CONFLICT AND THE COMING OF THE NEW DEAL: THE TRIUMPH OF MULTINATIONAL LIBERALISM IN AMERICA

Thomas Ferguson

In October 1929, the stock market crashed. Over the next few months the market continued dropping, and a general economic decline took hold. As sales plummeted, industry after industry laid off workers and cut wages. Farm and commodity prices tumbled, outpacing price declines in other parts of the economy. A tidal wave of bankruptcies engulfed businessmen, farmers, and a middle class that had only recently awakened to the joys of installment buying.

While the major media, leading politicians, and important businessmen resonantly reaffirmed capitalism's inherently self-correcting tendency, havoc spread around the world. By 1932, the situation had become critical. Many currencies were floating and international finance had virtually collapsed. World trade had shrunk to a fraction of its previous level. In many countries one-fifth or more of the work force was idle. Homeless, often starving, people camped out in parks and fields, while only the virtual collapse of real-estate markets in many districts checked a mammoth liquidation of homes and farms by banks and insurance companies.

In this desperate situation, with regimes changing and governments falling, a miracle seemed to occur in the United States, the country that, among all the major powers in the capitalist world economy, had perhaps been hit hardest. Taking office at the moment of the greatest financial collapse in the nation's history, President Franklin D. Roosevelt initiated a dazzling burst of government actions designed to square the circle that was baffling governments elsewhere: how to enact major social reforms while preserving both democracy and capitalism. In a hundred days his administration implemented a series of emergency relief bills for the unemployed; an Agricultural Adjustment Act for farmers; a bill (the Glass-Steagall Act, also sometimes referred to as the "Banking Act of 1933") to "reform" the banking structure; a Securities Act to reform the Stock Exchange; and the National Industrial Recovery Act, which in effect legalized cartels in American industry. Roosevelt suspended the convertibility of the dollar into gold, abandoned the gold standard, and enacted legislation to promote American exports. He also presided over a noisy public investigation of the most famous banking house in the world: J. P. Morgan & Co.

For a while this "first New Deal" package of policies brought some relief, but sustained recovery failed to arrive and class conflict intensified. Two years later, Roosevelt scored an even more dramatic series of triumphs that consolidated his position as the guardian of all the millions, both people and fortunes. A second period of whirlwind legislative activity produced the most important social legislation in American history—the Social Security and Wagner acts—as well as measures to break up public utility holding companies and to fix the price of oil. The president also turned dramatically away from his earlier economic nationalism. He entered into agreements with Britain and France informally to stabilize the dollar against their currencies and began vigorously to implement earlier legislation that empowered Secretary of State Cordell Hull to negotiate a series of treaties reducing U.S. tariff rates.[1]

After winning one of the most bitterly contested elections in American history by a landslide (and giving the coup de grace to the old Republican-dominated "System of '96"), Roosevelt consolidated the position of the Democrats as the new majority party of the United States.[2] He passed additional social welfare legislation and pressured the Supreme Court to accept his reforms. Faced with another steep downturn in 1937, the Roosevelt team confirmed its new economic course. Rejecting proposals to revive the National Recovery Administration (NRA) and again devalue the dollar, it adopted an experimental program of conscious "pump priming," which used government spending to prop up the economy in a way that foreshadowed the "Keynesian" policies of demand management widely adopted by Western economies after 1945. This was the first time this had ever been attempted—unless one accepts the Swedish example, which was virtually contemporaneous.[3]

Roosevelt and his successive New Deals have exercised a magnetic attraction on subsequent political analysts. Reams of commentary have sought to elucidate what the New Deal was and why it evolved as it did. But while the debate has raged for over forty years, little consensus exists about how best to explain what happened.

Many analysts, including most of those whose major works shaped the historiography of the last generation, have always been convinced that the decisive factor in the shaping of the New Deal was Franklin D. Roosevelt himself.[4] They hail his sagacity in fashioning his epoch-making domestic reforms. They honor his statecraft in leading the United States away from isolationism and toward Atlantic Alliance. And they celebrate the charisma he displayed in recruiting millions of previously marginal workers, blacks, and intellectuals into his great crusade to limit permanently the power of business in American life.

Several rival accounts now compete with this interpretation. As some radical historians pose the problem, only Roosevelt and a handful of advisers were farsighted enough to grasp what was required to save capitalism from itself.[5] Accordingly, Roosevelt engineered sweeping attacks on big business for the sake of big business's own long-run interest. (A variation on this theme credits the administration's aspirations toward reform but points to the structural constraints capitalism imposes on any government as the explanation for the New Deal's conservative outcome.)

Another recent point of view explains the New Deal by pointing to the consolidation and expansion of bureaucratic institutions. It deemphasizes Roosevelt as a personality, along with the period's exciting mass politics. Instead, historians like Ellis Hawley (in his latest essays) single out as the hallmarks of the New Deal the role of professionally certified experts, and the advance of organization and hierarchical control.[6]

Some of these arguments occasionally come close to the final current of contemporary New Deal interpretation. This focuses sharply on concrete interactions between polity and economy (rather than bureaucracy per se) in defining the outcome of the New Deal. Notable here are the (mostly West German) theorists of "organized capitalism," several different versions of Marxist analysis, right-wing libertarian analysts who treat the New Deal as an attempt by big business to institutionalize the corporate state, and Gabriel Kolko's theory of "political capitalism."[7]

These newer approaches provide telling criticisms of traditional analyses of the New Deal. At the same time, however, they often create fresh difficulties. "Organized capitalism," "political capitalism," or the libertarian "corporate state" analyses, for example, are illuminating with respect to the universal price-fixing schemes of the NRA. But the half-life of the NRA was short even by the admittedly unstable standards of American politics. The historic turn toward free trade that was so spectacularly a part of the later New Deal is scarcely compatible with claims that the New Deal institutionalized the collective power of big business as a whole, and it is perhaps unsurprising that most of this literature hurries over foreign economic policy. Nor are more than token efforts usually made to explain in detail why the New Deal arrived in its classic post-1935 form only after moving through stages that often seemed to caricature the celebrated observation that history proceeds not along straight lines but in spirals. It was, after all, a period in which the future patron saint of American International-ism not only raised more tariffs than he lowered but also openly mocked exchange-rate stability and the gold standard, promoted cartelization, and endorsed inflation.[8] Similarly, theorists who treat the New Deal chiefly as the bureaucratic design of credentialed administrators and professionals not only ignore the significance of this belated opening to international trade in the world economy, but they also do less than full justice to the dramatic business mobilization and epic class conflicts of the period.

Nor do any of these accounts provide a credible analysis of the Democratic party of the era. Then, as now, the Democratic party fits badly into the boxes provided by conventional political science. On the one hand, it is perfectly obvious that a tie to at least part of organized labor provides an important element of the party's identity. But on the the other, it is equally manifest that no amount of co-optation accounts for the party's continuing collateral affili-ation with such prominent businessmen as, for example, Averell Harriman. Why, if the Democrats truly constituted a mass labor party, was the outcome of the New Deal not more congruent with the traditional labor party politics of Great Britain and Germany? And, if the Democratic party was not a labor party, then what force inside it was powerful enough to contain the CIO and simulta-neously launch a sweeping attack on major industrial interests? These analyses also slip past the biggest puzzle that the New Deal poses. They offer few clues as to why some countries with militant labor movements and charismatic political leaders in the depres-sion needed a New Order instead of a New Deal to control their work force.

In this essay I contend that a clear view of the New Deal's world historical uniqueness and significance comes only when one breaks with most of the commentaries of the last thirty years, goes back to primary sources, and attempts to analyze the New Deal as a whole in the light of industrial structure, party competition, and public policy. Then what stands out is the novel type of political coalition that Roosevelt built.[9] At the center of this coalition, however, are not the workers, blacks, and poor who have preoccupied liberal commentators, but something else: a new "historical bloc" (in Gramsci's phrase) of capital-intensive industries, investment banks, and internationally oriented commercial banks.

This new kind of power bloc constitutes the basis of the New Deal's great and, in world history, utterly unique achievement: its ability to accommodate millions of mobilized workers amid world depression. Because capital-intensive firms use relatively less direct human labor (and that often professionalized and elaborately trained), they were less threatened by labor turbulence. They had the space and the resources to envelop, rather than confront, their work force. In addition, with the momentous exception of the chemical industry, these capital-intensive firms were both world and domestic leaders in their industries. Consequently, they stood to gain from global free trade. They could, and did, ally with important international financiers, whose own minuscule work forces presented few sources of tension and who had for over a decade supported a more broadly international foreign policy and the lowering of traditionally high American tariffs.

The Rise of the Multinational Bloc, 1918–1929

At the center of the Republican party during the System of '96 was a massive bloc of major industries, including steel, textiles, coal, and less monolithically, shoes, whose labor-intensive production processes automatically made them deadly enemies of labor and paladins of laissez-faire social policy.[10] While a few firms whose products dominated world markets, such as machinery, agitated for modest trade liberalization (aided occasionally by other industries seeking specific export advantages through trade treaties with particular countries), insistent pressures from foreign competitors led most to the ardent promotion of high tariffs.[11]

Integral to this "National Capitalist" bloc for most of the period were investment and commercial bankers. They had abandoned the Democrats in the 1890s when "Free Silver" and Populist advocates briefly captured the party. The financiers' massive investments in the mid-1890s and after, in huge trusts that combined many smaller firms, gave them a large, often controlling, stake in American industry, and brought them much closer to the industrialists (especially on tariffs, which Gold Democrats had abominated), and laid the foundation for a far more durable attachment to the GOP.[12]

World War I disrupted these close relations between American industry and finance. Overnight the United States went from a net debtor to a net creditor in the world economy, while the tremendous economic expansion induced by the war destabilized both the United States and the world economy. Briefly advantaged by the burgeoning demand for labor, American workers struck in record numbers and for a short interval appeared likely to unionize extensively.[13] Not surprisingly, as soon as the war ended a deep crisis gripped American society. In the face of mounting strikes, the question of U.S. adherence to the League of Nations, and a wave of racial, religious, and ethnic conflicts, the American business community sharply divided.

On the central questions of labor and foreign economic policy, most firms in the Republican bloc were driven by the logic of the postwar economy to intensify their commitment to the formula of 1896. The worldwide expansion of industrial capacity the war had induced left them face to face with vigorous foreign competitors. Consequently, they became even more ardent economic nationalists. Meeting British, French, and, later, German and other foreign competitors everywhere, even in the U.S. home market, they wanted ever higher tariffs and further indirect government assistance for their export drives. Their relatively labor intensive production processes also required the violent suppression of the great strike wave that capped the boom of 1919–20 and encouraged them to press the "Open Shop" drive that left organized labor reeling for the rest of the decade.

This response was not universal in the business community, however. The new political economy of the postwar world pressured a relative handful of the largest and most powerful firms in the opposite direction. The capital-intensive firms that had grown disproportionately during the war were under far less pressure from their labor force. By the end of the war the biggest of them had also developed into not only American but world leaders in their product lines. Accordingly, while none of them were pro-union, they preferred to conciliate rather than to repress their work force. Those which were world leaders favored lower tariffs, both to stimulate world commerce and to open up other countries to them. They also supported American assistance to rebuild Europe, which for many of them, such as Standard Oil of New Jersey and General Electric, represented an important market.

Joining these latter industrial interests were the international banks. Probably nothing that occurred in the United States between 1896 and the depression was so fundamentally destructive to the System of '96 as the World War I–induced transformation of the United States from a net debtor to a net creditor in the world economy. The overhang of both public and private debts that the war left in its wake struck directly at the accommodation of industry and finance that defined the Republican party. To revive economically and to pay off the debts, European countries had to run export surpluses. They needed to sell around the world, and they, or at least someone they traded with in a multilateral trading system, urgently needed to earn dollars by selling in the United States. Accordingly, along with private or governmental assistance from the United States to help make up war losses, the Europeans required a portal through the tariff walls that shielded Republican manufacturers from international competition.

The conflict between these two groups runs through all the major foreign policy disputes of the 1920s: the League of Nations, the World Court, and the great battles over tariffs, among others. Initially, the older, protectionist forces won far more than they lost. They defeated the League, kept the United States out of the World Court, and raised the tariff to ionospheric levels. But most trends in the world economy were against them. Throughout the 1920s the ranks of the largely Eastern internationalist bloc swelled.

Parallel to the multinational bloc's increasing numbers was its growing unity of interest, as problems with the British over oil and cables were resolved. As the bloc closed ranks, it discovered it could achieve its immediate foreign-policy objectives by working unofficially around the Congress with key executive-branch functionaries and New York Federal Reserve Bank officials.

Along with its increasing internal homogeneity, the multinational bloc enjoyed several other long-run advantages, which helped enormously in overcoming the new bloc's relative numerical insignificance vis-à-vis its older rival. The newer bloc included many of the largest, most rapidly growing corporations in the economy.

Recognized industry leaders with the most sophisticated managements, these concerns embodied the norms of professionalism and scientific advance that in this period fired the imagination of large parts of American society. The largest of them also dominated major American foundations, which were coming to exercise major influence not only on the climate of opinion but on the specific content of American public policy. And, what might be termed the "multinational liberalism" of the internationalists was also aided significantly by the spread of liberal Protestantism; by a newspaper stratification process that brought the free trade organ of international finance, the *New York Times*, to the top; by the growth of capital-intensive network radio in the dominant Eastern, internationally oriented environment; and by the rise of major news magazines. These last promised, as Raymond Moley himself intoned while taking over at what became *Newsweek*, to provide "Averell [Harriman] and Vincent [Astor] . . . with means for influencing public opinion generally outside of both parties."[14]

Closely paralleling the business community's differences over foreign policy was its split over labor policy. Analysts have correctly stressed that the 1920s were a period of violent hostility toward labor unions. But they have largely failed to notice the significant, sectorally specific modulation in the tactics and strategy employed by American business to deal with the labor movement.

The war-induced boom of 1918–19 cleared labor markets and led to a brief but sharp rise in strikes and the power of labor. A White House conference called by Wilson to discuss the situation ended in stalemate. John D. Rockefeller, Jr., and representatives of General Electric urged conciliatory programs of "employee representation" (company-dominated, plant-specific works councils). Steel and other relatively labor intensive industries, however, rejected the approach. Led by Elbert Gary, head of U.S. Steel, they joined forces, crushed the great steel strike of 1919, and organized the American Plan drives of the 1920s.

Rockefeller and Gary broke personal relations. Rockefeller supported an attack on the steel companies by the Inter-Church World Movement, an organization of liberal Protestants for which he raised funds and served as a director. Later he organized a consulting firm, Industrial Relations Counsellors, to promote nonconfrontational "scientific" approaches to labor conflict. Industrial Relations Counsellors assisted an unheralded group of capital-intensive firms and banks throughout the 1920s—a group whose key members included top management figures of General Electric and Standard Oil of New Jersey, and partners of the House of Morgan. Calling themselves the "Special Conference Committee," this group promoted various programs of advanced industrial relations.[15]

Industrial Relations Counsellors worked with the leading figures of at least one group of medium-sized firms. Perhaps ironically, they were organized in the Taylor Society, once the home of Frederick Taylor's well-known project for reorganizing the labor process. Two types of firms comprised this group: technically advanced enterprises in highly cyclical (hence, in the 1930s, highly depressed) industries like machine tools, and medium-sized "best practice" firms in declining sectors. Mostly located in the Northeast, these latter firms hoped that the introduction of the latest management and labor relations techniques would afford them cost advantages over burgeoning low-wage competitors in the American South. Forming a sort of flying buttress to the core of the multinational bloc, most of these firms strongly favored freer trade, while several future New Dealers, including Rexford Tugwell and Felix Frankfurter, worked with them.[16]

The leading figures in Industrial Relations Counsellors and their associates (who included, notably, Beardsley Ruml, head of the Spelman Fund, a part of the Rockefeller complex that began funding the first university-based industrial relations research centers) played important roles in virtually all major developments in labor policy across the 1920s. These included the campaign that forced the steel industry to accept the eight-hour day; the milestone Railway Labor Act; and the increasing criticism of the use of injunctions in labor disputes (a legal weapon that was an essential element of the System of '96's labor policy) that eventually led to the Norris-LaGuardia Act.

Under all these accumulating tensions the elite core of the Republican party began to disintegrate. The great boom of the 1920s exacerbated all the tensions over labor and international relations just described, while it greatly enhanced the position of the major oil companies and other capital-intensive firms in the economy as a whole (see table 1.1). Though their greatest effects came after the downturn in 1929, other "secondary"—that is, idiosyncratic or transitory—tensions also multiplied during the boom. One, which affected partisan competition even in the 1920s, concerned investment banking. A flock of new (or suddenly growing) houses sprang up and began to compete for dominance with the established leaders: the House of Morgan and Kuhn, Loeb. In time these firms would produce a generation of famous Democrats: James Forrestal of Dillon, Read; Averell Harriman of Brown Brothers Harriman; Sidney Weinberg of Goldman, Sachs; John Milton Hancock and Herbert Lehman of Lehman Brothers.[17]

In commercial banking, rivals also began to contest Morgan's position. The Bank of America rose rapidly to become one of the largest commercial banks in the world. Though the competition did not yet take partisan form, the bank bitterly opposed Morgan interests, which attempted to use the New York Federal Reserve Bank against it. Morgan also was hostile to Joseph Kennedy and other rising financial powers.

The cumulative impact of all these pressures became evident in the election of 1928. Some of the investment bankers, notably Averell Harriman, turned to the Democrats. Enraged by the House of Morgan's use of the New York Fed to control American interest rates for the sake of its international objectives, Chicago bankers, led by First National's Melvin Traylor, organized and went to the Democratic convention as a massed body. These were portentous developments indeed. At the time, however, they were overshadowed by the dramatic, but brief, effort of major elements of the strongly protectionist chemical industry, notably several members of the DuPont family, to try to take over the Democratic party. Repelled by Al Smith's shocking embrace of tariffs, most of the multinational bloc stayed with Republican presidential hopeful Herbert Hoover who, though still ostensibly committed to the traditional GOP position on tariffs, signaled his willingness to countenance several multinational-supported policies: German (and other) foreign investment in the United States, American investment abroad, and "unofficial" American intervention in European affairs.[18]

Economic Catastrophe and "National Recovery," 1929–1935

The onset of the Great Depression opened a new phase in the decay of the now creaking System of '96. As the depression grew worse, demands for government action proliferated. But Hoover opposed deficit-financed expenditures and easy monetary policies.[19] After the British abandoned the gold standard in September 1931

Table 1.1

Largest American Industrials, 1909–1948
(Ranked by Assets)

Company	1909	1919	1929	1935	1948
U.S. Steel	1	1	1	2	3
Standard Oil of N.J.	2	2	2	1	1
American Tobacco	3	19			17
Int'l Mercantile Marine	4	12			
Anaconda	5	14	8	8	19
Int'l Harvester	6	13	17	14	18
Central Leather	7				
Pullman	8				
Armour	9	3	14	20	
American Sugar	10				
U.S. Rubber	11	8			
American Smelting & Refining	12	17			
Singer	13				
Swift	14	4	19	19	
Consolidation Coal	15				
General Electric	16	11	11	13	9
ACF Industries	17				
Colorado Fuel & Iron	18				
Corn Products Refining	19				
New England Navigation	20				
General Motors		5	3	3	2
Bethlehem Steel		6	5	7	12
Ford		7	6	6	10
Socony Mobil		9	7	4	5
Midvale Steel		10			
Sinclair Oil		15	16	16	15
Texaco		16	9	11	6
DuPont		18	12	9	7
Union Carbide		20			14
Standard Oil of Ind.			4	5	4
Standard Oil of Calif.			10	10	11
Shell			13	15	
Gulf			15	12	8
General Theater Equip.			18		
Kennecott			20	18	
Koppers				17	
Sears Roebuck					13
Westinghouse					16
Western Electric					20

Source: A.D.H. Kaplan, *Big Enterprise in a Competitive Setting* (Washington, D.C.: Brookings Institution, 1962), 140ff.

and moved to establish a preferential trading bloc, the intransigence of Hoover and the financiers locked the international economy onto a collision course with American domestic politics. Increasingly squeezed industrialists and farmers began clamoring for government help in the form of tariffs even higher than those in the recently passed Smoot-Hawley bill; they also called for legalized cartels and, ever more loudly, for a devaluation of the dollar through a large increase in the money supply.

Concerned, as Federal Reserve minutes show, at the prospect that the business groups and farmers might coalesce with angry, bonus-marching veterans, and worried by French gold withdrawals and fears that not only farmers and workers, but leading bankers, might go bankrupt, the Fed briefly attempted to relieve the pressure by expansionary open-market operations. But after a few months, the policy was abandoned as foreigners withdrew more gold and bankers in Chicago and elsewhere complained that the drop in short-term interest rates was driving down interest rates on short-term government debt (and thus bank profits, which, given the scarcity of long-term debt and the disappearance of industrial loans in Federal Reserve districts outside of New York, now depended directly on these rates).[20]

Hoover's commitment to gold, however, began driving inflationist, usually protectionist, businessmen out of the GOP to the Democrats. Their swarming ranks triggered a virtual identity crisis among Republican party regulars. As familiar rules of thumb about the growth of the world economy grew increasingly anachronistic, the mushrooming sentiment for monetary expansion and economic nationalism scrambled the calculations of the contenders for the Democratic nomination.

The developing situation called for the highest kind of political judgment from aspiring presidential candidates. At this point a legendary political operative came out of retirement to advise Franklin D. Roosevelt. Colonel Edward House had been a longtime adviser to Woodrow Wilson and was normally an ardent champion of low tariffs and the League of Nations; but, perhaps most important for the first New Deal, he was now closely associated with Rockefeller interests.[21] Along with the more famous Brains Trust, which functioned largely as a transmission belt for the ideas of others, including, notably, investment bankers from Lehman Brothers, House helped chart Roosevelt's early path. It was calculated to blur his image and make him acceptable to all factions of the party. Making overtures to William Randolph Hearst and other like-minded businessmen, Roosevelt repudiated his earlier strong support for the League of Nations, talked rather vaguely of raising tariffs, and began showing an interest in major revision of the antitrust laws.[22]

The tactics were successful. Coming into office at the very darkest moment of the depression, with all the banks closed, Roosevelt moved immediately to restore business confidence and reform the wrecked banking structure. The real significance of this bank reform, however, has been misperceived. With the world economy reeling, the shared interest in a liberal world economy that normally (i.e., when the economy was growing) bound powerful rivals together in one political coalition was disappearing. In this once-in-a-lifetime context, what had previously been secondary tensions between rival financial groups now suddenly came briefly, but centrally, to define the national political agenda. With workers, farmers, and many industrialists up in arms against finance in general and its most famous symbol, the House of Morgan, in particular, virtually all the major non-Morgan investment banks in America lined up behind Roosevelt. And, in perhaps the least appreciated aspect of the New Deal, so did the now Rockefeller-controlled Chase National Bank.

In the eighteen months previous to the election, relations between the Rockefeller and Morgan interests had deteriorated drastically. After the crash of 1929 Equitable Trust, which Rockefeller had purchased and in the late 1920s had sought to build up, had been forced to merge with the Morgan-oriented Chase National Bank. The merger caused trouble virtually from the beginning. Thomas W. Lamont and several other banking executives allied with Morgan attempted to block the ascent of Winthrop Aldrich, the brother-in-law of John D. Rockefeller, Jr., to the presidency of the Chase. Their efforts, however, proved unsuccessful, and Aldrich quickly, if apparently rather tensely, assumed an important role in Chase's management. But when Rockefeller attempted to secure a loan for the construction of Rockefeller Center (which threatened [Pierre] DuPont and Raskob's Empire State Building, already under construction and unable to rent all its space with the collapse of real-estate values), the bank seems not to have gone along. The chief financing had to come instead from Metropolitan Life. An old dispute between two transit companies, one controlled by the Morgans and the other by the Rockefellers, also created problems.[23]

Though sniping from holdover employees continued for several years, operating control of Chase passed definitely out of

Morgan hands in late 1932. With longtime Chase head Albert Wiggin retiring, Aldrich was announced as the next chairman of the bank's governing board, and plans were made to reorganize the board of directors.

In the meantime, the East Texas oil discoveries dropped the price of oil to ten cents a barrel. This quickly brought the entire oil industry to the brink of disaster. Becoming more interested in oil and domestic recovery, and less in banking, the Rockefeller interests urged a substantial relief program on Hoover, who brusquely rejected it. Almost simultaneously top Rockefeller adviser Beardsley Ruml, then still at the helm of the Spelman Fund and a prominent Democrat, began promoting a complicated plan for agricultural adjustment. At Chicago the Roosevelt forces accepted some of its basic concepts just ahead of the convention.[24]

Only a few days before the 1932 presidential election, Morgan discovered that high Chase officials were supporting Roosevelt.[25] Colonel House's daughter was married to Gordon Auchincloss, Aldrich's best friend and a member of the Chase board. During the campaign and transition period, House and Vincent Astor, Roosevelt's cousin and also a member of the reorganized Chase board, passed messages between Roosevelt and Chase.[26]

A few days after Roosevelt was inaugurated, Chase and the investment bankers started their campaign, both in public and in private, for a new banking law. Aldrich made a dramatic public plea for the complete separation of investment and commercial banking. Then he began personally to lobby Roosevelt and high administration officials. As Secretary of Commerce Daniel Roper reported to Roosevelt in March 1932:

> I have had a very interesting and refreshing conversation with Mr. W. W. Aldrich. . . . I also suggest that you consider calling in, when convenient to you, Senators Glass and Bulkley and Mr. Aldrich to discuss the advisability and necessity for dealing not only with the divorcement of affiliates from commercial banks but the complete divorcement of functions between the issuance of securities by private banks over whom there is no supervision and the business of commercial banks. We feel that this suggestion should be incorporated in the Glass Banking Bill.[27]

Aldrich also joined the ancestral enemies of the banks—William Randolph Hearst, Samuel Untermeyer, South Dakota senator Peter Norbeck, and others promoting Ferdinand Pecora's investigation of J. P. Morgan & Co. He cooperated fully with the investigation, promoted "reforms," and aided investigators examining the Wiggin era at Chase. "I found Aldrich sympathetic to the last degree of what the president is trying to do," noted Colonel House to Roper in October 1933. House continued:

> I advised him to tell the Banking Committee the whole story. He is prepared to do this, and has gone to the country today to write his proposed testimony in the form of a memorandum, a copy of which he is to send me tomorrow morning. He intimated that if there was any part of it that I thought should be changed he would consider doing so. . . . He tells me that his Board is back of him and some few of the leading bankers. However, most of them are critical and many are bitter because of what they term his not standing with his colleagues.[28]

These efforts came to fruition in the Glass-Steagall Act. By separating investment from commercial banking, this measure destroyed the unity of the two functions whose combination had been the basis of Morgan hegemony in American finance. It also opened the way to a financial structure crowned by a giant bank with special ties to capital-intensive industry—oil.

With most of the (Morgan-dominated) banking community opposed to him, Roosevelt looked toward industry for allies. By now an uncountably large number of firms, for reasons discussed earlier, were actively seeking inflation and, usually, an abandonment of the gold standard. For more than a year, for example, Royal Dutch Shell, led by Sir Henri Deterding, had been campaigning to get Britain, the United States, and other major countries to remonetize silver. At some point—it is impossible to say exactly when—Deterding and his American financial adviser Rene Leon began coordinating efforts to secure some kind of reflation with James A. Moffett, a longtime director and high official of the Standard Oil Company of New Jersey, and a friend and early supporter of Roosevelt.[29]

While they campaigned to expand the money supply, a powerful group of industrialists, large farm organizations, and retailers organized separately for the same general end. Led by Bendix, Remington Rand, and Sears Roebuck, they called themselves "The Committee for the Nation." As Roosevelt took over in the spring of 1933, contributions from Standard Oil of New Jersey and many other industrial firms were swelling this committee's war chest.[30] The committee was vigorously pushing the president to go off the gold standard.

Working closely with sympathizers in the Treasury Department, the banks fought back. Federal Reserve minutes show the Executive Committee of the System Open Market Committee distinguishing between "technical" and "political" adjustments of the money supply, with the political adjustments designed to head off demands for reflation.[31] But the industrialists could not be denied. Moffett and Leon found legal authority for Roosevelt to go off gold during the banking crisis, when even the banks conceded the step to be briefly necessary. Later the same pair teamed up to reach Roosevelt at the crucial moment of the London Economic Conference and persuaded him to send the famous telegram destroying the hope for informal agreements on currency stabilization devoutly wished for and almost achieved by James P. Warburg and other international financiers.[32] Still pressured by the Committee for the Nation and the oil companies, Roosevelt embarked on his famous gold-buying experiments in the autumn, driving most of the banks to distraction. Roosevelt also continued with the National Recovery Administration, whose name wonderfully symbolized the truly national character of the political coalition forged by the extreme economic circumstances of the early 1930s: protectionist industrialists (whose ranks had been swelled by the collapse of world trade), oilmen desperate for price controls, anti-Morgan and pro-oil-industry bankers, and farmers.

Phoenix Rises: Economic Upturn and the Return of the Multinational Bloc

This first New Deal was desperately unstable. Once the worst phase of deflation ended and the economy began slowly to revive, industries with good long-term prospects in the world economy would start exploring ways to resume profitable overseas business. In time, this search would necessarily bring them back in the direction of the international banks, which (with the obvious exceptions noted above) generally opposed the NRA, and away from the economic nationalists, for most of whom the NRA initially represented the promised land. In addition, the NRA's halfhearted and incoherently designed attempt to supplement price mechanisms with administrative processes for the allocation of resources bitterly divided its natural constituency of protectionist businessmen.

Not surprisingly, therefore, the NRA began to self-destruct almost from the moment it began operations. Free traders fought with protectionists; big firms battled with smaller competitors; buyers collided with suppliers. The result was chaos. The situation was especially grave in the oil industry. There the majors and the smaller independent oil companies stalemated in the face of massive overproduction from the new East Texas fields.[33]

As the industries fought, labor stirred. A bitter series of strikes erupted as the ambiguous wording of the National Recovery Act's 7a clause, guaranteeing employee representation, came to be interpreted as securing "company" rather than independent trade unions.[34]

With the pressure beginning to tell on Roosevelt, he looked around for new allies. He sponsored an inquiry into foreign economic policy conducted by Beardsley Ruml, which recommended freer trade. Simultaneously he allowed Secretary of State Cordell Hull to promote reciprocal trade treaties in a series of speeches. The prospect of a change in U.S. tariff policy drew applause from segments of the business community that had mostly been hostile to Roosevelt. The Council on Foreign Relations sponsored a symposium at which journalist Walter Lippmann declared that freedom itself could probably not be maintained without free trade.[35]

As the first New Deal coalition disintegrated under the impact of interindustrial and class conflicts, Roosevelt turned more definitely toward free trade. He pushed through Congress a new bill (bitterly opposed by steel, chemicals, and other industries) giving Hull the authority to negotiate lower tariffs and then let him build support for the trade treaties.

The rest of the New Deal's program stalled. With their public support already eroded, the NRA and other measures were declared unconstitutional by the Supreme Court. Largely out of ideas, anxiously eyeing the activity of the Left, the prospect of strikes, especially in the steel industry, and sporadic urban disorders, Adolf A. Berle conveyed his deep pessimism to fellow administrators as they toured New York and New England:

> Mr. Berle stressed the need for prompt action in any program of economic security. He dreads the coming winter. While the City of New York has gotten along better in the past months than was to be expected, the City's finances are near the exhaustion point. Mr. Berle also states that the "market" was "jittery" about the credit

of the federal government. Another complete financial collapse is distinctly possible if "Wall Street" should decide to "dump" U.S. bonds, which Mr. Berle thinks it might be foolish enough to do. The Communists are making rapid gains in New York City and the one thing that can save the city is very prompt action which will give the people out of work something better than they now have. The fiscal situation is such that the total costs of taking care of these people cannot be increased. The prompt enactment of an unemployment insurance bill and, if possible, old age pension legislation would have a very wholesome effect.... Any unemployment insurance system adopted should be put into operation at once, both to give new hope to the unemployed and to bring in new revenue badly needed to take care of the large numbers of people to be cared for at this time.[36]

In this, the darkest point of the New Deal, at the moment in which other countries had terminated constitutional regimes, Roosevelt and part of the business community began to discover the logic of a (stable) winning political coalition. The first successful capital-intensive-led political coalition in history began dramatically to come together.

As national income continued its gradual rise, John D. Rockefeller, Jr., and his attorney, Raymond B. Fosdick, voted a special grant from the Spelman Fund to pay staff of Industrial Relations Counsellors while they worked on social welfare legislation within federal agencies. Then the capital-intensive big-business members of the Commerce Department's Business Advisory Council, led by Walter Teagle of Standard Oil and Gerard Swope of General Electric, joined leaders of the Taylor Society on an advisory committee whose task was the preparation of the Social Security Act. Backed by Aldrich, Harriman, Thomas Watson of IBM, George Mead of Mead Paper, the Filenes, and a huge bloc of retailers and other corporations, the group subcontracted preparation of the bill to Industrial Relations Counsellors (where Teagle and Owen D. Young, the board chairman of General Electric, were, or within months became, trustees). With slight changes, that bill, with its savagely regressive tax on payrolls, became the law of the land.[37]

Almost simultaneously, the decisive legislative struggle over the Wagner National Labor Relations Act came to a climax. Throughout 1934, strikes and work stoppages had mounted. In June 1935, the National Recovery Act was due to expire, threatening to leave the country without any machinery for processing class conflicts.[38]

As Armageddon approached, the conservative American Federation of Labor (AFL) was becoming increasingly desperate. Roosevelt had fairly consistently sided with business against it, and the federation was increasingly divided and rapidly losing control of its own membership. According to AFL memoranda of the period, top union officials were convinced that without a new labor relations law they were going to be destroyed.[39]

But while many big-business executives were sympathetic to the strongly conservative union's plight (Alfred P. Sloan, for example, wrote frankly that the AFL had to be preserved because it constituted a bulwark against communism),[40] they adamantly opposed any extension of the legal rights of unions. Caught between the warring groups, Robert Wagner of New York, the senator from the most perfectly representative capital-intensive state in America, began searching for compromise while Edward Filene's Twentieth Century Fund opened a special inquiry. Working closely together, the Fund and Wagner began considering alternatives. Shown drafts of a proposed bill, the general counsels of U.S. Steel and most other industries shifted into open opposition. Teagle and Swope, however, began meeting with Wagner. What happened next is too complex to be fully described here. All that can be said is that attorneys for the AFL pressed the Twentieth Century Fund for a stronger bill; Wagner took up some amendments Teagle and Swope proposed to the sections defining unfair labor practices; a number of mostly Northeastern textile and shoe firms, which were hoping to stop the flow of jobs to the South, promoted the legislation; and the Twentieth Century Fund trustees (who included not only E. A. Filene but important members of the Taylor Society and several other major business figures) joined Mead, several tobacco executives, probably Swope, and perhaps Teagle, in endorsing the bill. The fund then assisted the lobbying effort, arranging testimony and helping to defray some of the costs Wagner was incurring.[41]

Almost at the same instant, Roosevelt turned sharply away from the proposals for more inflation and stronger federal control of banking advanced by the Committee for the Nation and major farm groups. For some time the administration had been buying silver (to the great satisfaction of Western senators from silver-producing states, Shell, and silver speculators the world over) but holding the dollar firm against the pound. After ferocious infighting, the administration now accepted a compromise Federal Reserve Act of 1935.[42] The measure contained provisions (ardently promoted by Chase president Aldrich, who played a key role in the final negotiations) reconfirming the separation of investment from commercial banking. It also confirmed the supremacy of the Board of Governors in Washington over the New York Federal Reserve and the other regional banks, as the Bank of America and other leading non–New York banks (including the chain controlled by Fed chairman Eccles) had long desired.

Only days later, as Democratic party leader James Farley collected cash contributions from oil companies, Roosevelt overruled Interior Secretary Harold Ickes and established a compromise oil price control scheme. With its implementation, the greatest of major American industries achieved near-complete price control for a generation.[43]

The powerful appeal of the unorthodox combination of free trade, the Wagner Act, and social welfare was evident in the 1936 election. A massive bloc of protectionist and labor-intensive industries formed to fight the New Deal. Together with the House of Morgan (which had reasons of its own to oppose Roosevelt), the DuPonts recruited many of these firms into the Liberty League. They were joined by some firms hoping to find a Republican candidate to run a milder New Deal.[44]

But Standard Oil could not abide Alfred Landon, who had once been in the oil business as an independent in Kansas. On the eve of the Republican convention, Standard dramatically came out against him.[45] In addition, a furious battle raged in the Republican camp over Hull's reciprocal trade treaties. Landon, who was at the moment surrounded by advisers from major banks, including James Warburg and figures from both Chase and Morgan, originally favored them. But the Chemical Foundation and many industrialists were bitterly opposed. At the Republican convention the latter group prevailed during the writing of the platform. For a few weeks thereafter, however, it appeared that the free traders would nevertheless win out. Landon repudiated that part of the platform and ran as a free trader.[46]

But the protectionists did not give up. Organizing many businesses into the "Made in America Club," and backed by Orlando Weber of Allied Chemical and other top executives, Chemical Foundation president Francis Garvan and journalist Samuel

Crowther, author of a book called *America Self-Contained* who enjoyed close ties with many businessmen, began kamikaze attacks to break through the cordon of free-trading advisers who were attempting to wall off Landon. Eventually they succeeded in getting their message through. Crowther optimistically noted, in a letter to Garvan in 1936, that George Peek, Chemical Foundation adviser and staunch protectionist, had succeeded in getting Landon's ear:

> On the foreign trade and gold, Landon was extremely interested and he gave no evidence of ever before having heard of either subject. . . . George Peek went back and forth over this subject, in terms of Landon's own business, and Landon seemed thus to get a grasp of what it was all about. . . . Peek hammered the subject of the tariff and of our whole foreign trade program and, although he could not say positively that Landon accepted it as his paramount issue, he did believe that by the time he left, Landon had begun to realize something and that he would go further.[47]

Though Warburg and the other bankers repeatedly warned him against it in the strongest possible terms, Landon began to waver. In mid and late September his campaign began to criticize Hull's treaties.

His attacks alienated many multinationalists, who had watched with great interest Roosevelt's effort to stabilize the dollar. When, after speeches by First National's Leon Fraser and others, Roosevelt opened negotiations with Britain and France, the New Deal began to look like a good deal to them. It became still more attractive when the Tripartite Money Agreement was announced in September and after the Roosevelt administration raised reserve requirements on bank deposits, as many bankers had been demanding. As Landon's attacks on the trade treaties increased (but, be it noted, while many of his polls were holding up, including the *Literary Digest*'s, which had never been wrong), a generation of legendary American business figures began backing out of the Republican campaign. On active service in war and peace, Henry Stimson, who had already backed the treaties, refused to support Landon and withdrew from the campaign. On October 18, as spokesmen for the Rockefeller interests debated issuing a veiled criticism of the Liberty League, came the sensational announcement that James Warburg, who since his noisy public break with FDR two years before had waged unremitting war on the New Deal and frequently advised Landon, was switching to Roosevelt out of disgust with Landon's stand on the trade treaties. Only a couple of days after Warburg released his rapturous public encomium to Hull, Dean Acheson, Warburg's friend and former associate at the Treasury Department, did exactly the same thing. So did cotton broker William Clayton, who also resigned from the Liberty League. On October 29 at

> a mass meeting in the heart of the Wall Street District, about 200 business leaders, most of whom described themselves as Republicans, enthusiastically endorsed yesterday the foreign trade policy of the Roosevelt Administration and pledged themselves to work for the President's reelection.
>
> After addresses by five speakers, four of whom described themselves as Republicans, the Meeting unanimously adopted a resolution praising the reciprocal trade policy established by the Roosevelt Administration under the direction of Secretary of State Cordell Hull. . . . Governor Landon's attitude on the reciprocal tariff issue was criticized by every speaker. They contended that if Landon were elected and Secretary Hull's treaties were revoked, there would be a revolution among conservative businessmen.[48]

While the Republicans switched, the Democrats fought. The Bank of America and New Orleans banker Rudolph Hecht, who was just coming off a term as president of the American Bankers Association, bulwarked the "Good Neighbor League," a Roosevelt campaign vehicle. Lincoln and Edward Filene supported the president to the hilt, as did sugar refiner Ellsworth Bunker, a major importer from the Caribbean. Sidney Weinberg of Goldman, Sachs came back into the campaign and raised more money for Roosevelt than any other single person. Behind him trailed a virtual Milky Way of non-Morgan banking stars, including Averell Harriman of Brown Brothers Harriman; James Forrestal of Dillon, Read; and probably John Milton Hancock of Lehman Brothers.

From the oil industry came a host of independents, including Sid Richardson, Clint Murchison, and Charlie Roesser, as well as Sir Henri Deterding, James A. Moffett of Standard Oil of California, W. Alton Jones of Cities Services, Standard Oil of New Jersey's Boris Said (who helped run Democratic Youth groups), and M. L. Benedum of Benedum-Trees. Top executives of Reynolds Tobacco, American Tobacco, Coca-Cola, International Harvester, Johnson & Johnson, General Electric, Zenith, IBM, Sears Roebuck, ITT, United Fruit, Pan Am, and Manufacturers Trust all lent support. Prodded by banker George Foster Peabody, the *New York Times* came out for Roosevelt, as did the Scripps-Howard papers.[49]

In the final days of the campaign, as Landon furiously attacked social security, Teagle of Standard Oil of New Jersey, Swope of GE, the Pennsylvania Retailers Association, the American Retail Federation, and the Lorillard tobacco company (Old Gold), among others, spoke out in defense of the program. Last, if scarcely least, the firm that would incarnate the next thirty years of multinational oil and banking, the Chase National Bank, loaned the Democratic National Committee $100,000.

The curtain fell on the New Deal's creation of the modern Democratic political formula in early 1938. When the United States plunged steeply into recession, the clamor for relief began again as it had in 1933. Pressures for a revival of the NRA also mounted. But this time Roosevelt did not devalue the dollar. With billions of dollars in gold now squirreled away in the Fed, thanks to administration financial policies and spreading European anxieties, early 1930s fears of hoarding and runs on gold had vanished. As a consequence, reflation without formal devaluation or a revival of the NRA became a live option. Rockefeller adviser Beardsley Ruml proposed a plan for deficit spending, which Roosevelt implemented after versions won approval from Teagle and nearly all the important bankers, including Morgan. Aldrich then went on NBC radio to defend compensatory spending from attacks as long as it was coupled with measures for free trade (to the great annoyance of the DuPonts). Slightly later, the State Department, acting in secret with the Chase National Bank, and in public with the Catholic cardinal of Chicago and high business figures, set up a committee to promote renewal of the Reciprocal Trade Act in the wavering Corn Belt.[50] They were successful. National income snapped back and the multinational bloc held together. The fatal circle closed: for all the drama of the next half century, the national Democratic party was permanently committed: it was now a party of the comparatively advantaged, unified around the principle of comparative advantage, and simultaneously the party of the "people" (or "labor") opposed to the Republicans, the party of "big business."

While scarcely profound or "magical,"[51] this process created illusions that ran very deep. Cultivated by the press, nourished by increasingly affluent business groups, and fiercely protected by two generations of (often handsomely rewarded) scholars, this view of the Democrats and the New Deal left ordinary Americans alternately confused, perplexed, alarmed, or disgusted, as they tried to puzzle out why the party did so little to help unionize the South, protect the victims of McCarthyism, promote civil rights for blacks, women, or Hispanics, or, in the late 1970s, combat America's great "right turn" against the New Deal itself.[52] To such people, it always remained a mystery why the Democrats so often betrayed the ideals of the New Deal. Little did they realize that, in fact, the party was only living up to them.

NOTES

This essay is a greatly abbreviated version of my "From Normalcy to New Deal: Industrial Structure, Party Competition, and American Public Policy in the Great Depression," *International Organization* 38, no. 1 (Winter 1984), reprinted by permission of MIT Press. See also my *Critical Realignment: The Fall of the House of Morgan and the Origins of the New Deal* (New York: Oxford University Press, forthcoming).

1. The first of several New Deal reciprocal trade measures passed rather early in Roosevelt's first term, but, as explained below, it had virtually no immediate effect on the administration's essentially protectionist trade policy.

2. The "System of '96" is a reference to the discussion of "party systems" and American electoral behavior by analysts such as V. O. Key and Walter Dean Burnham.

3. The role of "Keynesian" public finance versus a bulging export surplus in leading the Swedish revival of the mid and latter 1930s has been extensively debated: the weight of the evidence suggests that the Swedish government did not vigorously implement the advanced monetary and fiscal proposals that were undeniably in the air. I should also note that this paragraph's clear distinctions and exact datings of the New Deal's "Keynesian Turn" are taken over unchanged from my "Normalcy to New Deal" essay. I therefore find inexplicable the recent claim by M. Weir and T. Skocpol that my essay "mistakenly conflates the labor regulation and social insurance reforms of 1935–36 with Keynesianism." See their "State Structures and the Possibilities for 'Keynesian' Responses to the Great Depression in Sweden, Britain, and the United States," in P. Evans, D. Rueschemeyer, and T. Skocpol, eds., *Bringing the State Back In* (New York: Cambridge University Press, 1985), 154.

4. See, for example, Arthur Schlesinger, Jr., *The Age of Roosevelt*, 3 vols. (Boston: Houghton Mifflin, 1957–60); William Leuchtenburg, *Franklin D. Roosevelt and the New Deal* (New York: Harper & Row, 1963); and Frank Freidel, *Franklin D. Roosevelt*, 4 vols. (Boston: Little, Brown, 1952–).

5. See, for example, Barton Bernstein, "The New Deal: The Conservative Achievements of Liberal Reform," in Bernstein, ed., *Toward a New Past: Dissenting Essays in American History* (New York: Pantheon, 1968), and Ronald Radosh, "The Myth of the New Deal," in Radosh and Murray N. Rothbard, eds., *A New History of Leviathan* (New York: E. P. Dutton, 1972), 146–86.

6. See, for example, Ellis Hawley's "The Discovery and Study of a Corporate Liberalism," *Business History Review* 52, no. 3 (1978): 309–20. In contrast, his classic *The New Deal and the Problem of Monopoly* (Princeton: Princeton University Press, 1962) does not emphasize these themes. See also Alfred Chandler and Louis Galambos, "The Development of Large Scale Economic Organizations in Modern America," in E. J. Perkins, ed., *Men and Organizations* (New York: Putnam, 1977). It appears that Weir and Skocpol's "Keynesian Responses," and other recent essays in the "state managers" vein, represent something of a synthesis of this view and the older "pluralist" approach—with the conspicuous difference that the state manager theorists rely almost entirely on secondary sources.

7. For a review of the West German work see H. A. Winkler, ed., *Die Grosse Krise in America* (Göttingen: Vandenhoech & Ruprecht, 1973). Perhaps the finest of the libertarian writings are those by Murray Rothbard—see his "War Collectivism in World War I" and "Herbert Hoover and the Myth of Laissez-Faire," both in Radosh and Rothbard, *New History of Leviathan*; for Kolko's views see his *Main Currents in Modern American History* (New York: Harper & Row, 1976). See also Kim McQuaid, *Big Business and Presidential Power* (New York: William Morrow, 1983) and Robert Collins, *Business Response to Keynes* (New York: Columbia University Press, 1980).

8. Some commentators, such as Elliot Rosen in his very stimulating *Hoover, Roosevelt, and the Brains Trust* (New York: Columbia University Press, 1977), have questioned the existence of "two New Deals." These doubts, however, are difficult to sustain if one systematically compares the policies pursued during each period, as, for example, in the incomplete inventory that opened this essay.

9. On the notions of coalitions and investor blocs, see my "Elites and Elections, or What Have They Done to You Lately: Toward an Investment Theory of Political Parties and Critical Realignment," in Benjamin Ginsberg and Alan Stone, eds., *Do Elections Matter?* (Armonk, N.Y.: M. E. Sharpe, 1986), 164–88, and "Party Realignment and American Industrial Structure: The Investment Theory of Political Parties in Historical Perspective," in Paul Zarembka, ed., *Research in Political Economy*, (Greenwich, Conn.: JAI Press, 1983), 6:1–82.

10. See my "Party Realignment," sec. 4. The shoe industry was singular because in contrast with most other charter members of the Republican bloc, its firms directly confronted a giant trust, United Shoe Machinery. As a consequence, they were far more likely to harbor doubts about the wisdom of "big business" and often went over to conservative Democrats.

11. This discussion neglects a modest movement for very limited trade liberalization promoted by several sectors in the pre-1914 period.

12. For the merger movement of the 1890s, see my discussion in "Party Realignment." Railroad mergers, organized by leading financiers, were also a part of the consolidation of this bloc.

13. For reasons of space, notes for most secondary sources have had to be eliminated in this section. See "Normalcy to New Deal." Also eliminated are that essay's lengthy theoretical sections and a detailed specification of which firms and sectors belonged to the various blocs discussed below.

14. For the *New York Times*, see below; the Moley question is from a June 13, 1936, entry in his "Journal," now in the Moley Papers, Hoover Institution, Stanford, Calif. Astor and Harriman were the most important of the magazine's owners. Moley later moved much further to the right. (Most archives used in this project are adequately indexed; box numbers are provided for the reader's convenience only where confusion seems likely.)

15. The sources for this and the following paragraphs are mostly papers scattered through several archives, including the Rockefeller Archive Center at Tarrytown, N.Y. For the dominance of Standard Oil and General Electric within the group, see J. J. Raskob to Lammot DuPont, November 26, 1929, Raskob Papers, Eleutherian Mills–Hagley Foundation, Wilmington, Del. Industrial Relations Counsellors seems to have coordinated the meetings of the group for most of the 1920s.

16. Several (Northeastern) textile executives played leading roles within this group, which produced the otherwise inexplicable sight of a handful of textile men supporting Franklin D. Roosevelt during the second New Deal, and which for a brief period generated some interesting, if ultimately unimportant, wrinkles in the Hull-Roosevelt trade offensive in the mid-1930s. Boston merchant E. A. Filene, who established (and controlled) the Twentieth Century Fund, and who ardently championed what might be labeled the "retailers' dream" of an economy built on high wages and cheap imports, was deeply involved with this group. The small businessmen of the Taylor Society differed very slightly with their big-business allies on entirely predictable issues: antitrust and financial reform. Supreme Court justice Louis D. Brandeis, who is usually credited as a major inspiration for many New Deal measures, had once served as Filene's attorney and remained closely associated with him and his brother A. Lincoln Filene.

17. Because many of these bankers were Jewish, the competition with Morgan almost immediately assumed an ugly tone. J. P. Morgan,

Jr., quietly encouraged Henry Ford's circulation of the notorious *Protocols of the Elders of Zion* in the early 1920s, and later his bank forbade Morgan Harjes, the firm's Paris partner, to honor letters of credit from Manufacturers Trust, a commercial bank with strong ties to Goldman, Sachs and Lehman Brothers. See Thomas Lamont to V. H. Smith at Morgan Grenfell, January 10, 1927, Box 111, Lamont Papers, Baker Library, Harvard University. For more on the astonishing Morgan-Ford interaction, see Henry Ford to J. P. Morgan, Jr., May 7, 1921, and Morgan to Ford, May 11, 1921, Ford Archives, Henry Ford Museum, Dearborn, Mich.

18. See "Normalcy to New Deal," 72–79. Historians of this period have typically made rather too much of Hoover's criticism of foreign loans, since in its later stages it was encouraged by the Morgan bank.

19. In her *American Business and Foreign Policy* (Boston: Beacon Press, 1971), 137–38, Joan Hoff Wilson cites a Hoover "diary" in the Hoover Presidential Library as the authority for an account in which Hoover worked against the bankers. Box 98 of the Lamont Papers contains transcriptions of the telephone conversations to which the "diary" refers. The transcriptions not only refute every detail of Hoover's account but actually record Lamont's specific instructions to the president to conceal the origins of the moratorium. (As Lamont signed off from the first conversation: "One last thing, Mr. President . . . if anything, by any chance, ever comes out of this suggestion, we should wish to be forgotten in this matter. This is your plan and nobody else's.") A mass of supporting correspondence in the file confirms the authenticity of these transcripts while raising many more questions about the "diary." (Hoover often harbored private misgivings about both his policies and his advisers—but he never consistently acted upon these doubts.)

20. See Gerald Epstein and Thomas Ferguson, "Loan Liquidation and Industrial Conflict: The Federal Reserve and the Open Market Operations of 1932," *Journal of Economic History* 44, no. 4 (1984) for details.

21. Rosen, *Brains Trust*, 113, argues that House's influence on Roosevelt ebbed after March 1932. But the aging House could scarcely be expected to provide the daily memoranda and speeches that Roosevelt then needed. There is a sense in which House and all of Roosevelt's early advisers were supplemented, and in part supplanted, by many other forces then coming to life in the Democratic party; however, House always remained a major actor in the New Deal.

22. The Newton Baker Papers now at the Library of Congress, Washington, D.C., and the Franklin D. Roosevelt papers at the Roosevelt Library in Hyde Park, N.Y., contain a mass of material on the primary and convention battles (e.g., the letters between Baker and Ralph Hayes in the Baker Papers). Rosen, *Brains Trust*, chaps. 9 and 10, presents considerable detail on the business opposition to FDR's nomination, and is very good on the stop-Roosevelt forces' manipulation of the press.

23. For Lamont's dramatic bid to block Aldrich, see Aldrich interviews, Chase Manhattan Bank Oral History Project, November 29, 1961, now in the Winthrop W. Aldrich Papers, Baker Library, Harvard University; for apprising me of the Rockefeller Center financing controversy I am grateful to Robert Fitch, whose own work on urban development and American political structures involved a lengthy period of work in the Rockefeller Archives. For the subway battle see the *New York Times*, July 31, and August 27 and 31, 1932; and Cynthia Horan, "Agreeing with the Bankers: New York City's Depression Financial Crisis," in P. Zarembka, ed., *Research in Political Economy* (Greenwich, Conn.: JAI Press, 1986), vol. 8.

24. Agricultural economist M. L. Wilson is normally identified as the author of the adjustment plan. For Rockefeller's role in financing Wilson's early work see Rosen, *Brains Trust*, 180; see p. 178 for Ruml's role in the famous Wilson-Rexford Tugwell meeting on the eve of the convention.

25. See the crucial letters of Thomas W. Lamont to various business associates and attached memoranda in Box 123 of the Lamont Papers and my discussion of them in "Elites and Elections."

26. Some of these are in the House Papers, Yale University Library; others, in the Aldrich Papers. See, for example, the House-Auchincloss correspondence in the former.

27. Secretary of Commerce Daniel Roper to Franklin D. Roosevelt, March 28, 1932, Roosevelt Library. This is one of many documents relating to Aldrich's vast lobbying efforts; others aspects of this legislation involved fairly heated exchanges between the Bank of America and the National City Bank of New York. While not as enduringly significant as the separation of investment from commercial banking, these conflicts persisted for some years and complicated the position of the National City Bank during much of the New Deal.

28. House to Roper, October 21, 1933, House Papers.

29. The chief source for most of what follows are the personal papers of Rene Leon, copies of which are now in my possession. See also the correspondence between Walter Lippmann and Leon, now in the Lippmann Correspondence at Yale, and between Moley, Leon, and Deterding in the Moley Papers. Moffett Later joined Standard of California.

30. The Frank Vandertip Papers at Columbia University, New York City, contain the financial records of the Committee for the Nation during this period. The Standard Oil contributions are plainly listed there.

31. See, for example, the Minutes of the Executive Committee of the Open Market Committee, September 21, 1933; these are in the George Harrison Papers, Columbia University and available at the Federal Reserve Bank of New York. Copies also appear in the Minutes of the Directors Meetings of the Federal Reserve Bank of Boston for October 4, 1933, and other dates.

32. When Mrs. Rene Leon originally told me of her husband's efforts to block the efforts of Warburg and the other financiers at the London Conference, she could not remember the name of the businessman who had assisted him. The Leon Papers make it obvious that Moffett was the man, as, independently, Mrs. Leon subsequently wrote me. A copy of what is perhaps the urgent telegram sent to warn FDR against Warburg's efforts, which Mrs. Leon remembers her husband dispatching, can be found in Raymond Moley's papers relating to the London Conference. When the telegram came into Moley's hands is not clear; but this and other files in the Moley Papers contain numerous messages from Leon and even Deterding himself.

33. See, among others, Norman Nordhauser, *The Quest for Stability* (New York: Garland, 1979), chap. 8. I have profited greatly from the material in the J. R. Parten Papers (in Parten's possession).

34. See, among many sources, Sidney Lens, *The Labor Wars* (Garden City, N.Y.: Doubleday, 1973), 288ff.

35. See Walter Lippmann, "Self-Sufficiency: Some Random Reflections," *Foreign Affairs*, January 1934.

36. "Memorandum on the Views Relating to the Work of the Committee on Economic Security Expressed by Various Individuals Consulted," National Archives Record Group 47, Public Record Office, Washington, D.C. The interviews reported in the memo occurred "on a trip to New England and New York on August 11–21, 1934." I am grateful to Janet Corpus for bringing this memo to my attention.

37. It is impossible to inventory all of the relevant citations here, but see the material in Record Group 47 of the National Archives and, especially, the material in Box 31 of the Ralph Flanders Papers, Syracuse University Library, Syracuse, N.Y.

38. Some authors suggest that because strike rates went from ionospheric in 1934 to merely stratospheric in 1935, the Wagner Act cannot have been adopted in response to pressure from labor. In fact, the expiration of the NRA determined when the soaring overall rate of class conflict would affect the statutes. The Supreme Court decision declaring the NRA unconstitutional came only days ahead of the law's lapse. Obviously, what follows on the origins of the Wagner Act hardly suffices as a treatment of the rise of labor during the New Deal. I largely discuss elite responses to mass protest; I do not pretend to be offering a theory of the labor movement.

39. See, for example, Charlton Ogburn to William Green, January 7, 1935, Box 282, W. Jett Lauck Papers, University of Virginia.

40. See Sloan's remarkable letter to J. J. Raskob. October 23, 1934, Raskob Papers.

41. In the Twentieth Century Fund deliberations, some railroad leaders, noting the Wagner bill's similarity to the Railway Labor Act, supported its passage; Industrial Relations Counsellors opposed some of its key provisions; and nearly all the businessmen

sought an equivalent "unfair labor practice" provision applying to unions. The AFL attorney Charlton Ogburn, however, won out. Some aspects of New Deal tax policy (which was certainly not radical) should probably also be viewed as evidence of labor's rising power.

42. Morgan had sought to repeal Glass-Steagall. Aldrich blocked this, but had to accept a shift of power within the Fed from the New York Bank to the Board of Governors in Washington, which the Bank of America and other non–New York bankers championed. The almost simultaneous legislation aimed at breaking up the public utility holding companies drove another nail into the coffin of the House of Morgan, for that bank totally dominated the industry, especially after Insull's bankruptcy.

43. The Parten Papers, along with those of Interior Secretary Ickes at the Library of Congress and those of Texas governor James Allred, now in the University of Houston Library, Houston, Texas, contain large amounts of material on oil issues. See, as one example, Franklin D. Roosevelt to Governor E. W. Marland of Oklahoma, May 17, 1935 (copy in the Allred Papers).

44. Despite the co-presence of the DuPont and most Morgan interests in the GOP in this period, I would caution against the interpretation, popular in the 1930s and now showing signs of revival, of the existence of a unified "Morgan-DuPont" group. A reading of much correspondence on both sides has persuaded me that this simply did not exist during this time period.

45. See Bernard Baruch to Eugene Meyer, May 20, 1936, Baruch Papers, Seeley Mudd Library, Princeton University. Meyer was at that time helping to run the Landon campaign. Note that in autumn 1935 Standard had helped turn aside Hoover's bid for the 1936 nomination (see Herbert Hoover to Lewis Strauss, September 23, 1935, Lewis Strauss Papers, Hoover Presidential Library).

46. The Chemical Foundation Papers at the University of Wyoming in Laramie contain much material on Francis P. Garvan's efforts to promote protectionism around the time of the convention. See especially Garvan's correspondence with F. X. Eble and Samuel Crowther, in Box 11-2.

47. Samuel Crowther to Francis P. Garvan, July 18, 1936, Box 11-2, Chemical Foundation Papers.

48. *New York Times*, October 29, 1936, 10.

49. The details of all the high-level switches around the trade issues and the complex positions of some large interests (such as the Rockefellers) cannot be discussed here for reasons of space. Note, however, George Foster Peabody to A. H. Sulzberger of the *New York Times*, December 5, 1935, on the importance of good coverage for FDR and Sulzberger's accommodating reply of December 12, both in the George Foster Peabody Papers, Box 50, Library of Congress. Peabody held a large demand note on Roosevelt's Warm Springs, GA., Foundation.

50. For some documentation on the trade committee, see Aldrich Papers, Box 67. For Ruml's role in the deficit spending plan, see Robert Collins, *Business Response to Keynes* (New York: Columbia University Press, 1981), 69ff.

51. "Ferguson," write Weir and Skocpol in "Keynesian Responses," p. 144, "[is] unmistakably a writer in the peculiarly American 'Beardsian' tradition" who attributes "magical powers" to business. Who could complain about a comparison with the greatest of all American political analysts (who, we now learn, was basically right about the founding fathers; see Robert Maguire and Robert Ohsfeldt, "Economic Interests and the Constitution: A Quantitative Rehabilitation of Charles A. Beard," *Journal of Economic History* 44 [June 1984]: 509–19)? Serious readers of this essay, however, will recognize that the only "magical" power possessed by the New Deal's business supporters is their ability to remain invisible to historians.

52. Thomas Ferguson and Joel Rogers, *Right Turn: The Decline of the Democrats and the Future of American Politics* (New York: Hill & Wang, 1986), analyze at length the movement of various industrial groups in and out of the party during the decline of the New Deal. The explanation put forward there can usefully be contrasted with, for example, Thomas Burne Edsall, *The New Politics of Inequality* (New York: W. W. Norton, 1984), which continues to portray the GOP as the party of big business, while analyzing the Democrats mainly in demographic terms.

POLITICAL RESPONSE TO CAPITALIST CRISIS: NEO-MARXIST THEORIES OF THE STATE AND THE CASE OF THE NEW DEAL

Theda Skocpol

DESPITE all that has been observed since Marx's time, as to the operations of elites, bureaucracies, etc., Marxists generally seek to reduce political phenomena to the "real" class significance, and often fail, in analysis, to allow sufficient distance between the one and the other. But in fact those moments, in which governing institutions appear as the direct, emphatic, and unmediated organs of a "ruling class" are exceedingly rare, as well as transient. More often these institutions operate with a good deal of autonomy, and sometimes with distinct interests of their own, within a general context of class power which prescribes the limits beyond which this autonomy cannot be safely stretched, and which, very generally, discloses the questions which arise for executive decision. Attempts to short-circuit analysis end up by explaining nothing.

E. P. Thompson[1]

This essay uses the history of New Deal politics during the Depression of the 1930s in the United States to assess the strengths and limitations of several kinds of neo-Marxist theories of the capitalist state. One purpose of the essay is to compare some alternative neo-Marxist approaches, asking which raises the most fruitful questions and offers the best explanations of New Deal politics. More basically, the essay sketches some of the ways U.S. political institutions shaped and limited the accomplishments of the New Deal and argues that neo-Marxists of all varieties have so far given insufficient weight to state and party organizations as independent determinants of political conflicts and outcomes. The formulations here are meant to be suggestive rather than conclusive. Theoretical debates on the state and politics in capitalist societies are still wide open. An exploratory essay that probes the interface between theories and a concrete historical trajectory may help to push discussion away from abstract conceptual disputes toward meeting the challenge of explaining actual historical developments.

Explaining the New Deal

Recent historiographic disputes have worried about the "conserva-tive" versus "radical" nature of the New Deal, often asking, in effect, whether or not the New Deal was intended to "save capital-ism." In truth, U.S. capitalism was not fundamentally challenged—not by the leaders of the New Deal and not by any powerful oppo-sitional political forces. While the question of why there was no such challenge remains an important problem, we need to devote more attention to understanding what actually did change politi-cally and socially during the 1930s and to understanding the limits placed on concretely present tendencies within the New Deal.

The massive Depression of the 1930s not surprisingly stimu-lated important political transformations in the United States. The Democratic party triumphed electorally and incorporated new popu-lar groups into its coalition. An unprecedented plethora of federal agencies was established to implement new welfare and regulatory policies. Labor militancy spread in the mass production industries. The Congress of Industrial Organizations enrolled millions of workers in industry-wide unions. And the federal government was transformed from a mildly interventionist, business-dominated re-gime into an active "broker state" that incorporated commercial farmers and organized labor into processes of political bargaining at the national level.

Still, certain changes that were conceivably possible failed to occur in the New Deal. Although urban-liberal elements gained major new ground within the Democratic party, they were not able to implement a truly social-democratic program. And increased state intervention in the economy, however significant as a break with the recent American past, nonetheless failed to achieve its overriding objective of full economic recovery. Not until after the United States had geared up economically for World War II did extraordinary unemployment disappear and national output fully revive.[2]

How can we account for New Deal transformations in the American state and politics? And how can we explain why full economic recovery was not induced despite the political changes? The orthodox "pluralist" paradigm in political sociology is not well equipped to handle such questions. Pluralism attempts to explain governmental decisions in terms of the conflicting play of orga-nized group interests in society and as such it offers little that would help to explain major institutional transformations in history. To be sure, some classic pluralist works, such as David Truman's *The Governmental Process*,[3] include rich descriptions of U.S. institutional patterns and allude to how they encourage or block governmental access for different kinds of groups and interests. Nevertheless, pluralists fail to offer (or seek) well-developed explanations of how economic and political institutions variously influence group formation and intergroup conflicts. Nor do they feel the need to go beyond vague, evolutionist schemes that posit institutional change in politics as an inevitable progression of ever-increasing democracy, governmental effectiveness, and the specialization of political arrangements, all occurring in smooth, adaptive responses to the "modernization" of the economy and society.[4] Thus, to explain transformations such as those that occurred in the U.S. during the 1930s, a pluralist would either have to refer to broad, amorphous evolutionary trends at one extreme or to immediate maneuverings of interest groups at the other. Explaining an increase in state intervention, the specific forms this took, and especially the limitations on the effectiveness of such intervention, would not be a congenial undertaking.

More promising than pluralism for explaining the transformations of the New Deal are neo-Marxist theories of "the capitalist state." They at least raise the right order of issues and establish some of the analytical terms necessary for understanding such periods of institutional change. At the very center of neo-Marxist analysis is the relationship of political process and state actions to the capitalist economy and to basic class relations in capitalist society. According to neo-Marxists, a period of economic crisis such as the Great Depression is certain to spur socioeconomically rooted political conflicts and to create pressures for unusual degrees and kinds of state action. Moreover, any neo-Marxist explanation of the ensuing political conflicts and state actions would refer (in one way or another) to class actions, class conflicts, class interests, and, above all, in advanced capitalist societies, to the actions, conflicts, and interests of capitalists and the industrial working class.

Beyond such fundamentals, however, there is not much agreement among the various neo-Marxist approaches.[5] To discuss the usefulness of these theories in any depth it is necessary to identify sub-types and select examples appropriate to the particular purpose at hand. My interest here is in the tools neo-Marxist theories may have to offer for analyzing political conflicts and processes of state intervention within the bounds of advanced ("monopoly") capitalism. For this purpose, I shall explore particular examples of three broad types of neo-Marxist theories: "instrumentalist," "political-functionalist," and "class struggle." For Marxist "instrumentalist" theory, I shall especially emphasize works by U.S. historians of "corporate liberalism."[6] For Marxist "political functionalism" (my label), I shall use theoretical arguments from the early work of Nicos Poulantzas.[7] And for one kind of "class struggle" theory, I shall use Fred Block's essay "The Ruling Class Does Not Rule," the arguments of which were developed with reference to twentieth-century U.S. history, including the New Deal.[8] Each of the three theories to be discussed posits a distinctive combination of class and state actions through which a major capitalist economic crisis, such as the Great Depression, should generate political transformations and government interventions sufficient to ensure sociopolitical stability and renewed capital accumulation. For each perspective, my concern will be to see what the theory and history of the New Deal have to say to one another. Particular emphasis will be placed upon the National Industrial Recovery Act (NIRA) of 1933–35 and the Wagner National Labor Relations Act, for these acts are especially relevant to any assessment of the interrelations of the capitalist class, the industrial working class, and the national government during the New Deal.

Passed in June 1933 at the end of the first "Hundred Days" of New Deal legislation, the National Industrial Recovery Act was envisaged as a joint business-government effort to promote national economic recovery. To ensure the political support of organized labor, a provision of the NIRA, section 7a, endorsed the right of industrial workers "to organize and bargain collectively through representatives of their own choosing." However, most of the act addressed the declared needs of businessmen. Industries were freed from antitrust restrictions and prompted to draw up "codes of fair competition" to be approved and enforced by a new National Recovery Administration (NRA). The codes regulated hours of work and wage rates for labor, and they raised prices and controlled levels of production in an effort to guarantee profits for capitalists. The idea was to bring about economic recovery by stabilizing levels of production and employment and restoring "business confidence."

The Wagner Act was the most innovative accomplishment of the second, reformist phase of the New Deal. Enacted in July 1935, it reiterated and put teeth into the promises earlier made in section

7a of the NIRA. Industrial workers could join unions and bargain collectively, free from harassment by their employers. A National Labor Relations Board was established with full legal authority to determine collective bargaining units, to hold elections to certify union representatives on a majority basis, and to investigate allegations of unfair labor practices by employers. Through the Wagner Act, in short, the U.S. national government gave legal and administrative support to the widespread establishment of industrial labor unions.

Corporate Liberalism and the New Deal

In any discussion of neo-Marxist theories of the capitalist state, Marxist instrumentalisms are the place to begin, for they have been the take-off point for most recent debates. The somewhat dubious honor of embodying the generic outlines of this much-maligned approach has invariably been accorded to the pioneering book by Ralph Miliband entitled *The State in Capitalist Society*. In truth this book invokes arguments about politics and the state that have since been crystallized into virtually every major neo-Marxist position on these topics. Nevertheless, Miliband's primary purpose in the book is to debunk pluralism by showing that it systematically underestimates the preponderant, self-interested political influence of members of the capitalist class. As Miliband puts it: "What is wrong with pluralist-democratic theory is not its insistence on the fact of competition [that is, open political competition over state policies in capitalist democracies] but its claim (very often its implicit assumption) that the major organized 'interests' in these societies, and notably capital and labour, compete on more or less equal terms, and that none of them is therefore able to achieve a decisive and permanent advantage in the process of competition."[9] On the contrary, argues Miliband, capitalists, particularly those who control major economic organizations, do enjoy decisive and stable political advantages because of their privileged positions both "inside" and "outside" the state. Inside the state, officials tend either to be from capitalist backgrounds or to enjoy close career or personal ties to capitalists. Such officials, moreover, almost invariably assume the inevitability and legitimacy of a capitalist economy. Furthermore, says Miliband, "business enjoys a massive superiority *outside* the state system as well, in terms of the immensely stronger pressures which, as compared with labour and any other interest, it is able to exercise in pursuit of its purposes."[10] For capitalists enjoy disproportionate access to organizational resources, and they can credibly clothe their policy demands in "the national interest" and back them up with potent threats of economic or political disruption.

Miliband's purpose is to sketch a broad frame of reference, not to explain any particular kind of political outcome in capitalist societies. However, since the emergence of a New Left historiography in the United States during the 1960s, there has been an especially "strong" variant of instrumentalism specifically designed to explain why and how state intervention has increased during the twentieth century in U.S. capitalism. James Weinstein, William Domhoff, and Ronald Radosh have been among the articulate proponents of this view,[11] and James O'Connor relies in significant part upon it in his recent *Fiscal Crisis of the State*.[12] As Fred Block points out, " . . . the heart of the theory is the idea that enlightened capitalists recognize that crises of capitalism can be resolved through an extension of the state's role."[13] Corporate liberalism, Block notes,

> is a reinterpretation of the meaning of American liberalism. . . . In [the liberal] view, the expansion of the role of the state during the 20th century was a consequence of popular victories that succeeded in making capitalism a more benevolent system. The new theory reversed the old view, arguing that liberalism was the movement of enlightened capitalists to save the corporate order. In this view, the expansion of the role of the state was designed by corporate leaders and their allies to rationalize the economy and society. Rationalization encompasses all measures that stabilize economic and social conditions so that profits can be made on a predictable basis by the major corporations.[14]

Corporate liberalism seeks to explain particular episodes of capitalist political intervention, those that occur under crisis conditions and involve the deliberate extension of state action by a class-conscious vanguard. Under normal conditions, capitalists may influence the state in disunified fashion in all of the ways Miliband outlines, often working at cross-purposes through leadership posts in the state, personal ties to particular policy makers, or interest-group pressures from without. But, say the theorists of corporate liberalism, when crises of accumulation occur or political challenges from below threaten, capitalists can be expected to act as a class. As James O'Connor puts it, "by the turn of the century, and especially during the New Deal, it was apparent to vanguard corporate leaders that some form of rationalization of the economy was necessary. And as the twentieth century wore on, the owners of corporate capital generated the financial ability, learned the organizational skills, and developed the ideas necessary for their self-regulation as a class."[15] Enlightened leadership for the capitalist class is likely to come from those holding the most strategic and powerful economic positions. These vanguard leaders will realize the necessity of stepped-up state intervention and will use their great resources and prestige to persuade many capitalists to go along and to pressure politicians to implement the needed programs. If necessary, minor co-optive concessions will be offered to small businessmen and workers. The resulting state intervention will, however, primarily work in the interests of large-scale corporate capital.

For theorists of corporate liberalism, therefore, the New Deal is envisaged as a set of clever capitalist strategies to stabilize and revitalize a U.S. economy dominated by large corporations. "The New Deal reforms," writes Ronald Radosh, "were not mere incremental gestures. They were solidly based, carefully worked out pieces of legislation."[16] Great stress is placed on the ultimate benefits that U.S. corporate capitalism gained not only from government interventions to stabilize particular industries, but also from such widely popular measures as unemployment insurance, social security, and the legalization of unions and collective bargaining. That such measures appeared to be won by democratic pressure only represents an added advantage for capitalists. For in this way, says Radosh, "the reforms were of such a character that they would be able to create a long-lasting mythology about the existence of a pluralistic American democracy. . . ."[17] Business opposition to the New Deal is seen by theorists of corporate liberalism as emanating from "small business types, with their own conservative mentality, [who] responded to the epoch in terms of the consciousness of a previous era."[18] By contrast, far-sighted leaders of big business strongly promoted the necessary reforms. "The moderates in the governing class had to put up a stubborn, prolonged fight until the law would be able to reflect the realities of the new epoch of corporation capitalism."[19]

The corporate-liberal explanation of the New Deal is highly misleading. It can only be substantiated through a purely illustrative and selective citing of facts. When the theory is subjected to a rigorous, skeptical examination, corporate liberalism fails to ex-

plain even those aspects of the New Deal that seem most conso-
nant with it.

There *are* facts that fit the corporate-liberal interpretation of
the New Deal; indeed, such facts are repeatedly recounted by proponents of the theory. The self-stated aims of the leaders of the
New Deal, including Franklin Roosevelt himself, could easily be
described as "corporate-liberal," in the sense that the top New
Dealers were all out to sustain American capitalism (and democracy) through reform, not to propel the country toward socialism.
More to the point, business leaders and spokesmen were visibly
involved in the New Deal. Their presence was all-pervasive with
respect to the early, comprehensive measure for economic recovery, the National Industrial Recovery Act of 1933–35,[20] and under
the National Recovery Administration, businessmen in each industry drafted and enforced the regulatory codes. Later in the New
Deal, the Social Security Act was endorsed by a "Business Advisory
Council" of prominent bankers and officers of major corporations.[21]
Finally, corporate-liberal theorists correctly point out that throughout the 1930s FDR never ceased wooing business support and that
there were always officials with business backgrounds and ties holding high-level positions in the federal administration.

But facts such as these represent only the loosest conceivable
evidence for validating the hypothesis that capitalist plans and influence caused the New Deal. (Indeed, by analogous criteria, one
could "prove" that Marxist theory was sponsored by capitalists
because of Marx's close personal and financial ties to Engels, the
son of a capitalist manufacturer!) If we hold corporate liberalism to
more rigorous standards of validation, then the key questions become: Was there at work during the 1930s a self-conscious, disciplined capitalist class, or vanguard of major capitalists, that put
forward functional strategies for recovery and stabilization and had
the political power to implement them successfully? Were most
corporate leaders (especially of big, strategic businesses) prepared
to make concessions to labor? Did business opposition to the New
Deal come primarily from small business? These questions go to
the heart of the corporate-liberal claims; if they cannot be answered affirmatively, then the theory does not adequately explain
the New Deal.

No part of the New Deal better appears to fit the corporate-
liberal model than the National Industrial Recovery Act and the
National Recovery Administration (NRA) established under it.

Capitalists, above all, those who ran the major corporations in each industry, were by all historical accounts able to get exactly what they wanted out of the NRA, that is, fixed prices and stabilized production. Nevertheless, despite the ubiquitous influence of big businessmen in the formulation and implementation of the NIRA, this part of the New Deal does not measure up as a class-conscious strategy for U.S. corporate capitalism. The policies pursued were inadequate to the needs of the economy and to the interests of big business in general. For the most important fact of all about the NIRA, though, curiously, one that is never discussed by corporate-liberal theorists, is that it *failed* to bring economic recovery through business-government cooperation. Yet if we probe a bit into the actual state of consciousness and discipline among U.S. capitalists at the time of the NIRA, this failure becomes more understandable. We can see that, ironically, the failure can be partially attributed to the strong and misdirected political influence of (by corporate-liberal criteria) *insufficiently* class conscious capitalists.

U.S. capitalists were ill prepared to act together as a class in the early 1930s.[22] During the height of the Progressive Era (and the heyday of the National Civic Federation), there had been a measure of class unity and discipline, at least among large-scale corporate capitalists. In large part this was because the House of Morgan, autocratically directed by J. P. Morgan himself, enjoyed strong influence on boards of directors of the major corporations in many key industries. By the 1930s, the Morgan hegemony was no longer so absolute. World War I and the patterns of economic growth during the 1920s loosened the dependence of industrial firms upon outside financing. Sheer competitive disunity increased in many industries. Within others there was more unity, as ties among firms were strengthened during the mobilization for World War I and through the trade-association movement sponsored by the Republican administrations during the 1920s. Thus by the end of the decade the highest level of consciousness and discipline that some (by no means all) capitalists enjoyed was focused within single industries, especially those like textiles, where active and reasonably effective trade associations had evolved.[23]

Not surprisingly, therefore, when the Depression struck and business spokesmen began to come forward with plans for government programs to help business, even the most comprehensive visions of "business planning" outlined by Gerard Swope, president of General Electric, and Henry Harriman, president of the

U.S. Chamber of Commerce, called primarily for coordination within industries.[24] The idea was to give government backing to the efforts of trade associations (or other industry-wide bodies) to regulate competition in the interests of all (and especially the more established) businesses. But these plans had very little to say about how problems of interindustry coordination were to be resolved in the interest of the capitalist class, and the accumulation process, as a whole. At most, Swope and Harriman envisaged mutual consultation by representatives chosen from each industry, but they did not say how particular industries (or dominant enterprises within industries) could be persuaded to accept plans not favorable to their short-term interests.

In truth, the supposedly class-conscious capitalists of the early 1930s were mesmerized by false analogies based upon their experience of business-dominated government intervention during World War I.[25] The War Industries Board (WIB) of 1918 had been run by businessmen-administrators in the interests of the dominant firms in each industry.[26] As William Leuchtenburg puts it, "perhaps the outstanding characteristic of the war [World War I] organization of industry was that it showed how to achieve massive government intervention without making any permanent alteration in the power of corporations."[27] U.S. capitalists applauded this experience of "government intervention." Not only was their autonomy respected, but the happy result was economic prosperity and plentiful profits. In the face of another national crisis after 1929, why not revive the methods that had worked so well in World War I? For the capitalists there was the added advantage that appealing to the "analogue of war" could provide an occasion for nationalistic propaganda: it could pull Americans of all classes together "to do battle against the economic crisis," a crisis that otherwise might have been blamed on the capitalists themselves.

Still, there was an enormous difficulty in modeling the NRA on the WIB. Government mobilization of industrial resources for war, which inherently involves increasing production through massive federal spending, is not at all equivalent to using government authority to raise prices and stabilize profits, production levels, wages, and employment. In the WIB, businessmen-administrators were asked to allocate plenty and to control rapid expansion in an orderly way, with government purchases offered as inducements. But in the NRA, the job was to discipline businessmen, and labor, in a situation of scarcity and with few positive sanctions. Such policies were certain to exacerbate and politicize economic conflicts. The WIB was therefore a very poor model for capitalists to draw upon in their plans, and demands, for government intervention in the Depression. Moreover, it was unrealistic to expect that the efforts of individual industries to enhance their own profits by increasing their prices would lead to a rise in total real output and employment. Yet business spokesmen convinced themselves and, initially, many politicians that recovery *would* come in this way. Their "trade association consciousness" and their infatuation with the inappropriate WIB model left U.S. capitalists ill prepared to advocate any other more realistic plan for government intervention in the 1930s. The result was prolonged economic crisis and continuing political uncertainties for capitalists.

If the failure of the NRA raises questions about corporate liberalism by demonstrating the inability of U.S. capitalists to pursue a class-conscious strategy for economic recovery, New Deal labor politics even more directly contradict the corporate-liberal model of political change. The history of these policies shows that major industrial capitalists were not prepared to grant concessions to labor; instead undesired policies were forced upon them through the workings of a national political process that they could not fully control.

Even during the honeymoon between business and government at the start of the New Deal, major capitalists and their spokesmen were very reluctant to make concessions to labor, especially not any that would facilitate independent labor unions. As Arthur Schlesinger points out, in the original passage of the NIRA through Congress, the prolabor section 7a was constantly on the verge of being defined out of existence: "The trade association group, evidently feeling that organization was a privilege to be accorded only to employers, accepted the idea of 7a with reluctance; even the more liberal among them, like Harriman and Swope, had made no provision for organized labor in their own plans. . . . Only the vigilance of Jerome Frank, Leon Keyserling and Senator Wagner and the fear [in Congress] of provoking labor opposition kept it in."[28]

Such good friends as labor had in the early New Deal were not from the ranks of major capitalists, but from within the government.[29] Labor Secretary Frances Perkins was a rallying point for politicians and professionals who wanted to promote welfare measures and national regulation of working conditions, wages, and hours. And Senator Robert F. Wagner of New York spearheaded efforts to guarantee labor's right to collective bargaining with employers through independent union organizations. Wagner was certainly not anticapitalist, but his ideas about reform, recovery, and the right of labor went well beyond the notions of even the most far-sighted U.S. capitalists. In August 1933, Roosevelt made Wagner the chairman of a National Labor Board (NLB) that was supposed to promote labor's rights under section 7a. The board tried to persuade employers to bargain with unions that were to be certified, after board-supervised elections, as representing a majority of workers. But major employers adamantly refused, and the NLB could not persuade either Roosevelt or the NRA to enforce its decisions. As Senator Wagner saw that friendly persuasion would not work, he and his staff began planning and lobbying within Congress and the Roosevelt administration for strong legislation to enforce union recognition. These efforts eventually culminated in the (Wagner) National Labor Relations Act of July 1935.

By the second half of 1934, business opposition to the New Deal was spreading and becoming more vocal and organized.[30] To be sure, smaller businessmen were among the earliest opponents, as they reacted against the competitive advantages secured for large corporations under the NRA.[31] But businessmen across the board were souring on "bureaucracy" and were growing increasingly apprehensive about government regulation as political demands were voiced on behalf of farmers, consumers, and industrial labor. While a few major capitalists continued to speak out for the Roosevelt administration as individuals and through the Business Advisory Council, a much larger number of major capitalists were becoming increasingly hysterical in their opposition to the New Deal. The American Liberty League, launched in 1934, drew its most important support from major financial and industrial interests clustered around DuPont Chemical and General Motors—hardly "small business"![32] What is more, the National Association of Manufacturers (NAM), which prior to the 1930s was predominantly a spokesman for small and medium businesses, was transformed during the early 1930s into an anti-New Deal vehicle dominated by big businesses.[33] This is important to note because supporters of corporate liberalism repeatedly dismiss NAM opposition to New Deal policies as representing only the stubbornness of small businessmen.

Many U.S. businessmen ended up opposing the Social Security Act, and virtually all large-scale industrial employers unequivocally opposed the Wagner Act.[34] To say this is not to deny that, eventually, these measures were accepted by most corporate capitalists in the U.S. Nor is it to deny that these measures ended up, *after* the 1930s, creating conditions favorable to smoother capitalist economic growth and more stable industrial labor relations. But U.S. capitalists did not plan or promote these measures: they could not foresee their ultimately favorable effects, and, in the depressed economic situation and uncertain political climate of the mid-1930s, they feared the immediate ill effects of increased government power within the economy. In the area of labor relations, in particular, U.S. capitalists were comfortably accustomed to running their corporations with a free hand; independent labor unions, they correctly understood, would only circumscribe one of the areas of managerial autonomy that they had enjoyed in the past. That the labor unions would be established through increased federal regulatory powers only made the prospect worse.

To be sure, U.S. capitalists enjoyed great political influence during the 1930s, as they did in previous decades, and have ever since. But corporate liberalism greatly overestimates what U.S. capitalists were able and willing to do during the 1930s to engineer effective, congenial political responses to a capitalist economic crisis. As Ellis Hawley writes:

> Since they [capitalists] seemed to have benefited most from the innovations of the period, the temptation was strong to conclude that they must have planned it that way and used the New Dealers either as their tools or as camouflage for their operations. In reality, so the evidence at hand indicates, they had neither the power, the unity, nor the vision to do this. They could, to be sure, push an initial program upon the new administration, limit the efforts at structural reform, and secure desired stabilization measures for certain types of industries. But they could not make the initial program work or retain the initiative; and instead of seeing that their long-range interests lay with the pattern taking shape after 1934 and moving quickly to adopt it, most of them spent the next six years fighting a bitter and expensive delaying action.[35]

Major New Deal measures were passed and implemented over the opposition of capitalists. Not only did capitalists fail to control the political process during the mid-1930s, they even lost their ability to veto major legislative enactments that touched directly upon their accustomed prerogatives. Corporate-liberal theory cannot explain why or how this could happen, just as it cannot account for the failures of the business-sponsored NIRA.

Quite evidently, U.S. politics in the 1930s was more complex than the corporate-liberal perspective maintains. Let us therefore proceed to the "political functionalism" of Nicos Poulantzas.

Political Functionalism and the New Deal

Nicos Poulantzas is well known for some basic disagreements with instrumentalist approaches. For Poulantzas, "the direct participation of members of the capitalist class in the State apparatus and in the government, even where it exists, is not the important side of the matter. The relation between the bourgeois class and the State is an *objective relation*. This means that if the *function* of the State in a determinate social formation [that is, in a given society] and the *interests* of the dominant class in this formation *coincide*, it is by reason of the system itself. . . ."[36] In Poulantzas's view capitalists do not need to staff the state apparatus directly; nor must they put deliberate political pressure on government officials. Even without such active interventions, capitalists will still benefit from the state's activities. For the state, by definition, is "the factor of cohesion of a social formation and the factor of reproduction of the conditions of production of a system."[37] State interventions will, in other words, necessarily function to preserve order in capitalist society and to sustain and enhance the conditions for capitalist economic activity.

According to Poulantzas, the state and politics work in opposite ways for the dominant capitalist class and for the working class (and other noncapitalist classes).[38] Because working-class unity is a threat to capitalism, Poulantzas posits that the state functions most fundamentally to "disunite" the workers. It does this, in part, by transforming them into privatized individual citizens, competitive in their economic relations and members of a classless "nation" in political terms. At the same time, the political system (in a democratic capitalist state) allows workers to vote and form interest groups and political parties through which they may be able to achieve limited concessions through nonrevolutionary political struggles. Thus the capitalist state controls workers (indeed all nondominant classes) by promoting their "individualization" and by making necessary co-optive concessions in ways that tend to divide noncapitalists into competing sub-groups.

Poulantzas's state functions the opposite way for the capitalist class. In sharp contrast to Miliband's instrumentalism and to cor-

porate liberalism, Poulantzas holds that neither the political interventions of self-interested capitalists nor the policies formulated by
an enlightened corporate vanguard will ensure that the political
system functions in the interests of capitalists. Instead this happens
only because of the interventions of a "relatively autonomous"
state not directly controlled by capitalists. This state organizes the
unity of the capitalist class itself, because it is "capable of tran-
scending the parochial, individualized interests of specific capitalists and capitalist class fractions."[39] Simultaneously, the relatively
autonomous state also enforces whatever concessions the current
state of the political class struggle makes necessary if the dominated classes are to be kept in line.

Poulantzas is not greatly interested in explaining exactly how
the capitalist state goes about performing its inherent functions.
Historical contingencies such as divisions within the capitalist class
and the vagaries of the political class struggle apparently determine, in Poulantzas's view, specifically how the state is structured
and how it functions. But, short of revolution, functional outcomes
are certain to occur: the bottom line for Poulantzas always seems to
be the stability of the capitalist system, the reproduction of capitalist production relations, and the continuation of capitalist class
domination. Poulantzas's capitalist state is basically a vehicle of
system maintenance.

Corporate-liberal instrumentalists, as we have seen, attempt
to explain New Deal measures as the strategies of class-conscious
capitalists. More appropriately, Poulantzian theory would stress
the political provenance of policies, even of a measure such as the
NIRA, which closely conformed to the declared preferences of
capitalists. From a Poulantzian vantage point, New Deal economic
policies were not simply a response to the demands of capitalists;
rather they addressed the interests of competing groups both within
the ranks of the capitalist class and between capitalists and
noncapitalists. This process of placating competing interests through
active state intervention was mediated by the Democratic party
after its massive electoral victories in 1932. If business strategies
and political influence had been all that was necessary to produce
an NIRA-type program, then it should have been enacted by the
Republicans in late 1931 or during 1932, when Swope and Harriman
were first urging their plans. Instead, the NIRA came only after the
Democrats and Roosevelt came to power, and even then, the NIRA
was not formulated until the end of the "Hundred Days" of early

New Deal legislation. The NIRA itself was presented as a consensual, national effort to help businessmen, workers, and consumers, all together. And it represented the culmination of a sweeping legislative program in which the needs of farmers, bankers, home owners, the unemployed, and local governments had been addressed.[40] Just as Poulantzas's theory would suggest, this over-all process of interest aggregation and consensus building, all within the bounds of a taken-for-granted effort to save the existing capitalist economy, no doubt could be undertaken only by the Democratic party led by Franklin Roosevelt. Compared to the Republicans led by Herbert Hoover, the FDR-led Democrats in 1933 were more popularly rooted and sufficiently "relatively autonomous" from pure business domination to enable them to take strong state initiatives in the economic crisis. These initiatives, in turn, promised benefits for practically everyone and rebuilt national morale.

Within the political context thus created, it was possible to formulate and enact the NIRA. In the drafting process, various proposals for the government action to promote recovery were melded together:[41] business schemes for government-backed industrial cartels were the primary basis for Title I of the act, yet there was also a Title II establishing the Public Works Administration, which incorporated plans calling for major government spending to stimulate industry. Moreover, section 7a of Title I made promises to labor, and there were also rhetorical concessions to consumers and small businessmen.

The origins, the political context, and the legislative content of the NIRA thus fit Poulantzian political functionalism very well: the state undertook to organize business to promote recovery, and it did so with all of the symbolic trappings and concessions to popular groups that were necessary to present the entire effort as a unified, national battle against the Depression. Indeed, if the early New Deal and the NIRA had only quickly achieved their declared purposes of sociopolitical stability and full economic recovery, then Poulantzian theory would appear to offer a perfect explanation for the New Deal. But in actuality, the NIRA blatantly failed to bring economic recovery, and it deepened conflicts within the capitalist class, between capitalists and the state, and between capitalists and labor. Poulantzian theory predicts functional outcomes of state policies and interventions. It offers little direct theoretical guidance for explaining why and how failures of state policies could occur, especially not failures threatening to capitalists. If offers little guidance for dissecting the concrete course of political and social struggles over time, especially not struggles that lead toward deepening political contradictions as opposed to functional resolutions of crises through stabilizing political actions.[42]

In the context of his polemic against instrumentalism, Nicos Poulantzas has insisted that it does not matter whether capitalists staff or pressure the state. Thus Poulantzas declared in a critique of Ralph Miliband, "If Miliband had first established that the State is precisely, *the factor of cohesion of a social formation and the factor of reproduction of the conditions of production of a system* that itself determines the domination of one class over the others, he would have seen clearly that the participation, whether direct or indirect, of this class in government *in no way changes things.*"[43] Obviously, this is an extreme formulation. Poulantzas is saying that, no matter what, the state functions automatically to stabilize and reproduce the capitalist system. Yet Poulantzas has also made statements about relations between capitalists and the state apparatus that, if posed as hypotheses about conditions that could vary historically and cross-nationally, would help us explain the failures of the NIRA. The "capitalist State," Poulantzas has suggested, "best serves the interests of the capitalist class only when the members of this class do not participate directly in the State apparatus, that is to say when the *ruling class* is not the *politically governing class.*"[44]

We have already seen that the NIRA as a piece of legislation was drafted and enacted in a way that conforms to the Poulantzian notion of a "relatively autonomous" political process producing state policies that both support capitalism and are democratically legitimate. This was possible in 1933 because the electoral system, the Democratic party, the Roosevelt administration, and the Congress operated to produce the "Hundred Days" and the NIRA legislation. But, interestingly enough, the "relative autonomy" of politics was much less evident in the implementation of the NIRA than it was in its enactment. A silent assumption of Poulantzas's functionalist theory is that there will always be a centralized, bureaucratic administrative apparatus to manage economic interventions on behalf of the capitalist class as a whole.[45] But for understandable historical reasons, the U.S. federal government in the early 1930s lacked any such administrative capacity. The failures of the NIRA to promote economic recovery and to stabilize relationships among businessmen can be attributed in significant part to the absence of effective capacities for autonomous economic inter-vention on the part of the U.S. federal administration.

The national government with which the U.S. entered the Great Depression was basically formed during the Progressive Era partly in reaction against, and partly upon the foundations of, the uniquely "stateless" governmental system that had held sway in America during the nineteenth century.[46] This nineteenth-century system has aptly been called a "state of courts and parties," because its basic governmental functions were divided between, on one hand, a potent judiciary branch and, on the other, a network of government offices staffed by locally rooted political parties ac-cording to their electoral fortunes and patronage requirements. In the expanding, decentralized capitalist economy of nineteenth-cen-tury America, this governmental system functioned remarkably well. The courts regulated and defended property rights, and the party-dominated electoral-administrative system freely handed out economic benefits and loosely knit together a diverse society. With the advent of corporate concentration and the emergence of a truly national economy and society, the government of courts and par-ties began to face national-administrative and policy-making tasks for which it was poorly suited. But the old system managed to remain intact, and block governmental "modernization," as long as its mass-mobilizing political parties were relatively balanced in their political competition (at the national level and in many states outside the South). Only after the massive electoral realignment of 1896 decreased party competition in many formerly competitive states and created a national imbalance strongly in the Republican's favor, was the way opened for the building of new national admin-istrative systems.

Such administrative expansion came slowly and in fragmented ways during the Progressive Era. Unlike Continental European nations with bureaucratic states inherited from preindustrial, mo-narchical times, the U.S. national government, starting late in the game and from a low level, developed autonomous administrative capacities only imperfectly and under central executive coordina-tion and control. Presidents (along with groups of professionals) took the lead in promoting federal administrative expansion and bureaucratizing reforms. But Congress resisted efforts at adminis-trative expansion and, at each step, contested the executive branch for control of newly created federal agencies. For, by the early twentieth century, the U.S. had, if anything, even more of a "Tudor polity"[47]—a polity of divided sovereignty among the legislative, executive, and judicial branches and among federal, state, and local governments—than it had during the nineteenth century. In the earlier government of courts and parties, political party discipline had provided a kind of coordination in government. But once parties were weakened and once administrative realms began to be set up beyond the direct patronage controls of the parties, institutional struggles between the president and Congress were unleashed, above all, over how much administrative expansion should occur and under whose control.

In this context, no centrally coordinated, executive-dominated national bureaucratic state could emerge, not even during World War I. Administrative expansion during that crisis was ad hoc and staffed by officials predominantly recruited from business.[48] Moreover, it was rolled back by Congress right after the end of the war. What remained were a few (increasingly uncontrollable) independent regulatory agencies and some restricted realms of federal administration with overlapping, cross-cutting lines of control and access to the executive and to Congress. During the 1920s, the Republicans governed within this system, making minimal efforts at institutional innovation and undertaking few federal interventions in the affairs of states, localities, or the private economy. When the Depression hit, therefore, the U.S. had (for a major industrial nation) a bureaucratically weak national government, and one in which existing administrative capacities were poorly coordinated.

This historical background on the U.S. state can help us understand what happened in the implementation of the NIRA during 1933–35 in two main ways. First, it becomes easy to see why the National Recovery Administration, set up under Title I of the NIRA to regulate the industrial economy, had to be created from scratch and through the emergency recruitment of administrators from business backgrounds. There was no pre-existing federal bureaucracy with the manpower and expertise needed to supervise a sudden, massive effort to draw up hundreds of codes to regulate wages, working hours, prices, and production practices in every U.S. industry from steel and automobiles to textiles and consumer services.

The head of the NRA appointed by Roosevelt was General Hugh Johnson, a man with business experience and connections, who had served in the WIB during World War I. Johnson moved quickly to set in motion the process of approving and enforcing codes of fair competition for the various industries. Not taking time to define regulatory standards, Johnson appointed many "deputy administrators." He followed the WIB precedent of recruiting officials from business, very often drawing his deputies from the same industries with which they were then supposed to negotiate over the codes. Moreover, once the codes were approved by the NRA, their enforcement was typically delegated to code authorities dominated by representatives selected by trade associations or other major interests within each industry.[49]

Hastily assembled in these ways from extragovernmental sources of manpower, expertise, and organization, the NRA ended by being, as a contemporary observer noted, little more than "a bargain between business leaders on the one hand and businessmen in the guise of government officials on the other."[50] Obviously there was no "autonomy of the state" in relation to capitalists within the Recovery Administration. In consequence, economically powerful corporations and established trade associations were able briefly to gain legal backing for their own short-term interests, disregarding the legislated provisions for labor to have its own union organizations and representatives on code authorities and overriding the interests of smaller businesses or beleaguered competitors.[51] Yet these short-term advantages came at a price. Government regulation without state autonomy soon left businessmen quarreling among themselves, with the winners unable to enforce their will except through cumbersome legal procedures, and with the losers able to bring counterleverage on the NRA through Congress and courts. (Indeed, the NIRA was eventually declared unconstitutional in response to a suit brought by a small poultry-processing company!) And the NRA codes, once captured by big business, simply functioned to freeze production, guarantee monopoly prices to dominant firms, and undermine general economic expansion. Arguably, a more autonomous form of state regulation could have kept prices down and facilitated expanded production. In any event, when businessmen themselves became the state, government intervention could do little more than reinforce and freeze the economic status quo, while simultaneously politicizing conflicts among businessmen.

The limited capacities of the U.S. federal government can be used to explain the failure of the NIRA in a second way. Title II of the act called for massive federal expenditures on public-works projects, something that supporters felt would provide employment and help stimulate industry through construction contracts and purchases of materials. General Hugh Johnson fondly hoped to head both the NRA and the Public Works Administration (PWA), and he envisaged quickly spending the $3.3 billion PWA appropriation to help expand the economy even as the industrial regulatory codes were put into effect. Historians often imply that Roosevelt made a mistake in putting the gung-ho General Johnson in charge of the NRA, while handing the PWA to "Honest Harold" Ickes, who proceeded to spend his agency's appropriation very slowly and only on projects of unquestionable soundness.[52] Apparently, historians dream (a bit anachronistically) of a quick, Keynesian fix to the Depression—if only the PWA had had the right man as director. But this fails to take sufficient account of the given administrative and political realities of the time. The administrative means to implement a huge, speedy public-works program were simply not available, as Herbert Stein points out in his remarks on the proposals for $1 billion- to $8.5 billion-dollar programs that were offered from 1929 on:

> As proposals of amounts of money to be spent for federal construction in a short period, perhaps a year or two, these suggestions could not be taken seriously. The federal government could simply not raise its construction expenditures quickly by one or two billion dollars a year, for instance, and have any structures to show for it. Federal construction expenditures were only $210 million in 1930—a small base on which to erect a program of several billion dollars. The larger proposals were intended to finance expansion of state and local public works expenditures, in addition to federal. . . . But even combined federal, state, and local construction expenditures in 1930 were less than $3 billion.[53]

Arguably, the Roosevelt administration should have thrown administrative regularity to the winds and, in the interests of promoting economic recovery, simply handed public-works funds to businesses or to local governments. This might or might not have rapidly expanded productive economic investments. But politically it would have been disastrous. Virtually everyone inside and outside government at the time believed in "balanced budgets," and especially in a time of national economic crisis, federal expenditures were subject to close critical scrutiny for signs of waste or corruption. In choosing the cautious Harold Ickes to head the

PWA, Roosevelt acted in the knowledge that conspicuously wasteful or foolhardy public works expenditures could put the entire program in danger in Congress and perhaps raise doubts about other New Deal legislation as well, including relief expenditures.

The NIRA, in short, failed to regularize relationships among businessmen and failed to promote the economic expansion needed by the capitalist class as a whole in significant part because there was little autonomous administrative capacity in the U.S. national government of the early 1930s. Insofar as Poulantzian theory tends to assume that all capitalist states will automatically have this capacity, or will rapidly generate it if it is needed, the theory becomes misleading. Governmental capacities vary with the political histories of various countries; in turn, these governmental capacities affect what can be done for capitalist economies and for capitalists both in "normal" times and in crisis situations. Functional, adaptive state interventions do not always occur, and a large part of the explanation for whether they do or not, and for the exact forms of state interventions, lies in the prior histories of the state structures themselves.

If Poulantzas's functionalist theory overestimates the automatic ability of capitalist states to unify, organize, and serve the class interests of capitalists, it also underestimates the extent to which political struggles and state actions in capitalist democracies can actually stimulate or accelerate challenges to capitalist prerogatives from below, rather than merely averting challenges from below through minimal, nonthreatening concessions. For labor policies under the NIRA ended up promoting the emergence, through bitter conflicts, of independent industrial labor unions. These unions not only encroached upon the formerly near-absolute control of capitalist managers over the workplace, they also organizationally unified industrial workers to a greater degree than ever before in U.S. history.

Of course, the NIRA as originally passed in 1933 was intended to pacify labor, not to encourage industrial conflicts. But the actual effect of the act was to intensify conflicts over its labor provisions among workers, businessmen, and politicians.[54] In part, the declared goals of the NIRA were simply not implemented in the business-dominated NRA. Labor representatives appeared on less than 10 percent of the industrial code authorities, and the probusiness NRA administrators refused to disallow the company unions that managers organized to circumvent section 7a's declaration of labor's right to organize. In many industries, workers went on strike in efforts to secure their rights under the NIRA. Indeed, the impact of the NIRA upon labor was not simply the denial of promises in the actual administrative practices of the NRA. The mere passage of the act raised hopes among labor-union organizers and industrial workers, who redoubled their efforts in the field. Given employer resistance, the predictable result was an accelerating strike wave. Thus the NIRA and the NRA, by their mere existence, tended to encourage and politicize industrial labor disputes—hardly a "functional" outcome for capitalists.

Finally, and perhaps most important of all, the NIRA set in motion an effort to put the full legal backing of the state behind independent labor unions. During the life of the NRA Senator Wagner failed to get cooperation from businessmen, or backing from Hugh Johnson, for his plan to have the National Labor Board supervise elections and certify labor unions on a majority basis as representatives for workers in negotiations with employers. But Wagner's failure simply spurred him to redouble his efforts to legislate this solution over business opposition. And given the independent political leverage available to members of the Congress, Wagner was able to pursue a policy-making strategy at odds with the official attitude of the Roosevelt administration.

For the sake of organized labor, it was a good thing that Wagner was able to push ahead of official New Deal policies. If Roosevelt as president or as head of the Democratic party had been able to control all policy initiatives, the stance of the U.S. state toward labor in the New Deal might have better conformed to Poulantzas's theoretical expectations. For FDR and his labor secretary, Frances Perkins, favored only "paternalistic" concessions to labor, such as legislative measures to regulate wages, hours, and working conditions. They were not particularly friendly to organized labor; nor would they sponsor government measures to increase its power.[55] Roosevelt invariably wanted to "balance" existing pressures from capital and labor, even though capital's economic and organizational power was vastly preponderant. During 1934, Roosevelt intervened in the NRA's consideration of disputes in the auto industry, essentially backing up management's position in favor of "proportional representation" for company versus independent unions, rather than supporting the policy of Wagner's National Labor Board in favor of unified representation through majority election.[56] Not until Wagner had carried his proposals to the verge of sure Congressional victory did FDR endorse strong prolabor measures.

Robert Wagner was a politician bred in the New York Tammany Machine during a period when the machine had begun to sponsor some measure of social reform.[57] During his political career, Wagner developed ties to the American Federation of Labor and to liberal policy associations. And as a senator during the 1920s, he was one of the first congressmen to build an independent staff and to employ and consult professional experts in drafting legislation. Wagner established himself even before the Depression as a major formulator of national economic policies, and he was unusually effective in piloting bills through the Senate.

Thus Wagner had the policy-formulating capacity, the political connections, and the legislative skills to promote what eventually became the Wagner National Labor Relations Act. His frustrations with the NRA sharpened Wagner's perception of the need for strong, one-sided legislation in favor of unions. And the looseness of presidential control over Congress and of discipline on policy matters within the Democratic party allowed him the political space to move aggressively ahead of Roosevelt. From a capitalist point of view, this meant that the U.S. political system not only inadvertently stimulated industrial conflict, as an unintended effect of the NIRA, but also generated an autonomous political effort, spearheaded by Wagner, to array state power against capitalist prerogatives and preferences. This kind of development does not seem to be envisaged by Poulantzas's theory, which predicts that the capitalist state will invariably act to make the working classes less, not more, threatening to capitalists. Poulantzas's perspective probably underestimates the potential democratic responsiveness of elected politicians in all capitalist democracies. It certainly underestimates for the U.S. political system of the 1930s both the responsiveness of liberals such as Wagner and the autonomous room for maneuvering that members of Congress could enjoy within the U.S. "Tudor polity." In effect, "the state" did not act in a unified way toward labor, and some elements within it were prepared to promote an entirely new system of industrial labor relations for the USA.

This system would ultimately—a decade later—prove acceptable to U.S. capitalists. But in the meantime, as the accompanying figure suggests, New Deal labor legislation (especially section 7a and the Wagner Act) tended to stimulate rather than dampen labor disputes. From 1934 through 1939 labor disputes were primarily about union recognition. Leftist scholars sometimes interpret union recognition as a conservative goal, because they treat struggles for socialism or total workers' control of industry as implicit alternatives, or because they anticipate the stabilizing functions that unions eventually came to play in the U.S. political economy. But in the context of the U.S. in the 1930s, the growth of (noncompany) unions threatened capitalist prerogatives in the workplace, and the disproportionate expansion of industrial as opposed to craft unions united broader sectors of industrial labor than at any previous period in U.S. history. Capitalists (with very few exceptions) regarded all of this as threatening and believed that the federal government was encouraging labor offensives whose results were not fully predictable or necessarily controllable. For the decade of the Depression, the capitalists were correct in their analysis: "functional" outcomes were by no means certain.

How shall we draw the balance on Poulantzas's political functionalism as an approach to explaining the New Deal? A very welcome aspect of this variant of neo-Marxism is its stress upon what politics and the state do "relatively autonomously" for the economy, for the capitalist class, and for (or to!) the noncapitalists, especially workers. But, unfortunately, what the theory offers with one hand it immediately takes back with the other, for it wants us to believe that the state and politics always do just what needs to be done to stabilize capitalist society and keep the economy going. If this were really true, then state structures, state interventions, and political conflicts would not really be worth studying in any detail, and politics as such would have no explanatory importance. All that we would need to know about the New Deal, or about the NIRA, would be that these were part of a flow of history that eventually worked out splendidly for U.S. capitalists. But, of course, this is not all we need to know, or all we need to explain. To penetrate more thoroughly into the political dynamics of the 1930s, we need a perspective that pays more attention to class and political conflict and assigns greater importance to the autonomous initiatives of politicians. Fred Block's "The Ruling Class Does Not Rule" meets these criteria, and we turn now to an exploration of the strengths and limitations of this third neo-Marxist approach.

Class Struggle, State Managers, and the New Deal

Like Poulantzas, Block launches his attempt to build a theory of
the capitalist state with a critique of instrumentalism. Block accepts
the reality of capitalist influence in the political process but argues
that Marxists must "reject the idea of a class-conscious ruling class"
and posit instead "a division of labor between those who accumulate capital and those who manage the state apparatus."[58] Within
this division of labor, capitalists are conscious of the specific, short-
term economic interests of their firms or sectors, but "in general,
they are not conscious of what is necessary to reproduce the social
order in changing circumstances."[59] Capitalists do not directly control the state, however, for the state is under the direction of the
"state managers," defined as "the leading figures of both the legislative and executive branches—[including] the highest-ranking civil
servants, as well as appointed and elected politicians."[60] Once we
accept the idea of a real division of control between the economy
and the state, Block asserts, "the central theoretical task is to explain how it is that despite this division of labor, the state tends to
serve the interests of the capitalist class."[61] It is not sufficient simply
to posit the "relative autonomy of the state." Instead, an adequate
structural theory must spell out causal mechanisms in two distinct
areas. "It must elaborate the structural constraints that operate to
reduce the likelihood that the state managers will act against the
general interests of capitalists."[62] And the theory must also try to
explain why, on occasion, state managers actually extend state power,
even in the face of capitalist resistance, in order to rationalize or
reform capitalism. Rationalization and capitalist reform, Block tells
us, refer "primarily to the use of the state in new ways to overcome
economic contradictions and to facilitate the [nonrepressive] integration of the working class."[63]

   According to Block, it is fairly easy to explain why state managers would normally be very reluctant to act against capitalist
interests, even without assuming that class-conscious capitalists
run the state. The state in a capitalist society does not directly
control economic production, and yet the state managers depend
for their power and security in office upon a healthy economy. The
state needs to tax and borrow, and politicians have to face re-
election by people who are likely to hold them responsible if the
economy falters. Thus state managers willingly do what they can to
facilitate capital accumulation. Given that most economic investment decisions are controlled directly by private capitalists, state

managers are especially sensitive to the overall state of "business confidence," that is, "the capitalist's evaluation of the general political/economic climate." "Is the society stable; is the working class under control; are taxes likely to rise; do government agencies interfere with business freedom; will the economy grow? These kinds of considerations are critical to the investment decisions of each firm. The sum of all of these evaluations across a national economy can be termed the level of business confidence."[64] Normally, state managers will not want to do anything that might hurt business confidence, and so instead of pursuing social reforms or attempting to expand the state's role in the economy, they will confine themselves to formulating policies that are generally supportive of capital accumulation and not seriously objectionable to any major sector of the capitalist class.

But "if the state is unwilling to risk a decline in business confidence, how is it then that the state's role has expanded inexorably throughout the twentieth century?"[65] Block is unwilling to accept the answer offered by corporate-liberal instrumentalists. On the contrary, Block holds that capitalists are almost by definition too short-sighted initially to accept, let alone to promote, major reforms or extensions of state power. Such changes come primarily in opposition to capitalist preferences. And they mostly come when, and because, state managers are strongly prodded to institute reforms by the working class. Class struggle, says Block, pushes forward the development of capitalism. It does this economically by raising wages and thus prompting capitalists to substitute machinery for workers. It does it politically by pressuring state managers to institute economic regulations and social reforms.

According to Block, the biggest spurts forward in state activity come during major crises such as wars or depression. During wars capitalists cannot easily undercut state managers, and during depressions the decline of business confidence is not such a potent threat. Moreover, especially during economic crises, class struggle and pressures from below are likely to intensify. Thus state managers may find it expedient to grant concessions to the working class. Yet they will do so only in forms that simultaneously increase the power of the state itself. What is more, over the longer run, especially as economic recovery resumes or a wartime emergency ends, the state managers will do the best they can to shape (or restructure) the concessions won by the working class in order to make them function smoothly in support of capital accumulation and existing class relations. Thus it can come to pass that reforms and extensions of state power originally won through "pressure from below" can end up being "functional for" capitalism and accepted by many of the very capitalists who at first strongly resisted the changes.

Block's theory of the capitalist state, especially his explanation of major thrusts of capitalist rationalization, is elegant and powerful. In a number of ways, Block's ideas add to our understanding of why the New Deal occurred as it did. Where imprecisions or ambiguities do remain in Block's approach as applied to the New Deal, we can readily pinpoint some promising lines for future theories about political reforms and rationalization within capitalism.

Thinking first about the early New Deal—the "Hundred Days" of legislation culminating in the NIRA—the Block perspective shares some inadequacies with Poulantzian political functionalism, yet also improves upon it in significant ways. To take the inadequacies first: Block does not seem to do any better than Poulantzas in explaining why the NIRA failed to achieve its objectives. Like Poulantzas, Block pitches his theorizing at a high level of abstraction, talking about capitalism in general, and does not investigate existing state structures as constraints upon what state managers can do when they attempt to facilitate capital accumulation (whether through reform or not).

Compared to Poulantzas, the strength of Block's approach as (it might be) applied to the early New Deal lies in Block's greater attention to specific causal mechanisms. Instead of merely positing that the state "must" intervene to save capitalism, Block suggests that U.S. governments during the Depression were spurred to do all they could to facilitate capitalist economic recovery because public revenues and politicians' electoral fortunes depended on such efforts. It also makes sense in terms of Block's theory that both the Hoover Administration and, at first, the Roosevelt administration tried to promote recovery in close cooperation with capitalists. For Hoover and Roosevelt wanted to revive business confidence and thus resuscitate private investments.[66]

What is perhaps less clear from Block's perspective is why only FDR and the Democrats (and not Hoover and the Republicans) were willing to promote recovery specifically through increased state intervention in the economy. We can, however, derive a kind of explanation from Block's theory—one that resembles

Poulantzas's tendency to root the relative autonomy of the state from capitalists in the pressures generated by "political class struggle" in favor of concessions for noncapitalists. We can argue that the Democratic victory over the Republicans in the elections of 1930 and 1932 was an expression, albeit highly politically mediated, of class-based pressures from below on the U.S. federal government. In response to this pressure, the argument would go, the Democrats were urged, and enabled, to use state power for reformist and regulatory efforts well beyond what the business-dominated Republicans had been willing to undertake, even after the crash of 1929. Since at first hopes were high for quick economic recovery through revived business confidence, Roosevelt made every effort to fashion his first "Hundred Days" of legislation (including the bold National Industrial Recovery Act) not only to meet the reformist demands of farmers, workers, and the unemployed, but also to meet the preferences of many specific groups of capitalists and to enhance the general confidence of businessmen as rapidly as possible. In short, a judicious use of Block's theoretical perspective can go a long way toward explaining the special blend of popular responsiveness and willingness to cooperate with capitalists that characterized the fledgling Roosevelt administration in 1933–34.

Yet, of course, where Block's theory really comes into its own is in the analysis of the major social welfare and labor reforms of the New Deal era. Using Block's theory, there is no need to attribute measures such as the Social Security Act and the Wagner Act either to the far-sighted planning of the capitalist class or to the automatic intervention of a capitalist state smoothly functioning to preserve order and promote economic recovery. Instead, according to Block, these measures were made possible by a conjunction of working-class pressures with the willingness of state managers to increase their own institutional power at a time when capitalist veto power was unusually weak. The reforms provided benefits to many members of the working class, strengthened the state in relation to the working class, and increased the state's capacity to intervene in the capitalist economy. The eventual result was that working-class struggle ended up contributing to the further development of American capitalism.

As a general "explanation sketch" of the causes of the major social reforms of the New Deal and their eventual consequences, this is impeccable. Still it must be emphasized that at the very points where Block's class struggle theory of capitalist rationalization becomes most analytically relevant, it also becomes quite vague. What exactly is meant by "class struggle" or "working-class pressure" for reforms? How do varying forms and amounts of working-class pressure affect political and economic outcomes? Equally important, what are the likely interrelationships between working-class pressures and the activities of state managers? Do the latter only respond, or are they likely, under certain kinds of circumstances, to *stimulate* pressure from noncapitalists as well?

Merely raising questions such as these suggests that to go from the general "structural" dynamics outlined by Block to actual causal explanations, one would need to specify cross-nationally and historically variable patterns in such things as: the occupational and community situations of the industrial working class; degrees and forms of union organization; the actual and potential connections of working-class voters and organizations to political parties; and the effects of party systems and state structures on the likelihood that politicians' responses to working-class unrest or demands will be reformist rather than repressive.

In the case of the New Deal labor reforms, a number of conditions influenced the nature and pattern of change. The U.S. industrial working class entered the Depression without strong unions and without a labor-based political party. There was, however, a large semiskilled manufacturing labor force consisting of relatively settled immigrants and their children—a force ripe for mobilization into industrial unions.[67] The Democratic party, meanwhile, was "available" to come to power in the Depression. And insofar as its leadership took a reformist course, it was splendidly positioned to attract industrial working-class votes into a national political party that, nevertheless, could and would remain procapitalist and in many ways quite conservative.

Working-class pressure leading to reforms can entail very different scenarios. It can mean that strong labor unions and a labor or social democratic or Communist political party impose a more or less anticapitalist reform program on (and through) the government. Or it can mean that spontaneous working-class "disruption," especially strikes, forces specific concessions out of a reluctant government.[68] Neither of these scenarios really fits what happened in the United States during the 1930s. Obviously the industrial working class was organizationally too weak for the first scenario to happen. And we have already seen enough historical evidence on what happened with labor reforms in the New Deal to see that the "disruption" scenario is also inaccurate. Section 7a of the NIRA was originally achieved not by working-class disruptions, but by political lobbying by the American Federation of Labor and by the legislative efforts of Senator Robert Wagner. Once enacted, even though not successfully implemented, section 7a as a specifically political measure had a strong positive impact on labor-union growth in two main ways. First, it encouraged union organizers and emboldened rank-and-file workers with the belief that the national government would now support their efforts to unionize and bargain for economic gains. Second, it started Senator Wagner and others on the road toward the formulation of the Wagner Labor Relations Act, which ended up enforceably legalizing labor unions.

While labor's experiences under the NRA also fueled a growing strike wave in 1933–34, it cannot be plausibly argued that these strikes directly produced the Wagner Act of 1935. By 1934, rising numbers of labor disputes, and the inability of the National Labor Board (set up under the NIRA) to resolve them, did cause Roosevelt and Congress to become increasingly concerned with legislating new means for managing such disputes.[69] But, as the figure on page 88 shows, the immediate fruit of this concern, passed just as strikes came to a peak in mid-1934, was not the Wagner Act. Rather it was Public Resolution number 44, a measure cautiously designed to offend as little as possible major industrialists and conservative politicians.[70] A National Labor Relations Board was set up under the resolution, but it enjoyed no greater power to make employers accept independent unions than had the National Labor Board. Nevertheless, for whatever reasons, strikes fell off significantly (see the figure on page 88) from the time of the resolution until after the enactment of the Wagner bill a year later, in July 1935.

If working-class pressure helped to produce the Wagner Act, it was pressure registered not only through strikes but also through the major Democratic electoral victories in Congress during the fall elections of 1934. This election strengthened liberals in the Congress and virtually eliminated right-wing Republicans.[71] It came, moreover, just as business opposition to the New Deal was becoming bitter and vociferous. Half a year later, in June 1935, the Supreme Court declared Title I of the NIRA—the early New Deal's major piece of recovery legislation—unconstitutional. It was at this extraordinary political conjuncture, one marked by rhetorical class conflict as well as by FDR's last minute conversion to the Wagner

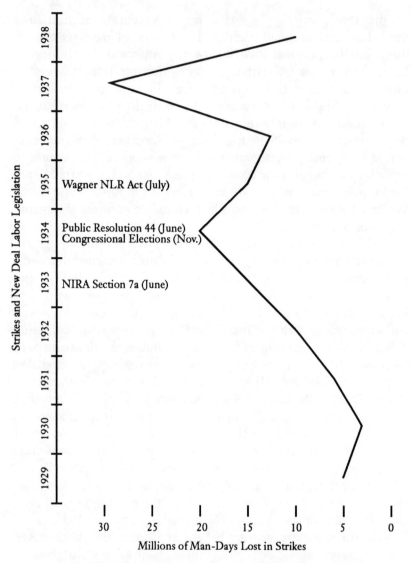

Strikes and New Deal Labor Legislation

Wagner NLR Act (July)

Public Resolution 44 (June)
Congressional Elections (Nov.)

NIRA Section 7a (June)

30   25   20   15   10   5   0

Millions of Man-Days Lost in Strikes

SOURCE: U.S. Bureau of Labor Statistics, *Monthly Labor Preview* (Washington: Government Printing Office, 1939), vol. 48, p. 1111.

Act (both because of its Congressional support and because he saw it as a partial substitute for the NIRA), that the various politicians and labor-board administrators who had all along pushed for pro-union legislation were finally able to carry the day and put through Congress the single most important reform of the New Deal era.

Block's theory fits these historical developments, to be sure, but with the important provisos that independent initiatives by liberal politicians within the Democratic party were decisive in the entire sequence from section 7a of the NIRA to the Wagner Act and that the significant working-class pressures were registered electorally as well as expressed in industrial unrest. The U.S. industrial working class of the 1930s was not strong enough either to force concessions through economic disruption alone or to impose a comprehensive recovery program through the national political process. It depended greatly on friendly initiatives and support from within the federal government and the Democratic party. It got these not simply through disruption, but because it represented an attractive potential for electoral mobilization and an interest group that, among others, FDR wanted to conciliate if possible. It also helped labor enormously that business panicked about the New Deal after 1933 and, by going into political opposition, gave liberals like Wagner even more space for legislative maneuver.

Turning from the causes to the consequences of the labor reforms of the New Deal, we arrive at other important queries that can be raised about Block's general explanation sketch. Do reforms enacted partially in response to demands from below invariably end up "rationalizing" capitalism by allowing state power to be used "in new ways to overcome economic contradictions and to facilitate the integration of the working class?" What determines and, possibly, limits the capacities of state managers to turn reforms and the concomitant enhancement of state power into effective supports for the capitalist economy as a whole?

In his theoretical statements on these issues, Block is not only imprecise; he actually points in contradictory directions. At various places in his article, he asserts that state managers almost by definition have the capacity to work for the general good of the capitalist class and economy:

> Unlike the individual capitalist, the state managers do not have to operate on the basis of a narrow profit-making rationality. They are capable of intervening in the economy on the basis of a more general rationality. In short, their structural position gives the state managers both the interest and the capacity to aid the investment accumulation process.[72]
>
> The more power the state possesses to intervene in the capitalist economy, the greater the likelihood that effective actions can be taken to facilitate investment.[73]

But, at other points, Block admits that the pattern in which working-class pressures that ultimately enhances the state's capacity to manage capital accumulation "is not a smoothly working functional process."[74] He rather weakly alludes to "time lags" and "friction" in the over-all process, yet also offers some stronger antifunctionalist formulations:

> There might, in fact, be continuing tensions in a government program between its integrative interest and its role in the accumulation process. [S]ome concessions to working-class pressure might have no potential benefits for accumulation and might simply place strains on the private economy.[75]
> The increased capacity of state managers to intervene in the economy during these periods [of crisis and reform] does not automatically rationalize capitalism. State managers can make all kinds of mistakes, including excessive concessions to the working class. State managers have no special knowledge of what is necessary to make capitalism more rational: they grope toward effective action as best they can within existing political constraints and with available economic theories.[76]

With this last statement, Block has come 180 degrees from the notion that the state managers are "capable of intervening in the economy on the basis of a more general rationality" because "their structural position" gives them "both the interest and the capacity to aid the investment accumulation process."[77] Obviously, Block can't have it both ways. Either state managers enjoy the automatically given capacity to rationalize capitalism or their capacities are determined by "existing political constraints." Given that Block footnotes the final quote reproduced above with a reference to the New Deal, it is apparent that he believes "existing political constraints" were important then.[78]

Indeed, during the New Deal, U.S. state managers could not automatically use state power to ensure full economic recovery (and thereby ensure social and political stability). Their efforts were always channeled, shaped, and limited by existing state and party structures not conducive to fully effective state interventions. We have already seen the limitations that an absence of strong, autonomous administrative institutions placed upon the effectiveness of the National Industrial Recovery Act of the early New Deal. Furthermore, even after pressures from below and state initiatives had combined to put through the major social and labor reforms of the post-1934 New Deal, "existing political constraints" still stymied the efforts of the state managers to turn such measures and the political and state power generated by them into effective means for promoting capitalist economic recovery.

Block's theory of capitalist rationalization through class struggle and state-sponsored reforms silently assumes that social democracy is the highest evolution of capitalism and that any major crisis of advanced capitalism resulting in important reforms will ipso facto entail a breakthrough toward what C. A. R. Crosland once called a "full employment welfare state."[79] Perhaps the pattern of state intervention implied here could aptly be called "social-democratic Keynesian," because state interventions, regulatory and fiscal together, would promote private accumulation of capital and, at the same time, further the social welfare, the full employment, and the political-economic leverage (that is, through strong unions) of the working class. Now, the interesting thing about the reformist phase of the New Deal (1935–38) is that, although tendencies existed that might conceivably have added up to a social-democratic Keynesian breakthrough, the existing governmental and party structures so patterned political conflicts and so limited the possibilities for political transformations as to prevent any such breakthrough from actually occurring. Instead, the direct consequence of the labor reforms, and of the enhanced labor and liberal power that accompanied them, was not economic recovery through social-democratic Keynesianism but increased social and political tension, leading by 1938–39 to an insecure impasse for the domestic New Deal.

What were the tendencies present in the reformist New Deal that pointed toward a social-democratic Keynesian breakthrough? For one thing, as Block's theory would suggest, the social and labor reforms of the New Deal generated new nexes of political power and interest, binding liberal-Democratic politicians into symbiotic relationships with the welfare and relief agencies of the federal government and binding both urban-liberal politicians and trade-union leaders into a symbiotic relationship with another new organ of state power, the National Labor Relations Board (NLRB). NLRB administrators achieved their entire raison d'être through the spread of labor unions; they had a natural institutional bias (as well as a legal mandate) in favor of protecting all legitimate unions and union drives.[80] Labor unions, in turn, certainly benefited from the protections thus afforded them. Union membership had declined to below 3 million in 1933 but started rising thereafter and shot up, especially from 1935, to over 8 million in 1939.[81] Both labor unions and the NLRB depended upon liberal-Democratic support in Congress and within presidential administrations. And, of course, liberal-Democratic politicians benefited from monetary contributions and from the electoral mobilization of workers' votes. This mobilization was organized, from 1936 on, through political committees established by union leaders grateful for benefits from the Roosevelt administration and hopeful that further gains could be made for workers (including those unemployed and on relief) through the strengthening of liberal forces in the Democratic party.[82] Indeed, it did seem that liberal Democrats, workers, unemployed people, people on welfare, and federal administrators could all work together fruitfully after 1935–36. Voices like Robert Wagner's called for economic recovery through bolstering the spending power of the working class. Urban liberals in general advocated increased welfare and public works expenditures and proposed substantial new efforts in public housing.[83]

Another major tendency that might have helped produce a breakthrough to social-democratic Keynesianism came from the president himself. After the 1936 election, Roosevelt introduced an executive reorganization plan drafted by a committee of academic experts on public administration. As drafted, this plan was well designed to overcome many built-in obstacles to any strategy (whether social-Democratic or not) of coordinated state intervention in the society and economy.[84] The reorganization plan called for the consolidation of federal administrative organs (including formerly independent regulatory bodies) into functionally rationalized, centrally controlled cabinet departments. It would have enhanced presidential powers of planning and policy coordination by: increasing executive versus Congressional control over the expenditure of budgeted federal funds; establishing a National Resources Planning Board for comprehensive, long-range planning and coordination of federal programs; and greatly expanding the White House staff directly responsible to the president. All of these measures, taken together, would have gone a long way toward reversing the historically inherited fragmentation of the U.S. federal administration. Since the start of the New Deal, the U.S. federal bureaucracy had, of course, expanded significantly. But the expansion had been piece-meal and, given the competing lines of authority between Congress and the president and the paucity of institutional means of executive coordination available to Roosevelt, the expanded federal government was becoming increasingly unwieldy.

Given that FDR and the Democrats were re-elected by huge popular margins in 1936, the time looked ripe to enhance the Roosevelt administration's ability to institutionalize and expand its reforms. And, to engage in a bit of counterfactual historical speculation, imagine that such a system not only could have been achieved but also that it could, in turn, have been harnessed to a disciplined and thoroughly liberal Democratic party, one devoted to the pursuit of full economic recovery through social spending. Then the institutional and political conditions for a true social-democratic Keynesian breakthrough in the U.S. would have been established. But, of course, things did not turn out this way, largely because of the nature of the Democratic party and the structure of the U.S. national government. The Democratic party absorbed, contained, and rendered partially contradictory the political gains of organized labor and liberals in the 1930s, and the national government blocked FDR's comprehensive scheme for administrative reorganization.

To begin with the failure of comprehensive reorganization, Roosevelt's plan met defeat in Congress above all because it threatened to disrupt well-established patterns of institutional power.[85] Senators and representatives were jealous of Congress's traditional power to "pre-audit" the expenditures of federal agencies, for through such power individuals and committees in Congress could influence programs affecting their state or local constituencies. In addition, both members of Congress and administrators of federal agencies were very nervous about administrative reorganizations that would disrupt existing symbiotic relationships among Congress, bureaucrats, and organized interest groups in the society at large. Predictably, the most intense opposition came from conservatives, for these people worried about the kinds of programs Roosevelt (and the New Dealers in general) might generate through a reorganized federal executive. But not only conservatives opposed the plan; some of Roosevelt's own Cabinet members, acting like any traditional U.S. cabinet heads jealous of their bureaucratic domains, opposed reorganization or failed to support it. Interestingly enough, the "urban liberal" par excellence, Senator Robert Wagner, also opposed the reorganization plan. He was worried about Congressional prerogatives and the administrative independence of the National Labor Relations Board.[86]

The Democratic party also functioned as an obstacle to a social-democratic Keynesian breakthrough in the 1930s. The most basic fact about the New Deal Democratic party was simply that it worked pretty much as all major U.S. political parties have done since about the 1830s.[87] U.S. parties do not formulate explicit, coherent national programs that their members in Congress are then disciplined to support. Rather U.S. parties "aggregate" blocs of voters through very diverse appeals in different parts of the country. Their overriding function is to compete in single-member-constituency, majority-take-all elections in order to place politicians in office from the local to the state to the national level. Once in office, parties exhibit some discipline (especially on procedural matters), but members of Congress are remarkably free as individuals (or ad hoc coalitions) to pursue whatever legislation or whatever administrative measures they believe will appeal to local constituents or to organized groups of financial contributors and voters. Members of Congress may, of course, be unusually attentive during periods of crisis to directives from the president and from House and Senate leaders; this was the case during the "Hundred Days" of 1933. But such extraordinary coordination rarely lasts for long, and there is still unlikely to be a disciplined pursuit of an over-all party program, if only because U.S. presidents, senators, and representatives are elected in diverse ways and by differently structured constituencies.

These institutional givens meant that as liberals, especially from northern urban areas, made gains within the national Democratic party, they could hope to gain *some* legislative and administrative leverage for their various constituents. They could not expect, however, to formulate comprehensive national strategies for a Democratic president and Congress to enact. The existing Congressional-executive system would frustrate any such efforts. Even more important, the Democratic party could maintain a semblance of national unity only by avoiding too many head-on clashes between its entrenched, overwhelmingly conservative southern wing and its expanding liberal urban-northern wing. There were also nonsouthern rural interests in the party, and their representatives were willing to support government programs for farmers but were usually not sympathetic to the needs of urban areas or labor.

Franklin Delano Roosevelt, an immensely popular President, gained the Democratic nomination in 1932 through southern and western support. By 1936 he also enjoyed strong support in urban areas and from organized labor.[88] But it became increasingly difficult for Roosevelt to manage all of these diverse interests under the Democratic umbrella. For a brief time in 1938, he attempted to make the party more consistently liberal by "purging" various very conservative Democrats who had opposed New Deal reforms.[89] But machines or special agglomerations of organized interests at local and state levels control nominations within U.S. parties, which are "national" only in label and for the purpose of electing presidents. So FDR's purge failed, and liberalism—even as an attitude, let alone as a comprehensive program of recovery and reform—could not take over the Democratic party.

Moreover, given the way that the operations of the Democratic party (and the Republican party) intersected with the operation of Congress, liberals (especially urban liberals) were unable to translate electoral support into truly proportional Congressional leverage. Ironically, efforts by labor and liberals to elect Democrats could even hurt politically, as Edelman explains:

> Both the House and the Senate greatly underrepresent urban areas. The emphasis on local needs therefore means that labor groups are underrepresented, for constituency pressures are more often exerted disproportionately on behalf of farmers and dominant local industries rather than on behalf of worker residential areas in the cities. This bias is greatly emphasized because the constituencies that are "safe" in the sense of predictably returning incumbents to office are also to be found almost entirely in predominantly rural areas: the South, Vermont, Maine, and some parts of the Middle West. Because an individual's influence in Congress depends so enormously on his seniority there, the congressmen from these areas gain disproportionately in influence when their parties win control. Thus a hard-fought Democratic victory in Pennsylvania, New York, Illinois, and California sufficient to enable the Democrats to organize the House and Senate does not benefit these states nearly as much as it benefits Alabama, Mississippi, Florida and other states in which there is little hard campaigning. To this extent AFL and CIO activity in congressional campaigns in the urban areas places some of the anti-labor rural congressmen in a stronger position.[90]

By the very nature of politics, conflicts intensify as a formerly weak interest in a situation of diverging interests grows stronger. As labor and liberal interests gained ground in U.S. policies during the 1930s, conservatives, whether businessmen or rural interests, were bound to oppose them, whatever the institutional arrangements had been. Yet above and beyond this inevitable opposition, the structure and operations of Congress and the Democratic party facilitated the formation of a "conservative coalition" to obstruct or modify many liberal New Deal measures, even as these arrangements made it difficult for liberals to become a national policy-making force.[91] Nor, as we have seen, could liberal programs supported by members of Congress always count on solid support from Roosevelt or his administration. For Roosevelt and his administrators had to worry about maintaining broad support in Congress and about balancing pushes and pulls within the Democratic party as a whole.

Given the structures of politics within which they had to operate, liberals during the New Deal had to settle for doing what pays off in the U.S. political system. They carved out domains of legislation and administration favorable to well-organized constituents and then did their best to defend these against bureaucratic encroachments or opposition within Congress or from the administration.[92]

In sum, "existing political constraints"—specifically, the U.S. government and political parties of the 1930s—limited the possibilities for politicians to use the new political energies and the new domains of state power generated by the reformist New Deal for the successful resuscitation of capitalist accumulation through state spending for (new or much expanded) domestic social programs. By the late 1930s, full economic recovery still eluded the national economy under the New Deal. In the absence of recovery, who could say where U.S. politics might go? Conservatives in Congress were gaining political strength and were increasingly able and willing to block policy initiatives coming from "urban liberals" inside and outside the government and to whittle down welfare and public-works measures sponsored by the president.[93] Labor unions were still not accepted by many industrial employers, and the NLRB and the Wagner Act were coming under increasingly vociferous political attacks.[94]

Yet, of course, the basic social and labor reforms of the liberal New Deal did survive. And full recovery, indeed, spectacularly accelerated growth, was achieved by the U.S. economy. But the intranational structural forces specified in Block's theory, that is, working-class pressures plus the initiatives of state managers, were not alone responsible for this outcome of the 1940s and after. Of the three neo-Marxist theoretical perspectives examined in this paper as a whole, only Block's repeatedly alludes to ways in which transnational structures and conjunctures affect the course of domestic politics in advanced capitalist nations. Even Block, however, fails to accord such transnational factors the systematic explanatory weight they deserve. It is not only the interplay of capitalists' economic decisions, working-class pressures, and state managers' initiatives that shapes political conflicts and transformations in advanced capitalism. International economic and politico-military relations also matter.

The case of the New Deal certainly dramatizes the importance of both international economics and international politics. Without the virtual collapse of the international monetary system and the sharp contraction of international trade in the early years of the Depression, it is highly doubtful that "political space" could have opened up in the United States for the pursuit of economic recovery and reforms through greater state intervention. Even more important was the impact at the end of the New Deal of the coming of World War II, starting in Europe. Everyone knows that "military Keynesianism"—growing federal expenditures on military preparedness and then war—jolted the national economy out of the lingering Depression at the end of the 1930s.[95] What is perhaps less well known are the crucial ways in which the turn toward military and foreign policy preoccupations and then into war overcame many of the domestic social and political impasses of the later New Deal.[96] There were several key developments. As the Roosevelt administration planned for (and later implemented) wartime industrial mobilization, it sought a rapprochement with big businessmen and tacitly agreed to cease pushing for new labor and social reforms in return for business cooperation. The institutionalization of labor unions was, at the same time, solidified during the war. In return for a no-strike pledge from union leaders, the government required employers to deal with unions and facilitated the enrollment of union members in industries doing war production. Finally, the issues of politics in Congress were partially transmuted from the domestic and economic questions that exacerbated conflicts between rural-conservatives and urban-liberals into more foreign-policy and military related issues that averted (or delayed) some of the old disputes over social reform. Reformers could no longer use economic crisis as a rationale for social welfare measures. Instead, both liberals and conservatives had to maneuver with the symbols of national unity evoked to sustain the wartime efforts at home and abroad.

What all of this, taken together, amounted to was not at all a defeat or a roll back for the reforms of the New Deal. Rather, most of the reforms were consolidated and retained, but within a new national political context in which business and government were again reconciled. Capitalists learned to live with and use many aspects of the New Deal reforms, even as they retained leverage in the U.S. political system to counter the power of organized labor and to limit future advances by liberals and labor. The full economic recovery, the new governmental tasks, and the new political climate brought by the war, all were important in allowing this denouement. Without the timely arrival of the war, the basic reforms of the New Deal might not have survived—and they might not have proved so "functional" for U.S. capitalism.

Conclusion

At the outset I declared three basic aims for this exploratory essay: to show that some current lines of neo-Marxist analysis are more promising than others for explaining the New Deal as an instance of political conflict and transformation within advanced capitalism; to argue that, for such explanatory purposes, no existing neo-Marxist approach affords sufficient weight to state and party organizations as independent determinants of political conflicts and outcomes; and to sketch some of the ways in which U.S. political institutions shaped and limited the accomplishments of the New Deal. In closing, I shall summarize my conclusions on each of these major themes and point out important areas for further investigation and critical discussion.

The evidence of the New Deal reveals the basic inadequacy of those lines of neo-Marxist reasoning that treat political outcomes in advanced capitalism as the enactments of a far-sighted capitalist ruling class or as the automatically functional responses of the political system to the needs of capitalism. Yet there are also more promising lines of analysis within neo-Marxism. Those theorists who assign explanatory importance to class struggle recognize that conflicts between capitalists and noncapitalists affect politics in capitalist societies. They also recognize that politicians (especially in liberal democracies) must respond to the demands of noncapitalists as well as to the demands of capitalists and the conditions of the economy. Moreover, those theorists who refer to the "relative autonomy of politics" or who assign "state managers" an independent explanatory role are moving toward an approach that can take seriously the state and parties as organizations of specifically political domination, organizations with their own structures, their own histories, and their own patterns of conflict and impact upon class relations and economic development.

Nevertheless, so far, no self-declared neo-Marxist theory of the capitalist state has arrived at the point of taking state structures and party organizations *seriously enough.*[97] Various ways of short-circuiting political analyses have been too tempting. Political outcomes are attributed to the abstract needs of the capitalist system, or to the will of the dominant capitalist class, or to the naked political side-effects of working-class struggles. It is often assumed that politics always works optimally for capitalism and capitalists, leaving only the "how" to be systematically explained. Even those neo-Marxists who have tried to incorporate state structures into their modes of explanation tend to do so only in functionalist or socioeconomically reductionist ways. What is more, almost all neo-Marxists theorize about "the capitalist state" in general, thus attempting to explain patterns of state intervention and political conflict in analytic terms directly derived from a model about the capitalist mode of production as such.

But capitalism in general has no politics, only (extremely flexible) outer limits for the kinds of supports for property ownership and controls of the labor force that it can tolerate. States and political parties within capitalism have cross-nationally and historically varying structures. These structures powerfully shape and limit state interventions in the economy, and they determine the ways in which class interests and conflicts get organized into (or out of) politics in a given time and place. More than this, state structures and party organizations have (to a very significant degree) independent histories. They are shaped and reshaped not simply in response to socioeconomic changes or dominant-class interests, nor as a direct side-effect of class struggles. Rather they are shaped and reshaped through the struggles of politicians among themselves, struggles that sometimes prompt politicians to mobilize social support or to act upon the society or economy in pursuit of political advantages in relation to other politicians. In short, states and parties have their own structures and histories, which in turn have their own impact upon society.

The New Deal is a difficult case, almost ideal for developing a macro-analytic perspective that points to all of the necessary factors to be considered in explaining transformations of the state and politics within advanced capitalism. Real political changes occurred in the New Deal: the inclusion of some popular interests in a more interventionist "broker state," the incorporation of the industrial working class into the Democratic party, and the expansion of urban-liberal influence within the party. But the political changes that occurred did not please capitalists or ensure capitalist economic recovery or consolidate the basic reforms that were enacted—not until World War II intervened to transform the overall political and economic context. By using various neo-Marxist explanatory approaches as foils for probing the politics of the New Deal, I have argued that many of the limitations on effective state intervention and on liberal reforms in the New Deal can be traced to the existing U.S. national administrative arrangements, governmental institutions, and political parties. These same structures, moreover, shaped the piecemeal reforms and the partially successful efforts to proffer relief and to promote recovery in response to the Depression. Capitalists, industrial workers, and farmers certainly helped to shape and limit the New Deal, as did the contours of the massive economic crisis itself. But economic and class effects were all mediated through the distinctive structures of U.S. national politics. The immediate changes were not fully intended by anyone, were not consistently in conformance with the interests of any class, and were not smoothly functional for the system as a whole. But the changes did make sense as the product of intensified political struggles and undertakings within given, historically evolved structures of political representation and domination. Such structures are the keys to any satisfactory explanation of the New Deal— and to other episodes, past, present, and future, of political response to economic crisis within capitalism.

NOTES

An earlier version of this article was presented in the session on "Political Systems" of the seventy-fourth Annual Meeting of the American Sociological Association, Boston, August 1979. In gaining historical background and formulating ideas for the paper, I especially benefited from the research assistance of Kenneth Finegold and from individual discussions with him and with Jonathan Zeitlin. Critical reactions and suggestions for revisions (not all of which I was able or willing to accept) came from Fred Block, William Domhoff, William Hixson, Christopher Jencks, John Mollenkopf, Charles Sabel, David Stark, and Erik Olin Wright.

1. E. P. Thompson, *The Poverty of Theory and Other Essays* (London: Merlin Press, 1978), p. 48.

2. See Lester V. Chandler, *America's Greatest Depression 1929–1941* (New York: Harper and Row, 1970).

3. David B. Truman, *The Governmental Process*, 2nd ed. (New York: Knopf, 1971; originally 1951).

4. Even a very sophisticated developmentalist argument, such as Samuel Huntington, "Political Modernization: America vs. Europe," chap. 2 in *Political Order in Changing Societies* (New Haven: Yale University Press, 1968), still tends to explain macrohistorical change (or its absence) in vague evolutionist terms, referring to the "needs" of society. Thus while Huntington brilliantly describes America's enduringly peculiar "Tudor" polity, his explanations for why America has no strong state is that it hasn't "needed" one, either to maintain national unity or to ensure economic growth. Aside from its crudeness, this explanation leaves one wondering about the Civil War, when unity broke down, and the Depression, when economic growth did. Society's "needs" must not be a sufficient explanation for political structures, their continuities and transformations.

5. Two good surveys of the literature are David A. Gold, Clarence Y. H. Lo, and Erik Olin Wright, "Recent Developments in Marxist Theories of the Capitalist State," *Monthly Review* 27, no. 5 (October 1975): 29–43, and 27, no. 6 (November 1975): 36–51; and Bob Jessop, "Recent Theories of the Capitalist State," *Cambridge Journal of Economics* 1, no. 4 (December 1977): 353–73.

6. I draw especially upon corporate-liberal arguments about the New Deal by Ronald Radosh, "The Myth of the New Deal," in *A New History of Leviathan: Essays on the Rise of the Corporate State*, ed. Radosh and N. Rothbard (New York: Dutton, 1972), pp. 146–87; and G. William Domhoff, "How the Power Elite Shape Social Legislation," *The Higher Circles: The Governing Class in America* (New York: Vintage Books, Random House, 1971), chap. 6.

7. Nicos Poulantzas, *Political Power and Social Classes*, trans. Timothy O'Hagen (London: New Left Books, 1973); and idem "The Problem of the Capitalist State," *Ideology in Social Science*, ed. Robin Blackburn (New York: Vintage Books, Random House, 1973), pp. 238–53. After these works Poulantzas evolved away from political functionalism toward more of a class-struggle approach. But I am only treating the earlier works here.

8. Fred Block, "The Ruling Class Does Not Rule: Notes on the Marxist Theory of the State," *Socialist Revolution*, no. 33 (May–

June 1977), pp. 6–28. Class-struggle versions of neo-Marxism are very diverse, and Block doesn't represent all of them. He just represents an example that I find particularly interesting because the state in Block's theory is not collapsed into class relations, as it appears to be, for example, in the more recent works of Nicos Poulantzas and in some of the German neo-Marxist theories surveyed in John Holloway and Sol Picciotto, eds., *State and Capital: A Marxist Debate* (London: Edward Arnold, 1978).

9. Ralph Miliband, *The State in Capitalist Society* (New York: Basic Books, 1969), p. 146.

10. Ibid.

11. James Weinstein, *The Corporate Ideal in the Liberal State: 1900–1918* (Boston: Beacon Press, 1968). For relevant works by Domhoff and Radosh, see note 6. In a private communication, Bill Domhoff has convinced me that his views about the Wagner Act have developed away from a strictly corporate-liberal position in publications subsequent to *The Higher Circles*. Thus my arguments here apply only to the cited parts of that book.

12. James O'Connor, *The Fiscal Crisis of the State* (New York: St. Martin's Press, 1973).

13. Fred Block, "Beyond Corporate Liberalism," *Social Problems* 24 (1976–77): 355.

14. Ibid., p. 352.

15. O'Connor, *Fiscal Crisis*, p. 68.

16. Radosh, "Myth of the New Deal," in *New History of Leviathan*, ed. Radosh and Rothbard, p. 186.

17. Ibid.

18. Ibid., p. 187.

19. Ibid.

20. See Ellis W. Hawley, *The New Deal and the Problem of Monopoly* (Princeton, N. J.: Princeton University Press, 1966), chaps 1–3; and Arthur M. Schlesinger, Jr., *The Coming of the New Deal* (Boston: Houghton Mifflin, 1958), chaps. 6–8.

21. Radosh, "Myth of the New Deal," in *New History of Leviathan*, ed. Radosh and Rothbard, pp. 157–58.

22. This paragraph draws especially upon David Vogel, "Why Businessmen Distrust Their State: The Political Consciousness of American Corporate Executives," *British Journal of Political Science* 8, no. 1 (January 1978): 70–72; and Gabriel Kolko, *Main Currents in American History* (New York: Harper and Row, 1976), pp. 100–117.

23. See Louis Galambos, *Competition and Cooperation: The Emergence of a National Trade Association* (Baltimore: Johns Hopkins University Press, 1966); and Robert F. Himmelberg, *The Origins of the National Recovery Administration* (New York: Fordham University Press, 1976).

24. Gerard Swope, *The Swope Plan* (New York: Business Bourse, 1931); Otis L. Graham, Jr., *Toward a Planned Society* (New York: Oxford University Press, 1976), pp. 24–25; and Kolko, *Main Currents*, pp. 116–20.

25. William E. Leuchtenburg, "The New Deal and the Analogue of War," in *Change and Continuity in Twentieth-Century America*, ed. John Braeman, Robert Bremner, and E. Walters (Columbus: Ohio State University Press, 1964). This article discusses the appeal of "analogies of war" to virtually all of the sets of actors in the early New Deal.

26. Robert D. Cuff, *The War Industries Board: Business-Government Relations during World War I* (Baltimore: Johns Hopkins University Press, 1973).

27. Leuchtenburg, "Analogue of War," in *Change and Continuity*, ed. Braeman, Bremner, and Walters, p. 129.

28. Schlesinger, *Coming of New Deal*, p. 99.

29. Good background on the labor policies of the New Deal is especially to be found in Irving Bernstein, *The New Deal Collective Bargaining Policy* (Berkeley and Los Angeles: University of California Press, 1950); and Murray Edelman, "New Deal Sensitivity to Labor Interests," in *Labor and the New Deal*, ed. Milton Derber and Edwin Young (New York: DaCapo Press, 1972), pp. 157–92.

30. Ellis Hawley, "The New Deal and Business," in *The New Deal*, ed. Braeman, Bremner, and Brody, vol. 1, *The National Level*, pp. 64–66; and Schlesinger, *Coming of New Deal*, chap. 30; William H. Wilson, "How the Chamber of Commerce Viewed the NRA: A Reexamination," *Mid-America* 44 (1962): 95–108; and Kim McQuaid, "The Frustration of Corporate Revival in the Early New Deal," *The Historian* 41 (August 1979): 682–704.

31. Small business opposition, pressed especially through Congress, is a major theme in Hawley, *New Deal and Problem of Monopoly*, chap. 4.

32. George Wolfskill, *The Revolt of the Conservatives: A History of the American Liberty League* (Boston: Houghton Mifflin, 1962); and Frederick Rudolph, "The American Liberty League, 1934–1940," *American Historical Review* 56, no. 1 (October 1950): 19–33. Rudolph writes (p. 22): "The membership of its national advisory council was drawn largely from the successful business interests of the industrial states of the North and East. . . ."

33. Philip H. Burch, Jr., "The NAM as an Interest Group," *Politics and Society* 4, no. 1 (Fall 1973): 100–105.

34. On social security see Edwin E. Witte, *The Development of the Social Security Act* (Madison: University of Wisconsin Press, 1962), pp. 89–90; and Schlesinger, *Coming of New Deal*, p. 311. On the Wagner Act see Bernstein, *New Deal Collective Bargaining Policy*, passim. The resistance of industrial employers is documented in Daniel A. Swanson, "Flexible Individualism: The American Big Business Response to Labor, 1935–1945," (Undergraduate thesis, Harvard College, Social Studies, 1974). See also Vogel, "Why Businessmen Distrust Their State," pp. 63–65.

35. Hawley, "New Deal and Business," in *The New Deal*, ed. Braeman, Bremner, and Brody, vol. 1, *The National Level*, pp. 75–76.

36. Nicos Poulantzas, "The Problem of the Capitalist State," in *Ideology in Social Science*, ed. Robin Blackburn (New York: Vintage Books, Random House, 1973), p. 245.

37. Ibid., p. 246.

38. Nicos Poulantzas, *Political Power and Social Classes*, trans. Timothy O'Hagen (London: New Left Books, 1973). See also Simon Clarke, "Marxism, Sociology and Poulantzas's Theory of the State," *Capital and Class*, no. 2 (Summer 1977), pp. 1–31.

39. Gold, Lo, and Wright, "Recent Developments," p. 38.

40. Actually, those whose needs were addressed earliest and most thoroughly in the New Deal were commercial farmers. This was not incidental in political terms, for Roosevelt had gained the presidential nomination in 1932 only through support from the South and West. Also, given the disproportionate weight of rural areas in the U.S. national political system of the 1930s, Roosevelt was bound to be especially desirous of attracting voters and placating Congressmen from these areas. It is noteworthy that neo-Marxist theories of politics in advanced capitalism tend to ignore farmers, concentrating instead only on industrial workers and industrial and financial capitalists. But a complete analysis of class and politics in the New Deal would definitely have to look at the relationships of farmers and agricultural laborers to industrial capitalists and workers.

41. The best discussion is Hawley, *New Deal and Problem of Monopoly*, chaps. 1–2. See also Schlesinger, *Coming of New Deal*, chap. 6.

42. Analogous criticisms (focused on Poulantzas's own concrete analyses of fascism) are offered by a historian in Jane Caplan, "Theories of Fascism: Nicos Poulantzas as Historian," *History Workshop* 3 (Spring 1977): 83–100. As Caplan says (p. 98), "we must . . . not turn history into a prolonged tautology." Poulantzas's functionalism constantly tends to do this.

43. Poulantzas, "Problem of Capitalist State," in *Ideology*, ed. Blackburn, p. 246.

44. Ibid., p. 246.

45. This is obviously a very "French" assumption!

46. This and the following two paragraphs build on Stephen Lee Skowronek's excellent "Building a New American State: The Expansion of National Administrative Capacities, 1877–1920" (Ph.D. diss., Department of Political Science, Cornell University, January 1979), to be published soon by Cambridge University Press.

47. This phrase comes from Huntington, "Political Modernization: America vs. Europe," in *Political Order in Changing Societies*, chap. 2.

48. Cuff, *War Industries Board*.

49. Good accounts of NRA administration include Hawley, *New Deal and Problem of Monopoly*, chap. 3; Schlesinger, *Coming of New Deal*, chap. 7; and Leverett S. Lyon et al., *The National Recovery Administration: An Analysis and Appraisal*, 2 vols. (Washington D.C.: The Brookings Institution, 1935), chaps. 4–9.

50. Quoted in Hawley, *New Deal and Problem of Monopoly*, pp. 56–57.

51. On the economic and political consequences of the NRA, see ibid., pp. 66–71 and chaps. 4–6; Chandler, *America's Greatest Depression*, pp. 229–39; and Schlesinger, *Coming of New Deal*, chaps. 8–10.

52. Schlesinger, *Coming of New Deal*, pp. 103–9, is the *locus classicus* of the Johnson-versus-Ickes comparison.

53. Herbert Stein, *The Fiscal Revolution in America* (Chicago: University of Chicago Press, 1969), pp. 23–24.

54. See Chandler, *America's Greatest Depression*, pp. 231–32; and, in general, the references cited in note 49.

55. Edelman, "Sensitivity to Labor Interests," in *Labor and the New Deal*, ed. Derber and Young, pp. 161–64, 178–82.

56. Bernstein, *Turbulent Years*, pp. 172–85.

57. This paragraph (and other discussion of Wagner) draws on J. Joseph Huthmacher, *Senator Robert F. Wagner and the Rise of Urban Liberalism* (New York: Atheneum, 1971); and Leon H. Keyserling, "The Wagner Act: Its Origin and Current Significance," *The George Washington Law Review* 29, no. 2 (December 1960): 199–233.

58. Block, "The Ruling Class Does Not Rule," p. 10.

59. Ibid.

60. Ibid., p. 8 (fn.).

61. Ibid., p. 10.

62. Ibid., p. 14.

63. Ibid., p. 7 (fn.).

64. Ibid., p. 16.

65. Ibid., p. 20.

66. Stein, *Fiscal Revolution*, chaps. 2–5, passim.

67. On the industrial working class see David Brody, "The Emergence of Mass-Production Unionism," pp. 223–62 in *Change and Continuity in Twentieth Century America*, ed. John Braeman, Robert Bremner, and E. Walters (Columbus: Ohio State University Press, 1964); Irving Bernstein, *The Lean Years* (Baltimore: Penguin Books, 1966); Bernstein, *Turbulent Years*; Derber and Young, eds., *Labor and the New Deal*; and Ruth L. Horowitz, *Political Ideologies of Organized Labor: The New Deal Era* (New Brunswick, N. J.: Transaction Books, 1978). I draw generally on these works in the discussions of labor that follow.

68. Such a portrayal of the process of change is offered by Frances Fox Piven and Richard Cloward in *Poor People's Movements: Why They*

Succeed, How They Fail (New York: Pantheon Books, 1977), chap. 3. An excellent critique of Piven and Cloward's analyses of events in the 1920s is offered in Timothy George Massad, "Disruption, Organization and Reform: A Critique of Piven and Cloward" (Undergraduate thesis, Harvard College, Social Studies, March 1978).

69. Bernstein, *New Deal Collective Bargaining Policy*, pp. 71–72, 77.

70. On the equanimity of a U.S. Steel vice president about Public Resolution no. 44, see the quotation in ibid., p. 81.

71. It is highly unusual for a party in power to gain in "off-year" Congressional elections, yet the Democrats did this in 1934. See John M. Allswang, *The New Deal and American Politics* (New York: Wiley, 1978), p. 30; and James T. Patterson, *Congressional Conservatism and the New Deal* (Lexington: University of Kentucky Press, 1967), pp. 32–33.

72. Block, "Ruling Class Does Not Rule," p. 20.

73. Ibid., p. 26.

74. Ibid., p. 23.

75. Ibid.

76. Ibid., pp. 25–26.

77. Ibid., p. 20.

78. Ibid., p. 26.

79. From C. A. R. Crosland, *The Future of Socialism* (London: Jonathan Cape, 1956), p. 61. I have taken the expression via Andrew Martin, "The Politics of Economic Policy in the United States: A Tentative View from a Comparative Perspective," Sage Professional Paper: Comparative Politics Series (Beverly Hills: Sage Publications, 1973). My thinking has been greatly influenced by Martin's paper.

80. Edelman, "New Deal Sensitivity to Labor Interests," in *Labor and the New Deal*, ed. Derber and Young, pp. 170–72.

81. Derber and Young, eds., Labor and the New Deal, pp. 3, 134.

82. On unions' political activities, see esp. J. David Greenstone, *Labor in American Politics* (New York: Vintage Books, 1790), chap. 2.

83. Huthmacher, *Wagner and Urban Liberalism*, chaps. 12–13.

84. Richard Polenberg, *Reorganizing Roosevelt's Government: The Controversy over Executive Reorganization 1936–1939* (Cambridge: Harvard University Press, 1966). Polenberg writes (p. 26): "A powerful president equipped with the personnel, planning, and fiscal control necessary to implement his social program—this was the Committee's aim."

85. Ibid., pts. 2, 3. Eventually, parts of the original executive plan were passed by Congress, but these parts simply strengthened the president's staff and modified the cabinet departments somewhat. The changes accomplished were piecemeal—far from the original plan for comprehensive reorganization.

86. Ibid., pp. 139–40. Polenberg cites Keyserling, "Wagner Act," pp. 203, 207–8, 210–12, on Wagner's views on the NLRB's administrative location. See also Huthmacher, *Wagner and Urban Liberalism*, pp. 243–45.

87. Theodore J. Lowi, "Party, Policy, and Constitution in America," in *The American Party Systems*, ed. William Nisbet Chambers and Walter Dean Burnham, 2nd ed. (New York: Oxford University Press, 1975), pp. 238–76.

88. Allswang, *New Deal and American Politics*, chaps. 2–4, passim.

89. On the attempted purge and the reasons for its failure, see ibid., pp. 121–26; and Patterson, *Congressional Conservatism*, chap. 8. On the paradoxical explanation for the one apparent success that FDR had in purging a conservative, see Richard Polenberg, "Franklin Roosevelt and the Purge of John O'Connor: The Impact of Urban Change on Political Parties," *New York History* 49, no. 3 (July 1968): 306–26.

90. Edelman, "New Deal Sensitivity to Labor Interests," in *Labor and the New Deal*, ed. Derber and Young, pp. 185–86.

91. Patterson, *Congressional Conservatism*, pp. 334–35.

92. On the resulting patterns of power see esp. Morton Grodzins, "American Political Parties and the American System," *Western Political Quarterly* 13, no. 4 (December 1960): 974–98; and Grant McConnell, *Private Power and American Democracy* (New York: Vintage Books, 1966).

93. Patterson, *Congressional Conservatism*, chaps. 6–10; and Richard Polenberg, "The Decline of the New Deal," pp. 246–66, in *The New Deal*, ed. Braeman, Bremner, and Brody, vol. 1, *The National Level*.

94. Ibid., pp. 315–24; and Huthmacher, *Wagner and Urban Liberalism*, chap. 14.

95. Robert L. Heilbroner, with Aaron Singer, *The Economic Transformation of America* (New York: Harcourt Brace Jovanovich, 1977), pp. 205–7.

96. David Brody, "The New Deal and World War II," pp. 267–309 in *The New Deal*, ed. Braeman, Bremner, and Brody, vol. 1, *The National Level*. See also Richard Polenberg, *War and Society: The United States, 1941–1945* (Philadelphia: J. B. Lippincott, 1972).

97. There are, however, some very promising pieces of comparative-historical analysis, including Martin, "Politics of Economic Policy in the United States"; Ira Katznelson, "Considerations on Social Democracy in the United States," *Comparative Politics* 11, no. 1 (October 1978): 77–99; Peter J. Katzenstein, ed., *Between Power and Plenty* (Madison: University of Wisconsin Press, 1978), esp. conclusion; and, perhaps the nicest example of all of an approach that combines class and political-structural analysis, Susan S. Fainstein and Norman I. Fainstein, "National Policy and Urban Development," *Social Problems* 26, no. 2 (December 1978): 125–46.

HERBERT HOOVER:
A REINTERPRETATION

Robert H. Zieger

Public Papers of the Presidents of the United States: Herbert Hoover. Containing the Public Messages, Speeches, and Statements of the President. (Published by the National Archives and Records Service.) Washington: Government Printing Office. 1974. Pp. xxxvi, 812.

Francis William O'Brien, edited and with commentary by. *The Hoover-Wilson Wartime Correspondence, September 24, 1914 to November 11, 1918.* Ames: Iowa State University Press. 1974. Pp. xxvi, 297.

Gary Dean Best. *The Politics of American Individualism: Herbert Hoover in Transition, 1918–1921.* Westport, Conn. and London: Greenwood Press. 1975. Pp. vi, 202.

Benjamin M. Weissman. *Herbert Hoover and Famine Relief to Soviet Russia, 1921–23.* (Hoover Institution Publications, 134.) Stanford, Calif.: Hoover Institution Press. 1974. Pp. xv, 247.

J. Joseph Huthmacher and Warren I. Susman, editors. *Herbert Hoover and the Crisis of American Capitalism.* (The American Forum Series.) Cambridge, Mass.: Schenkman Publishing Company. 1973. Pp. xiii, 138.

Martin L. Fausold and George T. Mazuzan, editors. *The Hoover Presidency: A Reappraisal.* Albany: State University of New York Press. 1974. Pp. vi, 224.

Edgar Eugene Robinson and Vaughn Davis Bornet. *Herbert Hoover: President of the United States.* (Hoover Institution Publications, 149.) Stanford, Calif.: Hoover Institution Press. 1975. Pp. xii, 398.

Joan Hoff Wilson. *Herbert Hoover: Forgotten Progressive.* (Library of American Biography.) Boston, Toronto: Little, Brown and Company, 1975. Pp. viii, 308.

Present concerns impinge upon analyses of the past, particularly the recent past. Events of the last decade and a half have shaken American liberals. The New Deal and social democratic traditions face heavy assault from both right and left. In their contributions to the reassessment of liberalism, historians have refurbished, not only heroes of the radical left, but conservative opponents of New Deal liberalism as well. Much of the literature on Herbert Hoover illustrates the simultaneous resurrection of the right and repudiation of liberal policies, both domestic and foreign. Indeed, so plausible and balanced does Hoover often appear in retrospect that it requires an effort to remember his political failure and the consistency with which the American people repudiated him and his associates at the polls.

The recent literature is highly respectful of and sympathetic toward Hoover. The only clear exception is Murray Rothbard's essay in the Huthmacher-Susman book, which pillories Hoover's deviations from market economics. At the other extreme, the Robinson-Bornet volume admits of virtually no faults in Hoover, aside from his failure to pander to popular whims. Gary Dean Best and Benjamin M. Weissman seek scrupulous neutrality, but both enhance Hoover's reputation. Joan Hoff Wilson's biography combines criticism of Hoover's rigidity, self-absorption, and defensiveness with sympathy for his views and a tone of presentist special pleading for his postpresidential career. In all, the most successful efforts to attain fresh insights into Hoover's career without overcompensation are those of Ellis Hawley, whose essays grace both the Susman-Huthmacher work and the Fausold-Mazuzan collection.

Hoover's collected papers for 1929 portray the man at the apex of his career. For most of that year he was a popular president with an energetic and positive program. No longer merely an influential advisor and not yet a political has-been, Hoover shows in the papers the optimism and purpose with which he entered the presidency. Press conference transcripts, speeches, letters and statements on particular issues, and presidential proclamations record the confident public face of his administration. Extensive supplements and appendices reprint speeches from the 1928 presidential campaign and his postelection trip to Latin America. A modest spread of photographs reveals the president in his official capacities, not yet ravaged by the Depression.

The public papers contain few surprises. The prose is leaden and difficult, attempts at humor heavy and unconvincing. Energy and seriousness are equally apparent. His messages on agricultural and tariff legislation, his background press briefings, and his special letters and statements reflect thorough preparation. Hoover's statements following the conferences with industrial, financial, and labor leaders held after the break in the stock market ring with a confidence born of his detailed knowledge of the economic system. The presidential papers reveal Hoover's reliance on expert opinion, special commissions and advisory groups, and voluntary action, as well as his repugnance for legislative initiatives. The *Public Papers . . . 1929* volume is a handsome addition to the National Archives' series and begins to fill an important gap in published presidential papers.

It is difficult to understand why the other volume of documents under review was published. Although *The Hoover-Wilson Wartime Correspondence* covers over four years, most of the communications are confined to the period of Hoover's actual service in the Wilson administration—June 1917–November 1918. Many of the communications deal with mundane matters and most would be of interest only to those concerned with the day-to-day activities of the Food Administration. Although historians have recently done much to link the two men ideologically, little in this collection touches directly on this theme. The letters and memoranda do remind the reader of the enormous complexity of food and agricultural problems during the war and reflect Hoover's decisiveness and vigor as an administrator. It is unclear, however, what broader purposes might be served by the publication of these items, especially since O'Brien's notes are largely limited to identification of references and discussion of immediate contexts. A monograph on Hoover, Wilson, and food and agricultural problems during the war would make sense; this collection of correspondence does not.

Other aspects of Hoover's early public career have already drawn monographic treatment. In *The Politics of American Individualism* Gary Dean Best follows him from his return from Europe to his entry into Harding's cabinet in 1921, while Joseph M. Weissman in *Herbert Hoover and Famine Relief to Soviet Russia, 1921–23* examines his humanitarian work as secretary of commerce. Although Best's book is unattractive in format, shockingly expensive, and narrowly focused, it makes some useful points. Carefully delineating the domestic and international strands of ideology that Hoover developed during and after the war, Best examines closely his service on the Second Industrial Conference, the abortive campaign in his behalf for the presidential nomination, and his decision to enter Harding's cabinet. Best argues that Hoover's concern with the economic consequences of the peace, both international and domestic, guided his attitudes toward the League of Nations, the labor problem, and his own political career. Seeking to promote intelligent debate over these issues and to propound his version of American exceptionalism, Hoover used his postwar fame to bring central questions of postwar political economy to public attention prior to joining the cabinet.

Although the book is solidly researched and intelligently presented, its narrow focus on three years of Hoover's life restricts its significance. Given this narrow focus and the previous appearance of important segments of the book in journal articles, this volume cannot be considered indispensable.

Herbert Hoover and Famine Relief to Soviet Russia, 1921–23 examines another aspect of Hoover's early public career. Weissman's detailed description of the American Relief Administration's enterprise focuses on Hoover's role and on the foreign-policy implications of this private body's activities. Based on archival sources, interviews, and scholarly and eyewitness literature in English and Russian, the book judiciously confronts the various ideologically tinged historical controversies associated with ARA efforts.

Weissman insists on the fundamentally humanitarian nature of the aid program. While the Hoover circle hated the Soviet regime and while some Americans were primarily concerned with trade expansion, neither counterrevolutionary purpose nor economic self-interest dominated ARA activities. Although Hoover and his associates clearly hoped that relief might encourage moderate forces in Soviet Russia, the United States government did not use the relief mission as a device for political interference. Nor does it appear that American policy-makers sought an early detente through famine relief.

Herbert Hoover and Famine Relief is clear, direct, and cogently argued. Frequent breaks in the narrative, however, and numerous undigested quotations clog Weissman's limpid prose. The book is not, as the publishers say, a philosophic essay, but it is a solid monograph on an important subject.

If these two monographs reflect favorably on Hoover's postwar activities, his tenure as cabinet member and president has generated sharp controversy. *Herbert Hoover and the Crisis of American Capitalism* contains four essays reflecting the mixed reactions of scholars to this phase of Hoover's career. Ellis Hawley, Robert Himmelberg, Murray Rothbard, and Gerald Nash in their respective papers and rejoinders, examine Hoover's ideology and his policy choices, both as cabinet member and as president. The result is a spirited uneven volume, unlikely to find the wide audience for which the American Forum Series is intended.

The editors provide a weak and careless introduction. Gaucheries of usage and spelling hint of haste and distractedness. The introduction contains irritating assertions that are either meaningless or questionable. Thus, we learn that among "the casualties of the First World War was the Progressive Era," a statement that is either tautological or historiographically dubious. In an apparent effort to make Hoover relevant to today's readers, the editors proclaim that his views of decentralization and voluntarism have gained new adherents, both with the right and with the New Left. This is a useful reminder, but Susman and Huthmacher confuse the issue, lumping these two categories of dissidents together and linking the resulting conglomeration with still another category of "Americans frustrated by the rise of giantism on all sides." To this hopelessly amorphous mélange of troubled people is attributed a reform program, a key ingredient of which is "corporate responsibility," a rubric that either expresses a pious hope for greater business morality or a greater regulatory role for government ("giantism"?). In any event, "corporate responsibility" may be a fond dream of good citizens, but it never sent Mark Rudd to the barricades. Against this left-right-frustrated-coalition the editors pit the "liberals of the 'unreconstructed' New Deal type [who] continue to advocate attempts to solve social problems by piling federal programs and appropriations still higher . . ."—hardly a fair statement of the goals or methods of the liberal-labor-civil rights bloc. Moreover, as Michael Harrington, Bayard Rustin, and others have demonstrated, there has been precious little real commitment of resources devoted to correcting social inequities.

Thus the editors start off with a confused and simplistic perception of the recent debate over public policy. This misleading focus is particularly annoying because this volume was commissioned expressly to stimulate debate and to introduce readers to relevant historical controversy. Left with little coherent direction by the editors, we must read the essays as separate pieces, gleaning from them what we can. Fortunately, they are frequently informative and provocative.

Robert Himmelberg's essay is informative. It reminds readers that for all of Hoover's associationalism, he often supported antitrust action. If the dominant motif of his public career was an apolitical, nongovernmental New Nationalism, he never entirely discarded the New Freedomite fear of cartelization. During his administration key antitrust suits were initiated and won, and the

Federal Trade Commission and the Department of Commerce scrutinized trade associations very closely.

Murray Rothbard's essay is provocative. A doctrinaire free-market economist, he sees Hoover as a fraud and a charlatan who compiled a record of governmental intervention in the economy throughout his tenure in the cabinet. For Rothbard, Hoover's involvement in labor matters, which other observers have seen as cautious, episodic, and limited, constitutes a coherent series of steps toward a form of corporate syndicalism. In the economist's view, America stood on the brink of fascism in 1932–33 when corporate leaders such as Gerard Swope pressed upon Hoover an NRA-like approach to recovery. In his "finest hour," Hoover rejected the Swope plan, although his career up until that point would seem to have been a preparation for it.

Rothbard sees Hoover as a practitioner of corporate liberalism, little different from any other major political figure. If even Hoover's brand of government-business cooperation and his kind of labor policies constitute drastic intervention in the market economy, the untrammeled functioning of which is vital to political liberty, the entire twentieth century—the entire modern world, for that matter—becomes a preface to fascism. If, however, there are degrees of regulation and intervention in political economy, and if governmental activity in the economic sphere is an inescapable aspect of any politics—especially democratic politics in which men and women seek advantage through organized public effort—Rothbard's essay is more dogmatic than convincing. This apocalyptical article is startling, superficially disturbing, and finally unsatisfying because it simply gives another name to actions and programs familiar under other rubrics.

The articles by Gerald Nash and Ellis Hawley are sedate when contrasted with Rothbard's sweeping claims. Nash stresses the role of science and Quakerism in the development of Hoover's ideology and contends that these forces bent him toward a moral absolutism that impeded him politically. Hawley tries to define Hoover's ideology. He stresses links to prewar progressivism and sketches Hoover's efforts to achieve a liberal capitalist order without resort to massive governmental intervention. Hawley adheres to the general view of prerevisionist liberal historians in his assessment of Hoover's performance as depression president, finding him ultimately guilty of an "intellectual rigidity [that] left him isolated from the main currents." But while Hawley's conclusions may be similar to standard liberal interpretations such as those offered by Carl Degler, Arthur M. Schlesinger, Jr., and Richard Hofstadter, his immersion in the Hoover papers and his sure grasp of twentieth-century economic policy enable him to understand Hoover on his own terms and to penetrate the complex substance of Hoover's ideology and programs. The reward of Hawley's essay lies not so much in his conclusions as in following him through the largely unexplored paths by which he arrives at them.

Hawley's depiction of Hoover as a link between power progressivism and the interest-group liberalism of the New Deal is amplified and sharpened in his essay in *The Hoover Presidency*. This volume contains nine papers delivered at a symposium at the State University College at Geneseo in April 1973. Donald McCoy's contribution stresses Hoover's political acumen in the 1928 campaign, while David Burner recalls the high hopes and systematic programs with which Hoover entered the White House. Essays by Frank Freidel and Albert B. Rollins focus on the interregnum of 1932–33. Freidel's account, a distillation of the exhaustive treatment of the subject in his biography of Roosevelt, contains few surprises, but Rollins argues that FDR had long envied and resented Hoover and had built his political career in the 1920s, in part in pointed opposition to his more successful erstwhile colleague of Wilson days. Roosevelt emerges from Rollins' account as an unusually devious and irresponsible public figure, exploiting Hoover's straitened circumstances and his forbidding public presence shamelessly in the 1932 campaign. The evidence is fragmentary at best, however, and there is no reason to abandon Freidel's more familiar version.

The heart of the volume is the section on Hoover's antidepression efforts. Hawley ably sketches both the hopes and limitations of his voluntary associationalism. The shift that occurred in the 1930s, he declares, "was not from laissez-faire to a managed economy, but rather from one attempt at management, that through informal private-public cooperation, to other more formal and coercive yet also limited attempts." Albert U. Romasco usefully surveys the Hoover historiography. He insists that a clear pattern of governmental response to economic downturn, as evidenced in 1907, 1914, and 1921–22, makes Hoover's responses to the Great Depression appear less innovative, thus complementing Hawley's effort to put Hoover's economic policies in context. Finally, in an excellent analysis based on his recent book, Jordan A.

Schwartz probes Hoover's political attitudes and finds him arrogant, contemptuous of Congress, and suspicious of the processes of elective government. Schwartz traces these attitudes to Hoover's engineering background and his long and successful career as an expert-administrator whose involvement in the practical realities of business, logistics, and economic problems left him with little aptitude for, or appreciation of, messy but equally practical political realities.

The volume closes with two essays on foreign policy. In one, Selig Adler casts a skeptical eye on the recent conversion of William Applemen Williams and New Left historians to the cause of Herbert Hoover. He suggests that Williams, in his eagerness to challenge the liberal consensus that dominated foreign-policy historiography until the 1960s, may have gilded the lily in Hoover's case, emphasizing out of context some of his anti-interventionist utterances while ignoring or slighting his economic expansionism, radicalism, and strident anticommunism. Adler maintains that, however much Vietnam may have revealed the limitations of interventionism in the 1960s, the menace of fascism and militarism left FDR with little room for maneuver in the 1930s, *pace* Hoover's objections. He calls for vigorous monographic examination of the claims for Hoover's foreign and domestic policies raised by Williams.

In her essay, Joan Hoff Wilson analyzes the economic aspects of Hoover's policies, stressing the link between his efforts in this field as secretary of commerce and those he undertook as president. Wilson evinces a sure grasp of such difficult and complex issues as reparations, tariff policy, and foreign exchange. Not content with rehabilitating Hoover's reputation as a shrewd and highly informed practitioner of economic foreign policy, Wilson also suggest the perspicacity of his overall approach to foreign policy, noting that many of his strictures against overextension have been borne out. Since the essay mentions the Manchurian crisis only in passing, however, and since its substance is confined to the 1921–33 period, the last two or three pages are a gratuitous exercise in political moralism. Wilson is barely able to suggest the outlines of Hoover's response to thirty years of world events, much less to explicate the complexities of foreign policy after he left office.

The Geneseo conference must have been rewarding for its participants if the high quality of the published results is any indication. It appears that neither Edgar A. Robinson nor Vaughn

Davis Bornet attended. If they did, none of the subtlety or ambiguity of recent scholarship concerning Hoover influences their book, *Herbert Hoover: President of the United States.* This is a curious volume, a homage to an old Stanford man by two historians with long associations with that university. While it cites much of the recent literature, and while the authors interviewed hundreds of people associated with Hoover, it is a simplistic defense of Hoover's entire course of action as president. Moreover, its authors' penchant for vapid generalizations and pronouncements is befuddling and irritating. What might have been a sympathetic, tightly argued reassessment of Hoover is a pretentious apology.

The authors perceive Hoover as a man so uniquely capable and so profoundly knowledgeable as to dwarf his contemporaries. They see a public yearning for reform, for freedom from special interests. At the same time, they see the nation's political structure—its parties and caucuses, its constitutional institutions—as hopelessly provincial, self-serving, and corrupt. Little is adduced in support of these claims; they are simply asserted, often in thick, cloudy language and with gratuitous moralisms. Theodore Roosevelt, they declare, "did not accept the doctrines of the ruling elements in the Republican party. In his middle course and his pragmatic approach, he never betrayed the basic meaning of earlier American political experience. Builders of a free society must be free" (p. 7). Again: "Perhaps nothing was so characteristic of the 'politics' of the period 1901–1929 as the slogan 'restore the government to the people.' This appealed to many of the electorate who felt that party organizations had become subservient to special interests. . . . The average citizen was quite content to believe that the managers of the great political enterprise they called the United States were the practical men known as 'politicians.'" The book is filled with such judgments that lack references and convey little meaning. A good editor might have corrected this tendency and steered the authors closer to their real purpose, informed rehabilitation of the Hoover presidency.

Such an editor might also have reduced the partisanship of the volume. A reader of *Herbert Hoover: President of the United States* would never realize that knotty, complex issues gripped the country in these years, issues over which honest people could differ and which they still debate. Everything is black and white: Hoover was invariably right, albeit at times guilty of the understandable lapses in patience that afflict a man surrounded by fools and charlatans;

his critics and opponents were invariably wrong. The authors use recent research where it suits their purposes but not as a means of elevating the debate to new levels of analysis. A taste of the authors' efforts at analysis is available on the last page. They ask "why the people rejected President Hoover's program for the new scientific era, a program rooted in voluntarism and cooperation rather than federal domination. . . ." Hoover, they aver, "conducted himself as an enemy of war and armaments; as a friend of constitutional government; as a supporter of voluntary methods; as a preserver of a partially regulated capitalist system that could hold its own. . . . President Hoover . . . was, above all, a determined spokesman for the traditional American virtues, hopes, and ideals of individual opportunity, personal freedom, and love of country." The back dust jacket lists encomia for the volume by such luminaries as Thomas A. Bailey, Frank Freidel, Norman Graebner, and Ellis Hawley. But these worthies notwithstanding, the book is neither "succinct" nor "lucid." It may, as Bailey suggests, "help swing the pendulum toward a fairer and more balanced appraisal of the thirty-first President," but only for those who have read nothing on Hoover for the past ten or twelve years. The book is a serious disappointment, given the authors' access to sources and their scholarly reputations.

With all the resurgence of interest in Hoover, there is not yet a comprehensive biography. Until one appears, Joan Hoff Wilson's *Herbert Hoover: Forgotten Progressive* will serve as a brief, competent introduction to his entire career. Based as it is on newly opened archival and manuscript materials and on recent scholarship, it is more sophisticated and analytical than previous biographies. *Herbert Hoover* portrays a man who combined great practical ability and intellectual consistency with a dour and almost reclusive personality. Wilson's discussion of Hoover's ideology, noting both its relationship to other strands of progressivism and its limitations, is fair, although it frequently lacks sharpness and clarity. While her observations on Hoover's ideas and policies on domestic issues in the 1920s parallel closely those of Hawley and other recent students, Wilson's examination of Hoover's foreign policy as president and his views of war and peace in the World War II era are fresh and particularly stimulating. An excellent bibliographical essay enhances the value of the book and partially compensates for the absence of notes, although at times materials drawn heavily upon in the text are not given attribution in the essay.

Wilson's discussion of Hoover's postpresidential career is lengthy and useful, especially in light of the lack of scholarly attention to this subject. She credits the thirty-first president with remarkable prescience for his warnings against the growth of a centralized state with vast, coercive powers and limitless international commitments. Although she acknowledges Hoover's extreme and often hyperbolic anticommunism, she notes that he never joined the McCarthyites. Her resurrection of his often trenchant and provocative critiques of foreign and military policy in the 1940s and 1950s is a great service, as is her discussion of Hoover's skepticism of bipartisanship in these areas. As Hoover did himself, however, Wilson leaves unanswered central questions about how the United States might hope to achieve the kind of expanding economy Hoover thought necessary for the maintenance of a unique social order without an aggressive foreign policy.

The chief flaw of the last part of the book lies in Wilson's largely implicit effort to enlist Hoover as a social critic. She contends that Vietnam and Watergate "have amply demonstrated his worst fears of a society and economy run from the top down by a coercive system of expertise and by what has recently been called an 'arrogant elite of political adolescents'" (p. 278).

This comment reflects the tone of the last part of the book. It also demonstrates some of the limitations of Wilson's prose and analysis. The use of the passive voice—a feature of her writing—obscures sources (there are no footnotes) and, in this case, substitutes a kind of cryptic rhetoric for thoughtful analysis. Hoover's penchant for expertise, his disdain for Congress, his contempt for the hurly-burly of the political process, and his compulsive self-containment hardly make him the model of the open, candid, and accessible chief executive. His faith in the public-spiritedness and ability of corporate executives certainly provided precedents for elitist decision-making. It is hard to see how either Vietnam or Watergate resulted from a "coercive system of expertise." True, Kennedy, Johnson, and Nixon relied heavily on their particular versions of the best and the brightest. But so did Hoover, whose whole public philosophy—as Wilson so correctly notes in an early chapter (pp. 72–3)—denigrated the elected representatives of the people and elevated the engineers, experts, and managers, whether governmental or private.

Moreover, Wilson seems to accept the same kind of facile assumptions shared by Susman and Huthmacher that the New

Deal and postwar liberal reform have foisted upon the American people some sort of coercive welfare state without their consent and against their interests. In reality, as Hawley and Otis Graham, Jr. (in his superb essay in Elkins and McKitrick, eds., *The Hofstadter Aegis*) remind us, New Deal reforms were partial, frugally funded, closely in line with prevailing conceptions about the role of government, and extremely sensitive to the rhetoric of decentralization and local control, often to the disadvantage of minorities, working people, and the poor. Far from creating a centralized welfare state, modern liberalism has fallen far short of its goals—always more modest than those of other Western states—in education, old-age security, health care, and many other areas.

For all of Hoover's rhetoric about grass-roots participation and the values of local decision-making, his reliance was always on elite groups. For all the limitations of post-1933 liberalism, it has been the New Deal and its heirs that have done the most to bring working people, blacks and other minorities, and the poor into decision-making processes. While it may be true that the country's international enterprises over the past generation have threatened domestic liberties, there is no easy linkage between the perniciousness of these activities and the creation of a partial welfare state. Just as the legacy of Hooverism is, as Wilson recognizes in the first two-thirds of the book, mixed, so is the inheritance of the New Deal era. If many contemporary Americans—primarily the liberals, radicals, and hirsute activists, with whom Hoover would have been, to say the least, ill at ease—might today see wisdom and good judgment in his broad strictures on foreign policy, few blacks, urban dwellers, laborites, or poor people would find much of use in his observations on government and public policy in the domestic field.

Wilson's biography accurately summarizes the interim conclusions of this round of Hoover scholarship. The limitations of Democratic liberalism, the agony of Vietnam, and second thoughts about the general efficacy of governmental solutions to social problems are conducive to favorable re-examination of men such as Hoover and Robert A. Taft. In addition, the opening of the Hoover presidential library at West Branch, Iowa, occurred when the graduate schools were swollen with eager Ph.D. candidates, many of whose lives inclined them toward a critical assessment of the previous generation's version of our recent past. At its worst, the current wave of scholarship simply updates and reinforces the self-serving and petulant tone of Hoover's own apologetics and those of his colleagues and associates in their defenses of the Chief. At its best, the current scholarship opens up to re-evaluation not merely Hoover himself, but a whole way of looking at the American social order. Let us hope that Hoover, now presumably rescued from the distortions and slurs of his political and ideological enemies, is not abstracted from his context and made to shoulder a burden of consistent public virtue and intellectual acuity that the record will not support.

Herbert Hoover rose from native stock to a position of wealth and power, first in private life, then as a public figure. Small-town Iowa and Oregon, Stanford University, the engineering profession, and private humanitarian service decisively shaped his preparation for the presidency. This background contributed personal qualities of energy, dedication, and integrity. It encouraged voluntarism, efficiency, and privatism. He never abandoned this background, nor did he transcend it. In certain respects, it would have stood the country in good stead after his fall from power; in other ways, it deserved to be rejected.

"Could it be true," asked Richard Hofstadter in his brilliant assessment of the 74-year-old former president in 1948, "that the great American tradition was nearing its end because the people had no ear for spokesmen of the old faith?" The rise of militant unionism, agitation over civil rights, the adoption of new regulatory and welfare-state devices, and the general reliance on federal action in a wide range of activities may have resulted from devious politicians, momentary frustrations, and temporary circumstances. But were not such programs and initiatives genuinely popular and even necessary for the preservation of the social order? "Perhaps, after all," Hofstadter wrote, "it was the spirit of the people that was not fundamentally sound." If historians are insensitive to and impressed by the fact that Hoover and his social vision have been frequently and resoundingly repudiated by the American electorate, they may find themselves sharing with Hoover, not only the more attractive aspects of his public thought, but some of the implicit distrust of the people that lurked beneath the surface of his rhetoric.

NOT SO "TURBULENT YEARS": ANOTHER LOOK AT THE AMERICAN 1930's

Melvyn Dubofsky

In sharp contrast to most descriptions and analyses of American workers and their labor movement during the 1930's, which stress the turbulence and conflict of the depression decade, this essay explores the passivity beneath the turbulent surface of violent events as well as the persistence of many predepression era beliefs and behavioral patterns among American workers. In order to understand why the industrial conflicts of the 1930's in the United States and the labor upheaval which created the CIO failed to produce a durable mass radical, or socialist, working-class movement, it is necessary to understand that the vast majority of American workers were never themselves involved directly in labor conflicts or violent events. It is equally important to comprehend precisely how underlying values and modes of behavior diluted working-class radicalism. Moreover, one must be aware of how Franklin D. Roosevelt's New Deal defused radical politics in the United States and also served as the American equivalent of North European social democracy. Finally, the essay suggests that a distinction must be drawn between class struggle as an historical reality and workers as a class subjectively aware of their historical role as agents of revolution or radical change.

Our conventional view of the 1930's was aptly caught in the title of Irving Bernstein's history of American labor during that decade, *Turbulent Years*, a title that the author borrowed from Myron Taylor's annual report to the Board of Directors of the United States Steel Corporation in 1938. That liberal historians and corporate executives perceive the 1930's as a "turbulent" decade should today occasion no surprise. For the American business elite especially, their social, economic, and political world had turned upside down during the Great Depression and New Deal. After nearly a full decade of corporate hegemony, class collaboration, and trade union retreat, the United States during the 1930's seemed chronically beset with class conflict, violence, and ubiquitous labor radicalism. In the words of one of the decade's radicals, Len DeCaux, a "new consciousness" awakened workers from lethargy. "There was light after the darkness in the youth of the movement," exulted DeCaux. "Youth that was direct and bold in action, not sluggish and sly from long compromise with the old and the rotten. There was light in the hopeful future seen by the red and the rebellious, now playing their full part in what they held to be a great working-class advance against the capitalist class. There was light, and a heady, happy feeling in the solidarity of common struggle in a splendid common cause."[1]

The picture one has of the 1930's, then, whether painted by a liberal scholar such as Bernstein, an activist like DeCaux, or a tycoon like Taylor, is of conflict and struggle. The foreground is filled with militant and radical workers, the masses in motion, a rank and file vigorously, sometimes violently, reaching out to grasp control over its own labor and existence.

Given the conventional portrait of the American 1930's, conventional questions arise, the most obvious of which are the following: 1) Why did labor militancy decline? 2) Why did militant, radical rank-and-file struggles produce old-fashioned, autocratically controlled trade unions in many cases? 3) Why did the turbulence create no lasting, mass radical political movement?

Before seeking to answer such questions, even assuming they are the best ones to ask about the thirties, I am reminded of a lesson contained in an American cartoon strip. A caveman reporter informs his stone-age editor that he has both good news and bad news. "Let's have the bad news first," says the editor. "There's only good news," responds the reporter. Need I add that American journalists had a field day during the 1930's and that their editors rejoiced in an abundance of "bad news;" frontpage headlines shrieked class war and wire photos depicted strikers in armed conflict with police and troops.

But were class war and violent pitched battles the reality of the 1930's? And, if they were, how do we explain the absence of a mass radical political movement?

Frankly, all of us realize how difficult it is to create or grasp historical reality. As historians, we work with the available evidence, always, to be sure, seeking to discover more about the past, but always aware that the *total* record of what happened is beyond our recall or recreation. Ultimately, then, just as man through his thoughts and actions makes history, historians, in the process of research and writing, create their own history.

In examining the 1930's, how should we go about creating the history of that era? Two convenient models are at hand. In one we can seek lessons for the present in an instrumental view of the past. That approach suggests the might-have-beens of history. If only Communists had behaved differently; if nonsectarian radicals had pursued the proper policies; if the militant rank and file had been aware of its true interests (as distinguished from the false consciousness inculcated by trade-union bureaucrats and New Deal Democrats); then the history of the 1930's would have been different and *better*.[2] The second approach to our turbulent decade has been suggested by David Brody. "The interesting questions," writes Brody, "are not in the realm of what might have been, but in a closer examination of what did happen."[3] Brody's approach, I believe, promises greater rewards for scholars and may even be more useful for those who desire to use the past to improve the present and shape the future. As Karl Marx noted in *The Eighteenth Brumaire*, "man indeed makes his own history, but only under circumstances directly encountered, given and transmitted from the past. The tradition of all the dead generations weighs like a nightmare on the brain of the living."[4]

One more preliminary observation must be made about recreating the past in general and the American 1930's in particular. We must be zealously on guard against falling victim to what Edward Thompson has characterized as the "Pilgrim's Progress" orthodoxy, an approach that, in his words, "reads history in the light of subsequent preoccupations, and not in fact as it occurred. Only the successful [. . .] are remembered. The blind alleys, the lost causes, and the losers themselves are forgotten."[5] In light of what I intend to say below and also what such theorists of "corporate liberalism" as Ronald Radosh and James Weinstein have written about the history of the American labor movement, it is well to bear in mind Thompson's comment that history written as the record of victors and survivors is not necessarily synonymous with the past as experienced by all of those who lived it and created it.[6]

I

Let us now see if we can uncover or glimpse the reality of the American 1930's. Certainly, the turbulence, militancy, and radicalism of the decade existed. From 1929 through 1939, the American economic and social system remained in crisis. Despite two substantial recoveries from the depths of depression, unemployment during the decade never fell below 14 per cent of the civilian labor force or 21 per cent of the nonagricultural work force.[7] Those workers who once believed in the American myth of success, who dreamed of inching up the occupational ladder, acquiring property of their own, and watching their children do even better occupationally and materially, had their hopes blasted by the Great Depression. As Stephan Thernstrom's research shows for Boston, the Great Depression thwarted occupational and material advancement for an entire generation of workers.[8] And what was true in Boston most likely prevailed elsewhere in the nation. If, in the past, American workers had experienced marginal upward social and economic mobility, during the 1930's they could expect to fall rather more often than to climb.

The thwarted aspirations of millions of workers combined with persistent mass unemployment produced a decade of social unrest that encompassed every form of collective and individual action from mass marches to food looting. One historian has pointed out that between February 1930 and July 1932, at least seventeen separate incidents of violent protest occurred. In Chicago in 1931, after three persons were killed during an anti-eviction struggle, 60,000 citizens marched on City Hall to protest police brutality. Indeed in nearly every city in which the unemployed organized and protested, violent confrontations with the police erupted.[9]

More important and more threatening to the established order than protests by the unemployed and hungry, which punctuated the early depression years, were the more conventional forms of class struggle which erupted with greater incidence after the election of Franklin Roosevelt and the coming of the New Deal. In 1934, after twelve years of relative quiet on the labor front, industrial conflict broke out with a militancy and violence not seen since 1919. In Toledo, Ohio, National Guardsmen tear-gassed and drove from the city's streets Auto-Lite Company strikers who had the support not only of the radical A. J. Muste's American Workers party and Unemployed League, but also of the citywide central labor council, an A. F. of L. affiliate. And the following month, July 1934, witnessed still more violent struggles. A strike by maritime workers in the San Francisco Bay area brought battles between police and longshoremen, several dead strikers, and the dispatch of state troops. In protest, the San Francisco central labor council declared a citywide general strike for July 16. Here, too, a labor radical, Harry Bridges, an Australian immigrant and a Marxist, led a strike unsanctioned by the A. F. of L. Only a day after the San Francisco general strike ended, Americans read in their newspapers of July 21 that on the previous day in Minneapolis, Minnesota, fifty men had been shot in the back as police fired on strikers. Within a week of the bloody July 20 battle between police and teamsters in the city's main square, Minnesota Governor Floyd Olson placed the Twin Cities under martial law. Once again, in Minneapolis, as earlier in Toledo and San Francisco, left-wing radicals led the strike, in this instance the Trotskyists, Farrell Dobbs and the brothers Vincent, Miles, Grant, and Ray Dunne. And only a week after the shootings in Minneapolis, on July 28, 1934, deputy sheriffs in the company town of Kohler, Wisconsin killed one person and injured twenty in what the New York *Times* characterized as a "strike riot."[10]

Few areas of the nation seemed untouched by labor militancy in 1934. In the spring a national textile strike called by the United Textile Workers of America brought out 350,000 workers from Maine to Alabama, and violent repression of the strikers proved the rule in the South's Piedmont mill towns. Throughout the spring auto and steel workers flocked into trade unions, like coal miners the previous year, seeming almost to organize themselves. And when auto manufacturers and steel barons refused to bargain with labor, national strikes threatened both industries. Only direct presidential intervention and the equivocal actions of A. F. of L. leaders averted walkouts in autos and steel.[11]

If 1934, in Irving Bernstein's chapter title amounted to an "Eruption," 1937 experienced an epidemic of strikes. The year began with the famous Flint sit-down strike in which the United Auto Workers conquered General Motors; saw United States Steel surrender to the Steel Workers Organizing Committee (SWOC)-CIO without a struggle less than three weeks after the General Motors strike ended; and culminated in the late spring with perhaps the most violent and bloodiest national strike of the decade: the Little Steel conflict that led to the Memorial Day "massacre" outside Republic Steel's South Chicago plant. In between Flint and Little Steel, more than 400,000 workers participated in 477 sit-down strikes. Twenty-five sit-downs erupted in January 1937, forty-seven in February, and 170 in March. "Sitting down has replaced baseball as a national pastime," quipped *Time* Magazine.[12]

The labor militancy and strikes of 1934 and 1937 created a solidarity that hitherto eluded American workers. During the 1930's, it seemed, the United States had developed a true proletariat, more united by its similarities than divided by its differences. Mass immigration had ended in 1921, and hence the last immigrant generation had had more than a decade to integrate itself into the social system and for its children to have been "Americanized" by the public schools and other intermediate social agencies. Male-female role conflicts appeared notable by their absence, and strikers' wives provided their husbands with substantial assistance as members of women's auxiliaries. "I found a common understanding and unselfishness I'd never known in my life," wrote the wife of one Flint sitdowner. "I'm living for the first time with a definite goal. [. . .] Just being a woman isn't enough any more. I want to be a human being with the right to think for myself."[13] "A new type of woman was born in the strike," noted an observer of the struggle in Flint. "Women who only yesterday were horrified at unionism, who felt inferior to the task of speaking, leading, have, as if overnight, become the spearhead in the battle for unionism."[14]

Even racial tensions among workers seemed to diminish during the 1930's, especially after the emergence of the CIO whose "new unionists" often crusaded for civil rights as vigorously as for trade unionism. The changes wrought by CIO led two students of black labor to conclude in 1939 "that it is easier to incorporate Negroes into a new movement [. . .] than to find a secure place in an older one." Surveying the impact of depression, New Deal, and CIO on black workers, Horace Cayton and George S. Mitchell suggested that

> in the readjustment of social patterns and ideologies, we find reflected a profound transition in Negro life as well as in the economic outlook of American workers generally. What has been for generations a racial stratification in occupation is, under present-day conditions, in process of transformation. Class tension and class solidarity have measurably relaxed racial tensions and, by so doing, have mitigated the divisive effects of racial antagonism.[15]

II

One must not, however, romanticize working-class solidarity and thus lose sight of the tensions that continued to pit American workers during the 1930's against each other rather than a common enemy. In New Haven, Connecticut, American-born workers still denigrated Italians as "wops," and "it's dog eat dog all right," retorted an Italian-American machinist, "but it's also Mick feeds Mick!"[16] A Hollywood film of the late 1930's, *Black Legion*, starring Humphrey Bogart as a frustrated white American-born Protestant machinist, captured the still lingering resentment harbored by the American-born against the foreign-born (and even their children), and depicted the sort of worker more likely to listen to Father Coughlin than to John L. Lewis, Franklin D. Roosevelt, or perhaps William Z. Foster. Or listen to an official of an A. F. of L. union with jurisdiction in an industry that employed many Afro-Americans. "I consider the Negroes poor union men. You know as well as I do that they are shiftless, easily intimidated and generally of poor caliber. [. . .] What should have happened is what is being done in Calhoun County, Illinois, where Negroes are not allowed to stay overnight. As a result there are no Negroes there and no Negro problem."[17]

But it was the CIO, not the A. F. of L., that symbolized the labor upheaval of the 1930's. And in 1937 when CIO organized autos, steel, rubber, and other former bastions of the open shop, between three and a half and four million workers joined the labor movement, a larger number than the entire A. F. of L. claimed as of January 1, 1937. Now, for the first time in its history, organized labor in America wielded power in the strategic core of mass-production industry, and it did so under the aegis of a labor federation (CIO) whose leaders consciously repudiated the A. F. of L. tradition of class accommodation and collaboration. The CIO during the late 1930's exemplified solidarity rather than exclusiveness, political action in place of nonpartisanship, biracialism and bisexualism instead of racial and sexual chauvinism, and militancy rather than opportunism. "CIO started as a new kind of labor movement," recalled Len DeCaux in his autobiography. "A challenge to the old AFL and the status quo it complacently guarded. It was new in its youth and fervor, new in the broad sector of the working class it brought into action, new in the way it accepted and integrated its radicals, new in its relative independence of corporate and government control, new in its many social and political attitudes."[18]

DeCaux was not alone among radicals in looking to CIO as the instrument through which to build a new America. Powers Hapgood, the Harvard-educated son of a wealthy Midwestern family, who worked as a coal miner in order to share the worker's plight, felt compelled in 1935 to seek an accommodation with his ancient enemy John L. Lewis, who was then organizing the CIO. "It's surprising how many radicals think I ought to see Lewis," Hapgood informed his wife, "saying it's much less of a compromise to make peace with him and stay in the labor movement than it is to get a government job and cease to be active in the class struggle."

To reject a reconciliation with Lewis in 1935, concluded Hapgood, would let the leftwing down.[19] After the CIO's first national conference in Atlantic City in October 1937, Adolph Germer, a former ally of Hapgood and then a Social Democrat evolving into a New Deal Democrat, wrote to an ex-associate in the Socialist Party of America: "I attended the Atlantic City conference and I assure you it was an educational treat. There was as much difference between that meeting and the A. F. of L. conventions I have attended as there is between night and day."[20] And Lee Pressman and Gardner Jackson, the former an ex-Communist and the latter a left-wing, socialist-inclined reformer, both of whom worked closely with Lewis from 1936 through 1940, observed that Lewis seemed a changed man in 1937, that the CIO experience had transformed him from "a labor boss of the most conventional kind, and a discredited one at that" into an eager, dedicated leader of a movement encompassing blue- and white-collar workers, farmers, small professionals and all sorts of "little people." Lewis, Pressman and Jackson believed in 1937, might well lead an independent populist or farmer-labor political movement in the event Roosevelt and the Democrats failed to implement full-employment policies and a welfare state.[21]

Had Lewis decided to lead such an independent political movement, the time never seemed riper. The Great Depression and the New Deal had wrought a veritable political revolution among American workers. Masses of hitherto politically apathetic workers, especially among first-generation immigrants and their spouses, went to the polls in greater numbers. And Roosevelt broke the last links that bound millions of workers across the industrial heartland from Pittsburgh to Chicago to the Republican party.[22] Lewis exulted at the results of the 1936 election in which for the first time since the depression of the 1890's, Democrats swept into power in the steel and coal towns of Pennsylvania and Ohio, winning office on tickets financed by CIO money and headed by CIO members.[23] A new consciousness appeared to be stirring among the nation's industrial workers. A social scientist sampling attitudes and beliefs among Akron rubber workers at the end of the 1930's discovered that the vast majority of CIO members valued human rights above property rights and showed little respect or deference for the prerogatives and privileges of corporate property. Akron's workers, and also many residents characterized as middle class, apparently distinguished between purely personal use-property and property as capital, which afforded its possessors power over the lives and labor of the propertyless.[24] Such an altered consciousness fed the dreams of Popular Fronters and third-party activists.

All this ferment, militancy, radicalism, violence, and perhaps even an altered working-class consciousness were part of American reality during the 1930's. Yet, as we know, American socialism expired during the depression decade, communism advanced only marginally, Roosevelt seduced the farmer-laborites and populists, the CIO came to resemble the A. F. of L., and John L. Lewis once again reverted to behaving like a "labor boss of the most conventional kind." Why? To answer that question we have to examine other aspects of social, economic, and political reality during the 1930's.

III

Just as one can claim that the 1930's represented a crisis for American capitalism that expressed itself most overtly in the eagerness and militancy with which workers challenged their corporate masters, one might just as easily assert that for most Americans, workers included, events during the decade reinforced their faith in the "justness" of the American system and the prospects for improvement without fundamental restructuring. For many workers capitalism never collapsed; indeed, for those employed steadily, always a substantial proportion of the work force, real wages actually rose as prices fell. For other workers, the tentative economic recovery of 1933–34 and the more substantial growth of 1937 rekindled faith in the American system. The two great strike waves of the decade, 1934 and 1937, erupted not in moments of crisis, but when hope, profits, employment, and wages all revived. Crisis, in other words, induced apathy or lethargy; economic recovery, a sign that the system worked, stimulated action. And when the recovery of 1936–37 was followed by the "Roosevelt depression," a more rapid and deeper decline than the Great Crash of 1929–33, the number of strikes diminished markedly and the more militant CIO affiliates concentrated in the mass-production industries suffered severe membership and financial losses.[25] Perhaps this final crisis of the depression decade left unresolved might have snapped whatever bonds still tied workers to the American system. That, however, remains a problematic historical might-have-been, as the coming of World War II resolved the contradictions in American capitalism and substituted patriotic unity for class conflict.

An analysis of the statistics of working-class militancy during the 1930's—the incidence of strikes, the number of workers affected, the man-days lost—also leads to divergent interpretations. One can stress the high level of strike activity, the fact that only 840 strikes were recorded in 1932 but 1700 erupted in 1933, 1856 in 1934, 2200 in 1936, and in the peak strike year, 1937, 4740 broke out.[26] One can argue that no area of the nation and, more importantly, no major industry escaped industrial conflict. For the first time in United States history strikes affected every major mass-production industry and paralyzed the towering heights of the economy: steel, auto, rubber, coal, electrical goods; the list goes on and on. For the nation and its workers, the 1930's were indeed "turbulent years."

But the statistics of industrial conflict reveal another story, an equally interesting one. When the 1934 strike wave erupted, President Roosevelt sought to understand its origins and implications. He asked the Commissioner of Labor Statistics, Isidore Lubin, to analyze and interpret the 1934 outbreak. Lubin prepared a report that he transmitted to the President in late August 1934. Seeking to place the 1934 strikes in historical perspective, Lubin acted logically. He compared what had happened in the first half of 1934 to the last previous year in which the United States had experienced such massive labor militancy, 1919. And he concluded that the 1934 strike wave could not match 1919 in intensity, duration, or number of workers involved. More than twice as many strikes began each month in the first half of 1919, reported Lubin, than in the same period in 1934; moreover, more than two and a half times as many workers were involved in the 1919 strikes. He then proceeded to assure the President that July 1934, the month of the San Francisco and Minneapolis general strikes, witnessed no mass working-class upheaval. Only seven-tenths of one per cent, or seven out of every thousand wage earners, participated in strikes. Only four-tenths of one per cent of man-days of employment were lost as a result of strikes. "In other words," Lubin reassured the President, "for every thousand man-days worked four were lost because of strikes." Selecting ten major industries for analysis, Lubin observed that only one-half of one per cent of the total number employed struck in July 1934. "Comparing the number employed with the number actually involved in strikes, one reaches the conclusion that for every thousand workers employed in those industries only five were affected by strikes. In terms of the number of man-days lost [. . .] it is estimated that for every thousand man-days worked [. . .] seven days of employment were lost because of strikes." And, in a final note of reassurance for the President, Lubin observed that the "recent strikes have been relatively short lived," less than half as long as the average duration during 1927 (24 compared to 51 days), a time of labor peace.[27]

But what of 1937, the decade's premier strike year, when more than twice as many workers struck as in 1934? Well, according to official statistics, only 7.2 per cent of employed workers were involved in walkouts (practically the same percentage as in 1934) and their absence from work represented only 0.043 per cent of all time worked.[28]

Questions immediately arise from a reading of such strike statistics. What was the other 93 per cent of the labor force doing during the great strike waves of 1934 and 1937? More important, how were they affected by the upsurge of industrial conflicts which did not involve or affect them directly?

Such questions are especially important when one bears in mind the continental size of the United States. Geography could, and did, easily dilute the impact of industrial conflict nationally. The United States lacked a London, Paris, Berlin, or Rome, where massive, militant strikes affected the national state directly as well as private employers. Few of the major strikes of the 1930's occurred even in state capitals, most of which were isolated from industrial strife. When teamsters tied up Minneapolis and longshoremen closed down San Francisco in July 1934, truckers continued to deliver goods in Chicago and Los Angeles, and waterfront workers remained on the job in New York, Baltimore, and San Pedro. For trade unionists and radicals it was exceedingly difficult, as Roy Rosenzweig has shown for A. J. Muste's Unemployed League, to transform well-structured local and regional organizations into equally effective national bodies.[29] Just as the millions of unemployed during the 1930's did not experience the shock of joblessness simultaneously, so, too, different workers experienced industrial conflict at different times and in different places. As we will see below, what workers most often experienced in common—participation in the American political system—was precisely what most effectively diluted militancy and radicalism.

Despite the continental size and diversity of the American nation, it is possible to glimpse aspects of working-class reality in local settings that disclose uniformities in belief and behavior which do much to explain the dearth of durable radicalism in the United States. We are fortunate that two truly excellent, perceptive sociological field studies were completed during the 1930's that dissect the social structure and culture of two characteristic smaller American industrial cities. We are even more fortunate that the two cities investigated—Muncie, Indiana, and New Haven, Connecticut— proved so unlike in their economic structures, population mixes, and regional and cultural milieus. Muncie was dominated by two industries—Ball Glass and General Motors—characterized by an almost totally American-born, white Protestant population, and situated in the heartland of American agriculture, individualism, and evangelical Protestantism. New Haven, by contrast, claimed no dominant employers, encompassed a population differentiated by nationality, race, and religion as well as class, and was set in a region traditionally urban (also urbane) and non-evangelical in culture. Yet after one finishes reading Robert and Helen Lynd on Muncie and E. Wight Bakke on New Haven, one is more impressed by the similarities rather than the differences in working-class attitudes and behavior.[30]

Let us examine Muncie first. The Lynds had initially gone to Muncie in the mid-1920's in order to discover how urbanization and industrialization had affected American culture, how the city and the factory had altered beliefs and behavioral patterns developed in the country and on the farm.[31] They returned a decade later in order to see what impact, if any, the "Great Depression" had had on local culture and behavior. Surprisingly, for them at least, they found labor organization weaker in 1935 than it had been in 1925, yet the Muncie business class seemed more united and more determined than ever to keep its city open shop (nonunion). The Lynds discovered objectively greater class stratification in 1935 than in 1925 and even less prospect for the individual worker to climb up the ladder of success (see Thernstrom on Boston's depression generation workers for similar findings), yet they characterized Muncie's workers as being influenced by "drives [. . .] largely those of the business class: both are caught up in the tradition of a rising standard of living and lured by the enticements of salesmanship." As one Middletown woman informed the sociologists: "Most of the families that I know are after the same things today that they were before the depression, and they'll get them the same way—on credit."[32]

Union officials told the Lynds a similar tale of woe. Union members preferred buying gas for their cars to paying dues, and going for a drive to attending a union meeting. Local workers were willing to beg, borrow, or steal to maintain possession of their cars and keep them running. Despite seven years of depression, Muncie's workers, according to the Lynds, still worshipped the automobile as the symbol of the American dream, and, as long as they owned one, considered themselves content.[33]

"Fear, resentment, insecurity and disillusionment has been to Middletown's workers largely an *individual* experience for each worker," concluded the Lynds,

> and not a thing generalized by him into a 'class' experi-
> ence.
> Such militancy as it generates tends to be sporadic,
> personal, and flaccid; an expression primarily of personal
> resentment rather than an act of self-identification with
> the continuities of a movement or of a rebellion against an
> economic status regarded as permanently fixed. The
> militancy of Middletown labor tends, therefore, to be
> easily manipulated, and to be diverted into all manner of
> incidental issues.[34]

So much for Muncie—what of New Haven with its more heterogeneous and less individualistic (culturally) working class, a working class that, in some cases, the investigator could interview and probe after the CIO upheaval of 1936–37? Again we see in E. W. Bakke's two published examinations of the unemployed worker in New Haven an absence of mass organization, collective militancy, or radicalism, despite an apparent hardening of class lines. New Haven's workers, unlike Muncie's, apparently did not share the drives of the business class and they did in fact develop a collective sense of class. "Hell, brother," a machinist told Bakke, "you don't have to look to know there's a workin' class. We may not say so—But look at what we do. Work. Look at where we live. Nothing there but workers. Look at how we get along. Just like every other damned worker. Hell's bells, of course, there's a workin' class, and its gettin' more so every day."[35] Yet New Haven, like Muncie, lacked a militant and radical working class. Why?

Bakke tried to provide answers. He cited the usual barriers to collective action and working-class radicalism:—ethnic heterogeneity; fear of the alien; fear of repression; and capitalist hegemony that was cultural as well as economic and political.[36] Yet he also discovered that answers to the absence of militancy and radicalism lay embedded deep within the culture of New Haven's workers. In most cases, their lives had disproved the American Dream; rather than experiencing steady upward mobility and constantly rising material standards of living, Bakke's interviewees had lived lives of insecurity and poverty. They regularly had had to adjust their goals to actual possibilities, which almost always fell far below their aspirations. As one worker after another informed Bakke, life involved putting up with it, grinning and bearing it, and using common sense to survive. Explaining how the unemployed managed in a period of general economic crisis, a brass worker noted in a matter of fact fashion, "The poor are used to being poor."[37]

As Eugene Genovese has remarked in a different context, an attempt to explain the relative absence of slave rebellions in North America,

> Only those who romanticize—and therefore do not respect—the laboring classes would fail to understand their deep commitment to "law and order." Life is difficult enough without added uncertainty and "confusion." Even an oppressive and unjust system is better than none. People with such rich experience as that of the meanest slaves quickly learn to distrust Utopian nostrums. As Machiavelli so brilliantly revealed, most people refuse to believe in anything they have not experienced. Such negativity must be understood as a challenge to demonstrate that a better, firmer, more just social order can replace the one to be torn down.[38]

Just so with New Haven's workers. For the majority of them, alternatives to the existing system seemed most notable for their absence. The only alternatives the city's workers cited, German Nazism, Italian Fascism, and Soviet Communism, none of which to be sure they had experienced, held no allurement, promised them "no better, more just social order." Workers repeatedly referred to Soviet Russia to explain both Socialism's and Communisms's lack of appeal.[39]

Lacking an alternative to the existing system, New Haven workers grabbed what few joys they could in an otherwise perilous existence. One worker explained his own resistance to Socialism in the following manner. He had fought enough losing battles in his life. But he knew one place where he could celebrate as a winner. As a Democrat or a Republican, at least once in a while he could get drunk on election night and act the part of a winner. But Socialists, he sneered, "when do you think they're goin' to have a chance to get drunk?"[40]

Ah, one might say, Muncie and New Haven were atypical and their working class more so. Look at Flint and Youngstown, Akron and Gary, Minneapolis and San Francisco. In those cities workers acted collectively and militantly. But a closer look at even such *foci* of labor struggle reveals a much more complex reality than suggested by conventional romanticizations of working-class solidarity and rank-and-file militancy.

Without militants, to be sure, there would have been no Flint sit-down strike, no San Francisco general strike, no walkout by Akron's rubber workers. Without rank-and-file participation, that is collective struggle, there would have been no union victories. Yet, in reality, solidarity rarely produced collective action; rather, more often than not, action by militant minorities (what some scholars have characterized as "sparkplug Unionism"[41]) precipitated a subsequent collective response. And rank and filers frequently resisted the radicalism of the militant cadres who sparked industrial confrontations. In Flint, as Sidney Fine has shown, only a small minority of the local workers belonged to the UAW and paid dues on the eve of the strike, and the sit-down technique was chosen consciously to compensate for the union's lack of a mass membership base.[42] The story was the same in Akron. When that city's rubber workers gained CIO's first major victory in March 1936 after a strike against the Goodyear Tire and Rubber Company, Powers Hapgood disclosed the following to John L. Lewis: "Confidentially, I can tell you that it was a minority strike, starting with only a handful of members and gradually building a membership in that Local Union to a little over 5000 out of 14,000 workers."[43] Lee Pressman, general counsel to the Steel Workers Organizing Committee, recalls that as late as the spring of 1937, after the UAW's success at Flint and United States Steel's surrender to SWOC, labor organizers had still failed to enrol in SWOC more than a substantial minority of the steelworkers employed by firms other than United States Steel.[44] For most rank and filers, then, militancy consisted of refusing to cross a picket line, no more. As one observer noted of the Flint sit-downers, a group more militant than the majority of auto workers, "Those strikers have no more idea of 'revolution' than pussycats."[45]

Even the most strike-torn cities and regions had a significantly internally differentiated working class. At the top were the local cadres, the sparkplug unionists, the men and women fully conscious of their roles in a marketplace society that extolled individualism and rewarded collective strength. These individuals, ranging the political spectrum from Social Democrats to Communists, provided the leadership, militancy, and ideology that fostered industrial conflict and the emergence of mass-production unionism. Beneath them lay a substantial proportion of workers who could be transformed, by example, into militant strikers and unionists, and, in turn, themselves act as militant minorities. Below them were many first- and second-generation immigrant workers, as well as recent migrants from the American countryside who remained embedded in a culture defined by traditional ties of family, kinship, church, and neighborhood club or tavern. Accustomed to following the rituals of the past, heeding the advice of community leaders, and slow to act, such men and women rarely joined unions prior to a successful strike, once moved to act behaved with singular solidarity, yet rarely served as union or political activists and radicals. And below this mass were the teenage workers caught halfway between liberation from their parental families and formation of their own new households, more attracted to the life and rituals of street gangs and candy-store cronies than to the customs and culture of persistent trade unionists and political activists.[46]

A word must now be added concerning those scholars who have argued that during the 1930's a spontaneously militant and increasingly radical rank and file was either handcuffed or betrayed by bureaucratic and autocratic labor leaders. For those who accept the Leninist thesis that trade unions are, by definition, economist and hence nonrevolutionary, there is no problem in comprehending the behavior of American trade unions and their members during the 1930's. But for those who seek to understand why the militant beginnings of the CIO terminated in an ideological and institutional dead-end, why, in David Brody's words, "the character of American trade unionism [. . .] made it an exploiter of radicalism rather than vice versa"—questions remain.[47] And it may seem easiest to answer, as Art Preis, Ronald Radosh, James Weinstein, and Staughton Lynd have done, that the blame for the failure of radicalism rests with such labor leaders as John L. Lewis and Sidney Hillman who sold out to the New Deal, collaborated with employers, and restrained rank-and-file militancy through the instrument of the non-strike union contract. That hypothesis, commonly subsumed under the rubric "corporate liberalism," contains a grain of truth.[48] But the small truth tends to obscure a greater reality. As J. B. S. Hardman observed a half century ago, labor leaders are primarily accumulators of power; and, need it be said, no man was more eager to accumulate power than John L. Lewis.[49] A businessman's power followed from his control of capital; a politician's from influence over voters and possession of the instruments of government; and a labor leader's power derived from his union membership, the more massive and militant the rank and file the more influential the labor leader. Bereft of a mass membership or saddled with a lethargic rank and file, the labor leader lost influence, and power. All labor leaders, then, necessarily played a devious and sometimes duplicitous game. Sometimes they rushed in to lead a rebellious rank and file; other times, they agitated the rank and file into action; whether they seized leadership of a movement already in motion or themselves breathed life into the rank and file, labor leaders obtained whatever power they exercised with employers and public officials as a consequence of their followers' behavior. Yet, while they encouraged militancy, labor leaders also restrained their troops, in John L. Lewis's phrase, "put a lid on the strikers." They did so for several reasons. First, not all rank-and-file upheavals promised success; and nothing destroyed a trade union as quickly or diluted a labor leader's power as thoroughly as a lost strike. Second, leaders had to judge at what point rank-and-file militancy would produce government repression, an ever present reality even in Franklin D. Roosevelt's America. Third, and more selfishly, rank-and-file upheavals could careen out of control and threaten a labor leader's tenure in office as well as strengthen his external power. Throughout the 1930's such labor leaders as John L. Lewis alternately encouraged the release of working-class rebelliousness and "put the lid back on." The labor leader was truly the man in the middle, his influence rendered simultaneously greater and also more perilous as a result of working-class militancy.[50]

A final word must also be said about the union contract, the instrument that allegedly bound workers to their employers by denying them the right to strike. With historical hindsight, such seems to be the end result of the union-management contract under which the union promises to discipline its members on behalf of management. But one must remember that during the 1930's ordinary workers, the romanticized rank and file, risked their jobs, their bodies, and their lives to win the contract. And when they won it, as in Flint in February 1937, a sit-down striker rejoiced that it "was the most wonderful thing that we could think of that could possibly happen to people."[51]

IV

Paradoxically, the one experience during the 1930's that united workers across ethnic, racial, and organizational lines—New Deal politics—served to vitiate radicalism. By the end of the 1930's, Roosevelt's Democratic party had become, in effect, the political expression of America's working class. Old-line Socialists, farmer-labor party types, and even Communists enlisted in a Roosevelt-led "Popular Front." Blacks and whites, Irish and Italian Catholics, Slavic- and Jewish-Americans, uprooted rural Protestants and stable skilled workers joined the Democratic coalition, solidifying the working-class vote as never before in American history. Roosevelt encouraged workers to identify themselves as a common class politically as well as economically. As with David Lloyd George in Britain's pre-World War I Edwardian crisis, Franklin D. Roosevelt in the American crisis of the 1930's found revolutionary class rhetoric indispensable. It panicked the powerful into concessions and attracted working-class voters to the Democratic party. Just as Lloyd George intensified the earlier British crisis in order to ease its solution, Roosevelt acted similarly in New Deal America. By frightening the ruling class into conceding reforms and appealing to workers to vote as a solid bloc, Roosevelt simultaneously intensified class consciousness and stripped it of its radical potential.[52]

The dilemma of John L. Lewis showed just how well Roosevelt succeeded in his strategy. During the 1930's no matter how much Lewis preferred to think of himself as an executive rather than a labor leader, however little he associated personally with the working class, he functioned as the leader of a militant working-class movement. Whereas Roosevelt sought to contain working-class militancy through reforms, militant workers pressured Lewis to demand more than the President would or could deliver. The more evident became the New Deal's economic failures, the more heatedly labor militants demanded a fundamental reordering of the economy and society, demands that Lewis, as leader of CIO, came to express more forcefully than any other trade unionist. "No matter how much Roosevelt did for the workers," recalls Len DeCaux, "Lewis demanded more. He showed no gratitude, nor did he bid his followers be grateful—just put the squeeze on all the harder."[53]

But Lewis, unlike the British labor leaders of Lloyd George's generation who found in the Labour party an alternative to the Prime
Minister's "New Liberalism," had no substitute for Roosevelt's
New Deal. In the United States, the President easily mastered the
labor leader.

Lewis's lack of a political alternative to the New Deal flowed
from two sources. First was the refusal of most American leftists to
countenance a third-party challenge to the Democrats and the
intense loyalty most workers felt to Roosevelt. Between the winter
of 1937–38 and the summer of 1940, however much Lewis threatened to lead a new third party, his public speeches and private
maneuvers failed to create among workers a third-party constituency. It was Lewis's radical speeches that made his eventual endorsement in 1940 of Wendell Willkie so shocking to many of the
labor leader's admirers. Had those Lewis sycophants known that in
June 1940, the CIO president plotted to win the Republican nomination for Herbert Hoover, they might have been even more
startled.[54] And it was his support first of Hoover and then of Willkie
that exposed the second source of Lewis's lack of a radical alternative to the New Deal. That was the extent to which Lewis, other
labor leaders, and perhaps most workers had assimilated the values
of a business civilization. This union, Lewis told members of the
United Mine Workers at their 1938 convention, "stands for the
proposition that the heads of families shall have a sufficient income
to educate [. . .] these sons and daughters of our people, and they go
forth when given that opportunity [. . .] they become scientists,
great clergymen [. . .] great lawyers, great statesmen [. . .] Many of
our former members are successful in great business enterprises."
And two years later in 1940, he told the same audience: "You know,
after all there are two great material tasks in life that affect the
individual and affect great bodies of men. The first is to achieve or
acquire something of value or something that is desirable, and then
the second is to prevent some scoundrel from taking it away from
you."[55] Notice the substance of Lewis's remarks to a trade-union
crowd, the combination of urging the children of the working class
to rise above it, not with it, and the materialistic stress on possessive individualism. Lewis, the most militant and prominent of the
depression decade's labor leaders, remained too much the opportunist, too much the personification of vulgar pragmatism and
business values to lead a third-party political crusade.

V

What, then, follows logically from the above description of the 1930's and the implied line of analysis? First, and perhaps obviously, however turbulent were the American 1930's, the depression decade never produced a revolutionary situation. Second, one observes the essential inertia of the working-class masses. Once in motion, the mass of workers can move with great acceleration and enormous militancy—but such movement remains hard to get started. Such social inertia combined with the inability of most workers and their leaders to conceive of an alternative to the values of marketplace capitalism, that is to create a working-class culture autonomous from that of the ruling class, was more important than trade-union opportunism, corporate co-optation, or New Deal liberalism (though the last factor was clearly the most potent) in thwarting the emergence of durable working-class radicalism. Third, and finally, it suggests that a distinction must be drawn between class struggle as an historical reality and workers as a class fully aware of their role, power, and ability to replace the existing system with "a better, firmer, more just social order [than] [. . .] the one to be torn down."

NOTES

1. Len DeCaux, *Labor Radical* (Boston, 1970), p. 230.
2. Staughton Lynd, "The Possibility of Radicalism in the Early 1930's: The Case of Steel," *Radical America*, VI (Nov.–Dec. 1972), 37–64; *idem.*, "Guerilla History in Gary," *Liberation*, XIV (Oct. 1969), 17–20; for a revised version of Lynd's views of the 1930's, one more in consonance with what actually happened, not what might have been, see "The United Front in America: A Note," *Radical America*, VIII (July–Aug. 1974), 29–37.
3. David Brody, "Labor and the Great Depression: The Interpretive Prospects," *Labor History*, XIII (Spring 1972), 231–244; *idem.*, "Radical Labor History and Rank-and-File Militancy," *ibid.*, XVI (Winter 1975), 122.
4. Karl Marx and Frederick Engels, *Selected Works* (London, 1968), p. 97.
5. E. P. Thompson, *The Making of the English Working Class* (London, 1965), p. 12.
6. Ronald Radosh, "The Corporate Ideology of American Labor Leaders from Gompers to Hillman," in James Weinstein and David W. Eakins, eds., *For a New America* (New York, 1970), pp. 125–152; R. Radosh, *American Labor and United States Foreign*

Policy (New York, 1969), pp. 18–29; James Weinstein, *The Corporate Ideal in the Liberal State* (Boston, 1968).

7. Stanley Lebergott, *Manpower in American Economic Growth* (New York, 1964), p. 512.

8. Stephan Thernstrom, *The Other Bostonians* (Cambridge, Mass., 1973), pp. 56, 59, 90, 203, 207, 233, 240, 249.

9. Bernard Sternsher, *Hitting Home: The Great Depression in Town and Country* (Chicago, 1970), p. 10; John A. Garraty, "Radicalism in the Great Depression," in *Essays on Radicalism in Contemporary America*, ed., Leon B. Blair (Austin, 1972), p. 89; Roy Rosenzweig, "Radicals and the Jobless: The Musteites and the Unemployed Leagues, 1932–1936," *Labor History*, XVI (Winter 1975), 52–77; Daniel J. Leab, "United We Eat: The Creation and Organization of the Unemployed Councils in 1930," *Labor History*, VIII (Fall 1967), 300–315.

10. Irving Bernstein, *Turbulent Years* (Boston, 1969), Ch. 6 remains the best description of the 1934 "Eruption." New York *Times*, July 17, 20, 21, 27, 28, 1934.

11. S. Lynd, "The Possibility of Radicalism," pp. 38–40, 49–51; Sidney Fine, *The Automobile under the Blue Eagle* (Ann Arbor, 1963), pp. 298–315.

12. Sidney Fine, *Sit-Down: The General Motors Strike of 1936–1937* (Ann Arbor, 1969), p. 331.

13. *Ibid.*, p. 201.

14. *Ibid.*

15. Horace R. Cayton and George S. Mitchell, *Black Workers and the New Unions* (Chapel Hill, 1939), v–viii.

16. E. Wight Bakke, *The Unemployed Worker* (New Haven, 1940), p. 87.

17. Cayton and Mitchell, *Black Workers*, p. 268.

18. L. DeCaux, *Labor Radical*, p. 303.

19. Powers Hapgood to Sweetheart, July 24, 1935, Powers Hapgood Papers, Lilly Library, Indiana University, Bloomington, Indiana.

20. Adolph Germer to Harry Hauser, Oct. 29, 1937, Adolph Germer Papers, Box 4, State Historical Society of Wisconsin, Madison.

21. Gardner Jackson, *Columbia Oral History Collection*, pp. 727–728; Lee Pressman, COHC, pp. 96–97.

22. See Paul Kleppner, *The Cross of Culture: A Social Analysis of Midwestern Politics* (New York, 1970), Chs. 5 and 7, and Richard J. Jensen, *The Winning of the Midwest* (Chicago, 1971), Chs. 9–10.

23. "Notes on CIO Meeting, November 7–8, 1938," Katherine Pollack Ellickson Papers, microfilm, Franklin D. Roosevelt Library, Hyde Park.

24. Alfred Winslow Jones, *Life, Liberty, and Property* (Philadelphia, 1941), pp. 250–279, 350–351, 354.

25. Walter Galenson, *The CIO Challenge to the AFL* (Cambridge, Mass., 1960), p. 585; Philip Taft, *The A. F. of L. from the Death of Gompers to the Merger* (New York, 1959), pp. 199–200; W. Jett Lauck Diary, Dec. 13, 1937, W. Jett Lauck Papers, University of Virginia Library; John Frey to W. A. Appleton, Apr. 13 and Aug. 1, 1938, John Frey Papers, Box 1, File 8, Library of Congress.

26. See, for example, James R. Green, "Working Class Militancy in the Depression," *Radical America*, VI (Nov.–Dec. 1972), 2–3.

27. Isidore Lubin, Memorandum to the President, August 29, 1934, Franklin D. Roosevelt Papers, OF407B, Box 10, Roosevelt Library.

28. Calculated from *Historical Statistics of the United States, Colonial Times to 1957* (Washington, 1960), Series D 764–778, p. 99.

29. R. Rosenzweig, "Radicals and the Jobless," p. 60.

30. E. Wight Bakke, *The Unemployed Worker*, and *Citizens Without Work* (New Haven, 1940); Robert S. and Helen M. Lynd, *Middletown in Transition* (New York, 1937).

31. R. and H. Lynd, *Middletown* (New York, 1929), pp. 3–6.

32. R. and H. Lynd, *Middletown in Transition*, pp. 42–43, 73, 203, 447–448.

33. *Ibid.*, pp. 26–28; cf., *Middletown*, p. 254.

34. *Middletown in Transition*, pp. 41–44.

35. E. W. Bakke, *Citizens without Work*, p. 102; cf. pp. 89–99.

36. *Ibid.*, pp. 59–66.

37. *Ibid.*, p. 69.

38. Eugene D. Genovese, *Roll, Jordan, Roll: The World the Slaves Made* (New York, 1974), p. 115.

39. E. W. Bakke, *Citizens without Work*, pp. 57–59.

40. *Ibid.*, p. 64.

41. Edward Shorter and Charles Tilly, *Strikes in France, 1830–1968* (London, 1974), *passim*.

42. S. Fine, *Sit-Down*, p. 117. The UAW had signed up 1500 out of more than 12,000 auto workers. Cf. Adolph Germer to John Brophy, Dec. 8, 1935, Germer Papers, Box 2.

43. Hapgood to Lewis, Mar. 29, 1936, Hapgood Papers.

44. Lee Pressman, COHC, pp. 193–194; David J. MacDonald, Oral History Transcript, p. 11, Pennsylvania State University Labor Archives.

45. S. Fine, *Sit-Down*, p. 331.

46. Peter Friedlander, *The Emergence of a UAW Local, 1936–1939: A Study in Class and Culture* (Pittsburgh, 1975), xiii–xx, pp. 27–28, 119–131, and *passim*.

47. D. Brody, "Labor and the Great Depression," p. 241.

48. See n. 6 above, and also S. Lynd, "The Possibility of Radicalism,"
pp. 50–51; *idem.*, Guerilla History in Gary," pp. 17–20; *idem.*,
"Personal Histories of the Early CIO," *Radical America*, V (May–
June 1971), 50; Alice and Staughton Lynd, *Rank and File* (Boston,
1973), pp. 4–5, 89–90; cf., Mark Naison, "The Southern Tenant
Farmers Union and the CIO," *Radical America*, II (Sept.–Oct.
1968), 36–54; and Art Preis, *Labor's Giant Step* (New York, 1964),
passim.

49. J. B. S. Hardman, "Union Objectives and Social Power," in J. B. S.
Hardman, ed., *American Labor Dynamics* (New York, 1928), p. 104.

50. Melvyn Dubofsky and Warren Van Tine, *John L. Lewis: A Biography* (New York, 1977), is a study of precisely that process and the
dilemma of trade-union leadership. Cf. P. Friedlander, *The
Emergence of a UAW Local*, pp. 119–131, *passim.*

51. S. Fine, *Sit-Down*, p. 307; D. Brody, "Radical Labor History," p.
125.

52. For the Edwardian British analogy, see Paul Thompson, *The
Edwardians* (Bloomington, Ind., 1975), pp. 260–262. On the
working-class core of the Democratic party, see Samuel Lubell,
The Future of American Politics (New York, 1965 ed.), pp. 179–182
and *passim*; A. W. Jones, *Life, Liberty, and Property*, pp. 314–317;
and P. Friedlander, *The Emergence of a UAW Local*, pp. 112–114.

53. L. DeCaux, *Labor Radical*, p. 295; L. Pressman, COHC, pp. 91,
96–97, 188, 191, 352.

54. L. Pressman, COHC, p. 380; Statement, Herbert Hoover Papers,
June, 1940, Post-Presidential Files, John L. Lewis, Box 98,
Herbert Hoover Library, West Branch, Iowa.

55. United Mine Workers of America, *Convention Proceedings, 1938*, p.
172; *1940*, p. 14; A. W. Jones observes of Akron's workers in 1939,
even the highly politicized ones, "Our measurements of opinion
and the comments of workers indicate clearly that most of them
do not want to feel that they have isolated themselves from the
general run of 'middle class opinion.' The general climate of
opinion bears in upon them and would make it impossible for
them to turn decisively away into a workers' world, even if such a
thing existed." *Life, Liberty, and Property*, p. 297.

AFL UNIONS IN THE 1930s: THEIR PERFORMANCE IN HISTORICAL PERSPECTIVE

Christopher L. Tomlins

The 1930s have been regarded as a pivotal period in the develop-ment of a modern organized labor movement in the United States. Historians have noted the rapid growth in membership of both old and new unions and the concomitant changes during these years in the political and economic environment of collective bargaining. In the course of their studies, these scholars have successfully ana-lyzed many of the factors that played a role in that growth.[1] By concentrating primarily on factors peculiar to the 1930s, however, these scholars have remained within the dominant tradition of American labor history that has been organized around events and has emphasized the simple dichotomies they appear to illustrate. Thus, analysis of the rapid growth of unionism in the 1930s has concentrated largely on strikes, contracts, federal legislation, and the effects of the confrontation between two rival federations on the institutional structure of the labor movement.

Operating from within this tradition, historians have gener-ally agreed that the 1930s saw the ascendancy of industrial over craft unionism.[2] The industrially organized unions of the Congress of Industrial Organizations (CIO) broke with the American Fed-eration of Labor (AFL), established themselves as a rival federa-tion, succeeded for the first time in organizing the workers em-ployed in mass production industries, and initiated a period of sustained rapid growth in labor unionism. As a result, the craft unions affiliated with the AFL were forced to reconsider their role in the labor movement. In order to survive, they began to admit less-skilled workers. Traditional interpretations hold that, in so doing, the craft unions altered their long-established strategy of organizing only skilled workers and changed their institutional structures to accommodate the new masses. These changes in AFL unions are thought to have been necessary preconditions for their subsequent expansion, for before the rise of the CIO the organized labor movement is thought to have been weak and structurally obsolete, with the unions isolated from the strategic sectors of a modern industrial economy. After the rise of the CIO, with industrial unionism in the ascendancy, the movement became powerful, self-assured, and capable of playing an influential role in American industrial society.[3]

While the political and economic circumstances of the period offer much support to this view of labor history, they do not by themselves provide a suitable framework for interpreting the distribution of membership gains in the 1930s. Although the unions affiliated with the CIO fought many bitter strikes, overcame the open hostility of management in the manufacturing sector of the economy, and succeeded, by and large, in organizing permanent unions in important areas of industry, it was the supposedly unregenerate "craft" unions of the AFL that contained the bulk of the organized labor movement's membership throughout this period. The affiliates of the AFL experienced substantial growth between 1933 and 1934. This growth was sustained despite the split in the AFL's ranks in 1936. Although it lost 1,104,900 members between 1936 and 1937 as a direct consequence of the suspension of the CIO unions, the AFL's major affiliates recruited over 760,000 new members in the same period. As a result, the AFL lost only 340,000 members overall. Even when the CIO unions were leading some of their most militant organizing campaigns, the AFL unions were able to achieve results little inferior.[4] Between 1937 and 1939 the CIO lost members, and entered a period of sustained growth only with the onset of the war boom in defense production. Over the same period the AFL quickly recovered from the split and expanded steadily. Between 1937 and 1945 nearly four million workers joined unions affiliated with the AFL. In the same years the CIO unions recruited slightly under two million.[5]

These figures indicate the need for reevaluation of the performance of AFL unions in the 1930s. A new analytic framework is needed, moreover, to help explain both the particular pattern of membership gains and the reasons behind the AFL's success. Analysis of the histories of AFL affiliates—as well as of the actual results of their organizing campaigns in the 1930s—indicates that traditional historiography exaggerates the extent to which competition between AFL and CIO was responsible for causing changes of strategy and structure in the AFL's affiliates. From the time of their founding the major AFL unions had exhibited a tendency to alter both organizing strategies and institutional structures to accommodate changes in the industrial environment in which they operated.

A long term perspective on the institutional development of major AFL unions helps to explain their success in recruiting and retaining new members in the 1930s. Such a perspective views the 1930s from within the "emerging organizational synthesis" in American history and relies to some extent on conclusions suggested by Alfred D. Chandler's studies of corporate development.[6] In application this approach confirms that the use of a simple polarity of "craft" versus "industrial" unionism, of AFL versus CIO, does not materially contribute to an understanding of the growth and development of the organized labor movement in the 1930s and after.

The AFL was formed in 1886 by national unions such as the Molders and the International Typographical Union and by numerous independent local unions that were not coordinated into single national organizations. These "basic building blocks" were predominantly unions of skilled workers.

Since before the Civil War, skilled workers had sought to enhance their economic power in confrontation with owners and management by organizing at the national level. This sometimes resulted in their isolation from less-skilled and unskilled workers who lacked the bargaining power and job control that craftsmen had.[7] But the impact of technological change, particularly the mechanization of production, on the division of labor and on industry's skill requirements weakened the ability of the craft unions to control their job territory (jurisdiction).

Unions responded in several different ways. Some resisted the mechanization of the production process or sought to compete with machinery by lowering their piece- or wage-rates. Others tried to control the introduction of machinery and to widen their jurisdiction to include craftsmen working on the same or related production processes, thus preserving their influence by building one union of all the strategic workers in one industry or group of industries. They also began to include particular strata of production workers (other than the skilled nuclei) where the organization of such groups was necessary to the preservation of job control.[8] Attempts to adapt to technological change through the alteration of jurisdiction and organizing strategy led both to the amalgamation of related crafts and to cautious organizing among selected sections of less-skilled workers.[9] As a result of these developments, by 1915 only 28 of 133 unions active in the labor movement, most of them affiliated with the AFL, could still be described as craft organizations. Of these, at least half were engaging in informal cooperation with other affiliates and were thus cutting across craft lines.[10]

The various AFL unions showed different rates of adaptation. Although the organized labor movement as a whole was directly and continuously confronted with the impact of technology on the organization of industry, different sectors of the economy were affected at different times.[11] Consequently, unions developed widely differing structures and jurisdictions.[12]

These varied responses by its affiliates in turn put great pressure on the federation itself, but for some years after the AFL was formed by the craft unions, its leadership continued to favor the creation of national unions of the pure craft type. Between 1886 and the early 1900s it encouraged the formation of as many autonomous craft unions as possible.[13] The jurisdictional boundaries between these small groups of skilled workers were frequently rather narrow—the Pocket Knife Grinders and the Table Knife Grinders were chartered as separate national unions, as were the Watch Case Makers and the Watch Case Engravers—and the policy led to constant jurisdictional squabbling among the small craft organizations.

At the same time the policy of the federation's leadership proved increasingly unpopular with the larger, well-established, and imperialistic affiliates—for example, the International Association of Machinists (IAM) and the United Brotherhood of Carpenters and Joiners (UBCJ)—which feared the division of their own more inclusive jurisdictions among a host of splinter groups of craftsmen claiming commonality of specific skills and refusing to be included in a more diffuse organization. The carpenters' union, in particular, put great pressure on the federation's leadership to end the practice of chartering small splinter groups and proposed a new policy that would reflect its own interests. The union sought the organization of different groups of skilled workers under the jurisdiction of the paramount craft in an industry or trade. Acceding to the carpenters' demands, the federation ended the process of jurisdictional division and subdivision, encouraged the amalgamation of related crafts, and in 1911 approved the policy of chartering only one organization for one trade: "The action of the 1911 convention of the AFL marks a turning point in its history. . . . After a decade of running strife the Atlanta convention of the AFL declared soundly for the principle of organization by the paramount craft in an industry, rather than for craft autonomy."[14]

Henceforth, the AFL was formally oriented not to the encouragement of pure craft unionism, but to the development of single organizations containing all the strategic workers of a particular trade or industry. Although the new policy allowed for the continued existence of craft unions where feasible, its major purpose was to encourage the formation of "craft-industrial" unions, like the carpenters and the machinists, in those industries where technological developments had weakened the position of craftsmen and required the extension of the union's jurisdiction in the interests of the paramount "policing" trade or craft.

The new policy was further reinforced by the creation of separate and autonomous divisions within the AFL known as departments. All the unions claiming jurisdiction over workers in a particular sector of the economy were affiliated to the relevant department. The Building Trades Department, for example, contained all the unions claiming the right to organize workers in the construction industry. The departments gave unions that were active in a particular industry a structure through which they could coordinate their activities, and thus complemented the organization of all crafts in an industry around the paramount craft or trade. At the same time the formation of the departments turned the federation into a bureaucratically decentralized and multidivisional organization that could service highly differentiated affiliates.[15]

Even after altering its structure, however, the AFL proved far too weak to impose an ordered adaptation to technological change on its affiliates. The major unions had no intention of allowing the federation to impede their own particularistic responses to developments in their industries. The principle of national union autonomy that governed the federation's relations with its member-unions meant that the AFL could never be a structurally coherent body. It was always less than the sum of its parts. The developments of the first decade of the twentieth century had resulted from policy changes of its major affiliates rather than a conscious attempt by the federation's leadership to initiate policy. After the 1911 Atlanta convention, the federation remained committed to "one trade, one organization," but the responses of the major unions soon took them beyond the Atlanta Declaration—beyond craft-industrialism—and toward multi-industrial organization.[16]

Because the federation was unable to exert real influence on the behavior of its affiliates, its policies provide an inadequate guide to the evolution of the organized labor movement in these years. It is at the level of the national union that significant changes in organizational policy may most precisely be discerned and the reasons for such changes isolated, for at this level occurred the most direct confrontation between labor unions and potentially disruptive alterations in the organization of industry and production.

The history of the carpenters' union affords an excellent illustration of these points. Originally a craft union with a membership mainly of construction workers, the UBCJ had, by 1902, begun a process of adaptation that eventually resulted in its transformation into a multi-industrial organization. This process was a direct response to on-going changes in the woodworking industry. The union was concerned above all to safeguard the position of the skilled carpenter. To achieve this goal it expanded its jurisdiction to cover first "all that's made of wood," and by 1914 anything "that ever was made of wood."[17]

The former claim took the union fully into the woodworking industry, which it sought to control on industrial lines.[18] The latter claim led the union to attempt to organize workers in metal-fitting manufacturing firms where it clashed repeatedly with the unions affiliated to the AFL's Metal Trades Department. A further logical development, confined in its fullest extent to the 1930s, was to enter the lumber industry, a move that gave the union control of the basic raw material of many of the industries in which it was active. At the same time the union remained the most powerful of the AFL's building construction unions and also organized woodworkers in railroad repair and maintenance shops. Each adaptation of jurisdictional policy inevitably meant alterations in the union's structure. As Robert Christie has observed: "Each of these alterations in union structure met a threat posed by changes in the organization of the [woodworking] industry, in the extent of the labor market, or in the tools of production. Whenever any one of these three factors has changed, carpenters' unions have had to change or cease to exist."[19]

While successfully widening the scope of its control to include diverse occupations and industries, the UBCJ continued to organize only those strata of workers that were strategic in any industry or trade in which it was active. In common with most AFL unions at this time it felt no obligation to organize "en masse." The union's policy was to control an industry in the interests of its skilled members and to organize only those less-skilled workers who could add to its power to "police" that industry.[20] In woodworking, the mechanization of the production process had led to the employment of less-skilled and unskilled workers in numbers sufficient to weaken the bargaining power of the craftsmen. The carpenters' union was therefore obliged to attempt to extend its control over all workers in the industry through selective organization of less-skilled workers; the union thus came to operate on an industry-wide basis. In the construction industry, where a number of unions were active, the carpenters' union organized only the skilled carpenters and their apprentices—and thus acted as a trade union. Unskilled workers in the construction industry had their own organization, the Hod Carriers' Building and Common Laborers' Union.

A similar process of structural evolution characterized the early history of the International Brotherhood of Electrical Workers (IBEW), the largest of the AFL's construction industry affiliates after the UBCJ. Like the carpenters' union, the IBEW's membership was not limited to skilled construction workers; although originally a multi-craft organization of construction workers and telephone and telegraph wiremen, the IBEW became occupationally diverse, "an amalgamation representing more than thirty different branches of the electrical trade."[21] In common with the other AFL unions, the IBEW attempted to control the industries and trades within its jurisdiction by organizing the strategic workers. It was prepared to admit less-skilled workers wherever technological change undermined the position of skilled workers. After 1912, for example, it had considerable success in organizing telephone operators, who were mainly unskilled women.[22]

Throughout its early existence the IBEW was pressed to keep up with the rapid technological development of the electrical industry and constantly widened its jurisdiction to cover new jobs. This meant that the IBEW had to find a way of controlling a great diversity of occupational groups, while admitting to membership only those workers who were strategic. It was evident, however, that an organization, the membership of which ranged from the erectors of telegraph poles to workers installing, maintaining, and repairing complex electrical equipment, could not have any definite national rules concerning membership. The union responded to this problem in 1903 by adopting a decentralized and multi-divisional structure.

The union was divided into three basic administrative divisions with separate jurisdictions: "outside" (workers in telephone and telegraph installation and maintenance, and power generation and distribution); "inside" (construction); and "shop" (production and maintenance workers in manufacturing). A fourth division was added later to cover IBEW members employed by the railroads. Each division was responsible for advising the locals affiliated to it on the criteria they should adopt for determining the eligibility of potential recruits.

The multi-divisional structure "simplified the question of jurisdiction."[23] By allowing the locals (through their respective divisions) to control the admission of new members, the union did away with many of the causes of internal disputes between different occupational groups competing for the control of new jobs. In this way the IBEW organized workers from remarkably diverse occupational backgrounds.[24] These structural developments early in its history enabled the IBEW to adjust to the rapid extension of the use of electrical power, and by 1923 the union had claimed a particularly extensive jurisdiction.[25]

The Teamsters' Union was confronted with a similar situation in the trucking industry. Until the 1930s the union's membership had consisted mainly of local draymen and haulers organized into occupationally distinct local unions, such as the Milk Drivers' Local Union or Coal Haulers' Local Union, operating within particular cities or metropolitan areas. Confronted with the emergence of highway trucking in the later 1920s and early 1930s, however, the union was forced to make fundamental changes in organizing strategy. Because of the nature of the job highway truck drivers could not be organized into locals covering such limited geographical areas. To bring these workers into the union the teamsters had to adopt new organizing policies.[26] Because of the strong tradition of local autonomy in the union, these policies were not initiated at the national level but were developed by local leaders. The regions rather than the national office introduced changes in strategy and structure.[27] By the mid-1930s organizing and administrative bodies intermediate between the national office and the virtually autonomous locals had emerged in the West (Highway Drivers' Council covering California and the Pacific Coast states) and the Midwest (Central States Drivers' Council).[28]

These developments were complemented in the later 1930s by the creation of the regional conference in the West. The Western Conference of Teamsters coordinated the local and district organizations of the union throughout the region; the conference served as a vehicle for the extension of teamster organization throughout a rapidly growing and increasingly diverse jurisdiction. Subsequently, the Western Conference served as a model for similar organizational innovations in the Eastern, Southern, and Midwestern regions (a process of adaptation that was substantially completed by the mid-1950s). By adopting the regional conference model, the Teamsters' Union was able to set up a multi-divisional structure and to coordinate on a national scale all of its members in different industries and occupations, including manufacturing and the retail trades.[29]

As these three examples demonstrate, AFL unions were capable of a significant degree of institutional flexibility. Other front-rank unions showed similar levels of "creative response" to changes in the industrial environment. The International Union of Operating Engineers, for example, responded to a widening product market in the 1920s and 1930s in the heavy and highway construction industry with a policy of centralization.[30] The Amalgamated Meat Cutters and Butcher Workmen (AMCBW), confronted with managerial hostility in the meat packing segment of its jurisdiction, responded by decentralizing and organizing retail butchers.[31] Finally, the IAM, originally a Southern-based organization of skilled railroad shop craft metal workers, early claimed jurisdiction over all skilled machinists, regardless of industrial boundaries, and from this base sought to control the industries in which its members were active. First developed during the presidency of James O'Connell (1893–1912),[32] this policy led the IAM in the early 1930s to organize industrially in those sectors where it had been granted an industry-wide jurisdiction by the AFL.[33]

Structural change thus occurred at many different times and involved a variety of AFL unions. The affiliates were each confronted with a particular technological and economic environment. Each faced alterations in the organization of the production process, in the extent of the labor market, in the "skill-mix" of the industry, and in relative factor prices. In some cases, as with the teamsters, innovation in the industry was fairly abrupt and demanded a swift and thorough institutional response. In others, a more gradual process of adaptation was sufficient to cope with changes in their respective industries. But all the major affiliates at one time or another came to terms with a complex and changing industrial environment.

This does not imply that AFL affiliates could deal effectively with all of the problems of industrial change which they faced. The AFL unions proved powerless to organize workers in those industries where the labor force was predominantly semi-skilled or unskilled—as throughout most of mass production. These industries remained unorganized until the unions that were to found the CIO grew tired of the vacillation of other AFL affiliates. The United Mine Workers (UMW)—a union determined to preserve its position in coal mining by extending its control to encompass steel, the major industry using coal as a producer good—finally launched the Steel Workers' Organizing Committee in 1936.[34] The UMW also supported the organization of workers in the automobile industry, while the garment trades unions sought the unionization of textiles. The subsequent achievements of the CIO underline the failure of AFL unions in the major manufacturing industries. Because the affiliates relied on organizing strategic nuclei to maintain and extend their control of jobs in an industry, they were unwilling to organize in situations where no such groups of workers could be found.

This should not, however, obscure the more successful adaptation of AFL unions to changing conditions in other sectors of the economy. The unions were best able to achieve and maintain control where industry was organized on a small-unit basis with comparatively little coordination between firms beyond the locality or region. This was the case, for example, in the trucking, retail, and construction industries. Here managerial hostility, which had complemented the weakness of the unions' strategies in the major manufacturing industries, was less coordinated. The unions were better able to maintain their positions and to keep abreast of technological innovations.

The AFL affiliates were not blindly committed to the organization solely of craftsmen or to the craft union structure. Between 1915 and 1939 the number of craft unions affiliated to the AFL diminished to 12 (out of 102 national unions).[35] In 1939 these unions contained only 0.68 percent of the AFL's total membership. Rather than remaining committed to craft unionism, the affiliates showed a tendency to adopt the form of organization that best suited the nature of their industries and best preserved their general bargaining position.

Structure followed strategy as unions altered their organizations in response to new threats. They were hindered by the opposition of management, by the opposition of elements within their own ranks, and by their general commitment to an organizing strategy applicable only to certain sectors of the economy. Nevertheless, it should now be apparent that to analyze the 1930s in terms of a victory of "industrial" over "craft" unionism is misleading. It obscures the fact that, although the majority of AFL unions were not "industrial" unions in the 1930s, they were certainly not "craft" unions either.

In the 1930s labor unions consolidated existing areas of strength and extended to new and important areas of the economy. The growing pressure to organize the unorganized exacerbated differences of ideology, strategy, and personality within the AFL. At the same time an important new factor affecting the structure and policies of labor unions appeared during this period, as the state began formally to intervene in collective bargaining.

In the case of AFL unions, quantitative analysis of their patterns of growth in the 1930s indicates that, until the war, the affiliates grew mainly in those areas of the economy—construction, transport and communications, and some of the manufacturing and service industries—where large-unit firms were comparatively rare. The factors highlighted by a long-term perspective on their institutional development thus continued to have a decisive influence on their performance, for it was on account of their decentralized wage-bargaining and administrative structures, adopted during the preceding era, that AFL unions were better equipped than the centralized CIO unions to handle the problems of organizing workers in these industries.

Traditional analyses of the growth of unionism in the 1930s tend, however, to underestimate the importance of AFL unions. Although historians have now recognized that the AFL grew faster than the CIO, they argue that the latter was more significant not only because its unions organized the center firms which set the general price and wage levels of the major manufacturing industries,[36] but also because the threat of a rival federation was instrumental in awakening the AFL unions from a state of "stunned inactivity" in 1936.[37]

The preliminary analysis of gross membership figures, earlier in this essay, has already disputed elements of this traditional view. Both federations contributed significantly to the "great leap forward" of the labor movement in 1936–1937. The campaigns of the CIO contributed a maximum of 53 percent of the total gains in membership experienced during this twelve-month period (886,000 of 1,673,000); those of the AFL unions at least 46 percent (768,000 of 1,673,000). This can hardly be called "stunned inactivity." Nor is it justifiable to imply that durable manufacturing is the only strategic area of the economy. This ignores the importance of transport and trade in a consumer economy and takes no account of the important secular trends toward growth of employment in the service sector and relative decline in manufacturing. It also neglects the importance of the construction industry and the long-term stability of employment in that industry.[38]

The traditional view is also inadequate because it conceives of the latter part of the 1930s as a contest between two rival blocs—one of craft unions and one of industrial unions. This concentrates the historian's attention on the attitudes and policies of the federation's top leadership. There is undoubtedly some truth in a description of the federation's national officers as "stunned" following the split. The AFL, however, unlike the CIO, was not a centralized body but a loose decentralized organization of widely differing and autonomous affiliates. It was the activities, reactions and organizing strategies of its member-unions that governed the AFL's overall pattern of growth. As the following analysis of their performance indicates, these unions met with considerable success.

The strength of the AFL in the later 1930s and 1940s owed much to the performance of its affiliates in industries outside manufacturing.[39] AFL unions in transport and communications grew rapidly; 1,000,000 workers in these industries joined unions between 1933 and 1945. The teamsters accounted for over 50 percent of this growth, expanding in membership from 71,000 to 644,000. Although concentrated in the trucking industry, this union also organized groups of manufacturing and retail workers. By 1956 it had become the largest union in the labor movement, with over 1,300,000 members.[40]

The AFL unions active in the construction industry expanded membership to a peak of 2,000,000 during the war. These unions, particularly the IBEW and the carpenters, also organized significant groups of manufacturing workers. The major period of growth occurred during the construction boom in the early 1940s.

Neither the teamsters nor the construction unions faced any competition from the CIO. Similarly, AFL unions in the service sector grew in areas where there was little confrontation with CIO unions. AFL growth here was based on the performance of its affiliates in consumer service industries and in public services. The Hotel and Restaurant Workers' Union grew from 26,000 to 282,000 between 1933 and 1945; the Building Service Employees added 76,000 members over the same period (18,000 to 94,000); unions of public service employees grew collectively from 145,000 to 300,000.

AFL unions were also successful in the retail trades. The Retail Clerks' Union expanded its membership from 5,000 to 96,000 between 1933 and 1945. By 1956 this union had a membership of 300,000. In the New York metropolitan area it faced competition from the Retail, Wholesale and Department Store Workers-CIO but elsewhere the clerks' union was less affected. Nor was the clerks' union the only AFL affiliate recruiting retail trade workers. The teamsters and meat cutters were also active in this field.[41]

In the manufacturing sector, unions of both federations grew most rapidly during the war. After the split in 1936, AFL unions added 400,000 members before 1940 and 2,000,000 in the next five years. Defense production and wartime labor shortages were clearly prime determinants of the growth of unionism in manufacturing, especially in the durable goods industries, where CIO strength was concentrated. In these industries CIO unions added 1,600,000 members between 1940 and 1945. AFL unions active here also grew substantially in the war years, but their rate of growth was slower than that of the CIO organizations.[42]

Outside durable goods the rates of growth of affiliates of the two federations in manufacturing were approximately the same. Between 1936 and 1937 the AFL lost 450,000 members in non-durable manufacturing industries when unions that had joined the CIO were suspended.[43] Thereafter, unions of both federations attracted approximately the same number of recruits overall, although the CIO lost members when the International Ladies Garment Workers' Union disaffiliated. This union rejoined the AFL in 1940.[44]

The non-durable goods industries were less affected by the expansion of defense-related production, and the overall rate of AFL union growth in these industries was approximately the same before and after 1940. By contrast, the CIO unions here enjoyed their greatest success after 1940. CIO membership rose by 400,000 between 1940 and 1945, with approximately 50 percent of the gain coming in textiles and in rubber and chemicals. As was the case elsewhere, unions of both federations expanded in areas where they had previously shown strength and did not compete to any great extent.[45]

The CIO's expansion in the manufacturing sector was thus primarily a function of the success of its affiliates in the durable goods industries. These unions were responsible for 80 percent of the CIO's gains in all manufacturing industries between 1940 and 1945. Their activities were also crucial to the performance of the labor movement as a whole in the manufacturing sector. Although they were not securely established until after the expansion of defense-related production,[46] these unions had organized many of the major manufacturing firms by 1940. In the next five years they contributed 68 percent of all union growth in durable goods and 51.5 percent of all union growth in manufacturing as a whole.

While the CIO expanded rapidly in manufacturing, its affiliates did not contribute materially to the general growth of the labor movement elsewhere in the economy. In 1937 48 percent of CIO members came from manufacturing (952,000 out of 1,900,000). By 1945 86 percent of its members were in unions active in this sector (3,300,000 out of 3,900,000). The three major durable good unions—United Electrical Workers, United Auto Workers, and United Steel Workers—together contained over half of the CIO's entire membership.

In contrast, the AFL's membership did not become concentrated in any one sector of the economy. Between 1933 and 1945 the AFL grew from 2,300,000 to 6,900,000 in membership. In 1933, 30 percent of its members were in manufacturing industries. In 1945, 35 percent came from these industries. Both in 1933 and 1945 the construction unions contributed 25 percent of the AFL's membership, and the service sector unions between 15 and 16 percent. Finally, the membership of unions active in transport and communications rose from 13.5 percent of the AFL's gross in 1933 to 20 percent in 1945.

As these figures indicate, AFL unions made major contributions to the growth of the organized labor movement in the 1930s and 1940s. Between 1937 and 1945 AFL affiliates added 3,700,000 new members. Approximately 2,000,000 of these recruits came from non-manufacturing industries, representing 90 percent of all union growth outside manufacturing. AFL unions were thus crucial to the success of the labor movement in important sectors of the modern American economy: because they were spread throughout the economy AFL affiliates were able to consolidate their positions across an unusually wide range of industries and occupations.

Outside of some manufacturing industries, the growth of AFL unions cannot be attributed to the stimulus provided by CIO competition; throughout the period in question the membership of the two federations continued to come predominantly from different sectors of the economy. Indeed, throughout the economy, competition appears to have been the exception rather than the rule. Between 1938 and 1946 unions seeking the right to represent groups of workers filed 47,600 cases with the National Labor Relations Board (NLRB), of which 29,700 had to be decided formally by holding an election or card count. Of these only 3,900—13 percent—involved direct electoral competition between AFL and CIO unions.[47]

While analysis of these cases calls into question the importance of AFL-CIO competition, the volume of the cases clearly indicates the importance of another element stressed in the traditional viewpoint—the influence of new political factors on labor union organization. Every historian of the period has noted the impact of the Wagner Act and NLRB on union organization and collective bargaining, and some have concluded that federal labor legislation played a more important role than CIO competition.[48] State intervention in collective bargaining, however, also had significant strategic and structural implications, for it permanently and substantially altered the environment in which unions operated. Increasingly, it was the NLRB rather than the union itself that defined the appropriate unit of organization and bargaining. By the 1940s, unions were constrained to operate in accordance with the board's criteria of efficient organization. They were no longer free to choose the strategy that best suited their particular industrial environment and their own institutional objectives.

The long-term structural implications of government intervention were noted in 1945 by President Paul R. Hutchings of the Office Employees International Union-AFL. Although recognizing that the Wagner Act had been a powerful stimulus to trade union growth, Hutchings criticized it for interfering with union autonomy:

Prior to the Act, unions were free to organize in whatever manner they found to be most effective. Frequently a union would build its membership in a shop by first organizing a small group of workers who had the fortitude to stand strong for the union. Upon the organization of such a group, certain job improvements would be obtained for them from management. And this working example of the gains to be achieved through organization frequently formed the most potent organizational appeal to other workers in the shop. . . . Now, trade unions must conform their organization to the appropriate bargaining unit patterns laid down by the [National Labor Relations] Board. They cannot organize and bargain for those workers in a plant who are interested in collective bargaining, they must organize and bargain for all workers within 'an appropriate bargaining unit.' The Board's measure of what constitutes 'an appropriate bargaining unit' is frequently far removed from what the union may recognize as the most propitious to protect its members and promote collective bargaining.[49]

As Hutchings observed, the passage of the Wagner Act added a new, and in the long term a crucial, political dimension to the environment in which unions operated. In the short term, of course, the major effect of federal labor legislation was to qualify the ability of management to oppose the spread of unionism. The extent to which AFL unions could take advantage of the opportunities that the Wagner Act presented was due primarily to their earlier creative responses to industrial change. In the long run, however, the government became the chief arbiter of how the unions would adapt to future economic changes—a subject that perhaps deserves more attention that it has received to date from labor historians.

That subject, however, leads far into the postwar economy and beyond the scope of this essay. For the present, a new perspective on union growth in the period from 1930 through 1945 must suffice. An examination of that growth calls into question the traditional argument that the AFL's success depended on the structural transformations of its affiliates in the face of CIO rivalry. Historically, AFL unions had already shown a tendency to adapt to the challenge of a changing industrial and economic environment. Similarly, the pattern of labor organization in the 1930s indicates that unions of the two federations were expanding in different areas of the economy and adopted strategies best suited to the varying structure of industry in their respective sectors. It is misleading, therefore, to regard the CIO's emergence as an apocalyptic event that decisively altered the shape and strategies of the entire organized labor movement. It is equally misleading to regard industrial unionism as a panacea or as an ideal toward which all unions should necessarily strive. Indeed, the history of the modern labor movement after World War II tends to confirm that industrial unionism is merely one phase in a continuing process of structural evolution rather than the final outcome of that process.[50]

These conclusions suggest the need for a new perspective on AFL unions in the 1930s. In concentrating on the newsworthy events of those years and on conflicts between the leadership of the two federations, historians have failed to account for some of the most important aspects of the growth of labor organizations in the 1930s. The history of the AFL's affiliates and the nature of the industries in which they were active must be studied to find explanations of the federation's achievements. Until such a perspective is adopted, the performance of AFL unions in the 1930s will appear anomalous because it cannot be fully explained by any of the factors traditionally emphasized.

NOTES

1. For example, see Irving Bernstein, *Turbulent Years: A History of the American Worker, 1933–1941* (Boston, 1969); Walter Galenson, *The CIO Challenge to the AFL: A History of the American Labor Movement, 1935–1941* (Cambridge, 1960).

2. A craft union is defined as consisting of "workers requiring identical skill and training who can carry through to completion a particular whole process." An industrial union is defined as including "the skilled, semi-skilled, unskilled [workers] and the auxiliary trades and occupations engaged in the performance of a particular service or the production of a particular commodity." See David J. Saposs and Sol Davison, "Employee Organizations and Elections: The Structure of AFL Unions," *Labor Relations Reference Manual*, 4 (Washington, 1940), 1044, 1047.

3. For example, Walter Galenson writes: "The shock of the CIO was necessary to the rejuvenation of the AFL. . . . If it had not been for the intense struggle between the two organizations, the U.S. might have entered the war with its labor force largely unorganized." Galenson, *CIO Challenge*, 644. See also James O. Morris, *Conflict within the AFL* (Ithaca, 1958), particularly 248; Mark L. Kahn, "Recent Jurisdictional Developments in Organized Labor," *Industrial Relations Research Association Publications*, 21 (New York, 1959), 5–6; Sidney Fine, "The History of the American Labor Movement with Special Reference to Developments in the

1930's," *Labor in a Changing America,* ed. William Haber (New York, 1966), 105–20; Jack Barbash, "The Rise of Industrial Unionism," *ibid.,* 143–57; Milton Derber, *The American Idea of Industrial Democracy, 1865–1965* (Urbana, 1970), 300–01.

4. The unions that left the AFL in 1936 to form an independent CIO were: United Mine Workers; United Mine Workers, District 50; United Textile Workers; Amalgamated Clothing Workers; International Ladies' Garment Workers; Mine, Mill and Smelter Workers; Iron, Steel and Tin Workers; Oil, Gas and Refinery Workers; United Automobile Workers; Fur Workers; Flat Glass Workers; Rubber Workers; Newspaper Guild. These unions had a total membership of 1,104,900. It is impossible to ascertain precisely how many future CIO members came from AFL ranks between 1936 and 1937, for a number of established AFL unions (such as the machinists and the carpenters) lost membership to the CIO, although the unions themselves did not change affiliation. If it is assumed that the CIO took more members from the AFL than those in the ranks of the major unions listed above, then the share of the CIO in the overall gain to the labor movement in dues-paying membership 1936–1937 will be smaller and that of the AFL correspondingly larger.

5. Table 1: Membership of American Labor Organizations, 1933–1945 (in thousands)

	All organizations	AFL affiliates	CIO affiliates	Independent unions
1933	2,973.0	2,317.5	—	655.5
1934	3,608.6	3,030.0	—	578.6
1935	3,753.3	3,218.4	—	534.9
1936	4,107.1	3,516.4	(1,204.6)*	590.7
1937	5,780.1	3,179.7	1,991.2	609.2
1938	6,080.5	3,547.4	1,957.7	575.4
1939	6,555.5	3,878.0	1,837.7	839.8
1940	7,282.0	4,343.0	2,154.1	784.7
1941	8,698.0	5,178.8	2,653.9	865.3
1942	10,199.7	6,075.7	2,492.7	1,631.3
1943	11,811.7	6,779.2	3,303.4	1,729.1
1944	12,628.0	6,876.5	3,937.1	1,814.4
1945	12,562.1	6,890.4	3,927.9	1,743.8

* Estimate

Table compiled from Leo Troy, *Trade Union Membership 1897–1962* (New York, 1965), Appendix 1-27 and Leo Wolman, *Ebb and Flow in Trade Unionism* (New York, 1936), 172–92. Both authors use the same criterion—the payment of dues—to establish the membership of each national union. The growth in AFL membership 1933–1936 is usually attributed to the activities of unions such as the UMW that later helped form the CIO. Unions that remained in the AFL, however, also began to grow in these years:

Table 2: Organizing Gains of AFL Affiliates, 1933–1936 (in thousands)

	Future CIO unions	All other AFL unions	Total gains	Col. 1 as a percentage of Col. 3
1933–34	448.4	264.1	712.5	62.9%
1934–35	57.7	140.7	198.4	29.1
1935–36	111.9	186.1	298.0	37.5

(The 1933–1934 figure is distorted by the affiliation to the AFL of the previously independent Amalgamated Clothing Workers with 135,000 members. This union was later a founding member of the CIO. Corrected to exclude this "gain" the 1933–1934 figure for Col. 1 is 313.4, for Col. 3 it is 577.5, and for Col. 4 it is 54.2 percent.) See Wolman, *Ebb and Flow*, 172–92, and Troy, *Trade Union Membership*, Appendix 1-27.

6. Louis Galambos, "The Emerging Organizational Synthesis in Modern American History," *Business History Review*, XLIV (Autumn 1970), 279–90; Robert D. Cuff, "American Historians and the Organizational Factor," *Canadian Review of American Studies*, IV (Spring 1973), 19–31; Alfred D. Chandler, *Strategy and Structure: Chapters in the History of the Industrial Enterprise* (Cambridge, 1962).

7. Lloyd Ulman, *The Rise of the National Trade Union: The Development and Significance of Its Structure, Governing Institutions, and Economic Policies* (Cambridge, 1955), 23–45, 49–52. The role of the skilled worker in the formation of the early unions is discussed in Benson Soffer, "A Theory of Trade Union Development: The Role of the Autonomous Workman," *Labor History*, 1 (Spring 1960), 141–63. The first part of this essay relies to some extent on the concept of the strategic worker. One definition of this term is a worker whose replacement would cost his employer more in lost production than the worker's wage demands. In manufacturing industries all skilled workers were strategic before the introduction of machinery. Less-skilled workers became strategic, as far as the unions were concerned, when mechanization gave them a role to play in the production processes previously dominated by craftsmen. Employers were able, however, to replace less-skilled workers much more easily than craftsmen, and where mechanization created an industrial labor force that was predominantly low-skilled—as in most of mass production—the unions had neither the power nor the inclination to organize. They only took in less-skilled workers where the division of labor resulting from technological innovations had split the job formerly performed by the craftsman into a number of related functions performed by "helpers," "assistants," or "specialists," without entirely displacing the skilled worker. The unions attempted to gain control of these new jobs so that they could preserve the wage-bargaining power of the craftsmen. In other cases the importance of particular jobs in an industry (for example, maintenance men in manufacturing firms) or the role of a particular industry in the economy (for example, trucking) made workers strategic and encouraged the unions to organize them. See Margaret Loomis Stecker, "The Founders, the Molders, and the Molding Machine," *Quarterly*

Journal of Economics, XXXII (Feb. 1918), 304–08; Elizabeth Faulkner Baker, *Printers and Technology: a History of the International Printing Pressmen and Assistants' Union* (New York, 1957); Mark Perlman, *The Machinists: A New Study in American Trade Unionism* (Cambridge, 1964), 229–33.

8. All three reactions are outlined in Ulman, *Rise of the National Trade Union*, 32–37. See also George E. Barnet, *Chapters on Machinery and Labor* (Cambridge, 1926), 139–61. The first two reactions were viable in the short-term only. In the long run unions that persisted in resisting or competing were severely weakened. See also Samuel Gompers, *Seventy Years of Life and Labor: An Autobiography* (2 vols., New York, 1925), I, 373.

9. Theodore W. Glocker, "Amalgamation of Related Trades in American Unions," *American Economic Review*, V (Sept. 1915), 574–75. See also Elizabeth F. Baker, "The Development of the International Printing Pressmen and Assistants' Union," *Industrial Relations Research Association Publications* (Madison, 1958), 159–61; Robert A. Christie, *Empire in Wood, a History of the Carpenters' Union* (Ithaca, 1956), 117–18; Garth L. Mangum, *The Operating Engineers: The Economic History of a Trade Union* (Cambridge, 1964), 42–45, 59; Michael A. Mulcaire, *The International Brotherhood of Electrical Workers: A Study in Trade Union Structure and Functions* (Washington, 1923), 28, 56–60; Perlman, *Machinists*, 23, 33–34; Frank T. Stockton, *The International Molders Union of North America* (Baltimore, 1921), 43–45.

10. Glocker, "Amalgamation of Related Trades," 554.

11. Historians have recognized the importance of technology as a factor in the development of labor unions, and the first part of this essay is based almost wholly on secondary sources. When approaching the question of the development of the organized labor movement as a whole over time, however, historians have generally ignored the findings of studies of individual unions, and resorted to the events and dichotomies of traditional historiography. Studies of union growth are an exception, for they recognize technology as one of a number of important general factors influencing the growth of the organized labor movement. See John T. Dunlop, "The Development of Labor Organization: A Theoretical Framework," *Insights into Labor Issues*, ed. Richard A. Lester and Joseph Shister (New York, 1948), 163–93; and Julius Rezler, *Automation and Industrial Labor* (New York, 1969), 119. But the occurrence of growth is not by itself a reliable index of adaptability to technological innovation. Many AFL unions were more concerned to control their jurisdictions by selective organization than to attempt to recruit en masse. The lack of rapid growth before the 1930s does not, therefore, prove the irrelevance of AFL unions to the modern American economy.

12. Saposs and Davison, "Employee Organizations and Elections," 1042–48.

13. Christie, *Empire in Wood*, 124–25.

14. *Ibid.*, 135–46.

15. *Ibid.*, 136. See also Albert Theodore Helbing, *The Departments of the American Federation of Labor* (Baltimore, 1931), 51, 121–34. The departments were the Building Trades Department, the Metal Trades Department, the Railway Employees Department, the Mining Department, and the Union Label Trades Department. Helbing concludes: "The affiliated unions are not looking toward the formation of single unions in the various industrial fields. In fact, it has been one of the chief concerns of the Department officers that the separate unions be kept intact. . . . The development of the Department idea provided the believers in autonomous national unions with a foundation on which to build if industrial conditions made local and national joint action necessary." *Ibid.*, 134.

16. Christie, *Empire in Wood*, 170–71, 182.

17. *Ibid.*, 106–19, 170–85.

18. Frank Duffy, the Carpenters' national secretary, declared at the union's convention in 1904 that "every man employed in the woodworking *industry* . . . ought to belong to the United Brotherhood [of Carpenters and Joiners]." Quoted in *ibid.*, 117–18.

19. *Ibid.*, xvii.

20. *Ibid.*, 196–97.

21. Mulcaire, *International Brotherhood of Electrical Workers*, 23.

22. *Ibid.*, 34–37.

23. *Ibid.*, 27.

24. *Ibid.*, 23.

25. IBEW claimed jurisdiction over all workers engaged in the manufacture, installation, maintenance, assembly, and operation of all electrical devices by which electrical power was generated, used or controlled. The bulk of its membership consisted of workers employed by telegraph and telephone, heat, light, power, and transport companies, the building trades, and the electrical manufacturing industry. *Ibid.*

26. Robert D. Leiter, "The Relationship between Structure and Policy in the Teamsters' Union," *Industrial Relations Research Association Publications*, 20 (Madison, 1958), 150.

27. *Ibid.*, 150–51. See also Donald Garnel, *The Rise of Teamster Power in the West* (Berkeley, 1972), 180–89. On the historically decentralized structure of the Teamsters' Union see Leiter, "The Relationship between Structure and Policy," 148–49; and Ralph C. James and Estelle Dinerstein James, *Hoffa and the Teamsters: A Study of Union Power* (Princeton, 1965), 16–17, 128–40.

28. Garnel, *Rise of Teamster Power*, 325–27; James and James, *Hoffa and the Teamsters*, 90–93.

29. The Western Conference of Teamsters was established in 1937, the Southern Conference in 1943, and the Central States and Eastern States Conferences in 1953. See Leiter, "The Relationship between Structure and Policy," 151.

30. Garth L. Mangum, "The Development of Local Union Jurisdiction in the International Union of Operating Engineers," *Labor History*, IV (Fall 1963), 257–72. Elsewhere Mangum comments: "The continuing mechanization of the construction process has been the most important determinant of the history of the International Union of Operating Engineers." See Mangum, *Operating Engineers*, 10.

31. David Brody, *The Butcher Workmen: A Study of Unionization* (Cambridge, 1964), 127. AMCBW's decentralized structure proved well-suited, after 1933, to the accommodation of the major development in retail food marketing of the 1920s and 1930s—the rise of the chain store. The union organized the chains by using its decentralized locals to apply boycott pressure to local chain store management, while at the same time approaching the centralized management of the large chains through its national officers. *Ibid.*, 130, 135, 141–46.

32. Mark Perlman writes: "O'Connell's administration saw the IAM grow from a quality-conscious organization into a 'pure-and-simple' type. It changed from a small railroad-craft-dominated organization to an industrial 'house of many mansions'. . . . [O'Connell's] eye was always on the facts of industrial development. Consequently, he steered a consistent and realistic course. He charted the IAM's development toward industrial control, while seeking to retain hegemony for the craftsmen." Perlman, *The Machinists*, 148.

33. Galenson, *CIO Challenge*, 495, 506–09.

34. *Ibid.*, 133.

35. Saposs and Davison, "Employee Organizations and Elections," 1044. See also Benjamin Stephansky, "The Structure of the American Labor Movement," *Industrial Relations Research Association Publications*, 9 (Madison, 1952), 46.

36. "The growth of organization in the traditional AFL trades, more imposing numerically, was less significant from a strategic point of view than the CIO concentration in vital centers of American industrial might." Galenson, *CIO Challenge*, 592.

37. *Ibid.*, 587.

38. See John P. Henderson, *Changes in the Industrial Distribution of Employment, 1919–59* (Urbana, 1961), 36–79.

39. Table 3: Membership of American Labor Organizations by Industrial Division and Federation, 1933–1945 (in thousands)*

	Manufacturing		Construction		Transport & Communications		Services	
	AFL	CIO	AFL	CIO	AFL	CIO	AFL	CIO
1933	692.9		617.7		314.6		359.8	
1934	1,008.4		639.6		352.7		393.7	
1935	1,001.0		498.5		469.8		445.2	
1936	1,142.0	(518.2)•	565.0	—	527.6	(44.1)•	509.3	(5.8)•
1937	837.5	952.1	743.5	—	727.8	95.5	673.8	71.9
1938	952.0	1,081.8	817.8	—	765.2	111.6	761.0	82.0
1939	1,022.1	1,060.6	891.1	2.5	844.1	118.4	857.0	86.3
1940	1,277.5	1,308.6	980.7	2.5	897.0	112.4	923.0	98.6
1941	1,525.6	1,798.3	1,354.8	2.5	1,034.0	110.2	981.9	111.0
1942	1,869.1	2,136.7	1,841.8	—	1,101.3	116.8	952.4	127.5
1943	2,326.4	2,873.5	2,066.9	—	1,092.5	138.5	947.7	147.8
1944	2,481.5	3,414.5	1,823.0	—	1,181.1	187.9	1,012.9	162.5
1945	2,393.9	3,361.2	1,723.9	—	1,381.0	204.9	1,112.8	178.4

*Table 3 does not include details of extractive industries—mining and agriculture. The latter remained unorganized. The former was dominated by the UMW, a founder of the CIO but independent after 1942.

•Estimates.

Table compiled from Wolman, *Ebb and Flow*, 172–92, and Troy, *Trade Union Membership*, Appendix 1-27.

40. "One of the most important single factors responsible for a revival of the AFL from 1933 on was the decision of the Teamsters Union to organize everything on wheels. It was during this period that the IBT became the most powerful union in the country." Robert D. Leiter, *The Teamsters' Union* (New York, 1957), 38.

41. In many cases the teamsters proved to be of decisive importance in aiding the unionization of the retail trades. See Marten S. Estey, "The Strategic Alliance as a Factor in Union Growth," *Industrial and Labor Relations Review*, IX (Oct. 1955), 41–53; and Marten S. Estey, "Patterns of Union Membership in the Retail Trades," *ibid.*, VIII (July 1955), 557–64.

42. Table 4: Comparison of the Membership of Affilitates of the AFL and the CIO in the Manufacturing Sector, selected years 1933–1945 (in thousands)

	1933	1936	1937	1938	1939	1940	1942	1944	1945
A. Metals, Machinery, Shipbuilding (Durables)									
AFL	186.9	284.9	336.9	355.5	371.6	435.6	870.0	1,355.7	1,184.7
CIO	—	(67.0)*	415.4	460.8	530.2	717.1	1,390.5	2,478.7	2,340.9
B. Other Manufacturing									
AFL	506.0	857.1	500.6	596.5	650.5	841.9	999.1	1,125.8	1,209.5
CIO	—	(451.2)*	536.7	621.0	529.9	591.5	746.2	935.8	1,020.3

*Estimates
Table compiled from Wolman, *Ebb and Flow*, 172–92, and Troy, *Trade Union Membership*, Appendix 1-27.

43. Unions in these industries which remained affiliated to the AFL recruited 100,000 members over the same period. Actual losses were thus 350,000.

44. Several other unions changed their affiliations between 1937 and 1945, thereby influencing gross membership figures. The UMW left the CIO in 1942; the International Typographical Union left the AFL in 1939 and rejoined in 1943; the Brewery Workers' Union left the AFL in 1942.

45. The major exception was the lumber industry where the carpenters' union competed with the International Woodworkers of America-CIO in the Pacific Northwest. Competition also occurred in the meat industry between the AMCBW and the Packing House Workers Organizing Committee.

46. "The situation . . . was still precarious five years after the formation of the CIO." David Brody, "The Emergence of Mass-Production Unionism," *Change and Continuity in Twentieth-Century America—the 1930s*, ed. John A. Braemen, Robert H. Bremner, and Everett Walters (Columbus, Ohio, 1964), 221–62; Barbara W. Newell, *Chicago and the Labor Movement: Metropolitan Unionism in the 1930's* (Urbana, 1961), 145–56.

47. Broken into three 3-year periods, the percentages of all formally decided cases that involved competition are:

1938–1940: 24%

1941–1943: 12.5%

1944–1946: 11%

   Between 1938 and 1946, 8.1% of all representation cases filed—decided both formally and informally—involved competition. These figures are compiled from Harry A. Millis and Emily C. Brown, *From the Wagner Act to Taft-Hartley* (Chicago, 1969), 77 (Table 1—"Cases Filed and Elections Held"); Joseph Krislov, "Organizational Rivalry Among American Unions," *Industrial and Labor Relations Review*, 13 (January, 1960), 218; and *Third Annual*

Report of the National Labor Relations Board (Washington, 1939), 50; *Fourth Annual Report of the National Labor Relations Board* (Washington, 1940), 54; *Fifth Annual Report of the National Labor Relations Board* (Washington, 1941), 7; *Sixth Annual Report of the National Labor Relations Board* (Washington, 1942), 37; *Seventh Annual Report of the National Labor Relations Board* (Washington, 1943), 88; *Eighth Annual Report of the National Labor Relations Board* (Washington, 1944), 95; *Ninth Annual Report of the National Labor Relations Board* (Washington, 1945), 85; *Tenth Annual Report of the National Labor Relations Board* (Washington, 1946), 86; *Eleventh Annual Report of the National Labor Relations Board* (Washington, 1947), 83.

48. For example, Perlman writes that "the fact of the NLRB caused the change within the IAM—far more than the 'fact' of the UAW, the SWOC (Steel Workers Organizing Committee), or the rubber workers." Perlman, *The Machinists*, 92.

49. Paul R. Hutchings, "Effect on the Trade Union," *The Wagner Act—After Ten Years*, ed. Louis G. Silverberg (Washington, 1945), 73.

50. See Arnold R. Weber, "The Craft-Industrial Issue Revisited: A Study of Union Government," *Industrial and Labor Relations Review*, 16 (April 1963), 381–404; Arnold R. Weber, "Craft Representation in Industrial Unions," *Industrial Relations Research Association Publications*, 28 (Madison, 1962), 82–92; Abraham L. Gitlow, "The Trade Union Prospect in the Coming Decade," *Labor Law Journal*, XXI (March 1970), 131–58; Kahn, "Recent Jurisdictional Developments," 21–23; Joseph Krislov, "Union Organizing of New Units, 1955–1966," *Industrial and Labor Relations Review*, XXI (Oct. 1967), 31–39; Joseph Shister, "The Direction of Unionism 1947–1967: Thrust or Drift?" *ibid.*, XX (July 1967), 578–601.

UNEMPLOYMENT DURING THE GREAT DEPRESSION

John A. Garraty

The Great Depression of the 1930s swept across most of the world like a blight or plague, swiftly and without warning. It produced much misery and suffering everywhere and eventually spread its poisons into every aspect of human existence—into politics, into social organization and culture, even into man's conception of himself. It came to an end only with the outbreak of a still worse catastrophe, World War II—of which the Great Depression was, indeed, a major cause.

The most obvious symptoms of the disease were a massive decline of monetary values, the shrinking of demand and therefore of production, and unemployment on a scale never before experienced. Of these the most intellectually challenging was the first, because this decline was most clearly within the capacity of governments to eradicate, if only they could find the proper medicine. The most baffling and frustrating was the decline of demand, for it created the paradox of poverty amidst plenty, of breadlines coexistent with overflowing granaries, and children in tatters while shelves bulged with goods. But the most tragic was unemployment, product of the others both in the sense "result" and in the sense that it reflected a multiplication of the stifling evils of the times.

Unemployment was in moral terms also the most unjust aspect of the depression because it concentrated economic losses that if even roughly shared would have been far more easily borne. Although the output of goods declined sharply over a period of many years and then revived with agonizing slowness, there were never any real shortages and the economic machinery never ground to a halt. There were idle factories and abandoned farms but even in the nations most profoundly affected the large majority of the people remained at work and able to support themselves. Put differently, in 1936 (when the Depression was wrongly believed to be over), Wladimir S. Woytinsky, an economist working for the International Labor Office, estimated the total economic losses of the period 1930–1934 as roughly equal to the cost of the Great

War of 1914–1918, between 100 billion and 120 billion 1913 American dollars, a heavy price but not beyond the resources of a world population of perhaps two billion persons.[1]

But the losses were not equally shared. By this I do not mean merely that some people were rich and others poor (for this was equally the case both before and after the depression) or even that workers as a class bore the brunt of the Depression. Rather I refer to the fact that its impact on workers was capricious. The metaphor of a plague is again apt. The Depression seemed to choose its victims blindly, crushing this person and sparing his neighbor without apparent reason. Few could feel safe while the plague raged and therefore it struck fear in nearly every heart, but those seriously touched remained a minority.

Workers in some industries were harder hit than others. In general those producing durable goods, such as machinery, clothing, and housing, suffered more severely than those in food processing, utilities, and public service. Regional variations were also enormous, a celebrated example being the invisible but very real separation that split Great Britain into a relatively prosperous south and east and an economically devastated west and north. Younger workers were more afflicted than older ones, although those beyond early middle age, if they lost their jobs, found it more difficult to find new ones. Groups with low social status, such as Blacks in the United States and foreign workers almost everywhere, were far more likely to be unemployed than others. On the other hand, those whose wages were traditionally depressed—women being the most notorious example—were somewhat less likely to be unemployed, other conditions being equal.

It is also true that many workers benefited from the Depression. Prices fell faster than wages, especially between 1930 and 1933. How many workers were in this fortunate position is impossible to say because statistics on part-time unemployment in the 1930s are almost non-existent. Certainly short-time work was very common. It must be re-emphasized however that the unemployed, while numbered in the millions, were a minority. Probably over half the world's wage earners actually improved their standard of living, at least in the early 1930s when the economic downturn was at its worst.

One result of unemployment, therefore, was to separate the interests of workers and the unemployed and to some extent to put them in conflict. Those with jobs were like diners eating a meal in the window of a restaurant while outside a hungry crowd stared at them silently; they were painfully conscious that many unemployed persons were eager to take their places. How deeply this awareness influenced particular workers is difficult to determine but it is possible to generalize about the attitudes of labor unions toward the unemployed. Most labor leaders, like the politicians and most other supposedly informed people in the 1930s, failed to grasp the dynamics of the Depression. A Dutch historian has described their combined record as marked by "inertia and lack of understanding," but these persons are surely not to be blamed for failing to find solutions to the unemployment problem. Union officials everywhere claimed to be deeply concerned about the fate of the jobless and there is no reason to doubt their sincerity. However, the fact remains that their first concern was nearly always for their own constituents. Since unemployed members tended to drop out of unions—and because of the aforementioned conflict of interest between workers and the unemployed—this meant that unions reflected the attitudes of those with jobs. With only a handful of exceptions unions rejected work-sharing as a means of coping with unemployment.[2]

The major European unions, although rhetorically supportive of radical change, offered few constructive suggestions about creating more jobs. Most paid lip service to the idea of expanding public works programs, but until late in the Depression tacitly accepted the prevailing conservative dogma that public works must be financed without unbalancing national budgets, which drastically limited their extent. Beyond this union proposals for dealing with unemployment were primarily self-protective. They advocated raising the school-leaving age, forcing married women out of the labor market, and instituting early retirement schemes—all measures that would reduce "unemployment" only by redefining the term—and they sought to "export" the problem: directly by calling for the repatriation of foreign workers, indirectly by advocating high protective tariffs and mounting campaigns urging consumers not to buy foreign-made goods. The faction-ridden French unions, for example, favored all these devices—some leaders even argued that unemployment could be reduced by birth control—and they stubbornly opposed efforts to rationalize antiquated French industry, insisting that mechanization would lead to wage cuts and reduce the number of jobs. But the relatively enlightened Norwegian unions, which in the early years of the Depression sought to ration work among as many people as possible and which later supported a "pro-production" policy aimed at increasing the number of jobs, also launched a "Buy Norwegian Goods" campaign and called for the exclusion of married women from the labor market.[3]

Organizations of those on the upper rungs of the vocational ladder, the professionals, were no different from the industrial workers and craftsmen in the unions. They used every means at their command to protect themselves, without regard for unemployed colleagues, present or future, domestic or foreign. In most countries doctors, lawyers, teachers, and other professionals sought to restrict entry into the universities, to stiffen examinations, to discriminate against women, especially married women, and to obtain stronger legal protections for professional titles of all sorts. Whereas before the Depression most nations had merely required proof of competence before allowing foreigners to practice a profession in their territory, after its outbreak most strove to keep foreigners out. In France, previously most liberal in its attitude toward foreign professionals, laws were passed making it almost impossible for a foreigner to study medicine in that country and limiting foreign doctors, even after becoming naturalized citizens, from practice until they had performed military service or endured a five-year waiting period. A law of 1934 prohibited foreign lawyers from practicing in France until ten years after naturalization. The resistance of American professional groups to the admission of German Jewish refugees after 1933 is another example of this.[4]

Nearly all trade unions advocated government relief for the unemployed. They also favored unemployment insurance and in most instances were prepared to back systems involving worker contributions to insurance funds.[5] But unemployment insurance was relatively rare in the early stages of the Depression; only in Great Britain and Germany were substantial percentages of industrial workers covered.[6] And union support for both insurance and outright relief was not unqualified.

The British Trade Union Congress fought hard, even when the Labour party was in power, against efforts to stiffen the requirements for obtaining public assistance and to reduce the amounts paid, but it is important to note that government doles also benefited unions by freeing them (as well as employers) from responsibility for supporting their discharged fellows and by reducing job competition that might further depress wages. The unions, in other words, implicitly accepted high unemployment as the price to be paid for maintaining the wage levels of persons with jobs. With the cost of living falling faster than wages, they "became more interested in increasing the rate of unemployment benefit than in increasing employment." British craft unions tightened already strict controls on the admission of apprentices and even objected when the sponsors of clubs for the unemployed tried to help idle workers to keep themselves occupied and earn a few shillings by tailoring, carpentry, and other handicraft work. The steelworkers' union refused to cooperate with labor-sharing proposals intended to spread available work among more men even though, since steelworkers were paid on a tonnage basis and output per worker in the industry was rising, their earnings were increasing.[7]

Of all the major labor organizations, the German Labor Federation (*Allgemeiner Deutscher Gewerkschaftsbund*) had by far the most enlightened attitude toward the unemployment problem. Its leaders included a number of excellent economists, most notably Wladimir S. Woytinsky—who was director of research for the Federation from 1929 to 1933, Fritz Baade—an agricultural marketing expert, and Fritz Tarnow—a carpenters' union member who was also a Reichstag deputy. Even in the 1920s the Federation was urging policies aimed at increasing consumer demand, Tarnow arguing in *Why Be Poor?* (*Warum arm sein?*, 1929) that greater purchasing power would mean more jobs. Although socialists by conviction, these men were prepared to work within the capitalist system; they saw unemployment insurance as an entering wedge, "a step forward on the road to socialism." The tragic result of their insights, however, was that when mounting unemployment put the insurance fund deep in the red in 1930, they rejected a compromise that involved a possible future reduction of unemployment benefits even though rejection meant the certain fall of the pro-labor Socialist government. The fall of the government led to new elections which made the Nazis a power in the Reichstag and also to the very reduction of insurance benefits that the unions had hoped to avoid.

German labor was not, of course, responsible for Hitler's rise. Indeed, Woytinsky, Tarnow, and Baade went on to develop the so-called W-T-B Plan for stimulating consumption by inflating the currency, which the unions finally endorsed in 1932. But union intransigence in 1930 was surely a mistake, and also not unrelated to the conviction of union economists that maintaining the level of insurance benefits would help maintain the level of wages. The tragedy was compounded by the fact that after 1930 the unemployed tended to desert the Socialist party for the Communists.[8]

In the mid-thirties the French labor federation (*Conféderation Général du Travail*) flirted with a number of rather imprecise "plans" for stimulating production, based on the Belgian Henri de Man's concept of a "mixed economy," one in which the state would control credit and nationalize certain key industries. In 1934 the CGT set up a bureau of economic studies to develop proposals. But the *planistes* (who included Georges Lefranc—secretary of the *Institut Supérieur Ouvrier*, Lucien Laurat—a prominent follower of de Man, the economists Etienne Antonelli of the University of Lyon and François Simiand of the Conservatoire des Arts et Métiers in Paris, and Jacques Duboin—author of the widely read *La grande relève des hommes par la machine* (1932) and other works advocating an "economy of abundance") never attracted much mass support for their ideas. They were also resisted by doctrinaire socialists ("before any plan, first . . . the total conquest of power by socialism") and other groups in the labor movement. In 1936, after the reunification of the communist and non-communist labor organizations, the CGT finally approved a plan on the de Man model that also called for large-scale public-works expenditures, but in the excitement following the political triumph of the Popular Front and the resulting wave of strikes the scheme was forgotten.[9]

As for the communist-controlled unions, they expressed particular sympathy for the unemployed as the ultimate victims of capitalism, but preferred to wait for what they saw as the approaching collapse of the system before trying to do anything about the job shortage. Communists (at least until 1934 after the Nazi seizure of power in Germany had caused a change in tactics) saw unions as mere agents of the party, designed to make workers class conscious and prepare them for the revolution; to concentrate on improving wages or working conditions would only delay the revolution by mitigating the evils of capitalism. The attitude of the French *Conféderation Générale du Travail Unitaire* was typical: it opposed unemployment insurance based on worker and employer contributions on the ground that wages were too low to support the payments: "Social insurance is a *right* of the worker. The *bourgeoisie*, as the privileged class, should pay the cost."[10]

Communist labor leaders did try to play upon the dissatisfactions of the unemployed. In France they organized regional Committees of Unemployed and published irregularly a paper, *Le Cri des Chômeurs.*[11] Especially in Great Britain and the United States, they attempted to organize the jobless to demand relief. In America the communist Trade Union Unity League created a network of Unemployed Councils and announced an International Day for Struggle Against Worldwide Unemployment (March 6, 1930). Well-attended protest meetings, some leading to violence, were held in most large cities and for a time the councils attracted many recruits. But the leadership soon diverted the movement to "abstract issues the jobless did not understand" and membership rapidly declined. Both the TUUL and the Unemployed Councils continued to exist and to support demonstrations by the unemployed, such as the Ford Hunger March of 1932, bloodily repressed by the Dearborn police and Ford company guards. But both organizations were essentially political groups, not labor unions, and had little effect on the attitudes of the unemployed. Similarly, the Unemployed Citizens' Leagues organized by A. J. Muste in 1932 attracted substantial support among the jobless of Ohio and Pennsylvania by working to improve relief programs and by organizing self-help projects. But the Leagues were gradually politicized and consequently had little appeal to unemployed workers. Muste began to complain that the unemployed were "devoted to mere self-preservation" and by late 1934 he and other leaders had moved into the Workers Party, a Trotskyite group interested in the jobless only as "shock troops" for the revolution.[12]

The British National Unemployed Workers' Movement was a far more formidable phenomenon. It had a much larger influence among the unemployed and its hunger marches and demonstrations against cuts in the dole attracted wide middle-class sympathy. It undoubtedly helped the jobless call attention to their suffering. But its communist affiliations made it anathema to the trade unions that represented the bulk of British labor. Moreover, the NUWM had little to say about getting rid of unemployment. It concentrated on obtaining more government relief for those out of work; about all it could suggest for "reducing" unemployment were the conventional proposals for defining it out of existence by keeping young people in school longer and retiring workers earlier.[13]

But if the unemployed were a minority and frequently ill-served, there was nonetheless deep concern throughout the world about the unemployment problem in the 1930s. The subject attracted the attention not only of politicians, economists, journalists, employers, and labor organizations, but also of sociologists, psychologists, and doctors. The unemployed were subjected to batteries of tests, questionnaires, and interviews. Nutritionists analyzed their diets; social scientists conducted elaborate field studies and persuaded unemployed persons to keep diaries and write their autobiographies; other experts pored over the records of relief organizations and national health statistics.

These studies varied greatly in scope and objectivity, and of course they revealed that individuals differed in the way they were affected by unemployment depending upon their intelligence, experience, and personalities, as well as upon the circumstances of their situation. As one researcher confessed, generalizing about the effects of unemployment was "like trying to summarize a Persian rug." Yet it seems fair to say that contemporaries had a clearer picture of the effects of unemployment in the Great Depression than they did of its extent—statistical information about unemployment was sketchy and inaccurate.

One of the surprising things revealed by research was that the Depression did not appear to have had any dramatic effect on public health. It did not cause an increase in death rates or even slow the long-range trend toward increased longevity characteristic of the industrial nations. In 1932 the Surgeon General of the United States announced that with regard to health, "the country has never been as prosperous in its history as during the year 1931, so far as we are able to ascertain by statistics," and he released figures showing that the mortality rate had fallen from 12 per thousand in 1929 to 10.6 per thousand in 1932. He attributed this happy state of affairs in part to the "devoted self-sacrifice of the medical profession" in treating poor patients "regardless of possible remuneration," but he provided no statistical evidence on this point. This is not to say that the health of many unemployed persons was not affected; common sense and much hard evidence indicate that it was. A British medical journal viewed the situation more realistically. "We know," it reported in 1933, "that at the present time a very large proportion of the population is imperfectly fed, but we cannot find the signs of it." In countries such as the United States that did not have national systems of relief in the early years, there were many cases of severe malnutrition and some of starvation, and even in Great Britain and Germany, where care of the needy was well-organized and reasonably comprehensive, investigators found countless families suffering from hunger and various dietary deficiencies. National health statistics, however, did not reflect this suffering to any marked degree. The effects of malnutrition appear only slowly, and it was probably also true that, statistically, the improved diet available to full-time workers because of lower food prices counterbalanced the deficiencies endured by the minority that was unemployed.[14] In countries where unemployment was relatively low the national diet actually improved during the early thirties. In France the improvement was startling; between 1931 and 1935 the per-capita consumption of food increased by five percent (more than the rise between 1913 and 1930) and meat, milk, and fruit consumption rose even more. Similar trends were discernible in many other nations, including Great Britain, despite its chronically high unemployment. When B. Seebohm Rountree replicated his classic 1899 survey of *Poverty* in York in the mid-thirties he found enough improvement in living standards to title his new book *Poverty and Progress*, although the numbers living in poverty were still shockingly high.[15]

Field studies of what unemployed families ate as well as estimates based on relief payments and the cost of food indicated that most of the jobless consumed enough calories to maintain weight. A French enquiry made in the middle of the Depression put the daily caloric intake of the unemployed at slightly over 2,700 calories (for workers it was 3,150), a total generally conceded to be adequate. A British investigation made at about the same time calculated the intake of the unemployed at 2,850 calories per day, about ten percent less than that of the typical worker. A German analysis of food prices and relief payments made during the grim winter of 1932–33 concluded that a jobless person could afford to purchase a little over 2,600 calories compared to about 2,850 for workers.[16]

However, the unemployed seldom obtained enough of the right kinds of food. Conditions varied from one country to another according to the amount of aid provided and the general standard of living, and among individuals. But their consumption of fruit, vegetables, and especially high-protein foods fell off everywhere. As early as December 1930, milk consumption in New York City was running a million quarts a week below normal. Even in France, where the unemployed usually ate enough proteins and vitamins, their intake of meat, dairy products, and vegetables was nevertheless much lower than that of workers. In poorer countries the dietary deficiencies of the unemployed were more serious. A team of Austrian sociologists headed by Paul F. Lazarsfeld discovered that seven of ten families in the town of Marienthal, where unemployment approached 100 percent, ate meat no more than once a week and that some of this meat was the flesh of cats and dogs. Pork consumption in Marienthal fell by about half, beef to only a small fraction of what it had been before the Depression. Flour consumption, on the other hand, increased. In Vienna the records of the Office of Markets revealed a considerable drop between 1931 and 1932 in the number of cattle and pigs slaughtered and in the sale of eggs and fruits. In Hungary, where the condition of agricultural workers was particularly bad and where many of them therefore flocked into the cities, by 1932 about 18 percent of the population of Budapest was on relief and getting, according to trade union estimates, only about half the money needed to maintain a minimum standard of living.[17]

The nutritional problems of the jobless were complicated by bad management and by their widely noticed tendency to "waste" money on non-essentials. George Orwell noted in *The Road to Wigan Pier*, a report on conditions in the so-called "distressed areas" of Britain, that the unemployed consumed large amounts of sweets, chips, and "the Englishman's opium," tea, and that they were inveterate gamblers. In Marienthal nearly half of the evening meals consumed consisted only of bread and black coffee. Although the coffee had no nutritional value, it was "considered a food and also a luxury, and for that reason holds a central place in the diet of the poorest classes in particular." An unemployed Polish worker told a pathetic story about a child who asked his mother for milk in his coffee. The mother replied that the milk was already in the coffee, but that the cows were now giving black milk. When the child asked why this was so, she answered that the cows were not getting enough to eat, and had become angry.

Investigations of unemployed French workers revealed a similar attitude toward "luxury" foods; they continued to devote substantial portions of their budgets to wine and coffee, despite the fact that a "purely rational analysis of their financial situation" should have led them to cut down on these items. A nurse who visited unemployed households in Alsace described a poor family that used the *prime à natalité* received at the birth of a baby to purchase a "uselessly luxurious baby carriage." Many Belgian unemployed workers spent money raising pigeons, not to eat but in hopes of winning a worthless prize, and Lazarsfeld reported the case of an almost destitute 50-year-old woman who bought a curling iron on the installment plan. The German journalist and sociologist Siegfried Kracauer, watching ragged groups of young people lay out 50 pfenning at a Berlin movie theater, decided that they attended "less for pleasure than to drive away the ghost of bad times." The film was a kind of medicine, he concluded.[18]

Descriptions of ragged clothes and bad housing conditions also fill the unemployment studies of the 1930s. Investigators reported finding children unable to go to school because they had no shoes, families living in crowded squalor or evicted for non-payment of rent. It was sometimes noted that landlords allowed tenants to stay on even when far in arrears, out of pity or because they preferred not to leave buildings vacant and at the mercy of vandals, but the sight of the poor living in tiny huts designed as toolsheds on garden allotment plots, and the mushrooming of shantytowns on wasteland on the edges of great cities from Australia to the Argentine—sardonically called Hoovervilles in the United States, *bidonvilles* (tin can cities) in France, humpies in Australia—suggests that eviction was far from uncommon. In the spring of 1935 two Indiana University sociologists found about 20,000 unemployed men living in state-operated shelters in the city of Chicago. Most of these unfortunates were ill-educated and of low intelligence, men who before the Depression were casual laborers at best. Many exhibited signs of emotional instability. But a number of them—a small percentage but several hundred nonetheless—were high school and college graduates who had held down good jobs before the Depression struck. In Budapest in the early 1930s hundreds of homeless unemployed professional workers were living in army barracks, and eating leftovers in the university cafeteria until the dean ejected them on the ground that they were having "a prejudicial effect, morally, on the students." Inadequate housing was, of course, a problem for many working families, in good times as well as bad, but the jobless, compelled to spend larger and larger proportions of their declining funds on food, often had to liquidate their meager possessions merely to stay alive.[19]

In a sense, demonstrating that many who were without work were inadequately fed, clothed, and sheltered was only documenting the obvious; the reports of researchers on the psychological effects of unemployment were somewhat more surprising. While individuals reacted in widely different ways, nearly every survey, whatever its scope, whatever the method of investigation, revealed essentially the same patterns. These were spelled out early in the

Depression by the Lazarsfeld team's analysis of Marienthal, in a field study of Greenwich, England, by E. Wight Bakke, an American sociologist, and in autobiographies of unemployed workers gathered by the Polish Institute for Social Economy. When workers lost their jobs their response, perhaps after a brief period of waiting for something to turn up, was to search feverishly for a new one. Then they became discouraged, sometimes emotionally disorganized. Finally, after months of continuous idleness, most either sank into apathy or adjusted to their condition, leading extremely circumscribed lives in apparent calm.

In *The Unemployed Man,* Bakke recorded the process as it evolved in the case of "A", a young Greenwich truck driver. Bakke met A at a political rally three days after he had been laid off. "There's plenty of jobs for a man with my experience," A said. "I've never been out more than a week or so before. I'll soon be back." Three weeks later, after having moved in with his parents and answered want ads without success, he was discouraged but still hopeful. After another five weeks, however, he told Bakke "I'm beginning to wonder what's wrong with me"; after another three, "either I'm no good, or there is something wrong with business around here. . . . Even my family is beginning to think I'm not trying." Finally, four months after losing his job, A became totally despondent, complaining to Bakke of "the hopelessness of every step you take."[20]

Lazarsfeld, who observed the people of Marienthal when they had already endured a long period without work, was more interested in their final adjustment to their situation. Studying closely the hundred most needy families in the village, he found four types. About half he classified as resigned to their fate; they had learned to accept a circumscribed existence, had no plans or expectations. Another quarter he called despairing—these were bitter, gloomy, frequently drunk, given to outbursts of misdirected rage. Another, smaller group were completely apathetic, heedless not only of the future but even of the present. Only about sixteen percent of these people could be classified as "unbroken," and they, significantly, had slightly higher incomes than the rest. They continued to hope for work and had an optimistic outlook despite their suffering. Conditions in Marienthal as a whole were not quite so bad as this analysis of its poorest citizens indicated. Lazarsfeld estimated that nearly a quarter of the families in the town were unbroken and about 70 percent merely resigned. The despairing and the apathetic made up the rest.[21]

Since Marienthal was an extreme case, the relative numbers who were crushed or maimed by unemployment there may have been larger than elsewhere, although it seems equally possible that the universality of unemployment may have sustained many individuals. What was clear, however, in that village and in every locale where investigators examined the state of mind of the jobless, was that few persons could survive long periods of enforced idleness without paying a psychological price, even if their basic economic needs were met.[22] A Canadian researcher spoke of the "lowered morale and broken spirits" of the unemployed, their "hopeless despair," their "dependent attitudes." When Henri Fuss, director of unemployment studies for the International Labor Office, visited a British employment exchange, he found "an air of lassitude." The jobless, he said, "walk heavily and slowly."[23] In Argentina, another writer noted, many of the unemployed "have gradually drifted away from all their connections and have come to look upon their past as another existence with which they have severed every tie."[24]

In 1931, New York City social workers, describing the reactions of their clients, stressed their general loss of pride and their tendency to avoid social contacts. In 1940, Mirra Komarovsky, who had studied a group of unemployed New York families in the late stages of the Depression, reported her general impression that "the [jobless] man suffers from deep humiliation." Unemployment, the psychologist Abram Kardiner noted in an article in *The Family*, produced feelings of shame and anxiety in its victims, leading eventually to apathy. When another psychologist administered a questionnaire designed to elicit social attitudes and personal values to 800 jobless men and women with records of previous steady employment, he also characterized their responses as apathetic; they appeared to react to the words of the items but not to their meaning. Still another psychologist gave a questionnaire prepared for the study of the mental state of psychotics to a group of English and Scottish unemployed workers. Many of the respondents displayed a "catastrophic" outlook toward life and were as "downcast" as mental patients.[25]

Novelists, reporters, and others who observed large numbers of the unemployed during the Depression described the psychological effects of idleness in the same terms. Orwell visited a family in a mining town, all of them out of work, "grown up sons and daughters sprawling aimless about . . . and one tall son sitting by the fireplace, too listless even to notice the entry of a stranger, and slowly pulling off a sticky sock from a bare foot." Elsewhere in *The Road to Wigan Pier* Orwell wrote of men "gazing at their destiny with the same sort of dumb amazement as an animal in a trap," and "haunted by a feeling of personal degradation." Siegfried Kracauer compared a Berlin shelter to the waiting room of a railroad station where "the train never comes." At a labor exchange he found the mood dark and subdued. Everyone spoke in whispers and with resignation. "I have observed that many scarcely listen to the announcements of jobs," Kracauer wrote. "They are already too numbed to believe in their chance of being chosen."

The American historian Ray Allen Billington, who was a director of the New Deal Writers' Project in Massachusetts in the late 1930s, interviewed scores of applicants. A quarter of a century later he still recalled "their bleak, downcast eyes, their broken spirit." Maxine Davis, a journalist, spent four months in 1935 driving across the United States talking to young people; she was struck by the "sheep-like apathy" with which they accepted their state. The writer Sherwood Anderson, who also toured America in this period, came to a similar conclusion. "There is in the average American a profound humbleness," he wrote. "People seem to blame themselves."

Although many Marxist novelists, especially in the United States, described the unemployed as militant, most novelists who wrote about the Depression without this particular political bias pictured them as crushed by unemployment. The Englishman Walter Greenwood, whose *Love on the Dole* (1933) was one of the most widely read novels of the 1930s, put it this way:

> It got you slowly, with the slippered stealth of an unsuspected malignant disease. You fell into the habit of slouching, of putting your hands in your pockets and keeping them there; of glancing at people, furtively, ashamed of your secret, until you fancied that everybody eyed you with suspicion.

Karl Lakner, the protagonist of the Austrian Rudolf Brunngraber's novel, *Karl and the Twentieth Century* (1933), emerges from World War I a cheerful, hard-working man fully capable of bearing misfortune. But repeated periods of unemployment and declining resources leave him with the "depressed look of the permanently unemployed." He becomes "utterly aimless," then "profoundly demoralized," and finally, after a futile attempt at robbery, he commits suicide. Johannes Pinneberg, the hero of the German Hans Fallada's *Little Man, What Now?* (1933), goes through similar experiences, reacts like Karl, and comes to almost as sad an end.[26]

Many Americans believed that the dependency resulting from unemployment was a more profound shock in their country than elsewhere because of the prevailing worship of self-reliance. In a nation that had almost no social insurance and provided relief for the destitute largely in the form of private charity until long after the economy had plumbed the depths, where labor unions preferred to obtain their goals by bargaining or striking rather than through legislation, unemployment was especially ego-eroding, or so the argument ran. Thus two sociologists wrote in 1936: "A man who has the traditional individualistic American idea that a man who is industrious and persevering can get and hold a job, receives a severe mental jolt when he finds himself unable to supply even the bare necessities of life." But there is much evidence that unemployment affected people in less individualistic societies in just the same way. "When for the first time I held out my hand for my 9 zloty of benefit," a Polish unemployed worker recalled, "I was filled with disgust for the whole of my previous existence."[27] Orwell, eager to rouse the British jobless to act against the conditions that had produced their misery, was "horrified and amazed" to discover "that many of them were *ashamed* of being unemployed."[28]

The effects of prolonged joblessness, and particularly its psychological effects, go far toward explaining why unemployment did not generate more political protest, let alone revolutionary activity, among its victims. Many practical considerations combined to keep the unemployed from revolting, some of these being the international character of the Depression, which made it difficult to believe that any one government was responsible for it; the lack of intellectually convincing suggestions as to how unemployment could be significantly reduced; the fact that the unemployed were everywhere a minority; fear of repression (which the majority seldom hesitated to apply when the jobless did make trouble); even gratitude for the aid which every society did provide for those without work. But the numbing effect of prolonged idleness, partly no doubt a result of diets low in proteins and also partly psychological, was also involved.[29]

Protest, of course, there was: mass meetings, hunger marches, rent strikes; countless cases of petty theft by the destitute; outright violence. Such disturbances attracted wide attention and roused profound fears. "Unemployment is making the world tremble," a French businessman wrote in 1932. "There [in America} is the 'bonus army,' hundreds of thousands of the unemployed who besiege the capital. Facing us are the 'hunger marchers,' who tie up the heart of the British Empire. Elsewhere races become emaciated, nations break up and lose their sense of proper order." The very logic of the situation increased the feeling of many observers that the world was teetering on the verge of chaos. "The present crisis is so widespread in its effects and so dire in its consequences to those who suffer from them," a German commission on unemployment reported in 1931, "that social consequences of the most serious nature . . . are to be feared."

But the protests of the jobless were sporadic, unfocused, and to a considerable extent merely rhetorical. A Washington reporter described the American Bonus Marchers of 1932 as "the army of bewilderment," their behavior marked by "a curious melancholy." When, gathered 8,000 strong before the Capitol, they learned that the Senate had rejected the Bonus bill, they meekly accepted the suggestion of their leader that they sing "America," and straggled back to their pitiful shacks on Anacostia Flats. Unemployed British hunger marchers occasionally used force to call attention to their plight, but most of the dozens of clashes between marchers and the police were provoked by the latter. In general the marchers conducted themselves with restraint and their leaders made great efforts to prevent breaches of the peace. They carried red banners, it is true, but most of their signs bore messages no more provocative than "down with the means test" and "against hunger and war." The culmination of the most successful of the great marches in early 1934 was the presentation of a petition to the House of Commons, phrased in the traditional language of petitioners ("[We] humbly desire to represent that great suffering has been caused to the unemployed . . . by the means test") and asking no more than "decent maintenance" or "employment at trade union rates." These most "militant" of victims of the depression were appealing for sympathy and succor, expressing, above all else, their dependency.[30]

Many students of unemployment in the thirties commented on the political passivity of the jobless, some with puzzlement, some with understanding. They collected innumerable individual statements expressing anger, resentment, and disillusionment with the authorities. "Unemployment is due to an agreement between the capitalists and the Government to crush the worker and make a slave of him," wrote a Pole. "I don't think things will improve until we have a revolution. . . . Just nationalise everything," said an Englishman. A researcher in an American municipal lodging house recorded the residents "giving the capitalist system hell in a big way." But such expressions were nearly always mere talk.

Yet those who studied the political attitudes of the unemployed also noted their lack of involvement. In Marienthal, always representative of the extreme case, the Lazarsfeld team reported a sharp falling off of *all* political activity. Elsewhere, however, most of the jobless displayed toward political issues the same apathy that characterized their whole lives. "When one is out of a job," a long-time-unemployed Dutch worker told an investigator in 1935, "one loses one's pleasure in politics." Bakke found few radicals among the unemployed of Greenwich and no difference in political attitude between them and those with jobs. *He* seemed more indignant about how society had treated these people than they were themselves. After a more detailed analysis of unemployment in New Haven Bakke came to the same conclusion. He attended a May Day meeting on the town common in 1934. A Communist orator delivered a powerful speech, but no one appeared to be following his argument and when he ended with a call for a protest march to city hall, only a handful followed him. Bakke concluded that despite the Depression nearly all the New Haven unemployed still accepted the capitalist system. On another occasion, after listening to several groups of men griping about conditions, he asked one of them where the local Communist headquarters was. The men bristled. "Take my advice and stay away from there," one of the men told him. To draw them out, Bakke began defending the Communist cause. Their response was twofold: Anyone who thought the Russian system was good was crazy. Communists were all foreigners; to support them was to be a traitor. "In the face of Communism," Bakke noted, "the most insecure American worker becomes a hero by defending American conditions."

The writer Matthew Josephson, radicalized by the suffering he observed and read about in the early thirties, began visiting the dingy municipal lodging houses of New York. He found not rebelliousness but defeatism and lassitude. Once he treated three down-and-outers whose confidence he had won to a meal. "Things can't go on like this," he said to them. They smiled faintly, but said nothing. Why didn't they complain about the dreadful conditions in the shelters? "We don't dare complain about anything. We're afraid of being kicked out." Why didn't they join the demonstrations that radicals in New York were organizing? They answered that they were "'good Americans' and didn't go for the 'communist stuff.'" Later in the Depression another American journalist who pictured himself as "frankly radical" and who described the efforts of various communist groups in glowing terms, spent seven months driving across the country and back taking the public pulse. As for the unemployed, he wrote, "the more I saw of them . . . the more I was depressed and outraged both by their physical and spiritual wretchedness and by their passive acceptance of their condition." The Polish autobiographies revealed still another aspect of the political passivity of the jobless. Two sociologists who studied them carefully remarked on the "inert" aggressiveness displayed in these accounts. The authors frequently manifested their rage and a desire for revenge, but often directed these feelings at their fellow sufferers, that is, at themselves. Of the 57 published accounts, only two blamed the capitalist system for unemployment, only four could reasonably be described as expressing revolutionary attitudes. "The unemployed," the sociologists concluded, were "scattered, loose, perplexed and hopeless . . . *a mass only numerically, not socially.*"[31]

Among other similar observations, Edwin H. Sutherland and Harvey J. Locke, describing the residents of Chicago shelters wrote: "While the men applaud anyone who makes a radical statement, they are generally indifferent to such radical programs as communism and fascism." Most of them insisted that all politicians were crooked and cynically sold their own votes on election day to the higher bidder, Democratic or Republican.[32] When young Lauren Gilfillan, full of sympathy for the downtrodden, went to live among the poverty-stricken striking coal miners of western Pennsylvania in the early thirties, she discovered many communists among them. But she portrayed the majority of the miners as anything but radical. "Oh, to hell with communism!" one of her new friends, himself an official of the Young Communist League, told her. "They're a lot of stupid lummoxes. Real miners ain't communists."[33] In his autobiography, *There Was a Time*, Walter Greenwood described a conversation at a Labour party headquarters during the period before he wrote his best-seller, *Love on the Dole*, a time when he was himself unemployed. He was talking to a militant friend, one James Moleyns, when two other unemployed men came in. One of the newcomers announced angrily that he was "Fed up. Fed up to the blooming teeth." His unemployment benefits had expired and a former friend, now a successful businessman, had refused him even a temporary job as a laborer, which would have enabled him after an interval to collect insurance again. The cynical Moleyns urged him to try to get a doctor to declare him eligible for such benefits, then added: "What the Government ought to do is freeze us solid, shove us in cold storage and bring us out when they need us." But the man merely continued to grumble about his faithless friend. "It was," Greenwood recalled, "as though he had not been listening."

In 1934 two American political scientists, Gabriel Almond and Harold D. Lasswell, published the results of an ingenious experiment that throws much light on the political responses of the unemployed. They observed large numbers of people on relief who came to the complaints desk of a relief office and evaluated the relative aggressiveness or submissiveness of their behavior in these confrontations with the authorities. They then chose 100 of each type and studied their case histories closely. They found, as might have been expected, that those in the aggressive group had displayed more assertiveness and had had more experience in manipulating people in their careers. They also had enjoyed higher standards of living than the submissive types. But the whole sample had shown little interest in radical politics; very few of those who behaved aggressively were affiliated with organized protest movements of any kind.[34]

These findings of contemporary investigators are confirmed by the most casual study of broad political trends. Nowhere, as we have seen, did the unemployed mount a substantial political movement of their own, nor did any significant number of them join communist or fascist parties. In Britain there were roughly three million unemployed in 1932–33 but only about 15,000 Communist party members. In the United States the best estimate of unemployment in late 1932 is about 13 million; in the presidential election of that year only 103,000 persons voted the Communist ticket and if the Socialist party can be considered an extremist organization in the American context, only 882,000 voters supported it, fewer than in 1912 when the electorate was only about one-third as large. Many of these voters, probably a large majority of them, were not unemployed.

After the successful strikes of 1936 in France the Communist party made large gains, but most of the recruits were *working* men. The French unemployed, according to one recent student, behaved somewhat like the typical French *fonctionnaire*, tending to rely on the established authorities to take care of them. Even in Germany, where the economic and social disintegration of the early 1930s favored extremist political movements, few of the unemployed were political activists. The Nazis strove mightily to recruit them, almost totally without success. By the fall of 1932 the jobless made up about 80 percent of the German Communist party, but the party had only 330,000 members, a small fraction of Germany's 6 million unemployed.[35] Many more unemployed Germans voted Communist, whereas the British jobless remained loyal to the Labour party and the American unemployed supported Franklin Roosevelt's New Deal. Political apathy did not apparently extend to total withdrawal from the political process, nor did it prevent the unemployed from voting their interests as they saw them. But they nowhere became an effective pressure group or an independent political force. Political activism was incompatible with joblessness. Insecurity caused the unemployed to be fearful and dependent. Fear and dependence eroded their confidence and destroyed hope. Lack of confidence and hopelessness undermined their expectations. Typically, when workers lost their jobs they had not suffered enough to become rebels. By the time they had suffered they had lost the capacity for militant protest.

The question remains: How did the experience of a decade of mass unemployment affect the industrial world? Fears that prolonged idleness would make millions *incapable* of working—that they were "done for as human material," as one observer put it in 1931—proved unfounded.[36] Similarly, the concerns of doctors and psychologists that the physical and mental health of the unemployed and their children had been permanently damaged were at least exaggerated. Vital statistics do not indicate that the jobless of the 1930s or their children died sooner or were more subject to disease than others. It has been argued that the anxieties of the Depression, reacting on the World War I-weakened egos of Germans in their twenties and thirties, made many of them Nazis, and that the Depression permanently checked the upward mobility of the generation of Americans of the laboring class that was born between 1900 and 1910,[37] but the question of what later happened to the unemployed—a very difficult one—needs more study. It is a commonplace that the Depression experience "marked" those who lived through it but there is no evidence that this influence was confined to the unemployed.

As for unemployment itself, very little was accomplished during the Depression to reduce it significantly. With the exception of Germany under the Nazis, no industrial nation got its unemployment rate even as low as ten percent (about double what is currently considered "acceptable") before the outbreak of World War II.[38] Keynes did not perfect his theory of full employment until 1936 and no government really accepted his analysis until after the exigencies of the war compelled them to adopt his proposals. The world did learn during the Depression how to cope with unemployment in the sense that governments expanded the amounts spent on relieving the victims, and most established more or less adequate systems of unemployment insurance. Many also undertook substantial public works programs to provide work for the jobless, although this method of dealing with the problem was abandoned in the postwar years.

It was commonly believed during the latter stages of the Depression that the compelling need to help the unemployed had destroyed laissez faire.[39] It would be more accurate to say that laissez faire happened to die during the Depression; as a practical strategy of government it had been expiring for generations. The theory of laissez faire, that is, the rational analysis developed by the great classical economists and codified late in the 19th century by Alfred Marshall was not undermined directly by the Depression except in the sense that observation of economic trends in the 1930s led Keynes and his followers to develop a new analysis—one that, for a time, provided some useful insights. Furthermore, despite Keynes' famous put-down of the "long run" effects of economic policies, much of what the economic establishment was saying in the 1930s—about the difficulty of manipulating complex business and commercial relationships by law or administrative fiat, about the dangers and injustices inherent in inflation, about the possible harmful impact of nationalist "solutions" on world peace—was correct.[40]

A decade of mass unemployment, however, made it politically impossible, once methods for stimulating the economy had been developed and convincingly demonstrated, not to make use of them. At least until 1933 and in most cases for years thereafter, the governments of the industrial powers placed a higher value on balanced budgets and preventing inflation than on increasing the number of jobs. As a result, those of their citizens who could not find employment bore a disproportionate share of the burdens of the Depression. Since World War II, most governments have given first priority to employment, though this has meant almost continuous inflation. As a result, joblessness has never remotely approached the levels of the 1930s. But inflation, the most glaring symptom of our contemporary economic ills, has proved to be almost as tragic and as unjust in its effects as was unemployment during the Great Depression. It creates the same general malaise and bears most heavily on a minority—the poor, the old, the "nonproductive." And thus it is no longer quite so certain that the measures that keep unemployment in bounds can prevent worldwide economic collapse "in the long run."

NOTES

1. W. S. Woytinsky, *The Social Consequences of the Economic Depression* (Geneva, 1936), 300. See also Karl Pribram, "Unemployment," *Encyclopedia of the Social Sciences*, 15: 153.

2. Jan Drondt, "Government, Labor and Trade Unions," in Herman van der Wee, ed., *The Great Depression Revisited: Essays on the Economics of the Thirties* (The Hague, 1972), 253. Edward L. Shorter and Charles Tilly argue, relative to France, that the bureaucratization of the unions in the 1920s and the growing willingness of employers to negotiate with them over wage rates conditioned labor leaders to concentrate their efforts in this relatively productive area rather than on such issues as hiring and firing that would rouse "irrational" employer resistance and thus threaten the new, orderly relationships that were developing. Shorter and Tilly do not concern themselves with union policies toward unemployment, but their argument would apply to this question and to union tactics in other nations. "Le déclin de la grève violente en France de 1890 à 1935," *Le Mouvement Social*, LXXVI (1971), 95–118, esp. 116n.

3. R. Dufraisse, "Le Movement Ouvrier 'Rouge' devant la Grande Dépression Économique de 1929 à 1933," in Denise Fauvel-Rouif, ed., *Mouvements ouvriers et dépression économique de 1929 à 1939* (Assen, 1966), 168, 173, 176–82, 185–7; Jacques Julliard, "Le Mouvement Syndical," in Alfred Sauvy, *Histoire économique de la France entre les deux guerres* (Paris, 1972), 3: 186–7; E. Bull, "The Norwegian Labour Movement, 1929–1939," *Mouvements ouvriers*, 346–9.

4. W. H. Kotschnig, *Unemployment in the Learned Professions* (London, 1937), 179–90, 223–31, 243–5; "Remedies for Unemployment among Professional Workers," *International Labour Review*, XXXIII (1936), 310–20.

5. An exception was the American Federation of Labor. As late as 1932 its official position was that relief "instills in those cared for a sense of irresponsibility and dependence that is harmful to society." *American Federationist*, XXXIX (1932), 61–2, quoted in E. T. Sweeney, "The A.F.L.'s Good Citizen, 1920–1940," *Labor History*, XIII (1972), 203. The AFL also opposed unemployment insurance until 1932.

6. *International Labour Review*, XXIII (1931), 48.

7. Robert Skidelsky, *Politicians and the Slump: The Labour Government of 1929–1931* (London, 1970), 23, 61–3, 142–52, 293–301, 351–2, 433; W. Campbell Balfour, "British Labour from the Great Depression to the Second World War," *Mouvements ouvriers*, 237, 247; C. L. Mowat, *Britain Between the Wars: 1918–1940* (Boston, 1971), 489–90. See also Lionel Robbins, *The Great Depression* (New York, 1934), 188–9.

8. Ursula Hüllsbüsch, "Die deutschen Gewerkschaften in der Weltwirtschaftskrise," in Werner Conze and Hans Raupach, eds., *Die Staats- und Wirtschaftskrise des Deutchen Reichs, 1929/33* (Stuttgart, 1967), 136–40; Helga Timm, *Die Deutsche Sozialpolitik und der Bruch der Grossen Koalition im März 1930* (Düsseldorf, 1952), 128–9, 178–87; R. N. Hunt, *German Social Democracy: 1918–1933* (Chicago, 1964), 185–7; Fritz Baade, "Fighting Depression in Germany," in E. S. Woytinsky, ed., *So Much Alive: The Life and Work of Wladimir S. Woytinsky* (New York, 1962), 61–8; R. Wagenführ and W. Voss, "Trade Unions and the World Economic Crisis: The Case of Germany," *Great Depression Revisited*, 260–1; Rudolf Vierhaus, "Auswirkungen der Krise um 1930 in Deutschland: Beiträge zu einer historisch-psychologischen Analyse," *Staats- und Wirtschaftskrise*, 165. Vierhaus writes: "In these years of crisis in Germany, society threatened to split into two groups: in one those still working . . . in the other those 'outside.'" He argues that the unemployed were a proletariat "in the old, pre-marxian sense" of a poverty-stricken mass, but that they did not constitute a unified and class-conscious social group. According to Woytinsky, Otto Wells, president of the Socialist party, opposed the W-T-B Plan on the ground that the party's first obligation was to the *employed*. Since so many unemployed voters were supporting the Communists and the Nazis, Wells said, let those parties look after their interests. W. S. Woytinsky, *Stormy Passage: A Personal History through Two Russian Revolutions to Democracy and Freedom, 1905–1960* (New York, 1961), 469.

9. V. R. Lorwin, *The French Labor Movement* (Cambridge, Mass., 1954), 71–2; Georges Lefranc, "Le courant planiste dans le mouvement ouvrier français de 1933 à 1936," *Le Mouvement Social*, LIV (1966), 69–89; Leon Jouhaux, *La C.G.T.: ce qu'elle est, ce qu'elle veut* (Paris, 1937), 169–87; Michel Collinet, "Masses et Militants: la bureaucratie et la crise actuelle du syndicalisme ouvrier français," *Revue d'histoire économique et sociale*, XXIX (1951), 70.

10. Antoine Prost, *La C.G.T. à l'époque du Front Populaire: 1934–1939* (Paris, 1964), 123–30; George Lefranc, *Le mouvement syndical sous la troisième république* (Paris, 1967), 275.

11. Archives Nationales, F[7] (13562). Police reports to the Minister of Labor, Jan. 13, 15, 1934.

12. D. J. Leab, "'United We Eat': The Creation and Organization of the Unemployment Councils in 1930," *Labor History*, VIII (1967), 300–15; Alex Baskin, "The Ford Hunger March—1932," *ibid.*, XIII (1972), 331–45; Roy Rosenzweig, "Radicals and the Jobless: the Musteites and the Unemployment Leagues, 1932–1936," *ibid.*, XVI (1975), 52–77; Irving Bernstein, *The Lean Years: A History of the American Worker, 1920–1933* (Baltimore, 1966), 416–35. See also E. W. Bakke, *Citizens Without Work* (New Haven, 1940), 71–84.

13. Wal Hannington, *Unemployed Struggles: 1919–1936* (London, 1936), 202–3, 232–3, 288; Noreen Branson and Margot Heinemann, *Britain in the 1930's* (London, 1971), 28–32, 87, 90. Of the twelve points in the NUMW's "unemployed charter" of 1929, only the vague number six, "introduce national plans of work schemes at trade union rates and conditions" could be said really to deal with reducing unemployment.

14. A Pennsylvania study of school children showed a 50 per cent increase in the number that were undernourished in a single year. J. M. Williams, *Human Aspects of Unemployment: With Special Reference to the Effects of the Depression on Children* (Chapel Hill, 1933), 54–5. For Britain and Germany, see Branson and Heinemann, *Britain in the 1930's*, 202–20; Pilgrim Trust, *Men Without Work* (Cambridge, 1938), 133–5; George Orwell, *The Road to Wigan Pier* (New York, 1961), 23, 60, 72–3, 89; Allen Hutt, *The Condition of the Working Classes in Britain* (London, 1933), *passim*; R. P. Lopes, "The Economic Depression and Public Health," *International Labour Review*, XXIX (1934), 793; Mowat, *Britain Between the Wars*, 492, 503–17. "No matter how much the statistics pointed to a general increase in real income," Mowat writes, "there was no doubt . . . that very many families were still, in the thirties, ill-fed, ill-housed, ill cared for when illness struck." (502).

15. Sauvy, *Histoire économique*, 2: 121; B. S. Rountree, *Poverty and Progress* (London, 1941).

16. Gabrielle Letellier, *et al.*, *Enquête sur le chômage* (Paris, 1938–49), 3: 310; Pilgrim Trust, *Men Without Work*, 135; Lopes, "Depression and Public Health," 795.

17. *The New York Times*, Dec. 6, 1930; Letellier, *Enquête sur le chômage*, 3: 202–3, 209; Marie Jahoda, P. F. Lazarsfeld, and Hans Zeisel, *Marienthal: The Sociography of an Unemployed Community* (Chicago, 1971), 26, 30; Lopes, "Depression and Public Health," 789–90; M. Incze, "Conditions of the Masses in Hungary," *Acta Historica*, III (1954), 12, 19–20, 25–32, 51–67; Mark Mitnitsky, "The Economic and Social Effects of Industrial Development in Hungary," *International Labour Review*, XXXIX (1939), 459–73.

18. Orwell, *Wigan Pier*, 84–9; Lazarsfeld, *Marienthal*, 27n, 55; Jean Rosner, "An Inquiry into the Life of Unemployed Workers in Poland," *International Labour Review*, XXVII (1933), 388; Letellier,

Enquête sur le chômage, 3: 41; Claude Thouvenot and Arnette Minot, "Incidence de la crise de 1929 sur les consommations en Meurthe-et-Moselle," *Annales de L'Est* (1970 no. 3), 239; Philip Eisenberg and P. F. Lazarsfeld, "The Psychological Effects of Unemployment," *Psychological Bulletin*, XXXV (1938), 360; Siegfried Kracauer, *Strassen in Berlin und anderswo* (Frankfurt-am-Main, 1964), 93. See also H. L. Smith, *New Survey of London Life and Labour* (London, 1930–35), 1: 14—"Different households . . . obtain different amounts of satisfaction from the same incomes, for there is an art of expenditure and household economy, no less than of acquisition."

19. Thouvenot and Minot, "Consommations en Meurthe-et-Moselle," 242; F. A. Bland, "Unemployment and Relief in Australia," *International Labour Review*, XXX (1934), 53; Enrique Siewers, "Unemployment in Argentina," *ibid.*, XXXI (1935), 798-9; Lopes, "Depression and Public Health," 788; E. H. Sutherland and H. J. Locke, *Twenty Thousand Homeless Men: A Study of Unemployed Men in Chicago Shelters* (Chicago, 1936), 34–5, 52–69; Incze, "Masses in Hungary," 87–8.

20. E. W. Bakke, *The Unemployed Man: A Social Study* (London, 1933), 64–7. After his more elaborate research in New Haven, Bakke described the process in greater detail. 1) *Momentum Stability*, marked by the expectation of regaining the lost position, economizing on luxuries, a negative attitude toward outside help. 2) *Unstable Equilibrium*, marked by hectic job-seeking, severe economizing, the use of credit. Blame is placed mainly on "fate" or "luck." 3) *Disorganization*, marked by abandonment of the search for a job, disregard for personal appearance, isolation from society, little concern for the future, willingness to accept charity. 4) *Experimental Readjustment*, marked by the resumption of job hunting without a sense of urgency, the spending of money when available but doing without it when it was not, the accepting of relief or charity as a matter of course, the development of new interests, such as hobbies, and the willingness to accept the reality of a dependent position. 5) *Permanent Readjustment*, the solidification of stage 4. Bakke, *Citizens Without Work*, 155–77. Analyzers of the Polish autobiographies, dealing with more impressionistic and subjective evidence, were satisfied with a simpler classification: 1) Feverish, optimistic search for work. 2) Pessimism. 3) Apathy. Bowhan Zawadski and P. F. Lazarsfeld, "The Psychological Consequences of Unemployment," *Journal of Social Psychology*, VI (1935), 224–51; Rosner, "Unemployed Workers in Poland," 384–5. British, Italian, and Belgian researchers reached almost identical conclusions. See H. L. Beales and R. S. Lambert, eds., *Memoirs of the Unemployed* (London, 1934), 26; Eisenberg and Lazarsfeld, "Psychological Effects," 378; Guillaume Jacquemyns, "Les chômeurs devant l'opinion publique," Institut Universitaire d'Information Sociale et Économique, *Bulletin* (1949), no 4, 8–9.

21. Lazarsfeld, *Marienthal*, 45–65.

22. The sociologist Karl Mannheim, who was familiar with the work of Lazarsfeld, Bakke, and other contemporary investigators,

related the apathy of the unemployed to the destruction of "the 'life plan' of the individual," the erosion of the hopes and expectations which are central to active participation in any society. *Man and Society in an Age of Reconstruction: Studies in Modern Social Structure* (New York, 1940), 104n, 181, 220n.

23. H. M. Cassidy, *Unemployment and Relief in Ontario, 1929–1932* (Toronto, 1932), 253; Henri Fuss and D. C. Tact, "Unemployment Benefits and Measures for Occupying the Unemployed in Great Britain," *International Labour Review*, XXVII (1933), 597–8. Lazarsfeld called Marienthal "*die müde Gemeinschaft*," the weary community. Its citizens had "forgotten how to hurry." When one of the researchers, timing the lethargic movements of the villagers on the main street, observed one person actually trotting along, he discovered that it was the village idiot. (36–44, 66–77, esp. 66–7.)

24. Siewers, "Depression in Argentina," 798.

25. Lillian Brandt, *An Impressionistic View of the Winter of 1930–31 in New York City* (New York, 1932), 17; Mirra Komarovsky, *The Unemployed Man and His Family—The Effects of Unemployment upon the Status of the Man in Fifty-Nine Families* (New York, 1940), 74; Abram Kardiner, "The Role of Economic Security in the Adaptation of the Individual," *The Family*, XVII (1936), 187–97; A. C. Tucker, "Some Correlates of Certain Attitudes of the Unemployed," *Archives of Psychology* (1940), no. 245; Nathan Israeli, "Distress in the Outlook of Lancashire and Scottish Unemployed," *Journal of Applied Psychology*, XIX (1935), 67–9.

26. Orwell, *Wigan Pier*, 60, 81; Kracauer, *Strassen in Berlin*, 81, 72, 74; R. A. Billington, "Government and the Arts: The W. P. A. Experience," *American Quarterly*, XIII (1961), 471; Maxine Davis, *The Lost Generation: A Portrait of American Youth Today* (New York, 1936), 27; Sherwood Anderson, *Puzzled America* (New York, 1935), 46; Walter Greenwood, *Love on the Dole* (London, 1969), 169; Rudolf Brunngraber, *Karl and the Twentieth Century* (New York, 1933), *passim*; esp. 68, 203, 259, 265; Hans Fallada, *Little Man, What Now?* (New York, 1933), *passim*. In *Die Ehe des Arbeitslosen Martin Krug* (Oldenburg, 1932), a novel with a similar theme, Bruno Nelissen Haken wrote: "If [the unemployed] speak of the future, they mean tomorrow or the next day. They do not think of anything beyond that. And if a year passes, that time becomes yesterday, the next year, tomorrow." (71)

27. Sutherland and Locke, *20,000 Homeless Men*, 150; Rosner, "Unemployed Workers in Poland," 385. After studying the Polish autobiographies, Rosner was struck by the "deep-seated love of work" that permeated them. (391).

28. Orwell, *Wigan Pier*, 80. Orwell claimed that by 1937 the unemployed were beginning to realize that they were not personally responsible for their dependent state.

29. For a general discussion of this subject, see J. A. Garraty, "Radicalism in the Great Depression," in L. H. Blair, ed., *Essays on Radicalism in American Life* (Austin, 1972), 102–13.

30. Maurice Duperrey, ed., *Le Chômage* (Paris, 1933), 94; Ministry of Labour, *The Unemployment Problem in Germany* (London, 1931), 8; Hannington, *Unemployed Struggles, passim*, esp. 219, 265, 282–3, 288; Allen Hutt, *Postwar History of the British Working Class* (New York, 1938), 213–16. The American Bonus Army, it should be recalled, represented a special interest group seeking immediate payment of veterans' benefits not due under the law until 1945. Most of the marchers were no doubt unemployed, but they were not demonstrating for general unemployment relief or for the payment of the bonus only to unemployed veterans. See Roger Daniels, *The Bonus March: An Episode of the Great Depression* (Westport, Conn., 1971).

31. Rosner, "Unemployed Workers in Poland," 390; Lambert and Beales, *Memoirs of the Unemployed*, 198; Sutherland and Locke, *20,000 Homeless Men*, 13; Lazarsfeld, *Marienthal*, 40–1; Jan Beishuizen and Evert Werkman, *De magere jaren: Nederland in de crisistijd, 1929–1939* (Leiden, 1968), 126; Bakke, *Unemployed Man*, 60–1, 149, 151, 236; Bakke, *Citizens Without Work*, 46–70, esp. 56–7, 60–1; Matthew Josephson, *Infidel in the Temple: A Memoir of the Nineteen-Thirties* (New York, 1967), 75–81; James Rorty, *Where Life is Better: An Unsentimental Journey* (New York, 1936), 9–10, 27–8; Zawadski and Lazarsfeld, "Psychological Consequences of Unemployment," 245–9. Rosner mentions reports of beggars "growl[ing] at each other like dogs." (391).

32. Sutherland and Locke, *20,000 Homeless Men*, 160–1. Maxine Davis recorded as typical the following exchange with an unemployed youth in Youngstown, Ohio: "If you don't like the way the President is doing things, why don't you men here organize and do something about it?" "Naw. What's the use? The politicians run everything, the dirty crooks. . . . An' the big boys run the politicians. I'm wise, lady, I'm wise." *Lost Generation*, 31–2.

33. Lauren Gilfillan, *I Went to Pit College* (New York, 1934), 259. The miners were not fascists either. They habitually referred to mine officials and other "capitalists" as "Mussolini." (19).

34. Walter Greenwood, *There Was a Time* (Middlesex, 1969), 150–2; Gabriel Almond and H. D. Lasswell, "Aggressive Behavior by Clients toward Public Relief Administrators: A Configurative Analysis," *American Political Science Review*, XL (1934), 643–55.

35. Annie Kriegel, *The French Communists: Profile of a People* (Chicago, 1972), 75–7; Dufraisse, "Movement ouvrier 'rouge,'" *Mouvements ouvriers*, p. 181; Werne Conze, "La crise économique en Allemagne entre 1929 et 1933," *ibid.*, 56.

36. Louis Adamic, *My America: 1928–1938* (New York, 1938), 298.

37. Peter Loewenberg, "The Psychohistorical Origins of the Nazi Youth Cohort," *American Historical Review*, LXXVI (1971), 1457–1502, esp. 1461–3, 1468, 1501; Stephan Thernstrom, *The Other Bostonians: Poverty and Progress in the American Metropolis, 1880–1970* (Cambridge, Mass., 1973), 233.

38. Walter Galenson and Arnold Zellner, "International Comparison of Unemployment Rates," in National Bureau of Economic

Research, *The Measurement and Behavior of Unemployment* (Princeton, 1957), 454–6. France may have been another exception—it is difficult to be sure because French unemployment statistics were particularly inadequate. See *ibid.*, 515–26, esp. 523.

39. See, for example, League of Nations, *World Economic Survey, 1935–1936* (Geneva, 1936), 149: "Perhaps the most fundamental, and certainly the most general of . . . trends is the increasing measure of social responsibility which is felt by public opinion, and therefore by Governments, for the welfare of the wage-earning classes of the population. . . ."

40. See, for example, Lionel Robbins, *Economic Planning and International Order* (London, 1937), *passim*, esp. 320–1; Robbins, *Great Depression*, 117, 144–9.

ALONG THE "AMERICAN WAY": THE NEW DEAL'S WORK RELIEF PROGRAMS FOR THE UNEMPLOYED

William W. Bremer

Because historians have accepted economic innovation as the standard by which to measure the New Deal's accomplishments, New Deal historiography has tended to discount the importance that reformers of the 1930s attached to the psychological effects of many federal programs.[1] Among American social work reformers, for example, stock manipulations and monopolistic business arrangements held less social significance than the traumatic psychic dislocation caused by simple joblessness. Unemployed, a man lost his "self-respect . . . ambition and pride," testified settlement headworker Lillian D. Wald.[2] New Deal Administrator Harry L. Hopkins noted, "a workless man has little status at home and less with his friends," a condition which reinforces his own sense of failure. Finally, Hopkins observed, "Those who are forced to accept charity, no matter how unwillingly, are first pitied, then disdained" by society in general.[3]

The antidote for joblessness was not charity but work. United by this belief and led by a group of New York reformers, American social workers campaigned for work relief programs at the local, state, and federal levels of government.[4] William Matthews, who founded New York City's Emergency Work Bureau in 1930, Homer Folks, who directed the legislative fight for the state's Temporary Emergency Relief Administration (TERA) in 1931, and Hopkins, who served as executive secretary and chairman of TERA before heading the New Deal's Federal Emergency Relief Administration (FERA), Civil Works Administration (CWA), and Works Progress Administration (WPA), espoused the idea that work conserved morale. "It was a habit [the unemployed] liked, and from which they chiefly drew their self-respect," Hopkins explained.[5] In addition to being psychologically valuable in itself, because it focused a person's productive energies and mental talents, work restored his social prestige, raised him in the esteem of his family and friends, and revitalized his self-confidence. "Give a man a dole and you save his body and destroy his spirit," Hopkins once proclaimed; "give him a job and pay him an assured wage, and you save both the body and the spirit."[6]

As Hopkins' statement suggests, the implementation of work relief programs during the Great Depression exemplified the New Dealers' concern with the psychological impact of their policies and programs. If general economic recovery and the physical well-being of the unemployed had been their overriding concerns, then New Dealers might have appropriately supported massive deficit expenditures for direct relief to give jobless people money to support the economy and themselves. New Deal administrators and their social work consultants, however, specifically rejected direct relief, because it threatened to undermine morale.[7] "The receipt of relief without work by an able-bodied person is inevitably humiliating, terribly distressing," argued Folks, "and idleness coupled with dependence [upon public charity] is a thoroughly abnormal experience and strongly tends to demoralization."[8] Work relief preserved "the initiative, the virility, the independence and sense of responsibility in the American people," according to Matthews.[9] Work relief was seen as an "American Way" to achieve these psychological goals, because it made public assistance something earned by work, not granted by charity, and because it thereby infused symbols of respectability into the stream of relief.[10] By employing people in jobs that utilized their skills, by compensating them according to the value of their labor, and by guaranteeing them regular incomes that would insure personal autonomy, work relief drew too upon American traditions of self-help and individual initiative. Thus, it also exemplified the New Dealers' acceptance and reinforcement of traditional cultural norms.

Specifically, the New Dealers' conception of work relief derived from values inherent in a capitalistic ethos and incorporated many of the practices of private employment. Therefore, despite the New Dealers' emphasis on psychological concerns, the history of work relief serves as a case study for their acceptance of capitalism and their proclivity to innovate within the confines of the capitalistic order. In the case of work relief, the New Dealers' desire to preserve the morale of the unemployed eventually collided with their assumption that they must maintain the capitalistic system, on which work relief depended for many of its distinguishing features. If work programs had precisely duplicated conditions of employment in private industry and fully satisfied the psychological needs of the unemployed, then the government would have entered into direct competition with private employers, possibly forcing more severe economic contractions and perhaps undermining the nation's private enterprise system. In addition, the unemployed might have become permanently dependent upon government for work. New Dealers responded to their dilemma by keeping work relief employment less attractive than private employment, thereby protecting private employers against public competition and assuring clear incentives to direct the unemployed back into private industry.

Primarily, however, New Dealers sought to make work relief more attractive than conventional forms of direct relief, which Matthews condemned as "so unpleasant, so disagreeable, in fact so insulting to decent people that they stay away from the places where it is given."[11] First, the unemployed were subjected to means tests to prove their destitution, a procedure that Hopkins described as fostering the "wholesale degradation of [their] finest sensibilities."[12] Second, direct relief was given in kind, so that others prescribed what the unemployed should eat and wear. Finally, relief investigators intervened in the lives of the unemployed, telling them "where and how they should live . . . [and] how they should order their relationships within the family group, with their relatives, neighbors and friends."[13] Viewed as charity, direct relief bore a stigma derived from traditional assumptions that workless people were personally responsible for their misfortunes and incapable of managing their own affairs.

For two reasons—because the Depression was a disaster that clearly transcended the individual's control and because the vast majority of its human casualties had been self-supporting before 1929—social workers hoped to transform traditional attitudes toward the jobless. To do so, they portrayed jobless persons as victims of untoward circumstances. Matthews depicted them as victimized by "a material progress which has failed to bring a sustained adequacy of life to all those able and willing to work."[14] Moreover, Hopkins declared, "Three or four million heads of families don't turn into tramps and cheats overnight, nor do they lose the habits and standards of a lifetime. . . ."[15] The victims of society's economic collapse, social workers argued, were not moral degenerates nor mental misfits, but normally hard-working and self-sufficient, average Americans. "They don't drink any more than the rest of us," Hopkins claimed "they don't lie any more, they're no lazier than the rest of us. . . ."[16]

Contending that the unemployed were normal Americans who still valued individual initiative and self-help as personal virtues of the highest order, social workers expressed both the insights that they had gained from working with the jobless and their justification for creating morale-maintaining work relief programs. The gist of their thinking was that it was unnecessary to alter the attitudes or behavior of normally productive people who avoided charity as the final, degrading proof of personal failure. Rather than further demean relief recipients, public welfare policies would have to be "more considerate of the spirit, the condition, the feelings of the people who come for relief," Folks explained.[17] And because America's unemployed themselves seemed to equate work with personal worth, the idea that every American possessed "a right to work" and a corresponding "right to a job" assumed a place at the forefront of New Deal welfare policies.[18] Providing a justification for work relief in the abstract, however, was only the first step toward establishing it as a program that could meet the psychological needs of the unemployed. Indeed, the social workers' major task was to assure the jobless that they were not charity cases obliged to accept the treatment traditionally accorded individuals who could not or would not fend for themselves.

In an effort to achieve this objective, social workers demanded that the unemployed be freed from the restrictions on personal freedom that accompanied conventional relief systems. Work relief recipients were to be paid wages. "Earning wages conserves morale," Folks argued; "it is a normal experience; it is constructive."[19] Moreover, wages were to be paid in cash rather than in kind, freeing families from constraints upon choice and stimulating their sense of self-sufficiency. As Matthews explained, cash "allow[s] people to shop where they want, holding up their heads and paying their own bills."[20] With the implementation of such policies, social workers believed, work relief would be set on a footing clearly different from that supporting other relief programs, making it possible for the unemployed to retain personal rights and privileges usually reserved for employed persons.

Social workers also demanded that work relief reinforce the sense of personal worth that the unemployed associated with normal employment. Employment on work projects, therefore, was to be offered before the jobless became destitute, in order to avoid the debilitating effects of advanced deprivation as well as the implication that work relief was a masked substitute for charity.[21] Men were to be assigned to projects for which they were physically and mentally suited. They were to be paid wages sufficient to preclude the need for additional relief and at rates that complemented the value of their labor in the normal employment market.[22] Continued employment on work projects was to be conditional upon satisfactory job performance, because this was a fundamental requisite for private employment. "The sooner work relief can be given as nearly as possible the same status as that of work under regular conditions of hiring and discharging," Matthews suggested, "the sooner it will command the respect . . . of the worker . . . [and] the sooner will the indifferent and lazy be sifted out of it. . . ."[23] Finally, work projects had to be useful—useful in the sense that work relief recipients felt that their efforts were well spent, and useful in the sense that other people respected them as contributors to the betterment of the community.[24] If work relief approximated the normal employment experience, social workers contended, then the unemployed would be able to view themselves as productive, responsible members of society, even though their work was supported by public funds.

The thrust of the social workers' demands was to maximize work relief's work aspects and to minimize its relief aspects as much as possible. Every provision that advanced a sense of personal worth and responsibility—cash wages, appropriate work assignments, business-like standards, and useful projects—was considered a step away from the stigma of charity and forward in the direction of conserving morale. Ideally, social workers themselves would "drop out of the picture," Hopkins once suggested, since the highly motivated, able-bodied unemployed did not need their services.[25] Thus social workers hoped to set in motion a program that would carry out their design of psychological uplift without requiring their direct intervention into the lives of the unemployed.

New Deal relief administrators frequently invoked the social workers' work relief ideal as their justification for federal work programs.[26] But the New Deal came close to achieving that ideal for only a few months during the winter of 1933–1934. In November 1933, confronted by the likelihood that millions of Americans would remain unemployed throughout his first winter as President, Franklin D. Roosevelt signed an executive order that enabled relief administrators to create a work program of their own design.

Hopkins and his colleagues boldly ignored the established machinery of relief, inviting two million Americans to apply for jobs with CWA without being subjected to means tests and investigations. Moreover, they paid workers the prevailing wage rates of private industry, adopted an hours schedule that resembled the normal working week, and organized self-help and production-for-use projects that utilized developed skills and produced basic consumer goods.[27] In effect, by avoiding relief procedures and by risking competition with private employers, CWA officials offered "real" jobs for work relief. Within weeks after CWA began, however, the President announced its termination.

In general, political pressures figured importantly in determining the fate of New Deal work programs. Recalcitrant taxpayers and budget-minded politicians refused to support costly expenditures for wages, materials, and equipment. Businessmen resisted government competition for surplus labor, contracts, and sales, while their workers feared that work relief would undermine private industry's jobs and wages.[28] New Dealers had to contend with the political reality that the primary concern of privately employed Americans was to maintain their own economic positions. In the case of CWA, however, such adverse political pressures seem to have been ineffective, since the popularity of work relief was at a high peak. When the New Deal reversed course and abandoned CWA, demonstrations were organized to protest Roosevelt's decision, letters poured into the White House and Congress, congressional hearings were called, and a bill was introduced in Congress to extend the life of the program indefinitely.[29] More important, an effective conservative coalition had not yet formed in Congress, business was still on the defensive, and what organized political pressure the New Deal did confront came from the left, which applauded CWA and urged its continuance.[30] Nonetheless, Roosevelt stuck to his decision to kill the program.

The President's motives were clear: he was influenced by a budget-conscious concern with the cost of CWA, and he feared that the program might "become a habit with the country."[31] But why did Hopkins and other social workers in the administration support this decision? Because they considered CWA an extraordinary measure, introduced temporarily to meet an emergency. "[I]t must be assumed in this office and everywhere else," Hopkins told his staff early in December 1933, "that Civil Works was set up purely as an emergency measure; that there is no implication in this of any permanent policy in the government." The most that might be expected was "a continuance of this thing through the middle of March, on a descending scale after that and out by the middle of May or the 1st of June [1934]."[32] From its beginning, therefore, New Dealers refused to champion CWA as permanent federal policy, and their refusal suggests that the work relief ideal probably violated their own cautious conception of the "American Way."[33] Perhaps their conservative assumptions and beliefs even thwarted later opportunities to free work relief permanently from the constraints of tradition. As late as February 1934, after Roosevelt announced his intention to terminate CWA, Hopkins might have used the public outcry that greeted that announcement to try to change the President's mind. Instead he and his associates retreated quietly to the policies and practices of FERA.

In keeping with traditional relief practices and in contrast to the abandoned CWA policies, both FERA and WPA—which together spanned the critical years from 1933 to 1939—required means tests and investigations to determine eligibility for public assistance.[34] Consequently, throughout the 1930s, social workers continued to be the primary agents through whom work relief was administered. They were called upon to study every aspect of a family's financial situation and were privy to the most intimate details of family life. During the period of FERA, for example, a "budgetary deficiency" approach was used to ascertain appropriate earnings: a family's existing income, if any, was subtracted from a budgeted estimate of its needs, and the difference between those figures became the amount to be earned through work relief.[35] Nor did social workers "drop out of the picture" when standardized earnings replaced budgetary allowances, as happened under WPA, because supplementary relief was still required by the many families whose needs exceeded WPA earnings, and these families remained dependent upon direct relief and the supervision of social workers.[36]

In addition to being bound by traditional relief procedures, FERA and WPA conformed to an unwritten, conservative rule that prohibited government interference with an ongoing capitalistic economy. "Policy from the first was not to compete with private business," Hopkins explained.[37] New Dealers banned construction projects that might take business away from private contractors as well as projects that would involve the government in the production, distribution, or sale of goods and services normally provided by private employers. Projects were restricted to work that "would not otherwise be done," and job assignments had to exclude such fields as manufacturing, merchandizing, and marketing.[38] Within these limits, New Dealers did make a concerted effort to provide work appropriate to the varying skills of the unemployed. In general, however, relief officials were pledged to pioneer a new realm of employment beyond the frontiers of private enterprise.

Furthermore, their ability to make the new frontier of public employment habitable was severely limited by a policy of noncompetitive earnings, designed to keep the government from vying with private business for the labor of the American worker. Indeed, the New Deal was committed to maintain incentives to guide relief recipients back to the settled world of private enterprise, and inferior earnings served as a most effective incentive. Yet relief wages had to be sufficient to sustain not only the bodies but also the morale of the unemployed, who were accustomed to hourly rates paid by private business.[39] The morale-maintaining capacity of high wages was stressed when CWA began paying workers at rates that conformed to the value of their labor in the general employment market. Copying CWA's pattern, WPA classified workers as unskilled, skilled, or professional, adopted a graduated wage scale for each of these categories, and paid workers the prevailing local hourly rates for the type of work they did.[40] These measures were intended to preserve occupational integrity and to emphasize the differing status accorded different kinds of work by a capitalistic economy.[41]

The New Dealers' determination to keep relief jobs and incomes noncompetitive, however, led them to impose maximums on monthly earnings at each level. This policy limited the number of hours a person could work at his prevailing wage, thereby assuring that he could not earn as much as his counterpart in private industry.[42] "I ask you," Hopkins demanded rhetorically, "is it reasonable to suppose that an American worker . . . will reject private employment to remain in such a situation?"[43] By instituting graduated wage scales and prevailing wage rates, on the one hand, and by limiting work hours and total earnings, on the other, work relief administrators essayed a delicate and precarious balancing act. The evolution of the New Dealers' wage-hour formula for keeping relief wages high and relief incomes low, therefore, clearly illustrated their commitment both to make work relief a morale-maintaining program and to protect capitalistic enterprise against public competition.

Clearly, FERA and WPA provided work, but was it "real" work and was it free of the stigma of charity? The political left attacked New Deal work programs as hypocritical reforms intended to save capitalism rather than the unemployed, while the right charged them with destroying American traditions of self-reliant individualism.[44] Neither of these political factions, however, assessed work relief with as much insight as social workers outside the New Deal, who understood the work relief ideal and closely observed various programs operating in cities and states across the nation. In their estimation, the New Deal failed on both counts: its work programs neither offered "real" work that complemented the aspirations of the unemployed nor eliminated the stigma of charity that undermined feelings of personal worth.

The social workers pointed out that, by retaining conventional relief checks on the unemployed, New Deal work programs departed significantly from the work relief ideal. The stringent application of means tests delayed assistance until destitution set in, which exposed the jobless to the demoralizing effects of advanced deprivation.[45] Moreover, it scarcely seemed plausible that the unemployed could avoid perceiving themselves as "charity" cases, since they were subjected to tests, investigations, and supervision traditionally applied to paupers and other unemployables.[46] Fundamentally, the critics observed, the New Deal did not offer employment in lieu of relief, because it did not guarantee work and jobs as rights afforded every American regardless of need.[47]

Even after a person was accepted for work relief, social workers complained, he was scarcely assured a job that utilized his physical and mental abilities. Since relief administrators could not establish jobs in competition with private enterprise, the occupations of individuals such as druggists, assembly-line workers, and securities analysts were not sustained by work programs. Moreover, the New Deal's categories of work were "jerry-built" classifications. Bank tellers, real estate agents, insurance salesmen, and other businessmen joined physicians, dentists, lawyers, and teachers in the professional category, which qualified them for jobs writing guidebooks, serving as nurses' aids, teaching immigrants the English language, and supervising children's playground activities. The unskilled category amounted to a hodgepodge of individuals for whom manual labor was the only common denominator. As a re-

sult, barbers, shoemakers, and tailors, along with semi- and unskilled workers such as machine operatives, teamsters, and janitors,
were directed to construction projects.[48] Indeed, much of the occupational dislocation that its critics associated with work relief derived from the New Deal's emphasis upon construction.[49] The
"very nature [of] the work . . . was outside the workers' experience,
if they had any other than that of common laborers," according to
a student of WPA's program in Illinois.[50] In fact, a Pennsylvania
study disclosed that 61 percent of WPA work assignments were
different from the workers' usual occupations.[51]

Social workers belabored the New Deal by questioning the
ability of its work programs to maintain morale. Did not inappropriate, unwieldy classifications and arbitrary work assignments destroy subtle distinctions associated with American conceptions of
job status? Was not a wheelwright demeaned when he was classified as an unskilled worker and assigned a job as a cement finisher?
Did not a sales manager lose respect among his peers when he
became a playground supervisor?[52] Why not continue CWA's innovative policy, turning the productive abilities of the unemployed
to the advantage of the unemployed by allowing them to provide
themselves with essential goods and services? Such a policy would
psychologically benefit dentists, barbers, tailors, and others who
could pursue their regular work. Even machine operatives might
be put to work in idle factories, producing goods needed by the
unemployed.[53]

Social workers also criticized WPA's wage-hour formula. Paying men high hourly wages while severely limiting their hours of
work, they observed, imposed idleness upon workers who earned
their maximum allotments after only a few days of employment. A
highly paid mechanic, for example, earned his WPA "security wage"
in one week, leaving him with three workless weeks each month.[54]
If it was work that maintained morale, critics argued, then such a
policy denied people the morale-sustaining value of regular employment. In addition, skills were not conserved by men who were
inactive for long periods of time. The policy encouraged ineffi-
ciency, because interrupting a worker's routine made him less productive on the job, and because staggered work schedules undermined continuity on work projects.[55]

In addition to questioning the quality of work provided by the
New Deal, social work critics charged that work relief programs
were economically inadequate. At no time did they employ more

than one third of the nation's jobless people.[56] The vast majority remained dependent upon direct relief, which, after August 1935, was provided by states and localities without the assistance of the federal government. In addition, initially high earning levels collapsed under the pressure of insufficient funding. Within three to four months after the beginning of CWA and WPA, monthly work relief incomes had fallen to the same level as direct relief, which meant that the man who worked for his relief received no more than the man who did not.[57] Moreover, 75 to 80 percent of the workers were employed as unskilled laborers and paid on the lowest wage scale.[58] This fact made the idea of graduated incomes to emphasize job status seem ludicrous, especially since many workers were not pursuing their normal occupations or earning incomes that supported their normal way of living. "The wage paid for [work relief] should be the same for all, irrespective of individual former standards of living or of former occupations . . . ," Matthews protested.[59] Finally, in an economy already characterized by depressed wage levels and straitened personal incomes, the New Deal's policy of noncompetitive earnings relegated work relief recipients to the cellar of subsistence living, which was a fact sufficient in itself to cause doubt that work relief did much to maintain morale.[60]

By the late 1930s, social work leaders like Matthews had become totally disillusioned with New Deal work programs. In his autobiography, New York's pioneer of work relief noted the continuing presence of an "army of the unemployed" still managed by an "army of welfare workers," in spite of the New Deal's promises both to return American workers to regular jobs and to eliminate the stigma of charity. Matthews also believed that, after years of being shuffled from one relief program to another, "many [of the unemployed had] lost the desire to plan and manage their own lives" and had "accepted the role of dependency on government." As he viewed the situation, the New Deal had created a ubiquitous relief "mechanism" that stood "in the way of natural human relations." Between an unemployed man and his work relief earnings stood need tests and investigations that violated his privacy, "made work" that frequently did not utilize his skills, and a wage-hour formula that seldom gave him a decent income on which to live.[61] Matthews articulated the views of many other social work observers, who concluded that the New Deal's complex policies and complicated techniques, in effect, denied many citizens the right to useful public employment at a respectable wage.[62]

It may well be impossible to determine whether or not the New Deal served the psychological needs and maintained the morale of those who were employed in its work relief programs. As a contemporary student of WPA observed, "A clear estimate of the spiritual benefits received from WPA by those whom it supports is [not] easily come by, for it is ... difficult to weigh such qualities as self-respect, morale, and the maintenance of skills."[63] Nonetheless, it is obvious that New Dealers made a gallant attempt to sustain the unemployed psychologically. Even at poverty levels of support, jobs and cash wages did infuse the stream of relief with morale-preserving symbols of respectability. As Hopkins put it, "the unemployed themselves want work," and the New Deal did create jobs.[64] In addition, New Dealers pointed to hundreds of new or refurbished buildings, thousands of miles of freshly paved roads, and countless paintings, plays, and books that demonstrated how productive those jobs had been.

Work relief as applied by the New Deal was, however, a gravely flawed conception. Derived from private industry's experience with rewards systems that manipulated the terms of work to enhance employee morale, work relief remained bound to the conservative assumptions of its business exemplar.[65] It treated the unemployed within the confines of a work-centered culture, emphasizing job status at a time when jobs were dear and the status associated with them a luxury. It reinforced private enterprise's values of self-reliance and individual initiative, values belied by an industrial depression that cost people their jobs regardless of personal merit. And it was expected to achieve the impossible result of eliminating the stigma of charity without simultaneously deterring people from seeking private employment. Taken together, these points reveal the upshot of the work relief ideal: its rewards method of maintaining morale derived from a model of private employment, but that method could not be perfected in public employment without inhibiting the movement of people back into private industry. As a WPA adviser noted in 1939, private employers used a rewards system, because "high morale inevitably leads to enthusiasm for the employing organization and a desire to remain with it"; and that likelihood was antithetical to the New Dealers' commitment to return workers to regular employment.[66]

Could the New Deal have done more to make work relief suitable to the needs of the unemployed? When accounting for the economic conservatism of many New Deal policies and programs, historians often stress the political obstacles that existed independent of New Deal authority and that inhibited major structural changes. They emphasize that the electorate never gave Roosevelt a mandate to transform America. And, as time passed, conservative opposition to the New Deal grew in intensity and influence, forcing New Dealers to seek political expedients that precluded radical innovations.[67] Yet historical arguments that New Dealers accomplished as much as could be expected overlook economically radical and, more importantly, psychologically meaningful programs like CWA, which were achieved and then rejected because of the New Dealers' own cautious conservatism. Although CWA demonstrated the viability of doing without means tests, investigations, budgetary allowances, and noncompetitive work projects, New Dealers willingly cancelled the possibility of making it permanent. Finally, in 1943, when war had solved the problem of mass unemployment, they abandoned work relief altogether.

In trying both to maintain the morale of the unemployed and to avoid competition with private enterprise, New Dealers tried "to live by contrasting rules of the game," which sociologist Robert S. Lynd found to be "one of the most characteristic aspects of our American culture" in 1939.[68] Despite their investment in work relief, New Dealers simply believed that private business was still America's most important institution and that people must "get on" eventually on their own—as did the "Middletown" Americans of their time.[69] "Our aim," Hopkins revealed, is "to supply to industry as many physically strong, mentally alert, skilled workers as we can." Moreover, work programs were never intended to be "a replica of the outside business world," where, New Dealers believed, the unemployed must eventually establish their dignity again.[70] As a consequence, they used work relief as a psychological weapon to fight a delaying action against demoralization and despair, while following an "American Way" that directed the unemployed back into jobs in private industry.

New Dealers never accepted work relief as a permanent national policy. Instead of guaranteeing a "right to work" by instituting programs to offer employment to people who experienced joblessness during good times as well as bad, they developed an unemployment insurance system to preclude the need to assist temporarily unemployed, able-bodied citizens at public expense. For work relief, the stigma of public dependency endured. Perhaps New Dealers even realized that their own intention to provide the unemployed with incentives to return to private employment reinforced the stigma of being "on relief," even when that relief aid was earned. They may have also feared, as did their President, the possibility of fostering dependency by creating an expectation among able-bodied people that the federal government would always provide jobs. Clearly, work relief did not conform fully to the American tradition of self-help, as its critics observed repeatedly. Nor did its New Deal designers ever expect it to fulfill the economic and social aspirations of Americans. It remained more relief than work, more charity than employment.

NOTES

1. Many historians stress the idea that the New Deal attacked economic problems head-on by giving more economic power to labor and government and less to business and by initiating limited experiments in income redistribution and deficit spending. See William E. Leuchtenburg, *Franklin D. Roosevelt and the New Deal: 1932–1940* (New York, 1963), 338–39; Richard Hofstadter, *The Age of Reform: From Bryan to F. D. R.* (New York, 1955), 316–18, 325; Robert H. Bremner, "Poverty in Perspective," John Braeman, Robert H. Bremner, Everett Walters, eds., *Change and Continuity in Twentieth-Century America* (New York, 1966), 275–76. Other historians have concluded that the New Deal did not curb business' powers markedly, did not redistribute wealth, and did not spend at a rate needed to propel the nation out of the Great Depression. See Barton J. Bernstein, "The New Deal: The Conservative Achievements of Liberal Reform," Barton J. Bernstein, ed., *Towards a New Past: Dissenting Essays in American History* (New York, 1968), 264, 273, 278; Paul K. Conkin, *FDR and the Origins of the Welfare State* (New York, 1967), 23, 50–52, 69–81.

2. Lillian D. Wald, *Windows on Henry Street* (Boston, 1934), 231.

3. Harry L. Hopkins, "They'd Rather Work," *Collier's*, XCVI (Nov. 16, 1935), 7; Harry L. Hopkins, *Spending to Save: The Complete Story of Relief* (New York, 1936), 109.

4. Joanna C. Colcord, William C. Koplovitz, and Russell H. Kurtz, *Emergency Work Relief: As Carried Out in Twenty-Six American Communities, 1930–1931, with Suggestions for Setting Up a Program* (New York, 1932), 15–18; Joanna C. Colcord, "Social Work and the First Federal Relief Programs," *Proceedings of the National Conference of Social Work* (New York, 1943), 382–94. See also William W. Bremer, "New York City's Family of Social Servants

and the Politics of Welfare: A Prelude to the New Deal, 1928–1933" (doctoral dissertation, Stanford University, 1973), 140–69, 280–82.

5. Hopkins, *Spending to Save*, 109.

6. Harry L. Hopkins, untitled address, March 14, 1936, United Neighborhood Houses Papers (Social Welfare History Archives, University of Minnesota).

7. See Harry L. Hopkins, "Federal Emergency Relief," *Vital Speeches of the Day*, I (Dec. 31, 1934), 211.

8. Homer Folks, "Planning Work Relief," address, June 25, 1931, Homer Folks Papers (Columbia School of Social Work Library). During 1935, the New Deal discontinued federal grants to the states for direct relief. According to Harry Hopkins, New Dealers were "overjoyed to get out of the depressing business of direct relief." Hopkins, "They'd Rather Work," 7. See also Josephine Chapin Brown, *Public Relief, 1929–1939* (New York, 1940), 150–51.

9. William H. Matthews, "Relief Can Be Too Cheap," *Survey*, LXXI (Jan. 1935), 6.

10. Don D. Lescohier, "The Hybrid WPA," *Survey Midmonthly*, LXXV (June 1939), 167.

11. William H. Matthews to Paul Kellogg, Feb. 5, 1932, Survey Papers (Social Welfare History Archives, University of Minnesota).

12. Harry L. Hopkins, "The War on Distress," Howard Zinn, ed., *New Deal Thought* (Indianapolis, 1966), 152.

13. Brown, *Public Relief*, 223.

14. William H. Matthews, *Adventures in Giving* (New York, 1939), 230.

15. Hopkins, "They'd Rather Work," 7.

16. Quoted by Robert E. Sherwood, *Roosevelt and Hopkins: An Intimate History* (New York, 1948), 84. During the 1930s, social work generated a series of studies showing "that the unemployed were like everybody else," that they were "virtuous and wronged," and their their suffering derived, in part, from "thwarted middle-classness." William Stott, *Documentary Expression and Thirties America* (New York, 1973), 145–48, 156–59.

17. Homer Folks, "Home Relief in New York City: A Look Forward and Backward," Dec. 11, 1933, Henry Street Papers (Columbia University Library).

18. Hopkins, "The War on Distress," 153–54, 158.

19. Folks, "Planning Work Relief," Folks Papers.

20. Matthews to Robert F. Wagner, May 13, 1932, William H. Matthews Papers (New York Public Library).

21. Colcord, Koplovitz, and Kurtz, *Emergency Work Relief*, 142; Matthews to Robert Fechner, April 10, 1933, Matthews Papers.

22. [New York] State Charities Aid Association and [New York] Department of Social Welfare, "Work as a Means of Unemployment Relief" [June 1931], Herbert H. Lehman Papers (Columbia University Library); Welfare Council of New York City, Committee on the Emergency Financing of Social Work, "Report," July 8, 1932, *ibid.*

23. William H. Matthews, "These Past Five Years," *Survey Midmonthly*, LXXIV (March 1938), 72.

24. Welfare Council of New York City, Vocational Guidance and Family Service Sections, "Report to the Coordinating Committee on Agreements Reached at Three Joint Conferences on Work Relief," revised, Sept. 21, 1932, Henry Street Papers.

25. Hopkins, *Spending to Save*, 114.

26. See Corrington Gill, *Wasted Manpower: The Challenge of Unemployment* (New York, 1939), 160–61. Hopkins' published speeches and writings consistently drew upon the work relief ideal when describing New Deal policies, as did the writings of Josephine Brown, Arthur Burns, and Jacob Baker.

27. William Hodson, "A Review of Public Relief—Federal, State, and Local—As It Affects New York City," (Nov. 1933), Henry Street Papers; Hopkins, "The War on Distress," 151–58; Jacob Baker, "Work Relief: The Program Broadens," *New York Times Magazine* (Nov. 11, 1934), 6, 17. FERA also supported self-help and production-for-use projects during 1934.

28. Nels Anderson, "The War for the Wage," *Survey*, LXXI (June 1935), 164–65; Lescohier, "The Hybrid WPA," 168.

29. Russell Kurtz, "An End to Civil Works," *Survey*, LXX (Feb. 1934), 35; Sherwood, *Roosevelt and Hopkins*, 50–57; Searle F. Charles, *Minister of Relief: Harry Hopkins and the Depression* (Syracuse, 1963), 46–65.

30. James T. Patterson, "A Conservative Coalition Forms in Congress, 1933–1939," *Journal of American History*, LII (March 1966), 767; Leuchtenburg, *Roosevelt and the New Deal*, 91–94; Arthur M. Schlesinger, Jr., *The Coming of the New Deal* (Boston, 1958), 273–77; Charles, *Minister of Relief*, 60–61.

31. Quoted in Leuchtenburg, *Roosevelt and the New Deal*, 122.

32. [FERA-CWA Staff, Minutes] Meeting of Wednesday—December 6th [1933], Harry L. Hopkins Papers (Franklin D. Roosevelt Library, Hyde Park).

33. Robert Sherwood, who sees CWA as "a clean sweep for the Hopkins theories of work relief," suggests that Hopkins and other New Deal relief administrators obeyed the President's order to terminate CWA "with utmost reluctance and deep disappointment." Sherwood, *Roosevelt and Hopkins*, 53, 56. Searle Charles, however, argues more convincingly that "Hopkins and other leading administration officials opposed the suggested expansion of CWA." Charles, *Minister of Relief*, 61.

34. Necessity prompted the use of means tests and investigations: faced by a volume of unemployment that greatly exceeded the capacity of their program budgets, officials required such devices to insure an allocation of relief moneys to those who needed them most. Hopkins, "They'd Rather Work," 7; Brown, *Public Relief,* 158. Under FERA and CWA, some labor unions, professional societies, and veterans' organizations were allowed to "certify" the need of members, thus circumventing means tests and investigations. Later, WPA dropped "follow-up" investigations, but more than 95 percent of its workers were certified through standard relief procedures. Harry L. Hopkins, "F. E. R. A.," *Congressional Digest,* XIV (Jan. 1935), 16; Russell Kurtz, "How the Wheels Are Turning," *Survey,* LXXI (Aug. 1935), 227–28; Brown, *Public Relief,* 160–61, 167; Gill, *Wasted Manpower,* 198.

35. Russell H. Kurtz, "Two Months of the New Deal in Federal Relief," *Survey,* LXIX (Aug. 1933), 286, 289; Arthur E. Burns and Edward A. Williams, *Federal Work, Security, and Relief Programs* (Washington, 1941), 26, 38.

36. Matthews, "These Past Five Years," 71. Gertrude Springer noted that WPA earnings were based upon a generalized assumption "that all families have the average of 4.1 children, that everyone has average good health, [and] that accidents don't happen. . . ." Gertrude Springer, "You Can't Eat Morale," *Survey,* LXXII (March 1936), 77.

37. Hopkins, *Spending to Save,* 163.

38. Harry L. Hopkins, "Social Planning for the Future," *Social Service Review,* VIII (Sept. 1934), 403; Hopkins, "The War on Distress," 157–58.

39. Baker, "Work Relief," 6; Lescohier, "The Hybrid WPA," 169; Burns and Williams, *Federal Work, Security, and Relief Programs,* 61.

40. "Employment Conditions and Unemployment Relief," *Monthly Labor Review,* XXXVIII (Feb. 1934), 312–14; Hopkins, *Spending to Save,* 164–65; "Wage Rates," *Survey,* LXXI (June 1935), 176–77; Burns and Williams, *Federal Work, Security, and Relief Programs,* 61–62.

41. Ewan Clague and Saya S. Schwartz, "Real Jobs—Or Relief?" *Survey Graphic,* XXIV (June 1935), 293–95; Lescohier, "The Hybrid WPA," 167–69.

42. Gill, *Wasted Manpower,* 161; Baker, "Work Relief," 6.

43. Harry L. Hopkins, "Employment in America," *Vital Speeches of the Day,* III (Dec. 1, 1936), 106.

44. Richard H. Pells, *Radical Visions and American Dreams: Culture and Social Thought in the Depression Years* (New York, 1973), 85–86; Hofstadter, *Age of Reform,* 317–18.

45. Lescohier, "The Hybrid WPA," 168.

46. Matthews, "These Past five Years," 71–72.

47. Gertrude Springer and Ruth A. Lerrigo, "Social Work in the Public Scene," *Survey*, LXXII (June 1936), 166–67; Dorothy C. Kahn, "Conserving Human Values in Public Welfare Programs," *Proceedings of the National Conference of Social Work, 1941* (New York, 1941), 309, 312–13, 317–18.

48. Grace Adams, *Workers on Relief* (New Haven, 1939), 310–13, 327–28, 330–33.

49. Construction work made up 75 to 80 percent of all WPA projects. See Harry L. Hopkins, Radio Address, *Cong. Digest*, XVII (June-July 1938), 177; Harry L. Hopkins, "The WPA Looks Forward: A Statement and a Forecast," *Survey Midmonthly*, LXXIV (June 1938), 198.

50. Maxine Davis, "On WPA, or Else . . .," *Survey Graphic*, XXVII (March 1938), 166.

51. Howard M. Teaf, Jr., "Work Relief and the Workers," *Survey Midmonthly*, LXXIV (June 1938), 199. Teaf also found that 70 percent of all project workers were classified and placed in jobs as unskilled laborers, even though only 17 percent had classified themselves as unskilled workers when they applied for work relief. *Ibid.* In New York City, however, two thirds of all WPA employees were placed in jobs that complemented their normal occupations. Lescohier, "The Hybrid WPA," 168.

52. In her examination of questions like these, New York social worker-psychologist Grace Adams reached the conclusion that work relief recipients often felt that their skills were unwanted and that the work they did was of little value. Adams, *Workers on Relief*, 273–85.

53. Anderson, "The War for the Wage," 164–65.

54. Lescohier, "The Hybrid WPA," 168.

55. Davis, "On WPA, or Else . . . ," 165; Lescohier, "The Hybrid WPA," 168–69.

56. Burns and Williams, *Federal Work, Security, and Relief Programs*, 40, 47, 74; Brown, *Public Relief*, 169–70; Gertrude Springer, "Border Lines and Gaps," *Survey*, LXXI (Nov. 1935), 332–33.

57. Joanna C. Colcord and Russell H. Kurtz, "Demobilization of CWA," *Survey*, LXX (March 1934), 91; Gertrude Springer, "X Equals?" *Survey Graphic*, XXIII (May 1934), 249–50; Beulah Amidon, "WPA—Wages and Workers," *Survey Graphic*, XXIV (Oct. 1935), 494.

58. "With the WPA," *Survey*, LXXII (May 1936), 147; "WPA, RA, Drought," *Survey*, LXXII (Sept. 1936), 272; Springer, "You Can't Eat Morale," 77.

59. William H. Matthews, "The Relief Issue: An Inside View," *New York Times Magazine* (Jan. 15, 1939), 20.

60. Springer, "You Can't Eat Morale," 76; "Relief Must Go On," *Survey Midmonthly*, LXXIV (April 1938), 112. "We let a man on work relief work only as many hours as are necessary to keep

himself alive and clothed," New Deal relief administrator Baker once admitted. Baker, "Work Relief," 6.

61. Matthews, *Adventures in Giving*, 222–31, 238, 243. See also Matthews, "The Relief Issue," 8, 20.

62. See Kahn, "Conserving Human Values," 309, 317–18.

63. Adams, *Workers on Relief*, viii.

64. Hopkins, "Federal Emergency Relief," 211. The appeal that work relief had among the unemployed was indicated by a public opinion poll, which revealed that four out of five people on relief preferred work relief to direct cash relief. See Gertrude Springer, "This Business of Relief," *Survey Midmonthly*, LXXIV (Feb. 1938), 36.

65. Social workers closely followed innovations in business theory and practice. See Paul Kellogg, "Shapers of Things," *Survey Graphic*, XXVII (Jan. 1938), 16–21; "Profits from Well-Being," *Survey*, LXIII (Oct. 1929), 105. The businessman's approach was central to work relief because it suggested that the collective problem of individual demoralization could be ameliorated through institutional expedients. See Beulah Amidon, "Ivorydale: A Payroll That Floats," *Survey Graphic*, XIX (April 1930), 18–22, 56–57, 61, 64.

66. Lescohier, "The Hybrid WPA," 169.

67. Carl N. Degler, ed., *The New Deal* (Chicago, 1970), 23; Jerold S. Auerbach, "New Deal, Old Deal, or Raw Deal: Some Thoughts on New Left Historiography," *Journal of Southern History*, XXXV (Feb. 1969), 21, 27; Otis L. Graham, Jr., ed., *The New Deal: The Critical Issues* (Boston, 1971), 174–75, 177–78.

68. Robert S. Lynd, *Knowledge For What? The Place of Social Science in American Culture* (Princeton, 1939), 59.

69. For an analysis of commonly held American beliefs about unemployment and relief during the Great Depression, see Lynd, *Knowledge For What?* 59–62; Robert S. Lynd and Helen Merrell Lynd, *Middletown in Transition: A Study in Cultural Conflicts* (New York, 1937), 406–15. See also Studs Terkel, *Hard Times: An Oral History of the Great Depression* (New York, 1970).

70. Hopkins, "Employment in America," 107.

NEW DEAL AGRICULTURAL POLICY: AN EVALUATION

Theodore Saloutos

Perhaps in no period of American history were the efforts of the federal government to resolve the almost unresolvable problems of the farm prosecuted with greater vigor and optimism than during the New Deal years. What administrators and politicians thought and did about the depressed state of the farmers more or less set the pace for policy making in the post-World War II decades and deserves serious study. Any attempt to assess or reassess the agricultural policy of the New Deal requires a definition of what one means by that policy and a statement of what historians have had to say about it.

New Deal farm policy included a series of complex and interrelated programs that aimed to elevate the long-range social and economic position of the farmers, rather than simply attain stated price objectives. The policy was as comprehensive in character as political considerations permitted, seemingly contradictory and inconsistent, and the product of many minds and influences at work outside and inside the Department of Agriculture before and after the Roosevelt administration took office. The Department of Agriculture was among the most prestigious of all federal government agencies of cabinet rank and played a crucial and dominant role in all this. But other agencies participated too; and since their actions had a definite bearing on the farmer, they and their programs must be considered a part of farm policy.

Agencies which liberal groups easily could believe were more constructive and creative in their approach than the Agricultural Adjustment Administration (AAA) included: the Federal Emergency Relief Administration (FERA), which during the course of its existence provided many rural communities with relief; the Resettlement Administration (RA), which became an official part of the Department of Agriculture only after Rexford G. Tugwell stepped down as its director, and which in turn was absorbed by the newly created Farm Security Administration (FSA); the Rural Electrification Administration (REA), which did extensive work before it became affiliated with the Department of Agriculture in 1939, in preparing the groundwork for the electrification of many farms; the Tennessee Valley Authority (TVA), whose influence on the agriculture of the South and many rural communities was incalculable; and the Farm Credit Administration (FCA), established as a private lending agency outside the government.[1]

Historians who have dealt with New Deal farm policy fall into three distinct categories: the textbook writers who because of the nature of their assignment treat the subject cursorily and who as a rule begin with some comments about the failure of the Federal Farm Board to stem the tide of falling prices and then generally discuss the depressed state of agriculture in 1933, the general character of AAA and what it sought to do, the drought of 1934, the failure of AAA to do much for the sharecroppers, tenants, and small family farmers, and normally end their discussion with the invalidation of the first AAA in 1936;[2] those who have written books, articles, masters theses, and doctoral dissertations on some phase of the New Deal era such as the farm holiday movement, the plight of the sharecroppers and tenants, or an agency such as RA or FSA;[3] and a few generalists who have done little, if any, primary research on the subject but have some broad statement to make about what was done and what was not done.[4] For good and understandable reasons historians have completed fewer in-depth studies of New Deal farm policy than have farm economists, whose main preoccupation has been with price goals.[5]

An assessment of the New Deal in agriculture may well begin with AAA, which was the most publicized of the farm agencies. The philosophy behind AAA was that farmers, who were in a highly competitive business, could improve their financial position by employing the same methods that prudent businessmen used— that is by adjusting their production to effective demand.[6] The general objectives of the much heralded first AAA were to overcome the disparities between farm and nonfarm prices by granting benefit payments to producers who cooperated with the federal government to balance production with demand and thereby bring farmers a return more in line with their incomes for the years between 1909 and 1914.[7]

Phase two began with the enactment of the Soil Conservation and Domestic Allotment Act of 1936, which placed emphasis on increasing the income of farmers, not through acreage controls and marketing agreements as had been the case with the first AAA, but through the adoption of land uses and farm practices that conserved and built up the fertility of the soil.[8] Phase three began with the adoption of a new AAA in 1938, which sought to steer "a middle course" between the programs of the first AAA and the Soil Conservation and Domestic Allotment Act of 1936. This was deemed necessary because of a conviction that the adjustment value of the program begun in 1933 had been obscured by the droughts of 1934 and 1936 which had a greater effect on acreage and marketing adjustments than had been planned.

The lesson learned from the droughts of 1934 and 1936 was that a more permanent solution to the price imbalance was likely to be found in conservation rather than in acreage reduction or marketing agreements. This belief was strongly reinforced by the Court decision declaring the first AAA unconstitutional. But then the unusually favorable growing conditions of 1937 and the prospects of excellent crops in 1938 exposed the administration and farmers to the inadequacy of the conservation approach in years of bumper crops and emphasized the need for a broader program based on the control of a larger reserves storage. AAA sought to meet these conditions by establishing an "ever-normal granary" to provide for larger reserves as added protection against drought and to substitute surplus control—that is through the control of marketing in interstate commerce—as a means of combating surpluses. The new AAA or phase three in addition provided for the beginnings of a federal crop insurance program for wheat.[9]

A reassessment of these three phases of AAA calls for an evaluation of the price goals it sought, the effectiveness of acreage restrictions as a production control measure, the conservation program and what it had accomplished by 1939, the ever-normal granary, and the federal crop insurance program for wheat.

Opinions naturally differed over the goals of the New Deal in agriculture and how these goals were to be achieved. Men such as Henry A. Wallace, Milburn L. Wilson, Henry Tolley, Mordecai Ezekiel, and members of the Wisconsin school of agriculture economics recognized that resolving the farm dilemma depended on more than the attainment of higher prices and incomes, although all agreed that the primary objective of AAA was to raise farm prices to parity levels. This being the case, it can be said that the New Deal had achieved its objective only in part by 1939. The prices of most farm commodities in August 1939, the month before the Nazis invaded Poland, were low in comparison with parity and

August 1929 price levels. Of the prices received for farm commodities, only one, that for beef cattle, had attained parity by August 1939. Corn was 59 percent of parity, cotton 66 percent, wheat 50, butterfat 59, hogs 60, chickens 93, and eggs 49. The income of the farm population, which had significant bearings on the purchase of farm products, after dropping to a low of $39,000,000,000 in 1933, had recovered to only $66,000,000,000 in 1939 but had not reached the $79,000,000,000 of 1929.[10]

Farmers still complained in the early 1940s about the cost of wages, which they blamed for the high prices of many of the articles they bought. The average farm tax bill in 1940 was $450 or twice that for the period from 1910 to 1915. Because of higher wages and rents, middlemen took a higher toll on the food products that passed through their hands, made them cost more to the consumer, and left less for the producer. In 1939 the farmer received only 41 percent of the average consumer dollar spent for food as compared with 52 percent in 1913–1915.[11]

The parity price formula did not create serious difficulties in the early New Deal years because it was employed as a broad, general directive to improve the economic status of agriculture and also because Congress had given the Department of Agriculture considerable latitude in applying the formula. But this period of grace came to an end. Beginning with the spring of 1941 Congress insisted on a more rigorous interpretation, as seen in the mandatory farm commodity loans of 85 percent of parity, the 90 percent loans, and the 110 percent ceilings that followed. The change that restricted the range of administrative decision came at a time when the economic effects of the war were beginning to be felt and made past price relationships unrealistic. The war and the violent changes that it brought in the values of goods and services exposed the weaknesses of parity prices.

Parity prices, in short, whether they took 1909–1914 or some other period as their base, whether they took regional and the quality differentials of a commodity into account—much as these refinements helped—were not suitable goals for a farm policy simply because the function of prices was to guide and direct economic activity. In the words of one farm economist parity prices were "backward looking" and represented "the dead hand of the past." It was difficult if not impossible to force agriculture into a set of price relationships that existed years ago.[12]

The efforts of the New Deal to control production through the restriction of acreages and the adoption of conservation and adjustment practices can hardly be adjudged a success. The New Dealers had been inspired to some extent by American manufacturers and industrialists who had been able to slow down the volume of their production in periods of low consumer demand; but they soon discovered, if they had been unaware of it before, that restricting production in agriculture where there were millions of producers was far more difficult to achieve than in manufacturing or industry where the producers were fewer in number.[13]

The farmer's instinct was to produce in order to feed, clothe, and otherwise furnish the world; he disliked cutting down his production deliberately. However expert he was in his work there was little that he could do to control the quality and the quantity of his wheat, raw cotton, leaf tobacco, and other crops. Proper seeding, spraying, and care in the harvest could and did help the bounty and character of the crop; but a great deal of this could be undone, sometimes overnight, by heavy storms, floods, droughts, untimely frost, or the ravages of crop pests—all beyond or largely beyond the control of man.[14] The droughts of 1934 and 1936 demonstrated that the forces of nature often were more significant than human planning in affecting the volume of the crop.[15]

Before World War II a shrinking farm labor force was able to produce a surplus for a growing population of consumers because of technical and mechanical advances that steadily increased productivity. Between 1930 and 1940 the census showed a gain of only 7 percent in the total population, but a gain of 12 percent in agricultural production and 28 percent in the productivity of each farm worker.[16] Clearly the New Dealers had been unable to retire land from cultivation fast enough to overcome the effects of mechanical and technical efficiency in increasing production. Ironically, one of the great contributions of AAA, especially to the agriculture of the South, was that it helped increase the yields from planting on better land and cultivating from improved methods.[17] The organized staple cotton growers of twelve counties in Mississippi, among the most prosperous cotton producers in the South, reduced their acreage from 1,700,000 acres in 1930 to 1,000,000 acres in 1939; but their yields increased from between 200 to 400 pounds per acre. In 1930 and again in 1933 about 581,000 bales of cotton were harvested and in 1938 some 835,000.[18]

One lesson learned from AAA was the difficulty of contracting production in a highly mechanized society. Expansion came
much more easily to the more developed countries with improvement in skills, techniques, and the accessibility of capital than to
the less developed nations. Agricultural production under such
circumstances was caught in the forward surge, and those who
spoke for agriculture were often prone to ascribe the emerging
surpluses to shortcomings in the market instead of maladjustments
in production.[19]

Soil conservation, which became a key objective during phase
two of AAA, always had attracted the attention of the more concerned citizen, but the interest of the general public was not aroused
until its attention was directed to the agricultural surpluses. The
reduction in the acreage of the basic crops under AAA reduced the
drain on soils which was recognized as being in the public interest.
This phase of AAA had greater appeal to nonfarm people than the
gaining of higher prices and income for farmers. Conservation
specialists furthermore employed the drought in the Great Plains
states and the resulting dust storms as a means of impressing farmers and the general public with the need for more effective measures. Under the stimulus of this new interest, research in conservation expanded rapidly and the more comprehensive surveys made
from year to year added to knowledge of the problem.

The progress made in conservation by the time the New Deal
came to an end was encouraging, at best. According to the Soil
Conservation Service (SCS), some 200,000,000 acres of crop land
in use in 1939 were subject to "moderate or severe erosion," but by
that time farm conservation plans had been developed for only
39,000,000 acres. Although there exists no objective measure of the
amount of erodible lands farmed in a manner aimed to maintain
fertility of the soil in 1939, it probably was less than the 39,000,000
acres for which plans had been developed. SCS estimated that as a
result of its program about 75,000 farm families were operating on
fully protected land. But when one compared these 75,000 farm
families with the total of 3,600,000 families on erodible land, it was
apparent that although an awareness had been developed, erosion
still was an unresolved problem when World War II broke out.[20]

Another development encouraged by the New Deal was the
cultivation of soil-improving crops such as legumes, lespedeza, and
soybeans. The range of these crops was extended northward, and
the production of soybeans became a major item. The growing of

flax likewise spread into a number of states, and experiments with other crops, particularly minor ones, were carried on over most of the United States. Hybrid corn was used more extensively and yields double previous ones were reported in many areas. These changes and experiments were expected to have far-reaching effects on the economy.[21]

The controversial ever-normal granary, which Wallace, its principal architect and exponent, defined as "a definite system whereby supplies following years of drought or other great calamity would be large enough to take care of the consumer, [and] under which the farmer would not be unduly penalized in years of favorable weather," also must figure in any evaluation of the New Deal. To avoid a repetition of the Farm Board experience of huge surpluses and sagging prices it became necessary, after the loan program had reached a certain point, "to keep the granary from running over by some practical program of production adjustment." Wallace considered storing grain in the soil instead of in the bin also a part of the ever-normal granary.[22]

Something akin to the ever-normal granary had been in operation from the beginning. During the drought of 1934 corn stored on farms under the first corn loan in 1933 helped provide feed supplies for livestock. In 1939 a loan and storage program was in effect for wheat, the primary food crop, and for corn, the number one feed crop. Wheat reserves were held in the ever-normal granary through a federal crop insurance program under which the wheat growers put aside a portion of their crops as premiums to offset possible crop failures. By storing corn, a nonperishable potential supply of pork, beef, dairy products, eggs, and other products was carried over.[23]

Administration leaders saw that the ever-normal granary system fitted into the defense requirements of the nation soon after the war began. For a time there was some "panic buying," especially of sugar, which ended when the public realized that the prevailing program and the ever-normal granary provided for production as well as for reserves.

The reserve supply of agricultural products was exceptionally strong by 1940. The total crop production in 1939, although about 1 percent lower than that of the previous year, was nearly 4 percent above the average of the 1923–1932 period. By the end of the 1939–1940 crop season, the nation had reserves appreciably larger than those of the period from 1935 to 1939, and this caused some to question the efficacy of the program. The adjustment of supply to demand was a continuing objective, and the first program of AAA was designed to reduce burdensome surpluses. The carry-over into 1940, however, of crops such as cotton and tobacco was in part a product of recent catastrophic changes in the world market, the difficulties the country had in making exports, and the fact that the ever-normal granary deliberately provided for carry-overs that were larger than those of the past, particularly of wheat and corn.

Wallace insisted that the planning for larger reserves was a product of the earlier years and not a response to the immediate war or national defense needs. He stated repeatedly that the droughts of 1934 and 1936 and AAA of 1938 had prepared the groundwork. The supplies of wheat and corn in 1940, Wallace said, were at the levels considered desirable by AAA. The wheat reserve was about twice and the corn reserve about three times pre-AAA levels. Supplies of some types of tobacco were in excess of their goals, in part because growers in 1939 chose not to use marketing quotas and because of the war. The supply of cotton was excessive mainly because the war cut off most of the foreign market.[24]

Passage of the Federal Crop Insurance Act of 1938 marked the start of a new, voluntary program, purely experimental in character, to apply initially only to wheat. Proponents viewed the crop insurance programs as the agricultural counterpart of the Social Security Act, which furnished unemployment insurance for nonagricultural workers.[25] During the first year of the program, 1939, about 56,000 farmers received in excess of 10,000,000 bushels of wheat or the cash equivalent in indemnities for crops destroyed by forces beyond their control; this provided them with income that otherwise would have been lost. About 94 percent of the losses paid on the insured crop in 1939 were paid in the principal wheat-producing counties of the nation, where wheat was the chief, and in many cases, the only source of income.[26] By 1940 many requests were received for the extension of insurance protection to crops such as corn, cotton, tobacco, citrus fruits, and vegetables which from an insurance standpoint posed difficulties not posed by wheat.[27] By 1941 the insurance program was extended to include cotton, a major commodity.[28]

These early experiences brought to the surface the weaknesses of the first crop insurance program. Many growers took advantage of the voluntary features of the insurance program, especially when the prospects for crops were poor. The result was a heavy participation in the potential loss areas and light participation in the areas where the prospects for crops were much better. Losses, as a consequence, were out of line with actuarial estimates. Plans naturally were contemplated for the future that required the grower to insure for a longer period of time and to insure all the acreage in which he had an interest, instead of only those acres in which a loss was likely to occur.[29]

The criticisms most frequently made of AAA and other programs of the New Deal were that they catered primarily to the commercial, wealthier, and more substantial members of the middle class; that they rendered little, if any, assistance to tenants and sharecroppers; and that AAA, in particular, reduced members of the low-income groups from tenants and sharecroppers to farm laborers or pushed them off the land completely.[30] According to Wilson, these criticisms were made especially by those who were not farmers and who did not live in farm communities or know much about farming. These apprehensions were not entertained by persons better acquainted with farming because of an underlying assumption on their part that AAA was temporary legislation, that prices were going to rise, that the Depression was going to end, and that the emergency legislation was going to disappear.[31]

One can argue that these changes had been going on for years prior to the New Deal and continued after the New Deal ended. Most difficulties of the small farmers came from technological changes that increased output per worker and substituted capital for human labor. Mechanization and the need for more capital had far more to do with consolidation of farms and increasing their size than the organization of AAA. AAA undoubtedly hastened consolidation of small farms into larger ones, especially in the cotton industry and in those types of farming that employed migratory labor; and it also concentrated attention on a situation which existed for some time and to which very little attention had been given.[32]

That AAA did little for tenants, sharecroppers, and farm laborers is beyond dispute, although an exception has to be made for those who came under the classification of managing farm tenants. Relief for farm laborers never was designed to become a part of AAA; consequently little, if anything, could have been expected from this direction. The failure of AAA to come to the aid of sharecroppers and tenants may be attributed to a way of thinking that prevailed in agricultural circles, including educators, farm lobbyists, farm journalists, congressional leaders, and other members of the so-called agricultural establishment.

The objective of the Department of Agriculture and the land-grant colleges all along had been to establish prosperous farm families through the application of practical research and science. The assumption had been that this assistance could be rendered most effectively to those farmers who were accustomed to the family farm system and had incomes from their operations that were sufficient to attain a satisfactory standard of living. Agricultural thinking, research, teaching, and extension work that concentrated almost exclusively on the well managed family farm strongly influenced AAA.[33]

Strong attitudes also prevailed in rural areas as well as in the Department of Agriculture regarding poor farmers and what should be done for them. These attitudes were brought to bear on congressmen and senators through the farm organizations to which the more successful farmers belonged, and they influenced decisions on the kind of assistance provided to tenants and sharecroppers. The general feeling of many landlords and employers was that if the rural poor received too much assistance, they would become independent and difficult to deal with. "If they moved away, the labor market would be tightened. If they became owners they also became competitors. If something had to be done, the last of these alternatives was preferable." This probably would not affect many, and those who climbed the ladder to proprietorship soon would acquire the outlook of their fellow proprietors.[34]

As a consequence persons associated with agricultural colleges, agricultural experiment stations, and the Department of Agriculture seldom bothered with sharecroppers, tenants, and other low-income farmers, largely from the belief that such people were not able to climb into "the good income group." Small wonder then that agricultural institutions of higher education and research were ill-informed or uninformed about the nature and the extent of poverty in rural areas and unprepared to consider the problem.[35] Had the Department of Agriculture chosen to face this problem directly, which was unlikely, it would have encountered a hardened resistance to it not merely from substantial and wealthier farmers, but from many others who believed that agriculture held a slim future for depressed elements.

The belief had been fixed firmly that too many farmers were attempting to scratch out an existence from the soil and that it would be to their best interests and those of agriculture for them to go to the cities for a livelihood. The Department of Agriculture and much, perhaps most, of the agricultural establishment more or less subscribed to this position, although ground was given on it after RA, FSA, and the Bankhead-Jones Act became law. Still, those who believed that the nation suffered from a surplus of farmers, as well as from a surplus of crops, had influential forces at work for them.[36] One, as already suggested, was a bloc of congressmen and senators from the South and Midwest who had the necessary votes and were in command of strategic committees.[37] A second was the mechanization of cotton farming, especially the introduction of the cotton picker, which came into prominence in the late 1930s and lessened the demand for tenants and sharecroppers.[38] And third was the ominous threat of war and the likelihood that the demands of the defense and civilian industries would absorb all available farm labor for their factories and assembly lines.[39]

A small, persistent, and less influential group opposed the view that the time had come to eliminate surplus farmers from the land. Especially before the threat of war became imminent, this group argued that the cities had unemployment problems of their own, that the problems of rural poverty could not be resolved by shifting or dumping the surplus farmers onto the cities, and that a genuine attempt had to be made to keep these people on the land, not through making available to them small, subsistence farms, but through the establishment of agricultural communities or collective farms.

But expecting the federal government to subsidize collective farms and colonies was expecting far too much, considering the state of public opinion and the fact that tenants and sharecroppers represented the least influential elements in the country; they further were handicapped by lack of good leadership, funds with which to contribute to the political parties, and large blocs of voters in the poll-states. The only friends they had in Washington, outside the Southern Tenant Farmers' Union whose influence was minimal, was the National Farmers' Union whose strength was concentrated in the northern Great Plains states and whose financial resources were slender by comparison with those of its more affluent rivals—the American Farm Bureau Federation and the National Grange.[40]

Despite limitations in the intentions and accomplishments of AAA in behalf of tenants, sharecroppers, and small farmers, and the acquiescence of rural public opinion toward such a policy, it would be a mistake to assume that the New Deal did as little for these elements as is sometimes imagined. There is much evidence to the contrary, especially when one looks at the works of agencies other than AAA. Between 1933 and 1935, when the Resettlement Administration finally came into existence, at least four governmental agencies tried to deal with various phases of rural poverty. Insofar as immediate relief was concerned, the most significant of these was the Federal Emergency Relief Administration, whose work was not confined exclusively to farmers.[41]

FERA came into existence on May 12, 1933, and same day AAA was placed on the statute books. By November 1933 its relief load included 11 percent of all rural farm families.[42] Besides work project jobs given rural people, FERA late in 1933 announced the purchase of over 200,000,000 pounds of meat obtained through AAA to be distributed in areas where relief standards were low.[43] Other commodities were given as a means of providing reasonable standards of sustenance.[44] Early in the spring of 1934 a new plan stipulated that on April 1 civil works and direct relief would be replaced in rural areas and towns of less than 5,000 people with a program of rural rehabilitation to help individual families become self-supporting.[45]

After February 1935, when almost 1,000,000 farm families, including farmers and farm laborers, were receiving relief grants or rehabilitation loans, farm families began to leave the general relief rolls rapidly, especially after expansion of the rural rehabilitation program and a partial resumption of agricultural prosperity.[46] Figures in June 1935 indicated that nearly three fourths of the heads of families on relief in June 1935 were farmers and that slightly more than one fourth were farm laborers. Tenants, other than sharecroppers, made up more than one half of the farm operators on relief; farm owners accounted for another one third and sharecroppers for nearly one eighth. In the cotton areas, sharecroppers were represented more heavily on the relief rolls than either owners or other kinds of tenants.[47]

Although RA was created for the special purpose of aiding the low-income groups that AAA was unable to reach, it encountered powerful opposition from the start. This opposition should not obscure the fact that the intention of the New Deal, if not that of influential elements within the agricultural establishment represented by AAA, was to assist the rural disinherited. If the New

Dealers can be faulted for anything, it would be for the unrealistic methods they employed rather than for insensitivity to the needs of low-income groups. According to Tugwell, RA probably would have been more acceptable if its approach had been more gradual, allowing time for consolidation and the opportunity to grow. A slower and seasoned growth conceivably would have reduced the magnitude of some of its administrative problems and made the task more manageable for those who assumed new duties. But one cannot help but wonder whether the functions objected to would have been any more palatable if they had been added piecemeal instead of as one original package.[48]

Officials of RA were also under the misapprehension that two generations of agitation in behalf of conservation had prepared the farmers for land-use programs and the retirement of submarginal lands from commercial purposes. The corollary programs RA was asked to administer and those subsidiary to its major rural operations generated hostility. The grants and loans extended after the drought of 1934, the subsidiary medical services they developed, and the payment of poll taxes infuriated critics. Matters were not helped any by the transfer of the Subsistence Homesteads Division from the Department of the Interior and the addition to its operations of the Rehabilitation Corporation, organized to establish communities in rural areas.

Besides these problems there were those of the Suburban Resettlement Division whose projects were expected to reflect good planning and decent construction and eventually supplant the crowded neighborhoods and the shabbily built houses of real estate promoters. RA came under such savage attack that plans for sixty projects had to be abandoned and confined to only three that never were finished. RA was also castigated for trying to do something for low-income families who, in the opinion of critics, had done nothing to deserve this assistance, and for high costs and standards, and employment provided those on relief rolls. Congress knew that RA had little support, and Democratic politicians hoped that the entire operation would be junked.[49]

RA eventually was transferred to the Department of Agriculture, which some viewed with serious misgivings and others with enthusiasm; Tugwell also resigned as the director of RA, and the name of it changed to the Farm Security Administration. Although RA personnel was retained to staff FSA, there was a noticeable shift in orientation. Resettlement and housing were phased out gradually in favor of a massive rural rehabilitation effort whose goal was greater security in farm tenure. The scale of FSA activities soon exceeded that of RA, and it worked more quietly. Its activities were less novel and spectacular, and for a time it appeared as thought it would enjoy a more tenable political position.[50]

The Bankhead-Jones Act, passed in 1937 in response to mounting pressure for tenancy reform, failed to come up to the hopes of the more optimistic reformers. From its inception in 1937 through the fiscal year 1947, the tenant-purchase program provided for under the act made available loans amounting to $293,876,733 to only 47,104 farmers. This was a very modest beginning considering the fact that there were still 1,858,421 tenants in the country in 1945. At the rate that tenant purchases were being made, it was going to take nearly 400 years to make them all owners. Yet the more hopeful viewed this as an encouraging demonstration of a program that was to be expanded on "a scale commensurate with the magnitude of the problem [and] as rapidly as our experience and resources will permit." However, the coming of World War II and the inflation of land prices that followed postponed the expansion of the program.

The slow progress of the tenant-purchase program under the Bankhead-Jones Act cannot be blamed solely on the Department of Agriculture. The loans were too small to make possible an efficient use of family labor or yield a "maximum-adequate" income. Public opinion and Congress would not tolerate significant improvement in the status of tenants, sharecroppers, and farm laborers "on the government." In five successive appropriations beginning with the act of 1941, Congress deliberately stipulated that no loan could be extended for the purchase of a farm of thirty acres or more in the county in which the farm was located. This was chiefly the work of Representative Malcolm C. Tarver of Georgia, chairman of the appropriations subcommittee, who believed that the loans, which averaged $3,900 in his state, were "twice too high." In the face of such opinion it became almost impossible to create adequate farm units.[51]

This unsympathetic attitude was reflected in others besides the large landowners and those who believed that the number of farmers had to be diminished. In the South public and congressional opinion objected to "setting up" a tenant-purchase borrower above his neighbor; hence, if the status of the borrower's neighbor was low that of the borrower would have to remain low too. The feeling also was widespread among FSA personnel in the South that "a very modest improvement in the position of the farmers was all that could be expected."[52]

The belated efforts of the federal government to improve the status of tenants and sharecroppers encouraged action at the state level as well. The Farm Landlord and Tenant Relationship Act passed by the Oklahoma legislature in 1937, but repealed in 1939, was a pioneer step in this direction. The governors of the states of Arkansas and South Carolina also requested appropriate agencies to study the farm tenancy situation and to report to the next sessions of the legislature; and comparable action was taken in Louisiana and Texas.[53]

Much has been made of the unwillingness of larger farmers and landlords under AAA to share the benefit payments fairly with their tenants. That many tenants—the exact number has never been known and probably never will be—were deprived of their just dues is beyond doubt. But even if these payments had been shared fairly, sharecroppers and tenants would not have experienced significant economic progress. These payments would have purchased a few more of the necessities of life and little else. The payments listed in the public record represent the landlord's share on land operated by a number of tenants, who in theory earned proportionate shares. Individual payments to the tenants do not appear in this record. Of significance is the fact that fully 46 percent of the almost 5,250,000 farmers receiving payments under AAA in 1938 received $40 or less for the year. Fully 33 percent received sums ranging from $40 to $100 annually, and less than 2 percent from $1,000 to $10,000. The numbers receiving sums of over $3,000 averaged a small fraction of 1 percent.[54] These incentive payments were nothing more than their name suggests, designed primarily to introduce better farming methods for those who had a stake in the land and were going to stay on it. There was little in the program, fraud or no fraud on the part of the landlords, that would have encouraged poorer farmers to remain on the land if they had alternatives other than farming.

The New Deal did show some response to the needs of tenants and farmers receiving small payments and to those who had been defrauded under AAA. An amendment to the Soil Conservation and Domestic Allotment Act sought to render greater assistance to tenants and farmers receiving small payments. The amendment protected tenants against lease changes that would increase the share of the landlord's payments; and they were assured a division of payments between landlords and tenants in proportion to the shares in the crop. Payments that amounted to less than $200 annually were to be scaled upward, according to a specific schedule. And beginning in 1939 all individual payments were limited to $10,000.[55]

Some of the criticism leveled against AAA was unfair and the product of hindsight rather than foresight. It was expecting far too much of the New Deal to undo within a few years a system of tenancy and sharecropping that had been years in the making. To accomplish this, years of painstaking research and planning, a high degree of cooperation, a sympathetic Congress and generous financial outlays over a long period of time, endless patience and goodwill, and some luck were needed. Unfortunately, these ingredients were not present in sufficient quantity. Ridding the nation of sharecropping and tenancy required something more, considerably more, than favorable decisions at the administrative level.

There were reasons, too, for the decline in the number of farms that cannot be attributed exclusively to New Deal farm programs and policy. One was the resumption of industrial occupations by those who took refuge on farms during the height of the Depression. In some cases this meant moving back to cities and towns or dropping minor agricultural operations without changing residence as soon as factories opened. Still another reason was the growing number of foreclosures during the 1930s.[56] The defense program also had its effect. Recruiting for service in the armed forces, the building of cantonments, and the expansion of industry offered job opportunities, especially for the farmers of the South.[57]

The most striking decrease in the number of farms occurred in the drought area that extended from the Canadian line to the Texas Panhandle. Part of this decrease was due to the droughts of 1934, 1936, and other unfavorable years. Many farmers who withstood the first drought were forced later to abandon their operations. Changes from grain farming, ranching, or cultivated crops also occurred. In some areas there were increases in part-time farming caused by persons moving from the cities back to the land.[58]

FSA must rank as one of the most forward-looking as well as one of the most bitterly fought agencies sponsored by the New Deal. Apart from the tenant-purchase program it administered under the Bankhead-Jones Act, FSA left a very impressive statistical record of assistance. Including the work of the predecessor organization, RA, FSA as of May 1, 1941, through the voluntary farm debt adjustment committees established in every farming county, helped work out debt reductions totaling almost $100,000,000 for 145,000 indebted farmers. This represented a reduction of nearly 23 percent on debts that originally amounted to more than $445,000,000.[59]

FSA discovered that many of the farmers who came for assistance were in difficulties because of illness and could not do a good day's work; and in cooperation with state and local medical societies, FSA worked out a special medical care program for borrowers. This proved so popular with both physicians and FSA clients that health associations were organized in 634 counties in thirty-one states during the late 1930s and early 1940s. By May 1, 1941, about 80,000 families or 300,000 people were obtaining medical care through these associations. In many cases FSA included enough money in its rehabilitation loans to enable the borrower to make his first annual payment to the county health association. This resulted in both swifter progress toward rehabilitation and, as the health and ability of the family to support itself improved, in larger payments on the loans.[60]

FSA further realized that small farmers could not compete on even terms with commercial farmers and encouraged borrowers to pool their resources to buy tractors, lime-spreaders, purebred bulls, seed fertilizer, and other farm and household supplies in large quantities at lower prices. Small farmers also began to sell their pigs, chickens, and truck crops cooperatively. Often FSA included enough money in a rehabilitation loan for a borrower to pay his share of the cost of a combine, feed mill, terrace, or other equipment he could use cooperatively with his neighbors. Originally the loan included a sum that enabled the borrower to join a long-established cooperative. More than 300,000 low-income farm families were taking part in about 16,000 small cooperatives started with FSA help.[61]

From 1935, when the rehabilitation program was initiated, until 1941, FSA loaned more than $516,000,000 to 870,000 farm families, many of whom, judged by normal standards, were among the worst possible credit risks. By May 1, 1941, they had paid $182,000,000 into the federal treasury, and the expectations were that fully 80 percent of the money loaned would be repaid eventually with interest. The annual cost of the rehabilitation loans including losses, according to FSA sources, amounted to less than $75 for each family assisted. This sum was low for relief of any kind; estimated costs of work relief ranged from $350 to $800 per year.

As a result of FSA assistance many farm families made rapid gains in their net worth, standard of living, and ability to support themselves. A survey made at the end of the crop year of 1939 to determine the progress of 360,000 regular rehabilitation borrowers disclosed they had increase their net worth beyond and above all debts—including obligations to the government—by almost $83,000,000 since they had obtained their first FSA loan. This was an average increase of more than $230 per family which meant a gain in new purchasing power in their communities in a single year.[62]

Obviously the efforts of FSA angered certain influential segments of the agricultural establishment, such as the leadership of the American Farm Bureau Federation and the Cooley Committee of the House of Representatives. FSA, it was evident, was seeking to help those who needed help the most to remain on the land, contrary to the beliefs of those who held that these impoverished elements, and farmers in general, would be better off if they left agriculture completely.[63]

In international trade some minor progress was made in unclogging the channels of commerce, especially in dealing with some of the nations of the Western Hemisphere, but little headway was made in finding new outlets for cotton, which depended heavily on the overseas market. The causes for this failure to find new markets were beyond the power of any single nation to repair in a period of international crisis. The demand for cotton probably would have been considerably greater had it not been for the production and use of synthetic fibers in Germany, Italy, and Japan where the drive for self-sufficiency was great. Military preparations, rising trade barriers, and economic rivalries discouraged the sale of American cotton. The total use of cotton in foreign lands had increased appreciably, but the demand for American cotton had diminished.[64]

Perhaps one of the greatest contributions the New Deal made to agriculture was in the increased use of electricity on farms. This, of course, was tied in with the achievements of the Tennessee Valley Authority. Beginning in 1935 on a modest scale and outside the Department of Agriculture, the Rural Electrification Administration expanded its activities in the years prior to the outbreak of

World War II and especially after peace was restored. The federal government under the New Deal assumed a responsibility that the private utilities had been unwilling to assume and which they continued to resist until they saw the futility of their actions. And because of the spread of electricity in the rural areas under REA auspices, crop and livestock production improved; a wider use of farm machinery became possible; labor costs decreased; greater use was made of modern, efficient techniques of farming; much back-breaking toil and drudgery came to an end; the use of indoor plumbing and refrigeration spread; improved means of rural communication became possible; rural education benefited; and the morale of the farm family was lifted.[65]

By 1940 progress also had been made in developing better living conditions and gaining more secure income for the commercial farm families of the South. Incomes from livestock and livestock products were larger and the expenditures for food and feed smaller as a result of a greater incentive to produce for home use. The rising production of livestock was accompanied by a very substantial trend toward the production of feeds which were expected to broaden further the net income base, reduce the cost of raising cash, and the dependence on it.[66]

Income from livestock, fruits, and vegetables in the southern cotton growing states in 1939 was not very far from what it had been in 1929, but income from cotton remained significantly below the 1929 level. North Carolina was a conspicuous example of the former and Mississippi of the latter. Mississippi still was dependent primarily on cotton even though income from that crop was less than one half of what it had been in 1929.[67]

Another significant New Deal contribution was the Shelterbelt Project, launched after the drought and dust storms of 1934 for the purpose of lessening the effects of these disasters, protecting homes and livestock, and providing jobs for residents of the stricken areas. Allowing for the hostility that the project encountered in the early years and other problems, such as insects, disease, and rodent pests, the Shelterbelt Project turned out to be a far greater success than its critics had anticipated.[68]

Nor can we overlook the role of the New Deal in broadening the base of agricultural credit. The Farm Credit Administration created in 1933 extended loans totaling billions of dollars to farmers and their business cooperatives to finance production, market farm products, and purchase farm supplies. Its production credit activities—that is loans to farmers to purchase livestock, machinery, and supplies—ranged from 230,000 to 250,000 in number annually and from $250,000,000 to $350,000,000 in money. The average amount advanced in 1940 was almost $1,500. District banks for cooperatives extended credit to farmers' cooperative associations marketing farm products, purchasing farm supplies, or furnishing farm business services to members. Loans by these banks reached a peak of slightly more than $100,000,000 in 1940, as compared with an annual average of about $90,000,000 during 1936–1939. Emergency crop and feed loans authorized by legislation in 1927 and later years helped farmers obtain assistance from other sources. Walter W. Wilcox estimated that by 1940 "If the land bank borrowers, production credit users, and emergency crop and feed loan borrowers had all been different people, about one million different farmers would have utilized credit made available by the FCA. . . ."[69]

Furthermore, FCA improved the farm credit market for the farmer through the leadership and competition it provided. Credit was made available at the lowest possible rate consistent with good credit market practices. Credit was obtained by thousands of borrowers who otherwise would have lost their property through foreclosures. Federal land bank real estate loans reached a peak of almost $2,850,000,000 in 1936 and then declined to $2,500,000,000 in 1940. As Wilcox observed, "Federal farm credit agencies pioneered in adopting a long-time amortized loan for real estate mortgages, in the use of long-time normal value as a basis for appraisal, and in the development of a budget plan for fitting the timing and the amount of the loan directly to the acquisition and liquidation of assets."[70]

Left-wing critics claim that the New Deal could have accomplished far more for farmers than it actually did. They further assert that the mood of the American people was such that the Department of Agriculture, Wallace, and all surrounding him and his department could have brought about long overdue fundamental reforms for low-income farmers.[71] Just what these reforms were to be is unclear, unless they were nationalization of the land and establishment of cooperative or collective farms. There is little evidence to support the claim that the American people were receptive to such proposals. The farm holiday movement, which was at its peak in the initial stages of the New Deal, did not advocate this kind of change. Even if the farm holiday movement was supposed to represent farmer or public indignation with the New Deal for its failure to provide greater assistance for farmers, it had very little support behind it. At best the farm holiday movement represented a splinter group broken off the main branch of the Farmers' Union, the smallest of the general farmer organizations.

In attempting to summarize the effects of the New Deal on the American farmer one has to keep several things in mind. The New Deal happened in one of the most distressed periods of American history, one in which economies around the world were racked by comparable economic pains. The New Deal also sought to achieve relief, recovery, and reform in a set of economic conditions that had been years in the making, that could not possibly be undone in a short span of time under a system of government controlled by those who had faith in the capitalist system and political establishment and who depended on Congress, farmers, and the general public for continuation in office. Finally, the programs of FSA, the Bankhead-Jones Act, rural electrification, crop insurance, and the ever-normal granary were just beginning to get off the ground when the New Deal came to an end.

Still when all is said and done those farmers who were able to remain in agriculture, especially those with capital and resources, had more to gain from the New Deal than those who lacked capital and resources. The New Deal revived and maintained the morale of most farmers after it had fallen to the lowest depths in history. Farm prices failed to rise to the parity levels designated by the lawmakers, but they were lifted from the low levels of 1932 and 1933, and many of these gains can be attributed to the programs of the New Deal. Both farmers and the general public were made more aware of the need of conserving the soil; a laudable start was made in furnishing electricity for rural areas long neglected by private industry; the Shelterbelt Project helped make life on the Great Plains more bearable for more farmers; and statesmanlike measures, although unsuccessful in accomplishing their purposes, were adopted to improve international trade.

Whether Wallace had the future defense needs of the nation in mind when hostilities broke out may be a moot point. But beyond debate is the fact that "the peacetime programs of research, education, credit, rehabilitation, conservation, and adjustment carried on by the Land Grant Colleges and the Department of Agriculture were important factors contributing to agriculture's ability to respond to war needs. . . ."[72] The New Deal with all its limita-

tions and frustrations, by making operational ideas and plans that
had been long on the minds of agricultural researchers and think-
ers, constituted the greatest innovative epoch in the history of
American agriculture.

NOTES

1. Donald C. Blaisdell, *Government and Agriculture: The Growth of
   Federal Farm Aid* (New York, 1940), 149–97; Carle C.
   Zimmerman and Nathan L. Whetten, *Rural Families on Relief*
   (Washington, 1938), 8, 110; A. R. Mangus, *Changing Aspects of
   Rural Relief* (Washington, 1938), 12–15; Edwin C. Nourse,
   Government in Relation to Agriculture (Washington, 1940), 904–37.
   See also Merle Fainsod and Lincoln Gordon, *Government and the
   American Economy* (New York, 1941), 328–30, 349–50; Robert T.
   Beall, "Rural Electrification," *Farmers in a Changing World: The
   Yearbook of Agriculture, 1940* (Washington, 1940), 790–809;
   Norman I. Wengert, *Valley of Tomorrow: the TVA and Agriculture*
   (Knoxville, 1952); Gordon R. Clapp, *The TVA: An Approach to the
   Development of a Region* (Chicago, 1955).

2. Representative of the long list of textbook writers are Samuel E.
   Morison, Henry Steele Commager, and William E.
   Leuchtenburg, *The Growth of the American Republic* (New York,
   1969), 489–94; George H. Knoles, *The United States: A History
   Since 1896* (New York, 1959), 402–03; John A. Garraty, *The
   American Nation* (New York, 1966), 733–34; T. Harry Williams,
   Richard N. Current, and Frank Freidel, *History of the United States
   Since 1865* (New York, 1959), 488–91, 508–10; and Samuel Eliot
   Morison, *Oxford History of the American People* (New York, 1965),
   957–58. Perhaps broader and more incisive in their treatment are
   Harry J. Carman, Harold C. Syrett, and Bernard W. Wishy, *A
   History of the American People Since 1865* (New York, 1961), 618–
   29; and John D. Hicks, *The American Nation* (Cambridge, Mass.,
   1958), 581–85.

3. Richard S. Kirkendall, *Social Scientists and Farm Politics in the Age of
   Roosevelt* (Columbia, Mo., 1966); Arthur M. Schlesinger, Jr., *The
   Coming of the New Deal* (Boston, 1959), 27–84; John T.
   Schlebecker, *Cattle Raising on the Plains 1900–1961* (Lincoln,
   1963), 134–68; Sidney Baldwin, *Poverty and Politics: The Rise and
   Decline of the Farm Security Administration* (Chapel Hill, 1968);
   John L. Shover, *Cornbelt Rebellion: The Farmer's Holiday Association*
   (Urbana, 1965); Wengert, *Valley of Tomorrow*; H. S. Person, "The
   Rural Electrification Administration in Perspective," *Agricultural
   History*, XXIV (April 1950), 70–89; Murray R. Benedict and Oscar
   C. Stine, *The Agricultural Commodity Programs—Two Decades of
   Experience* (New York, 1956); Charles M. Hardin, *The Politics of
   Agriculture: Soil Conservation and the Struggle for Power in Rural
   America* (Glencoe, 1952); David E. Conrad, *The Forgotten Farmers:
   The Story of Sharecroppers in the New Deal* (Urbana, 1965); Chris-
   tine McFadyen Campbell, *The Farm Bureau and the New Deal: A*

Study of the Making of National Farm Policy 1933–1940 (Urbana, 1962); Donald H. Grubbs, *Cry From The Cotton: The Southern Tenant Farmers' Union and the New Deal* (Chapel Hill, 1971).

4. Howard Zinn, ed., *New Deal Thought* (Indianapolis, 1966), xv–xxxvi; Alonzo L. Hamby, ed., *The New Deal, Analysis and Interpretation* (New York, 1969), 3–6; Paul K. Conkin, *The New Deal* (New York, 1967), 40–43, 49–50, 100–01.

5. Theodore W. Schultz, *Redirecting Farm Policy* (New York, 1943); Geoffrey S. Shepherd, *Agricultural Price Policy* (Ames, 1947); Theodore W. Schultz, *Production and Welfare of Agriculture* (New York, 1949), 14–29, 64–82; John D. Black, *Parity, Parity, Parity* (Cambridge, Mass., 1942).

6. A. G. Black to H. T. Outwater, Sept. 4, 1934, Records of the Agricultural Stabilization and Conservation Service, RG 145 (National Archives).

7. United States Department of Agriculture, Agricultural Adjustment, *A Report of the Administration of the AAA, May 1933 to February 1934* (Washington, 1934), 1–7; and United States Department of Agriculture, AAA, *Agricultural Adjustment 1937–1938* (Washington, 1939), 11–15.

8. *Agricultural Adjustment 1937–1938*, 15.

9. *Ibid.*, 17–18.

10. Walter W. Wilcox, *The Farmer in the Second World War* (Ames, 1947), 9; Bureau of the Census, *Historical Statistics of the United States . . . to 1957* (Washington, 1961), 283.

11. Black, *Parity, Parity, Parity*, 82–83.

12. Schultz, *Redirecting Farm Policy*, 16–18, 33–36.

13. Brookings Institute, *Essays on Research in the Social Sciences* (Washington, 1931), 82.

14. Ralph F. Breyer, *The Marketing Situation* (New York, 1934), 88.

15. *Yearbook of Agriculture, 1935* (Washington, 1935), 15–20; *Yearbook of Agriculture, 1937* (Washington, 1937), 33–47.

16. J. Clyde Marquis, "Agriculture," Walter Yust, ed., *10 Eventful Years* (Chicago, 1947), 24.

17. G. H. Aull, "Discussion," *Journal of Farm Economics*, XXIII (Feb. 1941), 123.

18. O. C. Stine, "Future of Cotton in the Economy of the South," *ibid.*, 119–20.

19. Theodore Schultz, "Food, Agriculture, and Trade," XXIX (Feb. 1947), 5.

20. Wilcox, *Farmer in the Second World War*, 14–16; Robert J. Morgan, *Governing Soil Conservation: Thirty Years of the New Decentralization* (Baltimore, 1966), 110–13.

21. Z. R. Pettit, "Highlights of the 1940 Census," *Journal of Farm Economics*, XXIII (Feb. 1941), 269–70.

22. Shepherd, *Agricultural Price Policy*, 40.

23, United States Department of Agriculture, *Agricultural Adjustment 1938–1939* (Washington, 1939), 7.

24. *Report of the Secretary of Agriculture, 1940* (Washington, 1940), 27–29.

25. *Report of the Secretary of Agriculture, 1938* (Washington, 1938), 37.

26. *Report of the Secretary of Agriculture, 1940*, pp. 58–60.

27. *Ibid.*, 61.

28. *Report of the Secretary of Agriculture, 1941* (Washington, 1941), 128.

29. *Report of the Secretary of Agriculture, 1942* (Washington, 1942), 149–50.

30. Conrad, *Forgotten Farmers*; and Grubbs, *Cry From The Cotton*.

31. Reminiscences of M. L. Wilson, 988 (Oral History Research Office, Columbia University).

32. *Ibid.*, 988–89.

33. M. L. Wilson, "Problems of Poverty in Agriculture," *Journal of Farm Economics*, XXII (Feb. 1940), 10.

34. Rexford G. Tugwell, "The Resettlement Idea," *Agricultural History*, XXXIII (Oct. 1959), 161–63.

35. Wilson, "Problems of Poverty in Agriculture," 10–11.

36. R. R. Renne, "On Agricultural Policy," *Journal of Farm Economics*, XXII (May 1940), 488; Wilcox, *The Farmer in the Second World War*, 12–13.

37. Wesley McCune, *The Farm Bloc* (Garden City, 1943), 36–57.

38. James A. Street, *The New Revolution in the Cotton Economy* (Chapel Hill, 1957), 125–57, 175–91.

39. *Ibid.*, 176–78.

40. Tugwell, "Resettlement Idea," 161–63.

41. *Resettlement Administration Program* (Washington, 1936), 74 Cong., Senate Doc. No. 213, p. 1; Rebecca Farnham and Irene Link, *Effects of the Works Program on Rural Relief* (Washington, 1938), xi.

42. Mangus, *Aspects of Rural Relief*, 14, 19.

43. Dorothy Carothers, *Chronology of the Federal Emergency Relief Administration, May 12, 1933 to December 31, 1935* (Washington, 1937), 16.

44. *Ibid.*, 20.

45. *Ibid.*, 16.

46. Berta Asch and A. R. Mangus, *Farmers on Relief and Rehabilitation* (Washington, 1937), xviii–xix; Chester C. Davis, "The Farmer's Income Has Increased," *Review of Reviews*, 91 (April 1935), 32, 36–37, 64–65; Mordecai Ezekiel to E. Clemens Horst, Sept. 23, 1935, Records of the Office of the Secretary of Agriculture, RG 16 (National Archives).

47. Asch and Mangus, *Farmers on Relief and Rehabilitation*, xiv–xvi.

48. Tugwell, "Resettlement Idea," 159–60.

49. *Ibid.*, 161–63.

50. *Ibid.*, 160.

51. Edward C. Banfield, "Ten Years of the Farm Tenant Purchase Program" *Journal of Farm Economics*, XXXI (Aug. 1949), 469–70, 474.

52. *Ibid.*, 474–75.

53. Joseph Ackerman, "Status and Appraisal of Research in Farm Tenancy," *ibid.*, XXIII (Feb. 1941), 277–78.

54. Report Submitted By Claude Wickard, Nov. 30, 1940, Executive Communication No. 2045; Report of all Payments Over $1,000 Under Sec. 384, AAA of 1938, HR 76A-F1, 1 #1542, Records of the United States House of Representatives, RG 233 (National Archives).

55. *Agricultural Adjustment, 1937–1938*, B-19. On the increase in small payments, see *ibid.*, 106; *Agricultural Adjustment, 1938–1939*, 107–08.

56. Pettit, "Highlights of the 1940 Census," 269.

57. Stine, "Future of Cotton in the Economy of the South," 119.

58. Pettit, "Highlights of the 1940 Census," 269–70.

59. United States Department of Agriculture, *Farm Security Administration* (Washington, 1941), 12.

60. *Ibid.*, 13–14.

61. *Ibid.*, 14.

62. *Ibid.*, 14–15.

63. Statement by C. B. Baldwin, FSA Administrator, before House Committee Investigating FSA, June 29, 1943, mimeographed. See also Grant McConnell, *The Decline of Agrarian Democracy* (New York, 1969), 128–77.

64. Bennett S. White, Jr., "Discussion," *Journal of Farm Economics*, XXIII (Feb. 1941), 131–37.

65. Deward C. Brown, "Rural Electrification," in Theodore Saloutos, ed., "The New Deal and the American Farmer" (unpublished manuscript).

66. Stine, "Future of Cotton in the Economy of the South," 118.

67. *Ibid.*, 119–20.

68. Theodore Saloutos, "The New Deal and Farm Policy in the Great Plains," *Agricultural History*, XLIII (July 1969), 351; E. N. Munns and Joseph H. Stoeckler, "How Are the Great Plains Shelterbelts?" *Journal of Forestry*, XLIV (April 1946), 257.

69. E. C. Johnson, "Agricultural Credit," *Farmers in a Changing World: The Yearbook of Agriculture, 1940* (Washington, 1940), 745–49; Wilcox, *Farmer in the Second World War*, 22–23; W. J. Myers,

Cooperative Farm Mortgage Credit, 1916–1936 (Washington, 1936), 12–23.

70. Wilcox, *Farmer in the Second World War*, 23.

71. Conkin, *New Deal*, 40–43, 59–61, 100–01; Zinn, ed., *New Deal Thought*, xv–xxxvi; Hamby, ed., *New Deal*, 232–40.

72. Wilcox, *Farmer in the Second World War*, 35–36.

THE NEW DEAL AND THE NEGRO COMMUNITY: TOWARD A BROADER CONCEPTUALIZATION

Christopher G. Wye

This essay received the Organization of American Historians' Pelzer Award for 1971. The author acknowledges the financial assistance of the Ford Foundation.

With rare exceptions, research that evaluates the significance of the New Deal public housing and emergency work programs for Negroes has been conceptualized around certain well-defined questions. Most scholars who have approached the subject have focused their attention on the extent to which Negroes were included in these programs in an effort to assess the degree to which the New Deal was successful in alleviating the problems which Negroes faced as a result of the Depression, especially unemployment and the need for low cost housing. These studies have noted that, although Negroes received less assistance than their relatively greater needs warranted, they also received more than their proportionate share. Largely on this basis scholars concluded that the New Deal symbolized a salutary turning point in the attitude of the federal government toward Negroes.[1]

However, if research is conceptualized on a broader basis to include not only questions relating to the extent of Negro participation in the New Deal programs but also questions concerning the impact of these programs on the anatomy of the Negro community, notable qualifications are added to this conclusion and new insight is gained into the problems which the government faced at the local level. If the experience of Cleveland Negroes is representative, it is apparent that the New Deal's inclusion of Negroes in programs designed to relieve the special problems created by the Depression must be balanced against certain adverse side effects which these programs had on the social structure of the black community, especially on patterns of residential and occupational distribution.

On the one hand, the housing projects provided many Negroes with inexpensive and well-maintained living accommodations and the public work programs furnished jobs for a large number of Negroes who would otherwise have been unemployed. On the other hand, the housing projects encouraged residential segregation, contributed to the disruption of the normal pattern of socio-economic differentiation within ghetto neighborhoods, and played a crucial role in spreading slum conditions to new areas of the city, while the public work program appears to have depressed the Negro job structure to lower levels by employing Negroes in occupational categories below those which had been open to them in the private sector of the economy.

In Cleveland, there is evidence to substantiate the familiar conclusion that the New Deal low cost housing program provided Negroes with more than their share of new dwelling units. First through the Public Works Administration (PWA) and later through its successor, the United States Housing Authority (USHA), the federal government sponsored the construction in Cleveland of seven housing projects comprising 7,192 apartments. Three of these projects totaling 3,223 units were eventually occupied by Negroes. Since these 3,223 dwellings represented nearly 50 percent of the total number of units erected and since Negroes made up just under 10 percent of the city's population,[2] this meant that Negroes received approximately five times their share of public housing (see Table I).

Table I

Distribution of Negro and White Families in New Deal Public Housing Projects in Cleveland

	Outh waite Homes	Outhwaite Exten- sion	Carver Park	Cedar Central Homes	Wood- hill Homes	Lake Shore Village	Berea Homes
Negroes	574	1,217	1,226	9	0	1	72
Whites	14	4	21	645	568	800	1,644

Compiled from Cleveland *Call and Post*, Oct. 14, 1937, Aug. 31, 1940, March 8, 1941; and Robert C. Weaver, *The Negro Ghetto* (New York, 1948), 171–72, 197–98.

At the same time, the experience of Cleveland Negroes also confirms the conclusion that the public housing provided for Negroes fell far short of meeting their need. The 3,223 slum clearance units made available to Negroes replaced only one third of the nearly 10,000 homes located within the ghetto which the city's Real Property Inventory classified as "unfit for human habitation."[3] Nevertheless, the fact that the housing projects did not entirely solve the problem of substandard housing in the Negro community should not obscure the fact that they did provide a substantial number of modern and relatively inexpensive homes in an area which had become notorious for its poor condition.

Yet, while the housing projects rejuvenated certain slum sections, their distribution also encouraged residential segregation. Before the advent of the New Deal, more than 90 percent of Cleveland's 72,469 Negroes were concentrated in twenty-nine contiguous census tracts, comprising a compact ghetto on the city's east side.[4] Generally referred to as the Central Avenue district, the ghetto was bordered on the north by Euclid Avenue, an important shopping thoroughfare which marked the fringe of white settlements; on the east by the city's exclusive Shaker Heights suburb; on the south by the New York Central Railroad tracks and the industrial zone beyond; and on the west by Cleveland's downtown shopping area. By constructing three projects—Outhwaite Homes, Outhwaite Extension, and Carver Park—in the very heart of the ghetto, designating them as "Negro projects," and then failing to ensure Negroes free access to "white projects" located outside the Central Avenue district, the federal government lent its considerable influence toward preserving the local pattern of segregated housing (see Map I).[5]

Moreover, several of the "white projects" actually had the effect of intensifying residential segregation. Cedar Central Homes, which was erected just inside the northwest border of the ghetto, and Woodhill Homes, which was constructed on the southeast boundary of the Negro district, were located in racially mixed neighborhoods. In both locations Negroes had constituted approximately 50 percent of the residents. However, when these projects were rented, only nine negroes were admitted to the Cedar Central projects and none were accepted at the Woodhill complex.[6] Cartographic data indicating the final residence of each family who moved to make way for the construction of Cedar Central Homes makes

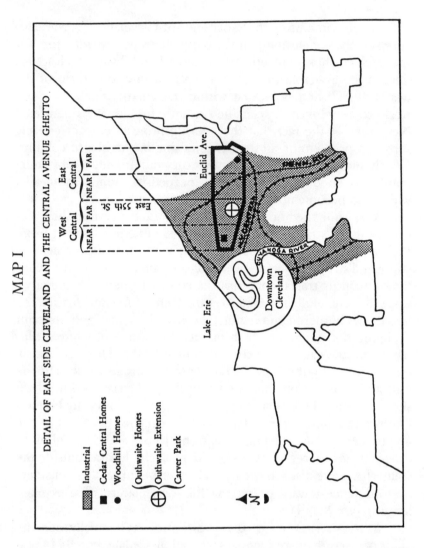

MAP I

DETAIL OF EAST SIDE CLEVELAND AND THE CENTRAL AVENUE GHETTO

Industrial
Cedar Central Homes
Woodhill Homes
Outhwaite Homes
Outhwaite Extension
Carver Park

it possible to establish with certainty that Negroes were pushed inward toward the center of the ghetto (see Map II). And, although similar data is lacking for the families who moved from the Woodhill Homes site, the absence of a significant increase in the number of Negroes in adjoining census tracts outside the Central Avenue district suggests that they too were forced deeper into the Negro section.[7] The influence of the two projects was reflected in the decline in the number of census tracts in which 90 percent of the Negro population lived from twenty-nine in 1930 to twenty-four in 1940.[8] Thus, as a result of the New Deal's housing program, ghetto borders were pushed inward, Negroes were even more heavily concentrated in the Central Avenue area, and segregation was increased.

Negroes were not silent. Protests made by the local National Association for the Advancement of Colored People (NAACP), the Urban League, and Negro politicians eventually resulted in a delegation that was sent to Washington to seek an end to the discrimination in the projects.[9] The director of PWA, Secretary of the Interior Harold L. Ickes, personally sought to assure the group that he was in sympathy with their cause. He pointed to his record as a former president of the Chicago NAACP and indicated that he was "in hearty accord that all groups must work together in the housing program." Moreover, at the conclusion of the meeting, Ickes made it clear that "PWA never had any intention of adopting a race segregation policy."[10] Yet, despite these assurances, Negroes never gained more than token representation in any of the projects located outside the Central Avenue ghetto (see Table I).

If PWA was in fact committed to opposing segregated housing, its practice of handling the actual construction and rental of the project units through local personnel sometimes worked at cross purposes to this policy. In Cleveland the man chosen to oversee PWA housing program, Warren C. Campbell, was a local businessman whose career in real estate offered very little to suggest that he was in sympathy with the principle of integrated housing.[11] As a past president of the Cleveland Real Estate Association, Campbell represented an organization which made it a policy not to rent or sell homes to Negroes in neighborhoods outside the ghetto.[12] Moreover, during World War II, the same organization was primarily responsible for the fact that needed defense housing units were not built for Negroes because it refused to approve the construction site selected by Washington officials.[13] At the same time, as a trustee of the Apartment House Owners Association, Campbell represented an organization which had opposed the slum clearance projects and had proposed to solve the problem of congestion in the Central Avenue district by sending recently arrived southern Negro migrants back to the South.[14]

Although the evidence concerning both Campbell's attitudes and the influence which they had on the housing program in Cleveland is circumstantial, it was under his administration that a variety of techniques were employed with the apparent purpose of ensuring that Negroes and whites were separated.[15] One such strategy was to open two units simultaneously, permitting Negroes to enter only one. This practice had the advantage of making it appear as though Negroes were being equitably included in the public housing program. When Cleveland's first two projects, Cedar Central and Outhwaite Homes, were made available in 1937, a special dedication ceremony featuring prominent Negro leaders was held at the Outhwaite complex, and a Negro project manager was appointed who conducted a special campaign to sell the units to the Negro community; no such activities attended the opening of Cedar Central Homes.[16]

For Negroes who persisted in seeking apartments at Cedar Central, other methods were used. Those who made their race evident by applying in person encountered the suggestion that apartments could be obtained more quickly at Outhwaite.[17] Those who applied by mail were compelled to answer a question asking for their "race or nationality" and found that their applications were transferred to the Negro project.[18] Moreover, as it became evident that Negroes were not being accepted at certain projects, a psychology of avoidance seemed to develop within the Negro community. Many Negroes refused even to apply at projects located outside the ghetto, feeling that "What's the use when we know they don't let Negroes live there anyway."[19]

The housing projects not only encouraged residential segregation but also disrupted the normal pattern of socio-economic differentiation within the ghetto neighborhoods, a process which eventually led to the spread of slum conditions into new sections of the city. Prior to the construction of the units, Negroes were distributed according to a definite pattern of socio-economic gradation within the Central Avenue ghetto. East 55th Street, a main thoroughfare which bisected the Negro community on a north-south axis, represented the dividing line between a lower-status area on the west and a higher-status area on the east. The West Central Avenue district was predominantly a slum and vice area. It was here that Negroes were most heavily congested, that educational and occupational levels were lowest, that disease and death

MAP II

FAMILIES WHO MOVED FROM THE CEDAR CENTRAL
HOMES CONSTRUCTION SITE

One Family

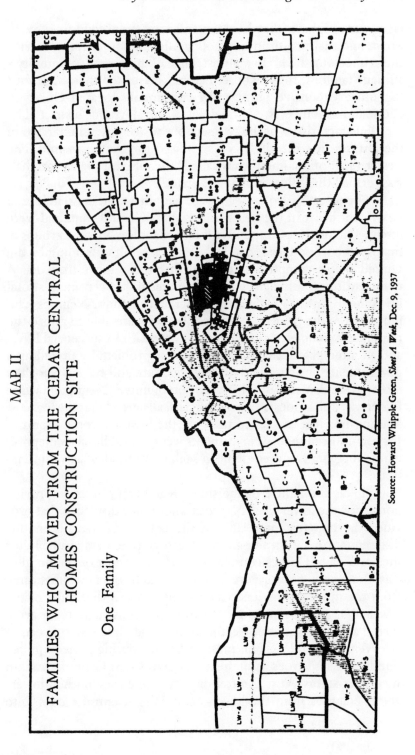

Source: Howard Whipple Green, *Sheet A Week*, Dec. 9, 1937

rates were highest, that housing and sanitation conditions were worst, and that prostitution, bootlegging, and other forms of vice and crime flourished.[20] In contrast, most of the Negro community's affluent families, those whose incomes permitted them to afford the more expensive homes and apartments located closer to Cleveland's suburbs, lived in the East Central Avenue district. The social characteristics of the two sections were aptly summarized in the phrases that the city's Negroes used to refer to them.[21] The western half of the ghetto was called "the jungle"; the eastern half was termed the "Blue Stocking District."[22]

The three Negro projects were built in a tight cluster close to East 55th Street in the heart of the West Central slum and were intended to provide inexpensive lodgings for low-income groups in that neighborhood (see Map I).[23] Yet, as a result of a ruling by the United States comptroller general that the returns from PWA units had to be sufficient to repay the federal government's total investment, only an estimated 10 percent of those Negroes who moved from the project construction sites were able to afford the rents in the completed apartments.[24] When USHA succeeded PWA and an attempt was made to remedy this problem by providing a government subsidy, the rental figures were still too high for the most bereft elements of the Negro community.[25] Negro and white leaders, as well as local housing officials, all agreed that the low cost housing projects had failed to reach the lowest income groups.[26] Instead, most of the new apartments went to middle-class Negroes whose incomes required them to seek more modest accommodations.[27]

It was the failure of the slum clearance projects to provide homes for the lower-class Negroes whom they displaced that provided the impetus for a shift in the pattern of socio-economic differentiation within the ghetto. Cartographic data available for the Outhwaite Homes complex disclose that most of the middle-class Negroes who were eventually housed in the new units came from the upper-status East Central district and that most of the lower-class Negroes who moved from the construction site were forced across East 55th Street into the same higher-status section (see Maps III and IV). This meant that the housing projects pulled middle-class Negroes from the upper-status East Central area into the lower-status West Central district, while they pushed lower-status Negroes from the lower-status West Central section into the upper-status East Central area. In effect, the construction of Outhwaite Homes led to a reversal of residential zones.

Other statistics add weight to this conclusion and suggest that the effects of Outhwaite Extension and Carver Park were similar. Data calculated for two socio-economic indices—education as measured by illiteracy rates and income as measured by median rental figures—reveal that before the projects were constructed there was a pattern of upward gradation from lower levels in the near West Central area through to higher levels in the far East Central area. However, in 1940 when all the three Negro units were completed, this pattern was no longer the same. Statistics for three socio-economic indices—education as measured by years of school completed, income as measured by median rental figures, and occupations as measured by percent of white collar workers—demonstrate that, while in all cases except occupations the near West Central area was still lower than the far East Central area, the two middle areas located on either side of East 55th Street were now reversed with the far West Central area higher than the near East Central area (see Table II).

Table II

Socio-Economic Areas in Census Tracts Over 50 Percent Negro Within the Central Avenue Ghetto, 1930–1940

	1930			
	Near West Central Area	Far West Central Area	Near East Central Area	Far East Central Area
Education by percent illiterate	7.5	5.5	5.0	2.0
Income by rent per month	23.0	27.5	29.7	34.2
	1940			
Education by years completed	7.2	8.5	7.7	8.7
Income by rent per month	16.3	20.3	16.3	21.6
Occupation by percent white collar	32.2	28.0	20.5	24.6

Both illiteracy and rental data for 1930 were derived from census tract statistics presented in Howard Whipple Green, *Population by Census Tract*, Cleveland Health Council, 1931. There were no data for occupations for 1930.

Of the data for 1940, those for education were derived from figures in Howard Whipple Green, *Sheet A Week*, February 11, 1943; those for rentals from Howard Whipple Green, *Cleveland Real Property Inventory, 1941*; and those occupations from *16th Census of the United States:1940. Population and Housing: Statistics for Census Tracts: Cleveland, Ohio and Adjacent Areas* (Washington, 1943).

To correlate the statistical areas indicated here with ghetto neighborhoods see Map I.

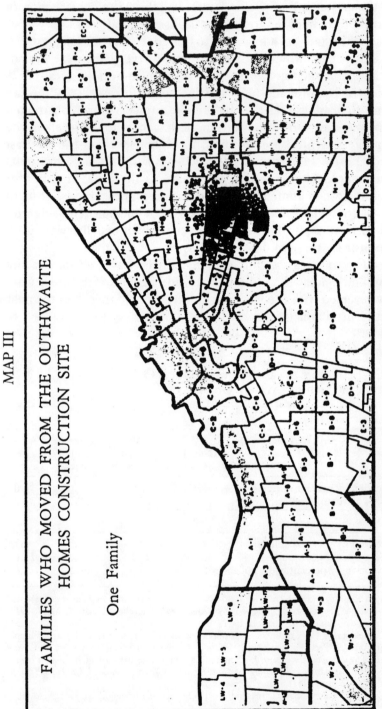

MAP III

FAMILIES WHO MOVED FROM THE OUTHWAITE
HOMES CONSTRUCTION SITE

One Family

Source: Howard Whipple Green, *Cleveland Real Property Inventory, 1936.*

The slum clearance housing projects, therefore, actually succeeded only in moving the slum area from one neighborhood to another. Both black and white observers agreed that the penetration of lower-class Negroes into the upper-status East Central section was attended by a marked deterioration in neighborhood conditions.[28] One and two family homes were converted into "kitchenette apartments," which usually consisted of one room with modest cooking facilities and which generally violated all of the city's building, safety, and sanitation codes.[29] In an area to which Negroes had once pointed with pride as "our showcase of progress ... [where] many of our outstanding businesses [as well as] several of our outstanding churches ... and fine homes add their dignity to the landscape . . ." surveys conducted by social agencies and the white press now found "shacks that even in the most vivid imagination never again can be termed houses . . ." with "holes in the walls and floors, paper falling off, lights out of order, plumbing faulty . . . [and] rats 'so big they look like cats.'"[30] Negro leaders commented bitterly that for those Negroes who had been forced to move by the housing projects, the notice posted on the construction sites which read "Property of the . . . United States Housing Authority" had become an "emblem of despair, desperation and disease."[31] Others went so far as to call USHA the "greatest menace to the Negro . . . in Cleveland today."[32]

Moreover, as lower-class Negroes moved into the East Central section, the "sporting element" appeared with greater frequency east of East 55th Street. Prostitutes, both Negro and white, plied their trade as far east as East 80th Street in a district referred to as "Little Hollywood."[33] Speakeasies dispensing liquor obtained from Cleveland's Italian bootleggers, the Mayfield Road Gang, which itself centered on the eastern fringe of the ghetto, became numerous along the Pennsylvania railroad tracks which cut across the area.[34] And policy, a form of nickle-and-dime gambling, was ubiquitous.[35]

While the New Deal low cost housing projects had both positive and negative effects on ghetto residential patterns, the public work program had a similarly mixed impact on the structure of Negro employment. Because Negroes were concentrated in jobs that were particularly vulnerable to dislocation in a contracting

MAP IV

FAMILIES WHO MOVED INTO OUTHWAITE HOMES

One Family

Source: Howard Whipple Green, *Cleveland Real Property Inventory*, 1936.

economy—primarily in unskilled labor and domestic service—the Depression hit Negroes with unusual severity. Although they made up only 10 percent of the available workers, they constituted 27 percent of the unemployed.[36] Within the Central Avenue ghetto unemployment averaged 50 percent and in some sections was as high as 90 percent.[37] Moreover, the effects of the Depression on Negroes were not relieved to any appreciable extent by the limited relief and emergency work projects sponsored by local agencies.[38] The seriousness of the Negroes' plight was summed up in reports made by the Negro community's two leading social welfare agencies. A survey conducted by the Phyllis Wheatley Association expressed the belief that "the race is standing on a precipice of economic disaster," while the Annual Report of the Cleveland Urban League for 1933 indicated that conditions among Negroes had "reached a state approaching chaos."[39]

Although the New Deal public work programs did not entirely meet the needs of the Negro community, Negroes received more than their share of the jobs which were provided.[40] The result was a substantial reduction in the high unemployment rate within the ghetto. Negroes generally constituted more than 10 percent of all workers assigned to the Civilian Conservation Corps from Cuyahoga County.[41] Central High School, which was located within the ghetto and was attended almost entirely by Negroes, regularly received larger grants from the National Youth Administration than any other single school in the city.[42] PWA—the same agency which built the low cost housing units—operated under a percentage formula which assured Negroes at least the number of jobs equal to their proportion of the total labor force.[43] And in the Works Projects Administration (WPA) activities, which accounted for the largest share of emergency work in Cleveland, Negroes averaged approximately 30 percent of the work force.[44] Moreover, Negroes held nearly 40 percent, or about four times their proportionate share, of all the jobs that were created by emergency work programs.[45] By at least the mid-1930s, New Deal public work projects had succeeded in reducing unemployment among Negroes from about 50 percent to 30 percent and the federal government had become the largest single employer of Cleveland Negroes as well as the most important new influence on the Negro job structure.[46]

However, while the federal government's emergency work programs significantly reduced the high rate of unemployment within the Negro community, they also appear to have depressed the Negro job structure by engaging many workers in job categories below those which they had filled in the private sector of the economy before the Depression began. A comparison of the occupational distribution of Negro workers with that of whites indicates that on eve of the Depression Negroes were underrepresented by from 30 percent to 80 percent in occupations above the skilled level, while they were overrepresented by from 20 percent to 300 percent in occupations below this category. As a result, 79 percent of all Negro males and 93 percent of all Negro females were employed below the skilled level, primarily in Cleveland's iron and steel mills and as servants in white homes.[47]

Yes, there is evidence to suggest that Negroes may have sunk to lower occupational levels. On public work projects the experience of Cleveland Negroes with PWA illustrates this point. PWA was especially important to Negro skilled workers in the building trades since, during the Depression-engendered lull in private building, it held a virtual monopoly over the available jobs in the construction industry. But at best the policies of PWA could have accomplished no more than to maintain the occupational color line.[48] This was evident from the terms of an agreement worked out between the Cleveland Urban League and the Department of the Interior that provided only that "the percentage of Negroes in each skilled craft shall equal the ratio that the number of Negro skilled workers bore to the number of white workers in each skilled craft as shown by the census of 1930."[49] Even this minimum standard, however, was widely disregarded.[50] The Negro press reported that "only four to five lonely Negroes are polka dotted among the hundreds of skilled workers" and concluded that "the percentage agreement from Washington . . . is apparently not being followed."[51] A survey conducted by the Cleveland Urban League confirmed this conclusion when it found that only five Negro carpenters, two cement finishers, six bricklayers, and one engineer were employed on all of PWA projects.[52]

More detailed information regarding the concentration of Negroes in unskilled occupations on the New Deal projects is available for WPA. The Cleveland Urban League in 1936 made a survey to determine what jobs Negroes held on eight sample public work projects, and the national *Census of Unemployment* in 1937 obtained information relative to the *former* occupations of Negroes temporarily employed on the government projects.[53] A comparison of these data shows that, while the former occupations of Negroes on emergency work constituted a representative cross section of the total Negro labor force, the jobs which Negroes held on government projects were disproportionately unskilled labor. Among Negro males, 819, or 16.7 percent, of those on public work had been formerly employed in skilled jobs, yet of these, only thirty-four, or .6 percent, held similar jobs on the emergency work projects. Similarly, among Negro females, 213, or 20.4 percent, of those in the public work programs had been formerly occupied in skilled jobs, but of these only five, or .3 percent, held comparable jobs on federal projects. Thus, in the private sector of the economy 79 percent of all Negro males and 93 percent of all Negro females were employed in unskilled labor, on eight WPA projects sampled by the Urban League these percentages increased to 99.4 percent for men and to 99.7 percent for women.[54]

The tendency for Negroes to be employed at lower job levels on the New Deal projects than those which they had occupied in private industry was the result of several factors. Of primary importance was the occupational design of the relief effort. Despite the attempts of government administrators to provide employment for skilled, white collar, and professional workers, the greatest number of federally sponsored jobs were in manual labor. For this reason occupation depression on the work projects was a characteristic of the white as well as the Negro labor force. The problems of black workers, however, were intensified by an apparently widespread pattern of discrimination in job classification at the local level. A survey by the Negro press both summed up this pattern and revealed the resentment Negroes felt toward it:

> Not a single Negro has a job on the state WPA staff. Not a single Negro . . . has an executive position on the WPA county staff. Out of the hundreds of clerks employed by the WPA headquarters not one is a Negro. Of the hundreds of foremen on the scores of projects that are being operated by the WPA here there are only two Negroes. Practically all of the jobs the WPA has to offer above the role of menial labor are given to whites. We have good ground for the charge that there is widespread and deliberate discrimination against our people. There

are practically no promotions of Negroes on projects.
When Negro workers reach the point where they are
eligible for promotion their jobs are abolished or some
trumped up charge against them brings their dismissal.
When Negroes are fortunate enough to be placed on a
project where the work is pleasant they are mysteriously
laid off. . . . All of our men are not ditchdiggers, neither
are all of our women domestics. . . . The administration
of WPA in Ohio and especially in Cuyahoga County has
about reached the point of scandal.[55]

Although a continuous stream of protest from Negro leaders
prompted Washington administrators to action on several occasions, very little improvement was effected. A conference in 1935
of the Cleveland Urban League and WPA officials resulted in the
employment of a "few Negro supervisors and foremen," mostly on
Negro projects.[56] Negroes continued to complain, however, and
three years later representatives of the national administration conducted an investigation of WPA operations in Cleveland which
confirmed the existence of discrimination but which resulted only
in a promise to employ Negroes in "several white collar jobs" and
to appoint "at least three [Negroes] in a supervisory capacity."[57] A
similar investigation made in 1939 ended with the dismissal of
several local white executives on charges of discriminating against
Negro skilled workers. But it appears that none of these actions
achieved more than temporary improvement. A Negro leader observed, "When there is a rumor of an investigation they seem to
find [skilled] Negroes from somewhere, but as soon as the heat is
off the Negroes . . . on the projects begin to disappear. It is about
as difficult for a skilled Negro operator to be assigned to a power
machine as it is for him to find a job in private industry."[58]

The failure of the federal government to curb discrimination
on the public work projects was due largely to its ineffectiveness in
dealing with lower echelon personnel. Washington officials might
attempt to eliminate the discrimination exhibited by administrators in executive positions at county headquarters, but only rarely
did they make a determined effort to curtail the discriminatory
practices of project leaders in the field, especially among foremen
and supervisors. Yet it was the project leaders who controlled the
allocation of jobs on the emergency work programs. Effectively, it
was they who determined the final job classification for most workers; it was they who determined who was to be laid off when

cutbacks were made; it was they who administered discipline (which could result in dismissal); and it was they who recommended promotions and demotions.

The variety of techniques employed by foremen and supervisors to restrict Negroes to unskilled occupations were frequently documented in the Negro press. Sometimes a project leader would refuse altogether to accept a skilled Negro. In one such instance, WPA county headquarters assigned two Negro typists to an indexing project, but the project supervisor wrote on the back of their assignment slips. "This project cannot use colored typists" and then sent them back to the county office.[59] More frequent was the practice of accepting a skilled Negro worker on a project and later demoting him to an unskilled job. This was the experience of a Negro electrician who was reclassified as a common laborer and put to work washing light bulbs.[60] Moreover, when Negro skilled workers who had been demoted to unskilled positions applied for reclassification their application forms were frequently lost between the office of the project foremen and the office of county headquarters.[61] And, Negroes who sought to register a complaint about their failure to be reclassified were threatened with dismissal, demotion, or a disciplinary reduction in pay.[62]

That lower echelon personnel in the field rather than executives at county headquarters were primarily responsible for the discrimination against Negro skilled workers on the public work projects was widely recognized by Negro leaders who considered them to be "czars" in the matter of job classification.[63] By the late 1930s comments of Negro leaders reflected a respect for the efforts of the county officials to secure a fair distribution of work for Negroes, while at the same time they displayed a certain resignation to the role of prejudiced foremen. In 1939 the Cleveland *Call and Post*, which had been one of the leaders in the campaign conducted by the Negro press to secure skilled jobs for Negroes, concluded that, "Despite the obvious efforts of departmental heads to do something about the violation of orders with reference to the classification . . . of workers . . . [their] efforts to secure a square deal for Negro skilled . . . workers . . . has continued to be obstructed by prejudiced foremen and office underlings."[64] A year later the same paper remarked that "while the central office WPA is innocent of responsibility for discrimination against Negro applicants, it is known that under officials at that office have turned their heads in the opposite direction while some underling supervisor or project foreman did the dirty work."[65]

These findings suggest that new perspectives on the relationship between Negroes and the New Deal are revealed if research is conceptualized on a basis broad enough to embrace both questions concerning the extent of Negro participation in government programs as well as questions relating to the impact of these programs on the social structure of the Negro community. Specifically, the Cleveland experience demonstrates that although the New Deal public housing and emergency work programs played an important part in alleviating the problems generated by the Depression, they also contributed to the preservation of perhaps the two salient components which combine to produce a caste-like Negro social structure—residential segregation and a distinctly racial occupational pattern.

NOTES

1. Richard Sterner and others, *The Negro's Share: A Study of Income, Consumption, Housing and Public Assistance* (New York, 1943); Gunnar Myrdal and others, *An American Dilemma: The Negro Problem and Modern Democracy* (New York, 1944); Leslie H. Fishel, Jr., "The Negro in the New Deal Era," *Wisconsin Magazine of History*, XLVIII (Winter 1964–1965), 111–26; Raymond Wolters, *Negroes and the Great Depression: The Problem of Economic Recovery* (Westport, Conn., 1970); St. Clair Drake and Horace R. Cayton, *Black Metropolis: A Study of Negro Life in a Northern City* (New York, 1945); Robert C. Weaver, *The Negro Ghetto* (New York, 1948); Robert C. Weaver, *Negro Labor: A National Problem* (New York, 1946); Robert C. Weaver, "Negro Labor since 1929," *Journal of Negro History*, XXXV (Jan. 1950), 20–28. These sources occasionally note that the New Deal housing program encouraged segregation and that the emergency work program employed Negroes below their level of ability or training.

2. Howard Whipple Green, *Census Facts and Trends by Tracts* (Cleveland, 1954), 5.

3. Howard Whipple Green, *Substandard Housing as Determined by the Low Income Housing Area Survey* (Cleveland, 1940), 5–6.

4. Green, *Census Facts and Trends by Tracts*, 108–10.

5. For reports of official references to the housing units as either "Negro projects" or "white projects," see *Cleveland Press*, Jan. 19, 21, 23, 1935; L. P. Mitchell to Harold L. Ickes [1935], National Association for the Advancement of Colored People Branch Files (NAACP Branch Files) (Library of Congress).

6. Howard Whipple Green, "Cedar Central Apartments are 100 Per Cent Leased," *Sheet A Week*, Nov. 26, 1937; *Cleveland Plain Dealer*, Jan. 22, 1935; Cleveland *Call and Post*, April 25, Oct. 21, Nov. 23, 30, 1937, Dec. 7, 1940; Cleveland *Gazette*, Oct. 30. 1937.

7. Green, *Census Facts and Trends by Tracts*, 108–10.

8. *Ibid.*

9. Cleveland *Gazette*, Feb. 2, 1935; Cleveland *Call and Post*, Jan. 26, 1935; Cleveland *Eagle*, Jan. 17, 1936; Cleveland *Press*, Jan. 22, 1935; Cleveland *Plain Dealer*, Jan. 22, 1935. See also Mitchell to Walter White, Oct. 6, 1937, H. A. Gray to White, Sept. 28, 1937, C. K. Gillespie to White [1935], NAACP Branch Files.

10. Cleveland *Gazette*, Feb. 2, 1935.

11. *Ibid.*, July 25, 1936.

12. Cleveland *Eagle*, April 3, 1936; Cleveland *NAACP Branch Quarterly*, NAACP Branch Files.

13. The Federal Housing Administration was ready to construct war housing for Negroes in Cleveland. A local financial institution was ready to finance the projects if the Cleveland Real Estate Board would approve the construction site. The board, however, failed to approve the location and the local source of finance then withdrew its offer. As a result, no units were built in Cleveland for Negroes. For details of this episode, see Weaver, *Negro Ghetto*, 216.

14. Cleveland *Gazette*, Sept. 24, 1932.

15. In 1940 when the Cleveland Metropolitan Housing Authority took over the management of the housing projects from the United States Housing Authority, Warren C. Campbell was replaced by Marc J. Grossman, a civic leader well known for his interest in philanthropic movements. But, the policy of segregating Negroes and whites did not change under his administration before 1944.

16. Cleveland *Call and Post*, July 12, 1937, Feb. 1, 1941.

17. Cleveland *Gazette*, Oct. 16, 1937; Cleveland *Call and Post*, Nov. 30, 1940. See also Gillespie to Ickes, Sept. 23, 1937, Campbell to Gray, Oct. 4, 1937, Mitchell to White, Oct. 22, 1937, NAACP Branch Files.

18. Cleveland *Gazette*, March 20, 1937; Cleveland *Call and Post*, Aug. 25, 1937.

19. Cleveland *Call and Post*, Feb. 15, 1941.

20. Robert Bernard Navin, *Analysis of a Slum Area* (Washington, 1934), 24–56; Howard Whipple Green, "Slums—A City's Most Expensive Luxury," *Sheet A Week*, Sept. 22, 1934; Gordon H. Simpson, "Economic Survey of Housing in Districts of the City of Cleveland Occupied Largely by Colored People" [mimeographed report of the Cleveland Chamber of Commerce, 1931], 20–50; "The Central Area Social Study" [mimeographed report of the Welfare Federation of Cleveland, 1944], 42–53, 124–46.

21. Simpson, "Economic Survey of Housing," 51–135; "Central Area Social Study," 42–53, 124–46; Wellington G. Fordyce, "Immigrant Colonies in Cleveland," *The Ohio State Archaeological and Historical Quarterly*, XLV (Oct. 1936), 320–40.

22. "Central Area Social Study," 124; Cleveland *Call and Post*, March 16, 1939.

23. Cleveland *Gazette*, May 16, 1931; Cleveland *Call and Post*, Feb. 6, 1936.

24. Cleveland *Gazette*, Feb. 1, 1936; Sterner, *Negro's Share*, 317; Cleveland Call and Post, Feb. 1, 1941.

25. Cleveland *Gazette*, Nov. 23, 1935; Cleveland *Call and Post*, March 21, 1940; Howard Whipple Green, "The Families That Moved to Make Way for the Outhwaite Housing Project," *Sheet A Week*, June 11, 1936.

26. Cleveland *Gazette*, May 28, 1938; Cleveland *Press*, Aug. 8, 1932. Grossman, who became head of the Cleveland Metropolitan Housing Authority on January 1, 1940, remarked in answer to a query from local Negro leaders: "The Housing projects built and to be built in the city of Cleveland do not and will not permit members of the lowest income group for whom they were first . . . [intended] to become tenants . . ." Cleveland *Gazette*, Nov. 25, 1939.

27. Cleveland *Press*, Nov. 23, 1932, June 2, 1933.

28. Cleveland *Gazette*, May 15, 1937; Cleveland *Press*, June 2, 1933.

29. Cleveland *Call and Post*, Nov. 8, 1941; Cleveland *Press*, Aug. 22, 1935, Dec. 1, 2, 3, 4, 1941.

30. Cleveland *Press*, March 12, 1934, Dec. 1, 2, 1941.

31. Cleveland *Call and Post*, Feb. 1, 1941.

32. *Ibid.*, Sept. 13, 1941.

33. Gordon H. Simpson to White, June 24, 1932, NAACP Branch Files; Cleveland *Press*, Aug. 12, 1930; Cleveland *Call and Post*, Oct. 24, 1935.

34. Cleveland *Press*, June 2, 1932.

35. *Ibid.*, March 14, 1935; David H. Pierce to Roy Wilkins, July 9, 1932, NAACP Branch Files; Cleveland *Gazette*, June 1, 1935; Cleveland *Call and Post*, Oct. 24. 1935.

36. *Fifteenth Census of the United States: 1930. Population: Occupations, by States: Reports by States, Giving Statistics for Cities of 25,000 or More* (Washington, 1933), 1269.

37. Weaver, "Negro Labor since 1929," 22; "Press Release," Cleveland NAACP, April 15, 1942, NAACP Branch Files.

38. Lucia Johnson Bing, *Social Work in Greater Cleveland: How Public and Private Agencies Are Serving Human Needs* (Cleveland, 1938), 14–26; Joanna C. Colcord, *Cash Relief* (New York, 1936), 59–63.

39. Cleveland *Call and Post*, Jan. 12, 1935; "Annual Report of the Negro Welfare Association, 1933," Cleveland Urban League Papers (Western Reserve Historical Society). The Negro Welfare Association was the Cleveland affiliate of the National Urban League.

40. Interview with Russell W. Jelliffe, Oct. 20, 1969.

41. "Minutes of the Board of Trustees of the Negro Welfare Association, June 1, 1936," Cleveland Urban League Papers; Cleveland *Call and Post*, July 14, 1936; C. V. Colwill to Clayborne George, June 11, 1933, NAACP Branch Files.

42. Cleveland *Call and Post*, July 6, 1939.

43. "Minutes of the Board of Trustees of the Negro Welfare Association, May 3, 1935," Cleveland Urban League Papers.

44. Cleveland *Press*, April 18, 1941.

45. Statistics derived from data in *Sixteenth Census of the United States: 1940. Population.* Vol. III, *The Labor Force: Occupation, Industry, Employment, and Income.* Part 4: *Nebraska-Oregon* (Washington, 1943), 639.

46. *Census of Partial Employment, Unemployment, and Occupations: 1937: States from North Carolina to Wyoming, Alaska, and Hawaii.* Part 4: *Nebraska-Oregon* (Washington, 1938), 71–75. "Annual Report of the Negro Welfare Association, 1938," Cleveland Urban League Papers.

47. These statistics were obtained by reclassifying all of the occupations of blacks and whites in the 1930 census according to the ranking system developed by Alba M. Edwards. This system involves a six category classification from unskilled labor at the bottom, through semiskilled, skilled, clerical, business, and finally to professional workers at the top. But for the purpose of brevity the procedure followed here has been to refer to all jobs in the skilled, clerical, business, and professional categories as simply skilled labor. The advantage of Edwards' system is that it permits an orderly ranking of jobs according to desirability and, therefore, provides a good basis for comparing the structure of Negro and white employment. The concept of a proportionate share, on which figures concerning underrepresentation and overrepresentation are based, assumes that all other things being equal Negro workers might be expected to approximate the percentage which they represent of the total labor force in each occupational category. Drake and Cayton, *Black Metropolis,* 223–32; Alba M. Edwards, *A Social-Economic Grouping of the Gainful Workers of the United States: Gainful Workers of 1930 in social-economic groups, by color nativity, age, and sex, and by industry, with comparative statistics for 1920 and 1910* (Washington, 1938).

48. Wolters, *Negroes and the Great Depression,* 203–12.

49. "Minutes of the Board of Trustees of the Negro Welfare Association, May 3, 1935," Cleveland Urban League Papers.

50. Interview with George W. Hanzly, Sept. 15, 1971.

51. Cleveland *Eagle,* Nov. 22, 1935.

52. "Minutes of the Organization of Building Trades Craftsmen [an organization sponsored by the Negro Welfare Association], Oct. 13, 1936," Cleveland Urban League Papers.

53. Cleveland *Eagle,* Jan. 3, 1936; *Census of Partial Employment,* 83.

54. These data were obtained by using the Edwards classification.

55. Cleveland *Call and Post*, Feb. 24, 1938.

56. "Minutes of the Board of Trustees of the Negro Welfare Association, Dec. 13, 1935," Cleveland Urban League Papers; *ibid.*, Jan. 10, 1936; Cleveland *Call and Post*, June 16, 1938.

57. Cleveland *Call and Post*, June 2, 1938.

58. *Ibid.*, Sept. 14, 1939.

59. *Ibid.*, June 23, July 7, 28, 1938, Feb. 1, 1940.

60. *Ibid.*, June 16, 1938.

61. *Ibid.*, July 14, 1938.

62. *Ibid.*, July 28, 1938.

63. *Ibid.* April 27, 1939.

64. *Ibid.*, July 14, 1938.

65. *Ibid.*, Feb. 1, 1940.

FRANKLIN D. ROOSEVELT'S SUPREME COURT "PACKING" PLAN

William E. Leuchtenburg

Franklin D. Roosevelt's proposal to "pack" the Supreme Court in 1937 bore the mark of a proud sovereign who after suffering many provocations had just received a new confirmation of his power. In November, 1936, the President had won the greatest electoral victory in the history of the two-party system. He had captured forty-six of the country's forty-eight states—all but Maine and Vermont—precisely as his campaign manager, James A. Farley, had predicted. Roosevelt was jubilant at the result. "I knew I should have gone to Maine and Vermont," he said, "but Jim wouldn't let me."[1]

Yet Roosevelt's sense of triumph was flawed by the realization that it was incomplete, for if he controlled the Executive office and could expect to have his way with Congress, where he had led his party to a smashing victory, the third branch, the Supreme Court, seemed intractable. Four of the justices—James McReynolds, Pierce Butler, Willis Van Devanter, and George Sutherland—were such staunch conservatives that almost every time Roosevelt's Attorney General, Homer Cummings, went into court, he knew he had four votes against him; if he lost even one of the remaining five he would be beaten. Three judges—Louis Brandeis, Harlan Fiske Stone, and Benjamin Cardozo—would approve most of the New Deal laws. But if either of the two justices in the center—Chief Justice Charles Evans Hughes or Owen Roberts—joined the conservative "Four Horsemen," Roosevelt's program might perish in the courtroom.

Early in the New Deal, except for a relatively minor ruling in the "hot oil" opinion,[2] the Supreme Court had appeared willing to uphold novel legislation. In two state cases and in the "gold clause cases," the Court sustained emergency acts, although each time by an uncomfortably close 5–4 margin.[3]

But in the spring of 1935 the roof fell in. Justice Roberts joined the conservative four to invalidate a rail pension law,[4] and thereafter Roberts voted with the conservatives on a number of crucial cases. Later that same month, on Black Monday, May 27, 1935, the Court, this time in a unanimous decision, demolished the National Industrial Recovery Act.⁵ In the next year the Court, in a 6–3 decision, struck down the Agricultural Adjustment Act in an opinion by Justice Roberts that provoked a blistering dissent by Justice Stone; took special pains to knock out the Guffey Coal Act in the *Carter* case; in the *Tipaldo* case invalidated a New York State minimum wage law.⁶ Of all the wounds the Court inflicted on itself, the *Tipaldo* decision cut deepest. It appeared to create, as Roosevelt said, a "no-man's-land," in which neither the federal nor state governments could act to protect the worker.⁷ At the end of the historic session, Justice Stone wrote: "We finished the term of Court yesterday, I think in many ways one of the most disastrous in its history."⁸

As Roosevelt contemplated his second term, a confrontation with the Supreme Court seemed inevitable. No doubt he wished to rebuke the justices for invalidating so much of the legislation passed in his first term, including the two big acts, the NIRA and the AAA. Even more important, the reasoning in such cases suggested that the Court would find still other laws unconstitutional when tests of these statutes reached it. In jeopardy in the next few months would be such landmarks as the Social Security Act and the Wagner National Labor Relations Act. But this was not all. Despite having won an unprecedented mandate, the President felt constrained in asking Congress for new legislation, such as a wages and hours bill, because the Court might very well strike down these new measures too.

Was there a way out of the President's dilemma short of a direct confrontation? The most obvious course would be for Roosevelt to wait until one or more justices resigned or died, but he could not foresee how long a period this would be. Not a single justice had left the bench in his entire first term. No president since Andrew Johnson had served a full term without being able to appoint at least one new member of the Court. Many New Dealers thought—perhaps with reason—that some aged justices would, in other circumstances, have retired, but were deliberately remaining on the bench to frustrate the President. Some believed that some justices were deliberately staying alive in order to thwart him.

Possibly, too, the President might have waited to see whether the election returns had helped to change the minds of the justices. But this seemed a poor risk, given the record of the Court as recently as the previous spring. Moreover, many of the New Dealers sensed a special urgency. They perceived the crisis of the depression as a priceless opportunity to advance social legislation and wished to exploit the President's stunning victory, which gave new momentum to the drive for reform. If Roosevelt hesitated, the sense of crisis might diminish and the momentum would be lost.

Given Roosevelt's determination to reform the Judiciary, what method was he to choose?[9] He had many choices before him, most of them embracing some kind of constitutional amendment. Some proposed that the Court be limited to invalidating statues only if it had a majority greater than 5–4. Others wanted to give Congress the right to re-enact laws by a two-thirds vote over an adverse decision. Still others wished to specify that Congress had broad authority to regulate labor conditions.

But these proposed constitutional amendments, it was argued, did not meet the problem posed by the Court's intransigence, or, if they did, they were not feasible politically. Roosevelt maintained that a constitutional amendment could not be ratified by a sufficient number of states, not at least in a reasonable period of time. "If you were not as scrupulous and ethical as you happen to be," he later wrote a prominent New York attorney who favored the amendment process, "you could make five million dollars as easy as rolling off a log by undertaking a campaign to prevent the ratification by one house of the Legislature, or even the summoning of a constitutional convention in thirteen states for the next four years. Easy money."[10]

Moreover, any legislation passed under the authorization of an amendment expanding the power of Congress would still be subject to review by the courts. "In view of what Mr. Justice Roberts did to a clause as broad and sweeping as 'the general welfare,'" observed the historian Charles Beard, "I can see other justices of his mental outlook macerating almost any clarifying amendment less generous in its terms. If there is any phrase wider than providing for the general welfare, I am unable to conjure it up in my mind."[11]

Roosevelt reasoned that it was not the Constitution that needed to be changed but the Court. Increasingly, he turned to the idea of reform by an act of Congress rather than by amendment and to basing the law on a court-packing procedure founded on the principle of the age of the justices. In coming to this decision, he was influenced by the British precedent earlier in the century in the threat to pack the House of Lords. The specific device which Roosevelt and Cummings hit upon was one originally proposed for lower court justices by none other than Justice McReynolds when he had been Attorney General, and the President took a keen pleasure in that fact. But Roosevelt, who delighted in dramatic surprises, kept his decision a closely-guarded secret, hidden not only from his congressional leaders but even from his Cabinet and some of his intimates.

After the election, the President went off on a cruise to South America, while the country waited in expectation to see what legislation he would recommend for his second term. In January, Roosevelt gave his inaugural address without indicating what he planned to do. The new Congress convened, and more days passed, and still he did not let on what he was going to say. Then, abruptly, without warning, the President, on February 5, 1937, dropped a bombshell. Instead of calling for new social reforms, Roosevelt caught the nation, his congressional leaders, and his closest friends by surprise with a bold, quite unexpected proposal—to add six justices to the United States Supreme Court.

Roosevelt sent his scheme for reorganizing the Judiciary up to the Hill in a special message. The President claimed that insufficient personnel had resulted in overcrowded federal court dockets and had occasioned great delay and expense to litigants. "A part of the problem of obtaining a sufficient number of judges to dispose of cases is the capacity of the judges themselves," the President stated. "This brings forward the question of aged or infirm judges— a subject of delicacy and yet one which requires frank discussion."

"In exceptional cases, of course," Roosevelt conceded, "judges, like other men, retain to an advanced age full mental and physical vigor. Those not so fortunate are often unable to perceive their own infirmities. . . .

"A lower mental or physical vigor leads men to avoid an examination of complicated and changed conditions. Little by little, new facts become blurred through old glasses fitted, as it were, for the needs of another generation; older men, assuming that the scene is the same as it was in the past, cease to explore or inquire into the present or the future." Life tenure for judges, the President declared, "was not intended to create a static judiciary. A constant and systematic addition of younger blood will vitalize the courts. . . ."

To achieve this end, the President recommended that when a federal judge who had served at least ten years waited more than six months after his seventieth birthday to resign or retire, the President might add a new judge to the bench. He would appoint as many as, but not more than, six new justices to the Supreme Court and forty-four new judges to the lower federal tribunals.[12] Since it seemed improbable that the justices would choose to resign, the plan was perceived to be an attempt to enlarge the Court.

The President's message generated an intensity of response unmatched by any legislative controversy of this century, save perhaps for the League of Nations episode. "No issue since the Civil War has so deeply split families, friends, and fellow lawyers," wrote one columnist.[13] Day after day, for the next half year, stories about the Supreme Court conflict rated banner headlines in the nation's press. One diarist noted: "Roosevelt's alteration plan of Supreme Court stirs America. Addresses, talks, arguments for and against it, everywhere."[14] The question was debated at town meetings in New England, at crossroads country stores in North Carolina, at a large rally at the Tulsa court house, by the Chatterbox Club of Rochester, New York, the Thursday Study Club of La Crosse, Wisconsin, the Veteran Fire Fighter's Association of New Orleans, and the Baptist Young People's Union of Lime Rock, Rhode Island.[15] In Beaumont, Texas, a movie audience broke out in applause for rival arguments on the Court plan when they were shown on the screen.[16]

Congressmen were inundated with communications from constituents on the Court bill. Senator Hiram Johnson of California reported: "I receive some hundreds of letters a day, all on the Court,—sometimes some thousands."[17] Senator Charles O. Andrews of Florida acknowledged: "We are receiving hundreds of letters regarding the Supreme Court and they have not been answered because it has been impossible to even read one-third, much less answer them. We have, however, answered many by working nights and Sundays."[18] Snowed under by 30,000 letters and telegrams, Senator Royal Copeland of New York said his office was "quite disorganized," and he pleaded for "some relief." "I feel fully informed of the wishes of my constituents," he added drily.[19]

No sooner was the message read in the House than the San Antonio congressman Maury Maverick raced down the aisle and dropped the bill in the hopper. But the Administration decided to concentrate not on the House but on the Senate, in part because it wished to avoid a clash with another Texan, Hatton Sumners, the hostile chairman of the House Judiciary Committee, and with Speaker William Bankhead of Alabama, who resented Roosevelt's failure to take congressional leaders into his confidence.[20] However, even opponents of the plan conceded that the bill would be approved in the House with many votes to spare.[21]

The situation in the Senate seemed almost as promising. FDR had so overwhelming a majority in the upper house that several Democrats were crowded across the aisle into the Republican section. The President figured to lose a few conservative Democrats, but he might make them up with progressive Republicans like Hiram Johnson and Gerald Nye and independents like George Norris.[22] Yet Roosevelt was unlikely to need these, for there were enough Democratic senators who owed their election to him to provide a comfortable margin. If every one of the sixteen Republicans rejected the measure, the opponents would still need more than twice that many Democrats to defeat it.

In the first week, numbers of Democratic senators announced themselves for the bill, including a phalanx of influential leaders like Majority Leader Joseph T. Robinson of Arkansas, the chairman of the Judiciary Committee, Henry Fountain Ashurst of Arizona, and such potent allies as Pat Harrison of Mississippi, James F. Byrnes, Jr., of South Carolina, and Key Pittman of Nevada. Men of rather conservative disposition, they received the plan with varying degrees of unenthusiasm but supported it out of loyalty to the President and the Democratic Party. More ardent backing came from such New Deal liberals as Hugo Black of Alabama and Sherman Minton of Indiana, both future Supreme Court justices. After assessing the situation, the White House concluded that no more than fifteen Democrats would oppose the bill in the Senate.[23] *Time* reported: "Newshawks who immediately made surveys of Congressional sentiment agreed that the bill would be passed without serious difficulty."[24]

Greeted in the press with anguished cries of outrage, the plan also elicited no little enthusiasm, especially from Roosevelt's admirers. They argued that the proposal was designed not to pack the Court but to "unpack" it, since the Court had been "stuffed" with corporation lawyers in previous Republican regimes.[25] The whole machinery of American government, they asserted, lay at the will of a single justice, Owen Roberts, who, by combining with the Four Horsemen, could nullify the wishes of the people.[26] A number of the bill's proponents charged that the Court had usurped its powers; some even denied that there was any constitutional sanction for judicial review.[27] Moreover, they claimed that there was ample historical precedent for altering the size of the Court.[28] Nor would they concede that Roosevelt was plunging the Court into politics; Rep. Thomas R. Amlie, a Wisconsin Progressive, contended: "The fact is that the Supreme Court has always been in politics up to its ears."[29]

Many shared Roosevelt's concern about the age of the justices, a feeling that had been intensified by the best-seller, Robert S. Allen's and Drew Pearson's *The Nine Old Men*.[30] One man wrote Chief Justice Hughes: "Seems to me if I were 75 I would be glad to enjoy life instead of working and taking a job away from some young family man."[31] Some Tennessee lawyers pointed out that a justice of 70 was an adult "before the telephone was invented, he was 35 before the automobile became of importance, and was over 40 before the airplane became a factor in national life. The golden of age of gasoline, electricity, chemistry, mass production, radio and education had not in the main begun when the man of 70 had reached the age of 45."[32] A Wisconsin man wrote: "Take it in my own case. I am assured by my acquaintances that I do not look any older than I did fifteen or twenty years ago. That may be true as to looks and mentality, but at my age (seventy seven), any sane man must know that physically I can not measure up to fifteen or twenty years ago. I could not possibly put in working hours that I did when serving in the State Senate eighteen years ago."[33]

Supporters of the plan scoffed at the worshipful attitude opponents took toward the Constitution and the Court. "A constitution is not an idol to be worshipped; it is an instrument of government to be worked," observed Senator Robert J. Bulkley of Ohio.[34] Many doubted the sincerity of the Constitution-worshippers. A South Carolinian noted: "If I got up tomorrow and advocated rigid adherence to the 14th and 15th [Amendments] of the Constitution, the same folks who are yelling 'Constitution' loudly now would fight among themselves for priority in applying the tar and feathers."[35] Henry M. Hart of the Harvard Law School contested the notion that Supreme Court opinions were like the pronouncements of a Delphic oracle, and Donald Richberg, former chairman of the National Industrial Recovery Board, asserted: "We need to be disillusioned of the idea that putting a black robe upon a man makes him a superior variety of human being."[36] Harold Ickes protested:

To listen to the clamor, one would think that Moses
from Mount Sinai had declared that God Himself had
decreed that if and when there should be a Supreme
Court of the United States, the number Nine was to be
sacred. All that is left to do now is to declare that the
Supreme Court was immaculately conceived; that it is
infallible; that it is the spiritual descendant of Moses and
that the number Nine is three times three, and three
stands for the Trinity.[37]

Although such sentiments strengthened the hand of the Administration Democrats in the Senate, the bill encountered even more vigorous opposition, far more than had been anticipated. Roosevelt must have expected the defection of Democrats like Carter Glass of Virginia and Josiah Bailey of North Carolina. Much more serious was the rebellion of party regulars like Tom Connally of Texas and of liberal Democrats like Burton K. Wheeler of Montana. The loss of Wheeler was a real stunner. After all, Wheeler had campaigned with Robert M. La Follette in 1924 on the Court reform issue. Since no one could dispute his credentials as a liberal, Wheeler, by denouncing the plan, made it difficult for the President to claim that his adversaries were the same bunch of economic royalists who had fought him in 1936.[38]

In fact, it quickly became apparent that opponents of the plan enjoyed widespread support. Marshaled by the publisher Frank E. Gannett's National Committee to Uphold Constitutional Government, they bombarded congressmen and newspaper editors with remonstrances comparing the President to Stuart tyrants and to European dictators. "Our President evidently has noted the apparent success of Hitler and is aiming at the same dominance," wrote a Saginaw businessman.[39] Opponents pointed out that Roosevelt had failed to suggest in his 1936 campaign either that the country faced a crisis or that he planned to remold the Supreme Court.[40] They argued that the President should seek to amend the Constitution, and emphasized that it had taken only ten months to ratify the 21st Amendment.[41] Above all, they protested that Roosevelt was not showing proper regard for the Judiciary. "As a boy I was taught to honor and revere the Supreme Court of the United States above all things," wrote a New Orleans insurance man.[42] "It seems strange to hear the Supreme Court discussed like a business, a going concern needing new capital to expand," commented a Charleston publisher. "We always were taught to think of it, with reverence be it said, as like the Church, where men selected for their exceptional qualifications presided as Bishops should."[43] A prominent Catholic layman compared the Court's authority to that of the Pope and added: "To all intents and purposes our Supreme Court is infallible. It can not err."[44]

Even friends of the proposal fretted about the deviousness of the President's argument that he was putting it forward because the age of the justices had resulted in crowded dockets, for it seemed obvious that FDR wished to pack the Court with justices of a liberal persuasion. Many took exception to Roosevelt's stress on the age of the justices. Congressmen over seventy were not entranced by the argument that men's faculties are impaired when they reach seventy. Other older people objected that the plan was an assault on the aged, who deserved respect, not opprobrium. One man counseled a Florida congressman: "If you think youth is more competent and reliable than the aged, remember Clemenceau who led France to victory, Chauncey Depew who died at 94 active to the last; Justice Holmes who at 90 gave a Supreme Court decision.

"Reflect how at 84 Hindenburg headed Germany; at 83 Edison was active, and at 86 Elihu Root was doing good work at his office."[45]

Another opponent of the proposal wrote the Washington *Post*: "Between the ages of 70 and 83, Commodore Vanderbilt added one hundred million dollars to his fortune.... At 74 Immanuel Kant wrote his 'Anthropology,' the 'Metaphysics of Ethics,' and 'Strife of the Faculties.' ... Marcus Portius Cato began the study of Greek when a youthful Roman of 80! Goethe at 80, completed 'Faust.' ... Tennyson wrote his divinely impressive farewell, 'Crossing the Bar' at 83.... At 98 Titian painted his historic picture of the 'Battle of Lepanto.' ... Can you calculate the loss to the world if such as they had been compelled to retire at 70?"[46]

The strategy of the crowded dockets–old age rationale turned out to be a blunder. Before long, the President virtually abandoned this line of argument and came out with his main reason: that the Court was dominated by a set of conservative justices who were making it impossible for liberal government to function.

This emphasis appealed to many of Roosevelt's New Deal followers, but others bristled at any attempt to alter the Court. They charged the President with tampering with the institutions established by the Founding Fathers. Although the number of justices had been changed several times before, many believed that the Constitution specified nine members. One writer encountered an elderly lady who protested. "If nine judges were enough for George Washington, they should be enough for President Roosevelt. I don't see why he needs fifteen."[47] In vain, supporters of the bill retorted that the Founding Fathers had been revolutionaries and that the opponents were attempting to escape modern problems by evoking nostalgia for a mythical past.

Still other critics like the historian James Truslow Adams valued the Judiciary as "the sole bulwark of our personal liberties." "If a President tries to take away our freedom of speech, if a Congress takes away our property unlawfully, if a State legislature, as in the recent case of Louisiana under the dictatorship of Huey Long, takes away the freedom of the press, who is to save us except the Courts?" he asked.[48] "If I were a Hebrew I would be scared green," asserted a Detroit businessman. "If I were a Negro I'd hate to have my precious amendment taken away from me—the one that put me on a equal footing with whites, thanks to Mr. Lincoln."[49] On the other hand, Southerners frequently warned that the Court was a bastion of white supremacy. "Our very social and racial integrity rest behind these 'checks and balances,'" a constituent wrote the Louisiana senators.[50] "Voices cry from every Confederate grave," declared another.[51]

So intensely did opponents object to the plan that a number of Democratic senators searched desperately for some device that would free them of the need to commit themselves. In particular, the freshman Democrats who had been swept into office in the Roosevelt tidal wave in 1936 looked for a way that would save them from voting for a scheme which many found repugnant and which they knew outraged many of their constituents, if they could do so without breaking openly with the President. Typical of these freshman Democrats were Prentiss Brown of Michigan, who took a resolutely noncommittal stance; Senator Andrews of Florida, who told his son: "It will be my policy, right on, not to commit myself to any particular course with regard to the Courts"; and John H. Overton of Louisiana, who raised straddling to an art.[52] Overton's standard release stated: "The importance of the subject, its many aspects, the high source of the recommendation and the contrariety of opinion throughout the United States suggest to me that the proper course is to with-hold any definite conclusion until the matter has been more thoroughly investigated, discussed and considered."[53] To one constituent, Senator Overton explained: "You state that you note that I am following Polonius' advice to 'reserve thy judgment,' I am going farther than this and, to paraphrase another precept of his, I am with respect to this matter, giving every man my ear and none, as yet, my voice."[54]

With the Democrats divided, the Republicans, at the urging of the canny Minority Leader, Charles McNary of Oregon, resolved to keep quiet and thus avoid offering an occasion that might re-unite the Democrats.[55] On the day after the President sent his message, Republican Senator Arthur Vandenberg of Michigan recorded in his diary: "This morning ex-President Hoover phoned me from the Waldorf-Astoria in New York, eager to jump into the fray. . . . Now here is one of the tragedies of life. Hoover is still 'poison'—(the right or wrong of it does not matter.). [William] Borah, McNary and I had a conference at 11 o'clock. Borah is prepared to lead this fight; but he insisted that there is no hope if it is trade-marked in advance as a 'Hoover fight' or a 'Republican fight.' McNary emphatically agreed. As a matter of fact, this already was my own attitude."[56] Men like Vandenberg, McNary, and Borah, senator from Idaho, managed to get most national GOP leaders to abide by the strategy of silence, although Hoover would not go along.[57] While the Republicans, by their restraint, were encouraging Democratic dissension, they held their own lines. Although the Administration had expected the support of some progressive Republicans, in the end every one of the sixteen Republican senators, including Johnson and Nye, rejected the bill.

The opponents made the most of the opportunity offered by the public hearings before the Senate Judiciary Committee. They led off with their most important witness, Senator Wheeler, who began with a discursive, disarming statement that gradually worked around toward the Administration's contention that aged justices were unable to keep abreast of their work. With a dramatic flourish, Wheeler then unfolded a letter from Chief Justice Charles Evans Hughes. The Chief Justice denied that the Court was behind in its business or that more justices would increase efficiency. Instead, he asserted, "there would be more judges to hear, more judges to confer, more judges to discuss, more judges to be convinced and to decide."[58] Hughes's unanticipated contribution not only effectively rebutted the President's crowded dockets argument, but suggested that henceforth Roosevelt, in pushing his proposal, would encounter not only the wily Wheeler but the formidable figure of the Chief Justice.

The Administration made the mistake of presenting its case briefly, and most of the hearings served to publicize the views of the opposition. The President's former aide, Raymond Moley, clergymen, law school deans, and spokesmen for farm organizations all testified against the measure. Professor Erwin Griswold of Harvard Law School protested that "this bill obviously is not playing the game. There are at least two ways of getting rid of judges," he observed. "One is to take them out and shoot them, as they are reported to do in at least one other country. The other way is more genteel, but no less effective. They are kept on the public payroll but their votes are canceled."[59]

Despite all the antagonism, it still seemed highly likely in the last week of March that the President's proposal would be adopted. Many of those who were skeptical of the scheme nonetheless did not want the Court to continue to invalidate New Deal laws, and if faced with a choice between Roosevelt's plan and the strangling of the New Deal, they would be likely to go along with the President. Roosevelt was certain to win unless Democratic senators, especially the freshmen, deserted him in droves, and it did not seem well-advised to break with a man who had been given so emphatic an endorsement just a few months before. Senator Andrews' son scolded his father: "I have noticed a decided dissatisfaction among the laymen for your straddling attitude regarding the Supreme Court. . . . I do not see how you can stand to go against the President and his Supreme Court proposal. Your being in Washington you cannot realize the absolute necessity of patronage and you have not gotten one little bit and you have got to have it. This Supreme Court proposal is the first test that will be placed upon your loyalty to the Democratic party. A year from now you might afford to 'bolt,' but right now I do not see how you can afford to have them place you on the first go-round as a 'bolter.'"[60]

A Michigan voter stated even more bluntly:

> I had never heard of Prentiss M. Brown until the last election, when I learned that a man by that name had been nominated for the United States Senate on the Democratic ticket.
>
> So I voted for Brown, not because he was Brown, but because he merely happened to be the candidate on the Roosevelt ballot, and I wanted to send to Washington every man possible to aid our President. . . .
>
> Now I read with amazement . . . this Senator Brown as saying that he has not made up his mind regarding just

how he'll vote on the proposal to change the Supreme Court.

Why does Senator Brown think we made him Senator Brown and sent him to Washington? We sent him there to support Roosevelt. Brown as Brown doesn't have to do any thinking or make any decisions. If he merely follows the policies outlined by our President he will be doing all the voters who voted for him will require.[61]

Men like Brown and Andrews continued to probe for a satisfactory compromise, but when it came to the showdown they figured to be on Roosevelt's side. At the end of March, *Time* wrote: "Last week the stanchest foes of the President's Plan were privately conceding that, if he chose to whip it through, the necessary votes were already in his pockets."[62] The undecided senators might not like the plan, but they could not justify frustrating the President while the Court persisted in mowing down New Deal legislation.

But the Court itself had some big surprises in store. On March 29, in a 5–4 decision in which Justice Roberts joined the majority, the Court upheld a minimum wage statute from the state of Washington which to most people seemed identical to the New York law it had wiped out in the *Tipaldo* case less than a year before.[63] Two weeks later, Roberts joined in a series of 5–4 decisions which found the National Labor Relations Act constitutional.[64] On May 24, the Court validated the Social Security law.[65] These decisions marked an historic change in constitutional doctrine. The Court was now stating that the state and federal governments had a whole range of powers which this same tribunal had been saying for the past two years these governments did not have.

The crucial development was the switch of Justice Roberts, which altered a 5–4 margin against New Deal legislation to a 5–4 edge in favor. Some analysts have argued that Roberts did not change at all. They explain that his response in earlier cases resulted from his unwillingness to rule on questions not properly brought before the Court.[66] This contention is not altogether unreasonable with respect to the relation of the *Tipaldo* to the *Parrish* decision, but if the Social Security opinions are compared to the rail pension ruling, or the Wagner Act opinions with the *Carter* decision, it seems unmistakable that the Court, and specifically Mr. Justice Roberts, had shifted ground.

Commentators differed, too, about why Justice Roberts joined the liberal majority. Some believed that Roberts had been brought in line by Chief Justice Hughes with the deliberate intent of defeating the President's plan by removing its main justification. A columnist asserted: "No insider doubts that the whole change of trend represented in the decisions was solely the work of Mr. Hughes. Everyone gives Mr. Hughes credit for arguing Associate Justice Roberts into position."[67] Others thought that Roberts had merely followed the election returns.[68] Roosevelt's Court proposal could not have been alone responsible, for the *Parrish* decision was reached before the President sent his message to Congress, although it was not handed down until afterwards.

Many observers, especially supporters of the plan, had no doubt that the Court had altered its views, and that it had done so because it had been baptized "in the waters of public opinion."[69] After the *Parrish* decision, one correspondent asked William Allen White: "Didn't the Welshman on the Supreme Court do a pretty job of amending the Constitution yesterday?"[70] George Fort Milton, the Tennessee editor and historian, observed: "The Supreme Court thing is quite amazing. Mr. Roberts changed his mind and so a law unconstitutional for New York is constitutional for the State of Washington."[71] Justice Roberts, said a national Democratic leader, "performed that marvelous somersault in mid-air. One day Mr. Roberts is at one side of the tent—the next day he grasps the trapeze, makes a far swing, turns a double somersault and lands on the other side of the tent. But there [is] no telling when he will swing back again."[72]

The switch by Roberts had ironic consequences. In one sense, it gave Roosevelt the victory he wanted, for the Court was now approving New Deal legislation.[73] But in another way, Roberts' "somersault" gravely damaged the chance of the Court plan. By eliminating the critical need for changing the membership of the bench, it erased the most important justification for the President's bill. Why change the Court now that you had the kind of decisions that you wanted? As someone said, "A switch in time saved nine."[74]

This argument became even more compelling when on the morning of May 18, while the President was breakfasting in bed, a messenger arrived at the White House with a letter from Justice Van Devanter announcing his resignation from the bench. Van Devanter's action was widely believed to have been the result of counsel from Senators Borah and Wheeler. Borah lived in the same apartment house on Connecticut Avenue; the two were on "Hello, Bill" and "Hello, Willis" terms.[75] The "conversion" of Roberts had given Roosevelt a 5–4 majority; soon he would be able to name someone to take Van Devanter's place and have the opportunity for a 6–3 margin.

Since it appeared that Roosevelt had won substantially what he wanted, he was now urged to call off the fight. "Why," it was asked, "shoot the bridegroom after a shotgun wedding?"[76] The *Parrish* and Wagner decisions turned some Senators against the plan, and encouraged others to press for compromise. Prentiss Brown stated that the switch of the Court took "a good deal of the ground work from under the arguments for the court bill and I believe it will open the way for friends and opponents to re-approach the issue."[77] By the end of April, the two sides were roughly even. One poll showed forty-four senators in favor, forty-seven opposed, four doubtful, with one seat vacant. The Social Security opinions and Van Devanter's resignation tipped the balance against the six-judge bill; thereafter, opponents held a narrow edge.[78]

Many of the Roosevelt leaders in Congress wanted to drop the whole project, but others argued that justices who would switch so easily in his favor could just as easily jump back once the pressure was off. One of the President's aides said: "No man's land now is Roberts land."[79] The Scripps Howard columnist Raymond Clapper noted in his diary that Roosevelt's press secretary had told him "that president is going ahead with fight—that don't know how long Hughes can keep Roberts liberal or how long Hughes will stay so."[80] Others reasoned that the switch of the Court had proven what FDR had been saying all along: there was nothing wrong with the Constitution, only with the Court. And if enlightenment was such a good thing, why not have more of it?[81] Senator Theodore Green of Rhode Island declared: "Again we learn that the Constitution is what Mr. Justice Roberts says it is. So what we need is not amendments to the Constitution, but a sufficient number of judges to construe it broadly, lest one man's mistaken opinion may decide the fate of a nation."[82]

Furthermore, Roosevelt believed the country was with him. After all, he had won a decisive victory only a half year before. "Why compromise?" Jim Farley asked. "The Democratic senators were elected on the basis of supporting the President's program. It is up to them to back it now."[83] To be sure, mail ran heavily against the bill, but since attitudes toward the plan divided sharply on class lines, and upper income groups were more articulate, this was not surprising. Members of Congress noted that opponents of the proposal often wrote on lithographed and embossed stationery, and when they analyzed their mail, they frequently found, too, that adverse letters came overwhelmingly from Republicans who in the recent campaign had been noisy but outnumbered.[84] If the press denounced the plan, 80 per cent of editorial writers had been against FDR in 1936, and look what had happened on Election Day. True, the polls also showed a small margin unfavorable to the bill, but remember how wrong the *Literary Digest* canvass had been a few months before. Only one significant election had been held since the President sent his message, and in that race a congressional seat in Texas had been won by a candidate committed to the plan, a newcomer named Lyndon B. Johnson.

Yet another reason compelled Roosevelt to push ahead. Although he could name a new judge to the Van Devanter vacancy, it was understood that he had promised the next opening on the bench to Senator Robinson. He could hardly avoid choosing the Majority Leader without inciting a Senate uprising. Yet Robinson was a 65-year-old conservative. If appointing Robinson was to be the climax of his campaign to bring young, liberal men to the Court, the enterprise would turn out to be a fiasco. It seemed more necessary than ever to balance the expected Robinson appointment by creating vacancies for liberal justices.

Well before the end of May, however, Roosevelt's lieutenants in Congress had to face up to the fact that they simply did not have the votes. One leader confided that five polls of the Senate had all come out with the same result: defeat.[85] Still Roosevelt temporized. Not until the night of June 3 at a two-hour conference at the White House did the President finally agree to permit Senator Robinson to seek a compromise. Acting as Roosevelt's broker, the Majority Leader worked out a revised bill which authorized the President to appoint an additional justice for each member of the Court who was 75; no more than one could be named in any calendar year. This meant that Roosevelt, besides filling the Van Devanter opening, might add four new judges, and this total could not be reached before 1941. By the time this measure had been pieced together, the President had lost much of the advantage of his willingness to bargain; deals that would have been appealing in April were no longer so by late May or June. "It is impossible today for the President to pass his six Judge Bill, and I seriously doubt whether he can pass a two Judge Bill," Senator Vandenberg claimed.[86]

By June, the fight had become very bitter, and although one opponent conceded that Robinson's compromise would win, the issue was close. The Senate divided so evenly that some predicted that when the roll was finally called, the outcome would be a tie which could only be broken by the vote of Vice-President John Nance Garner. The Vice-President had made no secret of the fact that he disapproved of the plan. When the President's message was being read in February, he had held his nose and pointed thumbs down. Now, in mid-June, Garner packed his bag and left to go fishing in Texas. Never before had he departed from Washington while Congress was in session.[87]

Two days after Garner decamped, the Senate Judiciary Committee published an adverse report which stunned Washington by the harshness of its censure of the President's plan. The report, signed by members of the President's own party, stated: "It is a measure which should be so emphatically rejected that its parallel will never again be presented to the free representatives of the free people of America."[88] The columnist Ray Clapper noted in his diary: "Bitter document, extremely rough. . . . It reads almost like a bill of impeachment."[89]

Everything now hung on the persuasive powers of Senator Robinson. A leader of his party, Joe Robinson had been chosen Democratic Vice-Presidential nominee in 1928, and in his many years on the Hill, he had put a number of men in obligation to him. A man of overbearing manner, he might intimidate some of the freshmen senators into going along. Besides, as *Time* noted: "Just as an expectant mother commands a certain ethereal prestige above other women, so Joe Robinson, as an expectant Justice of the Supreme Court, has become since Justice Van Devanter's retirement a sort of Super-Senator with a prestige all his own among his colleagues."[90] Through the sheer force of his own personality, the Majority Leader might be able to get Roosevelt those few uncommitted votes that could mean the difference between victory and defeat. Without Robinson, the President would be undone.

In the steaming month of July, the great debate in the Senate opened with no one certain how the final roll call would go. At the start of the debate, Administration leaders claimed a minimum of fifty-four senators, and on July 7, the Washington bureau of the Portland (Maine) *Press Herald* reported: "General opinion is the substitute will pass, and sooner than expected, since votes enough to pass it seem apparent, and the opposition cannot filibuster forever."[91] That same day, Hiram Johnson informed a confidant: "They have the votes at present to put it over."[92] Three days later, Senator

Kenneth McKellar of Tennessee wrote: "I am inclined to the belief that the bill substantially as advocated by the President's friends in the Senate will be passed."[93] With at least forty senators arrayed against the plan, opponents asserted that a filibuster could forestall a roll call indefinitely. But there were risks in resorting to a filibuster, especially when Roosevelt's foes purported to be embattled democrats. *Business Week* lamented: "Too many of them are not willing to run a real, organized filibuster. Too many of them are uncertain whether they would be justified in the eyes of their constituents."[94] Yet neither could the Administration be sure of its own ranks; many of the freshmen senators seemed shaky. On July 10, the Associated Press found seventeen votes still in doubt. On July 12, Senator Edward Burke of Nebraska circulated privately a tally which showed that a switch of four votes would produce a tie.[95]

To hold the waverers in line, Senator Robinson ran the debate with a whip hand. He invoked seldom-used rules to ward off the possibility of a filibuster, and even threatened continuous sessions, although members protested that such an ordeal would take its toll of the Senate, more than a third of which was over sixty.[96] Tempers grew short in the murderous Washington heat. Senator McNary wrote home: "We are having a hot spell and the weather is just as hot as ————, at least as hot as I think it is."[97]

On the opening day of debate, Robinson left the floor feeling ill. "No more questions today," he said. "Goodby!"[98] Several days later, the Majority Leader, in an angry exchange with an opposition senator, once again felt pain in his chest and had to leave the chamber. He did not appear on the Senate floor the next day. The following morning, his maid knocked on the door of his apartment and got no response. When she entered, she found Senator Robinson sprawled on the floor, dead.

The death of Joe Robinson doomed all hopes for Roosevelt's plan. "The Court issue went with Joe," concluded a Florida congressman.[99] "I think the death of Robinson will have a marked effect upon the Congress," wrote a former governor of North Carolina, "and I do not think that Robert E. Lee sustained a greater loss in the death of Stonewall Jackson than Roosevelt has lost in the death of Robinson."[100] A Minnesota editor reflected: "It is not unlikely that the death of Senator Robinson will be the turning point in the President's career."[101]

To anxious senators, already on edge from the strain of the long session, it seemed that Death had intervened to decide the fate of the Republic.[102] A Washington column reported: "The sudden passing of Robinson has brought the pressure of wives, families and physicians on many senators to hasten their departure from the sweltering capital."[103] Earlier in the session, one senator had died; two others were undergoing treatment at the Naval Hospital. Senator Copeland warned that, as a doctor, he could see on the faces of others in the chamber the same tell-tale signs of imminent death he had discerned in Senator Robinson's countenance in the past week. Senator Wheeler shouted that Robinson's death was a direct result of Roosevelt's Court bill. "I beseech the President to drop the fight lest he appear to fight against God."[104] (One correspondent wrote Wheeler: "Your bad taste is surpassed only by your conceit in assuming the role of God's spokesman."[105])

On the train returning from Senator Robinson's funeral in Little Rock, every compartment housed a caucus. In one compartment, three of the freshman senators decided that the game was over. When he returned to Washington, Prentiss Brown called together eight freshman Democrats, including Senators Overton and Andrews, who held the balance of power. After a two-hour conference on July 20, they marched across the hall in the Senate Office Building to Vice-President Garner's office to announce that they would vote to recommit the bill.[106] That did it. Hiram Johnson explained: "After the self-delivery of the freshmen Senators, we had fifty or fifty-one votes, but we did not have them until then."[107] The struggle ended so abruptly that Republicans who had worked for months on speeches they were to give in the Great Debate never had a chance to deliver them.[108]

But for FDR, all was not lost. Not only did he have a Court which was ruling in favor of the constitutionality of New Deal laws, but he still had the right to appoint someone to the vacancy created by Van Devanter's retirement. Once more, he kept the Capital in suspense. Day after day passed without his making a move. It was even suspected that he would not choose anyone until after the Senate had recessed. Then one day, again taking the country by surprise, he scrawled a name on a Court commission and sent it by messenger up to the Hill. The name was that of Senator Hugo Black of Alabama.

No appointment could have been better calculated to infuriate his opponents. Black had been an enthusiastic supporter of the Court plan, and he was one of the leading liberals in Congress. But senators who wanted to reject him could not bring themselves to turn down one of their own members. Despite rumors, subsequently confirmed, that Black had been a member of the Ku Klux Klan, the nomination went through fairly easily. Just a few weeks after Roosevelt had apparently been beaten, he had scored another victory.[109]

Black was only the first of a series of judges Roosevelt was able to name to the bench. Within two and a half years after the defeat of the Court proposal, the President had appointed five of the nine justices: Black, Stanley Reed, Felix Frankfurter, William O. Douglas, and Frank Murphy.

This new Court—the "Roosevelt Court" as it was called—ruled favorably on every one of the New Deal laws whose constitutionality was challenged. It expanded the commerce power and the spending power so greatly that it soon became evident that there was almost no statute for social welfare or the regulation of business that the Court would not uphold. While the Court had once held that the national government lacked the power to regulate even major industries, because it said these industries were not in interstate commerce, the Court now extended the range of the federal government to the most remote businesses. In one case, it held that a farmer was engaged in interstate commerce even when he grew wheat wholly for his own consumption on his own farm.[110]

Since 1937 the Court has not invalidated a single piece of congressional legislation regulating business. Although before 1937 only a few justices were committed to legal realism, after that almost the whole Court moved into that camp and the old doctrines of constitutional fundamentalism lost out. Whereas the beneficiaries of the Court before 1937 had been businessmen and other propertied interests, after 1937 they became the less advantaged groups in America. As early as the first week in June, 1937, *Business Week* was complaining: "The cold fact is that, for all practical purposes, the reorganization of the Court, sought by legislative process, has been accomplished by the ordinary process of court decision."[111] In the fall of 1937, Justice McReynolds grumbled: "The court starts off about as I expected. There is not much to be expected of it by sensible people of the former order."[112] By February, 1938, Frank Gannett was writing: "Since the President now controls the Supreme Court, our only hope lies in influencing the members of the Congress."[113] Little wonder that Roosevelt claimed he had lost the battle but won the war.

But there were other respects in which FDR lost the war. The Supreme Court fight spelled the beginning of the end for his New Deal coalition. To be sure, a number of congressmen were probably determined to split with him anyway, and simply used the controversy as an excuse, although even this assigns some importance to the Court battle. Too, the breakup of the coalition resulted, in part, from other developments: the recession of 1937–1938, anxiety over relief spending, resentment at sitdown strikes. But to attempt to explain the rupture of 1937 and ignore the Supreme Court donnybrook is like accounting for the coming of the Civil War without reference to slavery.

The Court struggle had a number of disruptive aspects:

1. It helped blunt the most important drive for social reform in American history and squandered the advantage of Roosevelt's triumph in 1936. In the spring of 1937, one observer noted: "Congress has been completely addled by the President's court proposal." The controversy, he added, had resulted "in the sidetracking of much useful legislation that otherwise might have been put through."[114] By the time the session sputtered to an end in "spasms of bitterness" in late August, it had been, as the *New York Times* commented, the "stormiest and least productive in recent years."[115] At the close of the "sock-Roosevelt" session, one reporter wrote: "Tonight the political 'master minds' of the capital gathering over their cups in relaxed reminiscence of the historic events of the last seven months, were mulling over one question: 'How did the President slide so far—so fast?'"[116] The Court struggle helped weld together a bipartisan coalition of anti-New Deal senators who dealt Roosevelt a series of rebuffs at the special session of Congress in the autumn of 1937 and at the regular session in 1938.[117] By the spring of 1938, the prospects for reform had diminished perceptibly, and for the next quarter of a century the advocates of social change would rarely win anything but minor successes in Congress.

2. It deeply divided the Democratic Party. In state after state, the Court squabble precipitated factional wars. In Massachusetts, the governor opposed the plan; his auditor and his attorney general favored it.[118] In Montana, the struggle triggered a primary contest between Senator Wheeler and a rival.[119] In numerous states—Indiana, Missouri, New Jersey, Ohio, Rhode Island, South Carolina, Texas, Utah, West Virginia—each of the two

Democratic senators pursued a diametrically opposite course on the bill.

Not only did the fight itself open wounds in the party, but it led to a series of later episodes, notably the purge campaign of 1938, which rubbed salt in the wounds. Some of the congressmen who broke with Roosevelt in 1937 were never to give him the same degree of loyalty they had in his first term, and others who were already disaffected soon helped forge a bipartisan anti-New Deal coalition. In April, Senator Bailey observed blandly: "I feel that the President made a mistake, but I am not disposed to criticise him or complain of him. He is on one side and I am on another, but the whole thing will pass." Less than four months later Bailey was writing: "We are engaged in a great battle in America. Do not be deceived about this. The lines are drawn. The issues are clear. Those who are not with us are against us.... Men must stand up now. The fight is not over. We have broken down the first big attack, but the attack will be made on many lines and ultimately there will be another attack on the Court. The socialistic forces of America are not confined to the Socialistic Party."[120]

3. Because of the Court dispute, Roosevelt lost that overwhelming middle class support he had mobilized in the 1936 campaign. Discord over the President's plan, coupled with other events, ended the brief era of great Democratic majorities. An attorney from Lake Charles, Louisiana, wrote: "I voted for President Roosevelt in both elections but would not have done so had he announced his intention to destroy the independence of the judiciary. These are the sentiments of everyone in this City that I have spoken to."[121] A Miami woman protested to a Florida congressman:

"Neither I, nor any of my friends who voted for him, gave him a mandate to destroy the independence of the court, nor of congress.

"I have actually lost faith in his honesty."[122]

A trade unionist from New York confided: "As a member of the Newspaper Guild of America, I have supported the President in the past, because of his humanitarian aims and his attitude toward organized labor. But his present effort to undermine the independence of the Judiciary has destroyed my confidence in his judgment."[123] In North Carolina, a former law school dean told Senator Bailey: "I was an enthusiastic supporter of Roosevelt last November. If an election was held tomorrow, I would not vote for him."[124]

4. The Court issue produced divisions among reformers of many types. It separated Senator Wheeler from labor supporters in Montana and resulted in a breach between Wheeler and the Administration that was never closed.[125] One of Roosevelt's lieutenants observed, "I've always granted to every man the right to his own opinions. . . . But to find Burt in the front ranks of those who were piously upholding the sanctity of the Supreme Court... well, that was really a sight to make the angels weep!"[126] In Minnesota, the controversy sundered the Farmer-Labor Party; many Farmer-Laborites were angered by the opposition of Senator Henrik Shipstead to the bill. The president of an organization of "independent" Minnesota lawyers wrote him: "Fake liberals are through[,] Shipstead; so is Burton K. Wheeler. Wait and see."[127] It alienated the publisher of *The Nation* from his editors; split Dr. Townsend from officers of his old age pension organization; and cut off old-line reformers like John Haynes Holmes and Oswald Garrison Villard from the main body of the New Dealers.

5. It undermined the bipartisan support for the New Deal. Many of the Republican progressives had become growingly apprehensive of the men around Roosevelt. The Court issue confirmed them in their suspicions that something alien, something fundamentally illiberal, had been introduced into the reform movement by the New Dealers—that, in the guise of solicitude for the common man, they were actually seeking self-aggrandizement. The President, too, seemed disturbingly eager to concentrate power in Washington. The Republican editor William Allen White, who admired much that the New Deal had achieved, wrote during the Court fight: "I fear him as I fear no other man in our public life."[128] The Court fracas, Hiram Johnson told Raymond Moley, "has forced me into a position of opposition to him, which will widen as the days pass."[129]

6. One tangential result of the Court dispute was that it also helped create distrust for Roosevelt's leadership in foreign policy. Writers frequently likened the Court fight to the League of Nations struggle and compared Hiram Johnson's stand, especially, to that of the original battalion of death. The President's

proposal fortified men like Johnson and Wheeler in their misgivings about FDR, for it seemed to reveal what they most deplored about his foreign policy—that it was devious, and that it sought too much power for the Executive.[130]

These multifold misfortunes were a fearful price to pay for the gains Roosevelt achieved. Yet none of these developments should obscure the President's one big success in the Court fight—that he secured the legitimization of the vast expansion of the power of government in American life. The Court struggle speeded the acceptance of a radical change in the role of government and in the reordering of property rights. It also had the probably unanticipated result of the appointment of a Court more interventionist in the field of civil liberties and civil rights. It is not surprising that historians speak of the "Constitutional Revolution of 1937." For in the long history of the Supreme Court, no event had more momentous consequences than Franklin Roosevelt's message of February, 1937.

NOTES

1. Walter Johnson, *1600 Pennsylvania Avenue* (Boston, 1960), p. 90.
2. Panama Refining Co. *v.* Ryan, 293 U.S. 388 (1935).
3. Home Building & Loan Association *v.* Blaisdell *et al.*, 290 U.S. 426 (1934); Nebbia *v.* New York, 291 U.S. 523 (1934); Perry *v.* United States, 294 U.S. 330 (1935), and related cases.
4. R.R. Retirement Board *v.* Alton R.R. Co., 295 U.S. 330 (1935).
5. A.L.A. Schechter Poultry Corp. *et al. v.* United States, 295 U.S. 553 (1935). That same day, the Court dealt a personal blow to the President in Humphrey's Executor *v.* U.S., 295 U.S. 609 (1935). William E. Leuchtenburg, "The Case of the Contentious Commissioner: Humphrey's Executor *v.* U.S.," in Harold M. Hyman and Leonard W. Levy (eds.), *Freedom and Reform* (New York, 1967), pp. 276–312.
6. United States *v.* Butler *et al.*, 297 U.S. 61 (1936); Carter *v.* Carter Coal Company, 298 U.S. 238 (1936); Morehead *v.* New York *ex rel.* Tipaldo, 298 U.S. 587 (1936).
7. Samuel Rosenman (ed.), *The Public Papers and Addresses of Franklin D. Roosevelt* (13 vols., New York, 1938–1950), V, 191–192.
8. Alpheus Thomas Mason, *Harlan Fiske Stone* (New York, 1956), p. 425.
9. The prelude to the 1937 fight is discussed at length in William E. Leuchtenburg, "The Origins of Franklin D. Roosevelt's 'Court-Packing' Plan," in Philip B. Kurland (ed.), *The Supreme Court Review* (Chicago, 1966), pp. 347–400.

10. Franklin D. Roosevelt to Charles C. Burlingham, Feb. 23, 1937, Franklin D. Roosevelt Library, Hyde Park, N.Y. (henceforth FDRL), PSF Supreme Court.

11. Charles A. Beard, "Rendezvous with the Supreme Court," *New Republic*, LXXX (Sept. 2, 1936), 93; Beard to Nicholas Kelley, Aug. 8, 1936, Mary Dewson MSS, FDRL, Box 6.

12. *Public Papers of Franklin D. Roosevelt*, VI, 51–66. The Court bill also called for a number of procedural reforms.

13. Paul Mallon, "Purely Confidential," Detroit *News*, Mar. 17, 1937.

14. Margaret Fowler Dunaway MS Diary, Early March, 1937, Schlesinger Library, Radcliffe College, Cambridge, Mass. See also notes for a speech, Dorothy Kirchwey Brown MSS, Folder 14, Schlesinger Library.

15. A. Roy Moore to John H. Kerr, Feb. 27, 1937, Kerr MSS, Southern Historical Collection, University of North Carolina, Chapel Hill, N.C., Box 9; S. R. Lewis to FDR, Feb. 19, 1937, National Archives, Dept. of Justice 235868; Rochester *Times Union*, Feb. 13, 1937, clipping, Frank Gannett MSS; Cornell University Collection of Regional History, Ithaca, N.Y., Box 2A; Mrs. C. I. Anderson to Merlin Hull, Feb. 19, 1937, Hull MSS, State Historical Society of Wisconsin, Madison, Wisc., Box 89; W. C. Cray to John H. Overton, Mar. 21, 1937, Overton MSS, Dept. of Archives and Manuscripts, Louisiana State University, Baton Rouge, La., Box 2; June Beliveau to Theodore Green, Apr. 30, 1937, Green MSS, Library of Congress, Washington, D.C. (henceforth LC), Box 33.

16. Beaumont *Enterprise*, Feb. 16, 1937, clipping, Arthur Vandenberg Scrapbooks, Michigan Historical Collections of The University of Michigan, Ann Arbor, Mich.

17. Johnson to John Francis Neylan, Mar. 21, 1937, Johnson MSS, Bancroft Library, University of California, Berkeley, Calif.

18. Charles O. Andrews to Charles Andrews, Jr., Mar. 2, 1937, Andrews MSS, P. K. Yonge Library of Florida History, University of Florida Libraries, Gainesville, Fla., Box 51.

19. *Knickerbocker News*, Feb. 20, 1937, clipping, Royal Copeland Scrapbooks, Michigan Historical Collections.

20. Stephen Early to FDR, Feb. 8, 1937, FDRL, PSF Supreme Court; Memorandum of Conference with Speaker W. B. Bankhead, Feb. 7, 1937, Lindsay Warren MSS, Southern Historical Collection, University of North Carolina, Box 17; Lawrence Lewis MS Diary. The State Historical Society of Colorado, Denver, Colo., Feb. 12, 1937; New York *American*, Feb. 19, 1937, clipping, Royal Copeland Scrapbooks.

21. Joe Hendricks to Wellborn Phillips, Jr., Feb. 25, 1937, Hendricks MSS, P. K. Yonge Library of Florida History, Box 2; Bert Lord to B. H. Chernin, Feb. 16, 1937, Lord MSS, Cornell University Collection of Regional History.

22. J. F. T. O'Connor MS Diary, Feb. 15, 1937, Bancroft Library, University of California.

23. Raymond Clapper MS Diary, LC, Feb. 8, 1937.

24. *Time*, XXIX (Feb. 15, 1937), 18–19.

25. William M. Fitch to Stanley Reed, Feb. 16, 1937, National Archives, Dept. of Justice 235868; Vyvian Faye Coxon to Joe Hendricks, Mar. 3, 1937, Hendricks MSS, Box 2.

26. A Wisconsin man wrote: "It is now possible, under a five to four decision, for one old man (whose mental and physical powers, as any honest authority will admit, are more than likely to be in process of deterioration) to nullify the acts of 435 congressmen, 96 senators and the President—all duly elected as the government of the people." C. W. Langlotz to Thomas Amlie, Feb. 12, 1937, Amlie MSS, State Historical Society of Wisconsin, Box 35. See also Henry Ware Allen to the editor, Washington *Post*, May 4, 1937; George Fort Milton to Homer Cummings, Mar. 17, 1937, Milton MSS, LC, Box 20.

27. Josephus Daniels to Frank Gannett, May 11, 1937, Gannett MSS, Box 16; *Congressional Record*, 75th Cong., 1st Sess., p. 307A.

28. Lex Green to C. E. Coomes, Feb. 15, 1937, Green MSS, P. K. Yonge Library of Florida History, Box 27.

29. Thomas R. Amlie to S. A. Jedele, Feb. 12, 1937, Amlie MSS, Box 35.

30. Thomas Reed Powell to William O. Douglas, n.d., Douglas MSS, LC, Box 20; Herbert Hoover to Charles Evans Hughes, Feb. 19, 1937, Hughes MSS, LC, Box 6; James A. Stone to William T. Evjue, Mar. 17, 1937, Stone MSS, State Historical Society of Wisconsin, Box 28; Thomas R. Amlie to Donald A. Butchart, Mar. 6, 1937, Amlie MSS, Box 36; *The New York Times*, Jan 27, 1937.

31. M. A. Hudak to Hughes, Apr. 13, 1937, Hughes MSS, LC, Box 164. For hostility to Hughes, see Chase Osborn to Daniel Willard, Dec. 22, 1937, Osborn MSS, Michigan Historical Collections; Mark Squires to R. L. Doughton, Feb. 10, 1937, Doughton MSS, Southern Historical Collection, University of North Carolina.

32. Nashville *Tennessean*, n.d., clipping in M. H. Berry to Kenneth McKellar, Feb. 10, 1937, McKellar MSS, Memphis Public Library, Memphis, Tenn., Box 202.

33. Al C. Anderson to Merlin Hull, Feb. 12, 1937, Hull MSS, Box 88.

34. *Congressional Record*, 75th Cong., 1st Sess., p. 405A.

35. Edmund P. Grice, Jr., to James F. Byrnes, Feb. 23, 1937, Byrnes MSS, Clemson University, Clemson, S.C. Another Charleston man wrote, "I get a kick out of the hypocritical reverence for the constitution on the part of some of my friends. They often prayed for deliverance from the eighteenth amendment tanked up on a jar of moonshine." Archie P. Owens to the editor, Charleston *News and Courier*, n.d., clipping in Owens to Byrnes, Feb. 21, 1937, *idem*.

36. Washington *Post*, May 5, 1937; Donald Richberg to Ray Clapper, Feb. 26, 1937, Richberg MSS, LC, Box 2.

37. Harold Ickes to William Allen White, Feb. 25, 1937, White MSS, LC, Box 186. Ickes was not wide of the mark. A Kansas City attorney who opposed the plan wrote: "The Constitution, by its separation of the trinity of governmental functions, Executive, Legislative and Judicial, vitalized the God concept." W. H. H. Piatt to Robert La Follette, Jr., William Allen White MSS, March 17, 1937, Box 187.

38. "The New Deal versus the Old Courts," *Literary Digest*, CXXIII (Feb. 13, 1937), 5–8; Henry Morgenthau, Jr., MS Diaries, FDRL, Feb. 15, 1937; Breckinridge Long MS Diary, LC, Feb. 15, 1937.

39. William B. Mershon to Arthur Vandenberg, Feb. 15, 1937, Mershon MSS, Michigan Historical Collections. See also Merton S. Horrell to Joe Hendricks, Feb. 12, 1937, Hendricks MSS, Box 2; Amy Armour Smith to Rush Holt, Mar. 18, 1937, Holt MSS, University of West Virginia Library, Morgantown, W. Va.; *Constitutional Democracy*, Apr. 5, 1937, copy in Hugh Ike Shott MSS, University of West Virginia Library, Box 38.

40. St. Louis *Post-Dispatch*, Apr. 11, 1937; Frank B. De Vine to Jesse S. Reeves, Reeves MSS, Michigan Historical Collections, Vol. 40. Administration supporters replied that the Court issue had been raised in the campaign—by Roosevelt's opponents; hence, the President did have a mandate. Secretary Harold Ickes wrote a Republican editor: "You raised these issues and the people brought in the verdict against you—an overwhelming verdict. Aren't you estopped from saying now that the question of judicial reform was not raised?" Harold Ickes to William Allen White, Feb. 20, 1937, White MSS, Box 186. See also A. F. Whitney to Frank O. Lowden, Apr. 17, 1937, Lowden MSS, University of Chicago Library, Chicago, Ill., Series 5, Box 25, Folder 2.

41. Advocates retorted that the amendment process was too slow; they pointed in particular, to the long, tedious odyssey of the Child Labor Amendment. One labor leader objected: "Amendments are O.K., except we start to save a kid in a So. Car. cotton mill when she is eight—she is 26 before we get the amendment." George B. Jackson to Joe Hendricks, Mar. 14, 1937, Hendricks MSS, Box 2. See also Breckinridge Long MS Diary, Feb. 15, 1937.

42. A. M. Savage to John H. Overton, Mar. 16, 1937, Overton MSS, Box 2.

43. W. W. Ball to "Lily," n.d., Ball MSS, Duke University Library, Durham, N. Car., July, 1936–Feb., 1937 folder.

44. Typescript of address by Joseph E. Ransdell, n.d. [July, 1937], Ransdell MSS, Dept. of Archives and Manuscripts, Louisiana State University, Folder 21, Box 3. Almost every Catholic Senator was arrayed against the plan; of all the elements, save for party, that might be associated with a Senator's position on the plan— class, ethnic group, etc.—the most telling was whether or not he was a Catholic.

45. Vincent P. Smith to Joe Hendricks, Mar. 2, 1937, Hendricks MSS, Box 2.

46. The Vicar to the editor, Mar. 10, 1937, Washington *Post*, Mar. 12, 1937. A Missouri country editor urged: "Let these men serve until they are taken by their maker or resign. . . . They have lived the span of life alloted them by Him, if they live longer it is because He has work for them to do." Raymond Lloyd to James F. Byrnes, Feb. 17, 1937, Byrnes MSS. A North Carolinian assured his elderly Congressman: "I am glad to say that your own constituents do not feel that a man is mentally decrepit at the age of seventy." Waller D. Brown to R. L. Doughton, Feb. 10, 1937, Doughton MSS. Admirers of Justice Brandeis resented the plan as an implied slur at the octogenarian justice.

47. Richard L. Neuberger, "America Talks Court," *Current History*, XLVI (June, 1937), 35.

48. Address, Mar. 8, 1937, Station WOR, J. T. Adams MSS, Columbia University Library, New York, N.Y.

49. Harvey Campbell to Arthur Vandenberg, Mar. 11, 1937, Vandenberg MSS, Clements Library, University of Michigan. See also Hugh L. Elsbree to Daniel Reed, Oct. 3, 1958, Reed MSS, Cornell University Collection of Regional History, Box 14; William F. Riley to his father, Mar. 3, 1937, in Riley to Clyde Herring, July 7, 1937, Riley MSS, University of Iowa Library, Iowa City, Iowa, Box 1; Oswald Garrison Villard to Maury Maverick, May 7, 1937, Villard MSS, Houghton Library, Harvard University, Cambridge, Mass. Advocates denied that the Court, and especially the Four Horsemen, had safeguarded civil liberties. Maury Maverick wrote: "If you look at the cases on sedition, espionage and the rest, . . . the courts declared pretty nearly every silly law constitutional during and following the World War. There was not much protection of civil liberties in this country." Maverick to John I. Palmer, Jan. 18, 1937, Maury Maverick MSS, Archives, University of Texas Library, Austin, Tex., Box 5.

50. Virgil Murdoch Rich to Senators Overton and Ellender, Feb. 10, 1937, Overton MSS, Box 2.

51. Edith Dickeymann to James F. Byrnes, n.d., Byrnes MSS.

52. Andrews to Charles Andrews, Jr., Feb. 26, 1937, Andrews MSS, Box 51; Charles O. Andrews to Hamilton Holt, Mar. 10, 1937, Holt MSS, Mills Memorial Library, Rollins College, Winter Park, Fla.; Detroit *News*, Feb. 6, 28, 1937. For other indications of straddling, or concern for public opinion, see F. Ryan Duffy to William B. Rubin, Feb. 11, 1937, Rubin MSS, State Historical Society of Wisconsin, Box 11; J. F. T. O'Connor MS Diary, Feb. 18, 1937; Portland *Press-Herald*, Feb. 6, 1937, clipping, Wallace White MSS, LC, Box 81; Fred Crawford to H. A. Douglas, Mar. 17, 1937, Crawford MSS, Michigan Historical Collections.

53. Mimeographed copy, John H. Overton MSS, Box 2.

54. Overton To Fayette C. Ewing, Feb. 20, 1937, *idem*.

55. Karl A. Lamb, "The Opposition Party as Secret Agent: Republicans and the Court Fight, 1937," *Papers of the Michigan Academy of Science, Arts, and Letters*, Vol. XLVI (1961).

56. Arthur Vandenberg MS Diary, Clements Library, University of Michigan, Feb. 6, 1937.

57. Herbert Hoover to Frank O. Lowden, Feb. 6, 1937, Lowden MSS, Series I, Box 58, Folder 5; Arthur M. Hyde to Paul Shoup, May 12, 1937, Shoup MSS, Stanford University Library, Stanford, Calif., Box 1. Too much has often been made of the Republican strategy of silence; men like Vandenberg spoke out after only a brief period of reticence.

58. U.S. Senate Committee on the Judiciary, 75th Cong., 1st Sess., *Reorganization of the Federal Judiciary*, Hearings on S. 1392 (Washington: Government Printing Office, 1937), Part 3, p. 491. Supporters of the plan retorted that if the Court was up to date on its calendar it was only because, ever since the enactment of a 1925 statute, the Court had been refusing to hear cases it should have heard. A federal district court judge from Los Angeles wrote: "I have never seen any logic in catching up with court calendars by shutting off the right to ask for justice, and that, in plain truth, is just what has been done. It is child's talk to say that the business of the court cannot be apportioned among fifteen so that more and better work can be turned out than through a court of nine." Albert Lee Stephens to William McAdoo, May 21, 1937, McAdoo MSS, LC, Box 435. But see Stanley Reed to FDR, Feb. 26, 1937, FDRL OF 10–F.

59. U.S. Senate, Committee on the Judiciary, *Hearings on S. 1392*, Pt. 4, p. 767.

60. Charles Andrews, Jr., to Charles O. Andrews, Mar. 11, 1937, Andrews MSS, Box 51.

61. F.R.L. to the editor, Mar. 2, 1937, Detroit *News*.

62. *Time*, XXIX (Apr. 5, 1937), 13.

63. West Coast Hotel Company *v.* Parrish, 300 U.S. 379 (1937).

64. The most important case was National Labor Relations Board *v.* Jones & Laughlin Steel Corporation, 301 U.S. 1 (1937).

65. Steward Machine Company *v.* Davis, 301 U.S. 548 (1937); Helvering *v.* Davis, 301 U.S. 619 (1937).

66. Merlo Pusey, *Charles Evans Hughes* (2 vols., New York, 1951), II, 757, 766–772; Felix Frankfurter, "Mr. Justice Roberts," *University of Pennsylvania Law Reviews*, CIV (Dec., 1955), 313–316. But see Edward F. Prichard, Jr., to the editor, Boston *Herald*, Apr. 2, 1937, copy in Theodore Green MSS, LC, Box 32.

67. Paul Mallon, "Purely Confidential," Detroit *News*, Apr. 13, 1937.

68. At least one justice did not anticipate that Roosevelt would win so handsomely; a number of judges might well have believed until that point that they were defending the people against an overbearing tyrant. The election results must have been a jolt. See Willis Van Devanter to Dennis Flynn, Oct. 19, 1936; Van

Devanter to Mrs. John W. Lacey, Nov. 2, 1936, Van Devanter MSS, LC, Vol. 52.

69. Detroit *News,* Apr. 13, 1937; Thomas Amlie to Mr. and Mrs. E. J. Klema, July 6, 1937, Amlie MSS, Box 39; J. F. T. O'Connor MS Diary, Apr. 12, 1937.

70. Tom Lewis to William Allen White, Mar. 30, 1937, White MSS, Box 187.

71. Milton to Joseph Greenbaum, Apr. 1, 1937, Milton MSS, Box 20.

72. Emma Guffey Miller, "Speech—Louisville [1937]," Miller MSS, Folder 36, Schlesinger Library, Radcliffe College.

73. Some conservatives believed that the Court's reversal had defeated the bill, but that too great a price had been paid. Newton Baker wrote: "The change of position by Mr. Justice Roberts is profoundly disturbing and distressing. I think the Court is already saved from the President's proposal, but how much of the old dignity and disinterestedness of the Court will remain as a tradition is a very serious question." Baker to John H. Clarke, June 9, 1937, Baker MSS, LC, Box 60.

74. Edward Corwin to Homer Cummings, May 19, 1937, Corwin MSS, Princeton University Library, Princeton, N.J.; Raymond Clapper MS Diary, June 10, 1937.

75. Willis Van Devanter to FDR, May 18, 1937, Van Devanter MSS, Vol. 54; *Time,* XXIX (May 31, 1937), 17; Stephen Tyree Early, Jr., "James Clark McReynolds and the Judicial Process," unpublished Ph.D. dissertation, University of Virginia, 1954, p. 102. Three months later, Borah wrote: "I made no effort to persuade anyone to get off the Supreme bench. I think I have a fair amount of nerve, but I would not undertake such a job as that." Borah to A. A. Lewis, Aug. 11, 1937, Borah MSS, LC, Box 414. The editor of the Boston *Herald* offered a different explanation: "That is a beautiful little controversy between the President and the C. J. Don't you suppose that Charles the Baptist persuaded Van Devanter to withdraw? Aren't the honors with the Chief Justice to date, rather than with the President?" Frank Buxton to William Allen White, June 8, 1937, White MSS, Box 189.

76. *Time,* XXIX (June 7, 1937), 13.

77. Saginaw *Daily News,* Apr. 13, 1937, clipping, Prentiss Brown Scrapbooks, St. Ignace, Mich. (privately held).

78. Detroit *News,* May 19, 1937; Frank V. Cantwell, "Public Opinion and the Legislative Process," *American Political Science Review,* LV (1946), 933–935. An advocate of the bill wrote: "The resignation of Justice Van Devanter has somewhat altered the situation and it is doubtful if the plan will pass the Senate with[out] some modification." Henry G. Teigan to Ross Blythe, May 20, 1937, Teigan MSS, Minnesota Historical Society, St. Paul, Minn., Box 16. On the same morning that Van Devanter resigned, the Senate Judiciary Committee voted, 10–8, to reject the plan.

79. Raymond Clapper MS Diary, Apr. 20, 1937.

80. *Ibid.*, May 24, 1937. One White House memorandum concluded: "The President has attained the most difficult of his *objectives*, i.e., the liberalization of the interpretation of the Constitution. He has yet to obtain these two objectives: (a) insurance of the continuity of that liberalism and (b) a more perfect judicial mechanism for giving a maximum of justice in a minimum of time." FDRL, PSF Supreme Court.

81. Address by Lewis Schwellenbach to Labor's Non-Partisan League, Minneapolis, Minn., Apr. 19, 1937, Schwellenbach MSS, LC, Box 1; Augustus L. and Alice B. Richards to Augustine Lonergan, Apr. 13, 1937, Richards MSS, Cornell University Collection of Regional History; Josephus Daniels to Joseph O'Mahoney, Apr. 7, 1937, O'Mahoney MSS, University of Wyoming Library, Laramie, Wyo.; William McAdoo to Walter Jones, Apr. 1, 1937; McAdoo MSS, Box 433; William Chilton to Roscoe Briggs, Apr. 1, 1937, Chilton MSS, University of West Virginia Library, Box 12; Philadelphia *Record*, Apr. 20, 1937, clipping, Frank Murphy Collection, University of Michigan Law School.

82. Statement of Theodore Francis Green, Green MSS, Box 32. George Fort Milton commented on the Wagner decisions: "It would be quite an unsafe thing to depend on the continuance of the present Robertian attachment as an anchor for a new constitutional attitude of the Government. Logically, Roberts' shift demonstrates so clearly the correctness of the Administration's position that the Constitution is all right; all that was wrong was an uncontemporarily-minded majority of the Court." George Fort Milton to Homer Cummings, Apr. 14, 1937, Milton MSS, Box 20.

83. *Time*, XXIX (May 24, 1937), 9.

84. Holland (Mich.) *Sentinel*, Feb. 16, 1937, clipping, Arthur Vandenberg Scrapbooks; Harold Ball to Joe Hendricks, Mar. 8, 1937, Hendricks MSS, Box 2; George Baldwin to Pat McCarran, June 2, 1937, McCarran MSS, Nevada State Museum, Carson City, Nev., File 672; B. H. Chernin to Bert Lord, Feb. 12, 1937, Lord MSS; M. E. Hennessy, "Round About," Boston *Globe*, clipping, n.d., David I. Walsh Scrapbooks, Holy Cross College Library, Worcester, Mass.; William Gibbs McAdoo to H. Hyer Whiting, Mar. 15, 1937, McAdoo MSS, Box 432. When Senator Green received a monster telegram from members of the Rhode Island bar opposing the plan, he had the signatures analyzed; of those who could be identified, 213 were Republicans, seven Democrats. Memorandum, Theodore Green MSS, Box 35. A Baltimore man wrote Senator Byrnes: "On my bended knees, I beg of you not to place the American people at the mercy of a man who seems to have only the interests of the lower classes at heart. . . . Please before it is too late consider the interests of your own class." Anon. to James F. Byrnes, Feb. 19, 1937, Byrnes MSS.

85. Lindsay Warren to A. D. McLean, May 23, 1937, Warren MSS, Box 17.

86. Arthur Vandenberg to William E. Evans, May 24, 1937, "Personal and Confidential," Vandenberg MSS.

87. Clippings in Scrapbook 13, John Nance Garner Papers, Archives, University of Texas Library. It created a deep rift between Garner and the White House circle. Raymond Clapper noted in his diary that Roosevelt's press secretary, Stephen Early, agreed with him "that Garner is at bottom of a lot of White House trouble now. Early says must be remembered that he is a millionaire and he has his goats and nut trees—is a plantation man." Raymond Clapper MS Diary, Aug. 3, 1937. See also, Joseph Guffey to FDR, July 29, 1939, Guffey MSS, Washington and Jefferson College Library, Washington, Pa.

88. U.S. Senate, Committee on the Judiciary, 75th Cong., 1st Sess., *Report No. 711* (Washington: Government Printing Office, 1937), p. 23.

89. Raymond Clapper MS Diary, June 14, 1937. Another political column noted: "The fury with which President Roosevelt's fellow Democrats on the Senate Judiciary Committee damned the New Deal's court plan today amazed this politically sophisticated capital. . . . What was not expected was the revelation that a group of Democratic Senators would scourge themselves into an emotional frenzy to denounce a head of their party who had carried 46 States only last November." John O'Donnell and Doris Fleeson, "Capitol Stuff," New York *Daily News*, June 15, 1937, clipping, Royal Copeland Scrapbooks.

90. *Time*, XXIX (June 14, 1937), 11.

91. Press Herald Bureau, Washington, Portland *Press Herald,* July 7, 1937, clipping, Wallace White MSS, Box 81.

92. Hiram Johnson to Garret W. McEnerney, July 7, 1937, Johnson MSS.

93. Kenneth McKellar to Charles T. Pennebaker, July 10, 1937, McKellar MSS, Box 97.

94. "How to Bust Court Filibuster?" *Business Week* (July 17, 1937), 14–15.

95. Memorandum, Frank Gannett MSS, Box 16.

96. Detroit *Free Press*, July 11, 1937.

97. McNary to Mrs. W. T. Stolz, July 10, 1937, McNary MSS, LC, Box 1.

98. *Time*, XXX (July 26, 1937), 10.

99. Lex Green to J. H. Scales, July 19, 1937, Green MSS, Box 27.

100. O. Max Gardner to B. B. Gossett, July 16, 1937, Gardner MSS, Southern Historical Collection, University of North Carolina, Box 15.

101. Elmer Ellsworth Adams to Theo Christianson, July 16, 1937, Adams MSS, Minnesota Historical Society, Box 42.

102. Middletown *Times Herald,* July 15, 1937, clipping. Royal Copeland Scrapbooks.

103. Doris Fleeson and John O'Donnell, "Capitol Stuff," Buffalo *Courier Press*, July 16, 1937, clipping, Royal Copeland Scrapbooks.

104. *The New York Times*, July 15, 1937.

105. *Ibid.*, July 16, 1937.

106. Detroit *Free Press*, July 21, 1937; Detroit *News*, July 21, 23, 1937, clippings, Prentiss Brown Scrapbooks; interview, Prentiss Brown, St. Ignace, Mich., July 7, 1965; Frank Gannett to J. P. Simmons, July 23, 1937, Gannett MSS, Box 3A; John H. Overton to Richard W. Leche *et al.*, July 22, 1937, Overton MSS.

107. Johnson to John Francis Neylan, July 24, 1937, Johnson MSS.

108. Detroit *Free Press*, July 23, 1937.

109. Raymond Clapper MS Diary, Aug. 4, 1937; Hiram Johnson to Lulu Leppo, Oct. 8, 1937, Johnson MSS; William Borah to Jess Hawley, Aug. 16, 1937, Borah MSS, Box 412; Rev. Edward Lodge Curran to Louis Brandeis, Oct. 6, 1937, Brandeis MSS, University of Louisville Law School Library, Louisville, Ky., SC 20.

110. Wickard *v.* Filburn, 317 U.S. 111 (1942); John W. Davis, Columbia Oral History Collection, Columbia University Library, pp. 165–166.

111. "What the Court Did to Business," *Business Week*, XVII (June 5, 1937), 17.

112. James C. McReynolds to Dr. Robert P. McReynolds, Oct. 30, 1937, McReynolds MSS, Alderman Library, University of Virginia, Charlottesville, Va.

113. Frank Gannett to E. A. Dodd, Feb. 5, 1938, Gannett MSS, Box 16.

114. Francis P. Miller to Herbert Claiborne Pell, Apr. 1, 1937, Pell MSS, FDRL, Box 8.

115. *The New York Times*, Aug. 22, 1937.

116. Blair Moody in Detroit *News*, Aug. 21, 1937, Blair Moody Scrapbooks, Michigan Historical Collections.

117. For a well-researched analysis, see James T. Patterson, *Congressional Conservatism and the New Deal* (Lexington, Ky., 1967). The seeds of the coalition had been planted before the Court message. Ralph Flanders to Warren Austin, Jan. 19, 1937, Flanders MSS, Carnegie Library, Syracuse University, Syracuse, N.Y., Box 20.

118. Springfield *Republican*, Mar. 14, 1937, clipping, David I. Walsh Scrapbooks.

119. Richard T. Ruetten, "Showdown in Montana, 1938" *Pacific Northwest Quarterly*, LIV (January, 1963), 19–29. I am indebted to Professor Reutten for permission to read his excellent unpublished study of Wheeler.

120. Josiah Bailey to Jas. R. Morris, Apr. 22, 1937; Bailey to Julian Miller, Aug. 4, 1937, Bailey MSS, Duke University Library, Political file.

121. J. E. Bass to John Overton, Feb. 24, 1937, Overton MSS, Box 2.

122. Helen St. Clair to Joe Hendricks, Apr. 17, 1937, Hendricks MSS, Box 2.

123. Walter Parkes to Theodore Green, Apr. 6, 1937, Green MSS, Box 34.

124. N. Y. Gulley to Josiah Bailey, Mar. 17, 1937, Bailey MSS, Political file. See also William F. Riley to Clyde Herring, July 7, 1937, Riley MSS, Box 1; Martha Washburn Allin to Henry Teigan, Feb. 13, 1937, Teigan MSS, Box 14; B. Agee Bowles to Carter Glass, Mar. 30, 1937, Glass MSS, Alderman Library, University of Virginia, Box 377.

125. William Brockway to Burton Wheeler, May 15, 1937, Theodore Green MSS, Box 33.

126. Frank Walker, "My Thoughts on President Roosevelt's Supreme Court Plan," Walker MSS, University of Notre Dame, Notre Dame, Ind.

127. Albert J. Stafne to Henrik Shipstead, July 23, 1937, Shipstead MSS, Minnesota Historical Society, Box 1. A Minnesota newspaper observed: "The Minnesota Farmer-Labor split was adding evidence of the havoc the court issue is working in party lines and in other previous congressional groupings." Duluth *Herald*, May 13, 1937, clipping, Shipstead MSS, Vol. 22.

128. William Allen White to John Finley, Apr. 29, 1937, White MSS, Box 187.

129. Hiram Johnson to Raymond Moley, Mar. 13, 1937, Johnson MSS; Edward Dickson to Hiram Johnson, Aug. 17, 1937, Dickson MSS, University of California at Los Angeles Library, Los Angeles, Calif., Box 8, Folder 9.

130. Hiram Johnson to John Francis Neylan, May 4, 1937, Johnson MSS.

THE NEW DEAL, COLLECTIVE BARGAINING, AND THE TRIUMPH OF INDUSTRIAL PLURALISM

Christopher L. Tomlins

This paper addresses what the author views as a prevailing misconception of labor law theorists and practitioners: that the goal of the Wagner Act was no more than the promotion of peaceful negotiating procedures and written agreements between organized interests—unions and employers—presumptively equal in power. The author argues that in fact the NLRA was drafted, and for a time implemented, with the avowed purpose of giving workers equality with employers in all aspects of industrial policy making, and that the now-prevalent approach became ascendant only after considerable conflict and the displacement of the Act's original administrators.

For the last forty years labor law discourse in the United States has been dominated by a set of values and assumptions that can conveniently be termed "industrial pluralism." Industrial pluralism connotes a systematic approach to labor relations, informed by liberal political and social theory, whose point of departure is the belief that industrial conflict in democratic societies is best dealt with through routinized procedures of negotiation and compromise leading to agreements formalized in contracts. Its adherents conceive of management and labor as self-governing equals who, through collective bargaining, jointly determine the terms and conditions of sale of labor power; and they see the historic purpose of labor relations law as nothing more than the facilitation of this process.[1]

Recently a new and skeptical school of labor jurisprudence, associated with what is known as the "critical legal studies" movement, has arisen to challenge the industrial pluralist paradigm. These scholars argue that the equality of labor and management in collective bargaining is purely formal, concealing a substantive inequality that renders pluralist explanations of the purpose of labor relations law incoherent. Indeed, once the false presumption of equality is removed, the critical scholars say, procedures represented as means to achieve peaceful labor-management cooperation stand revealed as "an institutional architecture" that actually serves to reinforce managerial domination of the workplace by narrowly confining unions to the role of "fiduciaries of an imagined societal interest in industrial peace" more or less forced to serve "specific managerial and disciplinary functions."[2] From this perspective the purpose of labor relations law is not to facilitate wide-ranging and socially constructive interactions between equals. Rather it is "to integrate the labor movement into the mainstream contours of pressure-group politics and to institutionalize, regulate and thereby dampen industrial conflict."[3]

At first sight, such observations appear little different from the "new left" analyses of the late 1960s and early 1970s that reduced all law and reform activity to an epiphenomenal reflex of capitalist productive relations. The critical scholars have avoided reductionism, however, by emphasizing that the legal outcomes they describe have been "systematically fashioned," a theoretical position that acknowledges the contingency of those outcomes. The leading figure of the genre, Karl Klare, has made this proposition the point of departure in his own work by arguing that the New Deal innovations on which modern labor relations law is based were "not a crystallization of consensus or a signpost indicating a solitary direction for future development," but "a texture of openness and divergency." Only by engaging in a conscious process of "deradicalization," a systematic and purposeful foreclosure of all options save those serving liberal pluralist values, did the courts achieve the structure of labor law we know today.[4]

Their efforts to avoid reductionism have not saved the critical labor law scholars from controversy. First, they have been faulted for their lack of attention to the social and political context in which legal events occur. Melvyn Dubofsky, for example, argues that the evolution of labor law "must be seen in light of shifts in the political balance of power and ebbs and flows in the labor movement."[5] Second, it is argued that once labor law has been placed in that context, attempts to portray it as the product of a successful judicial campaign to thwart the Wagner Act's radical potential become totally unconvincing. No dramatic "deradicalization" occurred in the 1930s and 1940s. Rather, the creation of a pluralistic labor relations law was the culmination of a consistent pattern of development in American industrial relations discourse. The savage conflicts that attended the birth of that law were between reactionaries and liberals contesting the very existence of unions and collective bargaining, not between liberals and radicals over what the right to self-organization and collective bargaining actually meant.[6]

Legal scholars should be castigated whenever they pay insufficient attention to the circumstances within which legal doctrine unfolds. In this case, however, historical investigation of these circumstances tends to confirm rather than rebut the critical scholars' contentions. To intimate that the Wagner Act might have been the most radical piece of legislation ever enacted by Congress[7] is, perhaps, unnecessarily extravagant. Certainly, however, the act's legislative history discloses a marked willingness on the part of at least some of its proponents to depart from the pluralist assumptions of American industrial relations discourse; certainly there ensued after its passage a struggle to impose a restricted pluralist meaning on it; and certainly the result was the eventual triumph of that restricted meaning in labor relations law.

The New Deal Collective Bargaining Policy

Background

Innovations in public policy, we have been reminded, do not occur in a vacuum. In the case of the New Deal collective bargaining policy, the legislative and administrative contests that determined its substance were fought out in a context structured by long-term developments in the practice of collective bargaining as pursued by the American Federation of Labor; the theories of collective bargaining embraced by labor economists; and the administrative strategies of state institutions vis-à-vis the labor movement.

Collective bargaining and the AFL. Collective bargaining became fully established as the axis of labor-management relations in AFL policy at the end of the nineteenth century. As the pace and scale of business accelerated after the 1893–98 depression, unions responded by shifting their organizational orientation away from local product markets to a regional and even national focus, diluting their strategic reliance on local craft control struggles and seeking instead to win material concessions from employers through negotiated guarantees of uninterrupted production. Such written "trade agreements" were not entirely twentieth-century innovations. Previous arrangements, however, had been predominantly informal and of restricted ambit. Not until the late 1890s did national unions begin acquiring sufficient centralized administrative and disciplinary capacity to be able to offer employers permanent routinized accommodations in exchange for uniform wages and conditions on a market-wide basis.[8]

Collective bargaining theories. Few employers responded to these early union initiatives. Greater interest was shown, however, by contemporary labor economists. Dismissive of classical political economy's individualistic faith in the market mechanism as a harmonizing agency, specialists in this new sub-field argued that economic activity was a *collective* phenomenon and was thus dependent on the development of social mechanisms that could adjust differing *collective* interests. They seized upon the trade agreement and collective bargaining as prime examples of such mechanisms. "[The trade agreement] implies the equal organization of employers [and employees] and the settlement of a wage scale and conditions of work through conferences of representatives," wrote the doyen of the field, John R. Commons, in 1907. "It is a form of constitutional government with its legislative, executive and judicial branches, its common law and statute law, its penalties and sanctions."[9]

This approach was taken up and developed further by William M. Leiserson, a student of Commons who would play a role of major importance in the debates over collective bargaining policy during the 1930s. According to Leiserson, trade agreements were "nothing less than constitutions for the industries which they cover, constitutions which set up organs of government, define and limit them, provide agencies for making, executing and interpreting laws for the industry, and means for their enforcement."[10]

Conceptualized politically, as a means of resolving conflicts over the employment relationship by imposing a redistribution of power on hitherto unequal parties, the trade agreement-as-constitution could have become an instrument of real industrial democracy. Commons and Leiserson, however, did not take this approach. In their hands the agreement and the institutions it created were procedural devices through which the *quid pro quo* of individual commercial exchange might be reproduced in contemporary social and economic relationships through the interaction of organizations presumed already to be equal in power.[11] Historically, both argued, industrial strife had developed not because relations of dominance and subordination were inherent in capitalist production but because the original organic mutuality of employers and employees had been disrupted by the growth of competition among employers during the nineteenth century's extension of markets. By setting up mechanisms to govern the sale of labor power throughout a given market, employers and employees could together eliminate destructive competition over wage costs. On this basis they could achieve industrial peace and reconstitute their former mutuality.[12]

Liberal-labor alliance. In the years after 1900, developments in the structure and ideology of the organized labor movement and in industrial relations theory became closely related; so much so, in fact, as to constitute a common program for the future development of collective bargaining. Within the organized labor movement the emergence in unions like the Machinists and the Carpenters of powerful national bureaucracies seeking routinized working relationships with employers confirmed the AFL's evolution from a locally based quasi-syndicalist movement of self-governing trades into a loose confederacy of self-interested organizations. Simultaneously, labor economists worked on refining their sketchy ideas about constitutional government into a comprehensive functionalist theory of cooperative dispute adjustment.

Key AFL officials endorsed this confluence of union practice and industrial relations theory. In 1923, for example, the Federation's executive council declared cooperative collaboration and the rejection of conflict to be the keystone of labor's relations with employers. Two years later William Green called on employers to endorse the establishment between themselves and the unions of "a proper regard for the functional exercise of each within their recognized spheres of jurisdiction."[13]

The associative state. Wider trends in the American political economy were creating the sort of environment in which these liberal-labor themes of industrial accommodation and self-government might become the basis for a new mode of labor-capital relations. Between 1890 and 1920 an astonishing efflorescence of collective organization and group activity—corporations, professional organizations and peak associations, reform movements, unions—swept aside nineteenth-century individualism and pointed the course of public life in a new direction. The nation's mode of government, in particular, underwent fundamental alteration as state institutions increasingly sought to accommodate these new nonpublic groups and organizations in the exercise of public power. This trend reached a climax during World War I, when the establishment of functional interdependence between public and private bureaucracies came to be regarded as the very sine qua non of a successful mobilization policy.[14]

Proponents of collective bargaining applauded the emergence of this "associative state" and looked forward to the acceptance of labor unions into the company of policy-making institutions. But in fact organized labor's role in the American political economy remained marginal. The Wilson administration, it is true, treated the AFL as the effectual wartime spokesman for the "labor" segment of American society in wartime manpower and dispute-adjustment matters, but the fruits of cooperation were soon forgotten in the savage labor-management conflicts of 1919–20. Even those employers ready at war's end to admit that some kind of continuing employer-employee relations might be desirable were overwhelmingly hostile toward the AFL and almost invariably chose to experiment with nonunion institutional forms: shop committees, employee representation plans, company unions. Nor were the architects of postwar domestic policy much more forthcoming, preferring to leave employers free to "reestablish an intimate relationship" with their employees unencumbered by guarantees to the unions.[15] Any lingering thoughts of policy innovations to encourage peacetime collective bargaining that they might have entertained were "regulated . . . to the periphery of national politics" after 1922 by the return of prosperity.[16]

Development

The onset of the Depression decisively altered the context of labor relations policy making. First, economic collapse comprehensively disrupted industry's existing labor policies. Second, as the crisis deepened it focused congressional attention more and more on the question of the distribution of national income. These circumstances offered proponents of collective bargaining new opportunities to seek legislative support. The result was a string of innovations endorsing collective bargaining and the right to organize: the Norris-LaGuardia Anti-injunction Act (1932); section 7(a) of the National Industrial Recovery Act (1933); Senator Robert F. Wagner's unsuccessful Labor Disputes bill (1934); and finally, in 1935, Wagner's National Labor Relations Act.

The legislation passed during the early stages of the burgeoning reform movement broadly embodied the liberal-labor consensus on union-employer collaboration that had been gathering force over the previous quarter-century.[17] Before this consensus could become a viable foundation for labor-capital relations, however, its proponents had first to persuade employers to entertain collective bargaining as an acceptable "associational" activity. The refusal of employers to do so undermined the authority of the liberal-labor

consensus and stimulated the emergence from within the embry-
onic federal labor relations bureaucracy of an alternative and less
accommodative approach to labor law reform predicated upon a
radical expansion of the state's legal authority and administrative
capacities in the labor relations arena and an uncompromising enforcement of workers' civil rights of collective organization and
representation. By early 1935 a contest for final authority to define
the precise direction of labor relations policy was under way *within*
Wagner's reform coalition between advocates of these two approaches.

   Early initiatives. The early rounds of the labor law reform
campaign were clearly dominated (on the reform side) by advocates
of the liberal-labor position. Their premises are easily stated. The
public interest lay in the stabilization of wages, hours, and working
conditions in industry at large. In the first instance this required
the resolution of "problems of economic control and government,"[18]
that is, terms and conditions of employment, arising within each
particular enterprise. Reform should thus be aimed at the establishment of mechanisms to facilitate joint determination and extend it to new areas of the economy. State intervention in the
substance of the parties' relationship, however, should be avoided.
Collective bargaining should remain a self-effectuating private process.

   The voluntarism of these early reform initiatives struck a
chord in a Congress still under the influence of the associative
ideology of the New Era. As Charles O. Gregory wrote many years
ago of the passage of the Norris-LaGuardia Act in 1932, "It is as if
Congress had said in this act: ' . . . We have instructed the judges to
withhold the use of the injunction against your self-help coercive
activities. . . . From now on it is up to you union people to promote
your own economic activities, as you see them, within the area of
conflict we have defined.'"[19] The National Industrial Recovery Act,
approved the following year, represented in large part a further
endorsement of the same approach. Unlike the Norris-LaGuardia
Act, however, the Recovery Act delegated substantial legislative
authority to the private sector to plan output, prices, wages, and
hours. This precipitated bitter conflicts between unions and employers over where the frontiers of associational involvement in the
planning process should lie.

   To the AFL the endorsement of collective bargaining in section 7(a) of the Recovery Act underlined the legitimacy of union

participation in policy making and implementation. Representation, code formulation, and code administration were to be matters for decision by the peak organizations of capital and labor in place on each side of industry. These would function in their own right in partnership with the government as regulators of both organized and previously unorganized areas of industry.[20]

Employers and Recovery Administration officials denied, however, that the act's guarantees required them to countenance any role for joint determination within the recovery program. In their eyes the industrial order that the act was designed to procure was predicated on cooperation among employers, not cooperation between employers and unions. This impasse meant a rapid escalation in industrial unrest, prompting calls in and out of Congress for the creation of dispute-resolving mechanisms. On August 5, 1933, Roosevelt established the National Labor Board, an ad hoc bipartisan body chaired by Senator Wagner, and gave it the task of addressing disputes over employee representation and other controversies impeding achievement of the act's purposes.

The half-year following the establishment of the National Labor Board was a period of considerable importance in the further development of the reform impulse. Initially the Board approached conflicts between employees claiming section 7(a) rights and employers refusing to acknowledge them with the methods and ideology of private dispute adjustment, primarily mediation. Its choice of this strategy was hardly surprising, for at this stage it was dominated by the liberal-labor allies of the 1920s, with AFL leaders sitting on the Board and William Leiserson serving as its chief administrative officer. But mediation proved increasingly incapable of coping with determined employer opposition.

Two important developments followed. Leiserson left to join the Petroleum Labor Policy Board and, largely at the instigation of General Counsel Milton Handler, the NLB moved to abandon adjustment of 7(a) disputes in favor of establishing representation and collective bargaining as rights to be enforced. Handler was successful in obtaining an executive order to this effect from the president in February 1934. Simultaneously a "Labor Disputes" bill giving statutory authorization to the new approach was drawn up by the Board's tiny legal staff under the direction of Senator Wagner's assistant, Leon Keyserling.[21]

The Labor Disputes bill. The move away from adjustment of 7(a) disputes to enforcement of 7(a) rights was of major importance to the development of federal labor relations policy. Initially Wagner tied the move to the requirements of the recovery program, particularly to the importance of creating a balance of power within the associative state. "The keynote of the recovery program is organization and cooperation," he said on introducing the Labor Disputes bill. "Employers are allowed to unite in trade associations in order to pool their information and experience and make a concerted drive upon the problems of modern industrialism. If properly directed this united strength will result in unalloyed good to the nation. But it is fraught with great danger to workers and consumers if it is not counterbalanced by the equal organization and equal bargaining power of employees. Such equality is the central need of the economic world today. It is necessary to ensure a wise distribution of wealth between management and labor, to maintain a full flow of purchasing power, and to prevent recurrent depressions."[22]

No matter how instrumental the rationale, however, a policy of enforcing rights still required its proponents to define what the rights which they proposed to enforce—the rights to representation and collective bargaining—actually meant. It was here that major differences were to emerge within the reform consensus.

To the AFL, the character of representation and collective bargaining was determined by its own jurisdictional structure and by the bargaining strategies of its member unions. In practical terms the right to representation and collective bargaining meant the right of a particular worker to join the union to which the federation had assigned jurisdiction over his job. The assignments themselves were based on a complex web of considerations internal to the organized labor movement: custom, bargaining history, and, above all, the distribution of power within the federation. Each affiliate was well aware of the precise extent of its jurisdictional "property" rights; each was perennially insistent upon its right to represent whatever workers occupied those particular jobs.

This interpretation of representation rights was shared by the unions' pluralist allies. Leiserson, for example, advised Wagner that his Labor Disputes bill should specify explicitly that employers bargain with "the labor organizations of [their] employees" through the officers "duly designated" by those labor organizations.[23] To the pluralists, as to the unions, exercising one's right to representation meant no more than enlisting the appropriate union to bargain on one's behalf. The real goal was the joint agreement,

whereby relations between the two sides of industry would be institutionalized in a system of countervailing power, and industrial
peace ensured.

The bill's attempts to enforce section 7(a), however, were
susceptible to a different interpretation, one that treated the designation of representatives not simply as a means to legitimize accommodations arrived at between union and employer but rather
as an expression by employees of a much broader civil right of
participation in industrial government.[24] Thus, the original draft of
the bill as introduced in the Senate stated in section 4 that employees "shall have the right to organize and join labor organizations,
and to engage in concerted activities, either in labor organizations
or otherwise, for the purposes of organizing and bargaining collectively through representatives of their own choosing, *or for other
purposes of mutual aid or protection*."[25] Advocating the bill's passage,
NLB member Francis Haas adverted to "the inherent rights which
all possess to participate in making regulations to govern them."
The rights the bill sought to protect were rights given by nature,
indistinguishable from the rights which "our Federal and State
constitutions declare that [workers] may exercise . . . to elect their
representatives in Government, whether local or national."[26]

Seen from this perspective, the bill presented the prospect of
using the power of the state to create an entirely new presence, a
citizenry of employees, in industry. Rather than a procedural means
to an essentially limited end—the "cooperative marketing" of labor[27] through the negotiation of stabilizing collective agreements—
the rights of employees to representation and organization were
treated in the bill as ends in themselves. They were "fundamental
rights," the unobstructed exercise of which comprised a non-nego-
tiable prerequisite for "frank and friendly relations in industry."[28]

Here, inconclusively, matters rested. Wagner was unable to
marshal sufficient congressional support to overcome the opposition of employers, and the Labor Disputes bill was shelved in favor
of a substitute "Industrial Adjustments Bill," introduced by Senate
Labor Committee chairman David Walsh. Subsequently the Walsh
bill was also discarded. Nevertheless, the debate over the Labor
Disputes bill had been of considerable significance. First, it had
revealed to all proponents of collective bargaining the depth of
opposition among employers to labor reform proposals of any sort;
this convinced Wagner that meaningful reforms could never be
achieved through compromise. Second, the debate had suggested

the existence of significant differences of emphasis and interpretation within the ranks of the coalition supporting labor law reform.

These differences grew firmer over the next six months. By the end of 1934 they had matured into two distinct programs for labor law reform, one focusing upon the strengthening of existing private institutions and the creation of mechanisms to encourage their interaction, the other geared to the protection of workers' civil rights and to the production of a transformed institutional order in industry.

The Wagner Act. The development of two distinct approaches within the reform coalition is relatively easy to trace, because by late 1934, when planning for new legislation began again in earnest, two separate centers of discussion and drafting had appeared. One was in Washington where, coordinated by Leon Keyserling and under the political direction of Senator Wagner, the legal staff of the Garrison Labor Relations Board[29] was engaged in completely rewriting the Labor Disputes bill. The other was in New York, where Edward A. Filene's Twentieth Century Fund had assembled a committee of lawyers, industrial relations experts, economists, social scientists, and progressive employers—William H. Davis (Chairman), the peripatetic Leiserson, Sumner Slichter, Robert S. Lynd, William Chenery, Henry Dennison, and others—to determine the appropriate role for government in labor relations.

The National Labor Relations Board staff's priorities in rewriting the Labor Disputes bill were clear and unambiguous. "The board wanted Congress to state clearly the obligation of the employer to bargain collectively, endorse and define the principle of majority rule, create a judicial and administrative agency 'wholly independent of any executive branch of the government,' provide for vigorous and prompt enforcement of the board's rulings, grant the board 'the widest scope . . . to permit it to build up a constructive body of labor law,' and apply the legislation to all workers in all industries engaged in interstate commerce."[30] This pointed the board away from associative concepts of the state and the ideology of adjustment among "interests" that informed those concepts. It placed the emphasis in labor relations policy squarely upon expansion of the state's administrative capacity to establish substantive rights and enforce correlative duties.

The priorities of the Twentieth Century Fund Committee contrasted in a number of respects. Whereas the NLRB stressed

the enforcement of individual rights, the Fund Committee continued to address itself to expediting the adjustment of group interests. "We are part of a competitive economy in which . . . various
groups are struggling for immediate economic advantage. The
government should create rules and mechanisms which will guarantee to both parties to the industrial bargain a fair field in negotiations."[31] The committee accepted that those rules and mechanisms
should be founded on effective implementation of 7(a), but it tied
enforcement specifically to the peaceful adjustment of disputes and
the promotion of agreements. As Slichter put it, "What we are
trying to get in the report is a public policy. That public policy has
two main parts: one is the encouragement of organization and
collective bargaining. . . . [The other] is the promotion of industrial
peace."

In the same vein, Leiserson argued that simply denouncing
the sins of employers and creating a powerful new agency to stamp
them out was not a realistic approach to industrial relations. The
government should instead concentrate on developing procedures
that parties to collective bargaining should be obliged by law to
follow. Leiserson proposed that the Committee make a particular
point of recommending that "a definite procedure should be laid
down which must be gone through before any group may assume
the right to strike."[32]

The divergence between the positions of the two groups was
accentuated by the absence of any sustained contact between them.
Each expressed considerable interest in the work of the other, but
little concrete information was exchanged until relatively late in
the day; the Fund Committee decided early on that none of its
findings should be communicated to anyone until its report and
proposals were complete, while for its part the Board group did not
provide the Fund with a draft of its bill until the middle of February
1935, three months after the two groups had begun their separate
discussions and only five days before Wagner was to introduce the
bill in the Senate.

The Twentieth Century Fund Committee's reaction to the
Wagner bill, one it had finally seen a copy, is extremely interesting.
"It was the consensus of the committee that the Wagner bill was in
all probability a bargaining bill. Mr. Dennison expressed the opinion that the committee should not throw their recommendations
into the discussion of the Wagner bill, but that they should be
released to the public after the Wagner bill had been introduced

and the opposition had launched its fight against the bill. The committee's recommendations might then become the basis for a compromise bill." The committee's minutes report "general agreement" with these proposals.[33] Plainly, the committee thought the bill should not pass as it stood.

The Fund Committee underscored its opinion of the Wagner bill by offering amendments during the Senate hearings that diluted the bill's emphasis upon the use of public authority to entrench fundamental employee rights. Acknowledging that employees had a right to freedom of association and self-organization, the committee simultaneously qualified its acknowledgment by arguing that the right should be affirmed *insofar as to do so would advance the purposes of peaceful and constructive collecting bargaining.* "We believe . . . that it is possible and desirable to go beyond the mere assertion of right and prohibition of interference, in the direction of positive and useful encouragement of collective agreements between management and labor. *The organization of workers and their choice of representatives, are, after all, only means to an end—the establishment and observance of written agreements.*"[34]

To that end the committee proposed that the act include a "more comprehensive definition of unlawful practices,"[35] by which it meant the inclusion of provisions regulating employee and union behavior. It also proposed that the "Federal Labor Commission," which it advocated as a replacement for the NLRB, be empowered to register collective bargaining agreements and enforce compliance with them.[36] In addition, the committee's amendments narrowed somewhat the definition of employee rights contained in section 7 of the Wagner bill,[37] and opened the door to employer suits against employees and employee organizations engaging in disputes.[38]

The Twentieth Century Fund Committee was wrong, however, in assuming that the Wagner bill could not be enacted as it stood. The failure of the Fund's amendments, moreover, meant that the three-year labor law reform drive had culminated in legislation geared to lawyerly preoccupations with the precise definition and active enforcement of workers' rights and employers' correlative duties rather than to the pluralists' instrumental insistence on legislative prescription of procedures whereby collective contracts might be written, executed, and enforced. As the reconstituted NLRB approached the task of implementing labor relations policy, it tended to accent further those aspects of the act most characteristic of its lawyerly provenance. The result was a mode of administration and an articulation of goals profoundly disturbing to the pluralist element in the reform coalition. Within a few months of the act's passage, Leiserson, for one, could be heard privately expressing his "grave doubts" as to whether members of the new Board could be successful "under the procedure that they have adopted."[39]

Conflicts over Policy

Despite the development of two distinct reform strategies within the coalition supporting collective bargaining, there were no open quarrels during the congressional debates. Labor leaders, the nascent federal labor relations bureaucracy, and pluralist industrial relations experts remained sufficiently united to ensure passage of the Wagner Act. Once the new Board moved to implement the act, however, rifts began to emerge. The fault line lay between the established, liberal-labor constituency, on the one hand, and the NLRB and its lawyers on the other. The immediate occasion for these strains exploding in conflict was the split within the labor movement between the AFL and the CIO and the controversy which this provoked over the NLRB's exercise of its powers to intervene in representation disputes. Board policy was condemned both by liberal pluralists and by AFL unions as an assault on union custom and practice. In 1938–39, AFL hostility toward the Board peaked in a campaign for legislative curbs on the NLRB's authority.

The appointment of William Leiserson to the NLRB in 1939 added a crucial new dimension to the controversy by providing a focus *within* the federal labor relations bureaucracy around which critics of the Board's reform strategy could coalesce. It was here that the struggle climaxed with the replacement in November 1940 of the incumbent chairman, J. Warren Madden, by the labor economist and arbitrator Harry A. Millis. Millis's appointment confirmed the defeat of the line followed by the Board during its first five years and marked the ascendancy of the industrial pluralists and the triumph of their paradigm in American labor relations.

The AFL and the NLRB. Compared with the contributions of the Twentieth Century Fund Committee and of the NLRB's legal staff, the role of the AFL in the 1934–35 debates was a minor one. AFL representatives were kept informed of the general nature of the Washington discussions, and the Federation's general counsel,

Charlton Ogburn, sat in on some sessions, but the Federation satisfied itself comparatively early on that the proposed legislation was in its interests, and from then on limited its participation in the policy-making process to attempts to amend the legislation so as to retain a degree of procedural initiative over employment of the act's sanctions in its own hands. Rejection of its amendments did not appear to weaken the AFL's overall support for the bill.[40]

Elements within the AFL leadership, however, were always uneasy about particular facets of the bill, notably the sections giving the NLRB final authority over the structure of labor representation. With the development, by mid-1935, of serious challenges to the authority of the incumbent leadership over the allocation of representation rights in mass production industries, assurances were sought that determination of representation questions would not enter the public domain and thus move beyond the incumbent leadership's control. Once given, these assurances temporarily restored to the legislation the quantum of ambiguity necessary to quiet the AFL's unease and ensure harmony in the reform coalition.[41] But the question reemerged almost immediately after the act was passed. By the end of the year, prompted by the formation of the minority CIO faction within the Federation and the threat, ultimately realized, of a split, AFL leaders had embarked upon what would become an increasingly bitter campaign to ensure that the Board's discretion in determining representation would be subordinated to the dictates of official Federation policy.

The main points at issue between the AFL and the NLRB are illustrated in *Shipowners' Association of the Pacific Coast.*[42] In this case the International Longshoremen's and Warehousemen's Union–CIO sought certification as the bargaining representative for all Pacific Coast longshoremen over the opposition of the International Longshoremen's Association–AFL, which sought recognition as the bargaining representative of longshoremen in four ports in the Pacific Northwest. The Board found that the entire Pacific Coast constituted one bargaining unit and certified the ILWU.

The AFL challenged the Board's authority to make such a determination on the grounds that the decision deprived the ILA of its "right to engage in business as a labor organization." According to AFL general counsel Joseph Padway, unions, once recognized, acquired vested interests—property rights—in their contractual relationships with employers that no merely administrative agency could vacate. The AFL accepted that passage of the

Wagner Act had made it "a necessary and vital prerequisite or condition of the proper functioning of any labor organization seeking to represent employees for the purpose of collective bargaining" that it first obtain the Board's certification that the group of employees for whom it sought to bargain was an appropriate group. But, the AFL argued, as long as the union could show that it had the support of a majority of the group it had designated, it was "entitled" to be certified so that it might retain its property rights.[43]

The Board argued differently. First, the right to organize and bargain collectively was not a property right of unions but a civil right of workers. Where challenged, it was to be exercised through administrative action in accordance with statutory prescriptions. Second, a union could have no legal claim to a particular certification. The Board's "finding of fact" was the only basis upon which assertions of union right might be made, and then only by a union already certified as the designated representative of workers in a unit found by the Board to be appropriate.[44]

Pre-enactment ambiguity gave rise to conflicts other than that over representation. Union behavior was similarly affected. Section 8 of the Wagner Act, for example, prohibited employers from "dominating or interfering with the formation or administration of any labor organization" and from entering into an exclusive agreement with any organization that was not the certified representative of employees in a collective bargaining unit approved by the Board. The purpose of this provision was to ensure disestablishment of company unions. The Senate Labor Committee report on the Wagner bill had recommended, however, that the provision be interpreted also as prohibiting exclusive agreements made by independent unions that did not represent a majority of the employees concerned.[45] The NLRB's concurrence meant that a collective bargaining technique employed by unions for many years was rendered illegitimate.[46] Henceforth, any employer who signed a closed shop contract without proof that the union in question represented the majority of his workers in an appropriate bargaining unit could be held guilty of improperly assisting a labor organization. Under such circumstances, said the Board, it would "restore the status quo by obliterating the illegal contract."[47]

To the AFL, such policies threatened the entire panoply of collective bargaining practices and union-employer accommodations that it had been trying to develop since 1900. Consequently, in April and May of 1939 its leadership appeared before the House and Senate Labor Committees to press a series of amendments to the Wagner Act designed to force the Board to move toward a more accommodating model of labor relations. These amendments required the Board to grant workers representation in accordance with the jurisdictional structure of their unions; guaranteed unions the opportunity to seek enforcement of the act in independent actions; denied the Board power to intervene in jurisdiction disputes; required it to respect contracts made by bona fide unions on behalf of minority groups of workers pending final determination of a majority representative, even where it found that the employer had been partial; and provided that unions should have unrestricted rights to seek review of Board decisions that affected their interests.[48]

The appointment of Leiserson. The AFL's campaign against the NLRB failed to bring about the substantive limitations on the Board's discretion that the Federation sought. It did, however, alarm the Roosevelt administration. Conscious in the wake of the 1938 elections of waning domestic support, Roosevelt sought to appease the AFL by denying retiring Board member Donald W. Smith reappointment, and put William Leiserson in his place. Already known as a critic of the current Board, Leiserson was under instructions from Roosevelt to "clean up" the NLRB's administration of the act.[49]

Leiserson's appointment precipitated bitter conflicts within the Board, for Leiserson arrived determined to rebuild labor relations law around the private process of accommodation engaged in by the organized parties. By undertaking to "protect by law the wage earners who cannot by their own strength overcome the oppressions of their employers," Leiserson argued, the Wagner Act had projected public authority into a field already occupied by nonpublic rule-making bodies: unions and employers. For government policy to succeed, the public agency created to administer it should learn from the institutions already established in the field and seek harmony with their environment, not "impose new rules [based] on [its] own notions of reasonableness."[50]

The struggle was played out in the arena of bargaining unit determinations. Here, diametrically opposed views of how an appropriate unit should be determined contested for dominance.

To Leiserson the Wagner Act had been passed to secure stable and responsible collective bargaining. Hence the appropriate unit in any case was that which best afforded the parties an opportunity to develop a stable and responsible bargaining relationship. The best guide to what was appropriate was provided by the parties' own customs and practices. In particular, if the parties had already arrived at a contract, that contract should define the unit. Leiserson repeatedly condemned "units established by Board members on the basis of their own opinions as to appropriateness" in disregard of arrangements already established and functioning. Only units developed in the course of dealings between unions and management could form the basis for "sound labor relations."[51]

Leiserson's colleagues rejected his contention that their discretion was limited by private contractual arrangements entered into by the parties. "I do not agree . . . that the Board 'is not authorized by the Act' to find a different bargaining unit from that which has been previously embodied in an exclusive bargaining contract," wrote veteran NLRB member Edwin S. Smith. "I think the past history of collective bargaining in a plant . . . is an important . . . factor in the determination of the appropriate bargaining unit. But I do not believe that the Board is precluded by anything in the Act from finding a different unit to be appropriate."[52] For his part, Smith argued that the Board's statutory obligation was to find the unit in every case that would most nearly match the bargaining power of the employees in question with that of their employer.

The chairman, J. Warren Madden, also denied that the Board's authority could be vacated by the arrangements entered into by unions and employers. "The development of the proper unit for collective bargaining," Madden believed, "is an evolutionary process." The Board should encourage and accommodate this evolution by allowing employee groups to design and redesign their bargaining arrangements with a minimum of restriction from any quarter.[53]

These differing approaches clearly illustrate the major difference of principle separating Leiserson on the one hand from Smith and Madden on the other. Smith and Madden believed that the Wagner Act gave the Board widespread power to protect the self-determination of employees and, crucially, to establish them in bargaining relationships that maximized their opportunity for further substantive self-determination. Leiserson, in contrast, held that the act did not authorize the Board to exercise independent judgment as to the appropriateness of units but only gave it fact-finding powers to, in effect, register and certify whatever units organized labor established in its relations with organized employers. His emphasis upon the determinative influence of the contract further expressed his conviction that the Board's overriding function was to achieve stability, order, and efficiency in collective bargaining and that the proper way to do that was for the Board simply to lend its imprimatur to whatever working arrangements had been established by the parties concerned.[54]

The Board remained in a state of fundamental disagreement on the unit issue throughout the first fifteen months of Leiserson's term. This did not prevent it from making decisions. It was even able to achieve unanimity on many occasions. Nevertheless, its disagreements were more than sufficient to obstruct the further development of the unit policies it had pursued before Leiserson's appointment.[55]

The obstruction was not destined to last. Both Madden and Smith were close to the ends of their terms of office, and in each case renewal was refused. Madden, the first to go, was retired after the 1940 election; his replacement as chairman was an avowed pluralist, the University of Chicago economist and labor arbitrator Harry A. Millis. Smith remained for another year but was rendered powerless by the pluralist axis of Millis and Leiserson. Leiserson was delighted that the conflict of the previous fifteen months had at last been resolved so decisively in his favor. "Now if the President only appoints Ed Witte next August when Smith's appointment expires, then we would have a real Board," he wrote to John R. Commons a week after Millis's appointment had been announced. "You would have all three of the Board members your boys—and you would be sure that the administration of the law was both proper and intelligent."[56]

The Triumph of Industrial Pluralism

The appointment of Harry A. Millis as chairman left the NLRB committed to the achievement of stable collective bargaining relationships as the sole object of federal labor relations policy. Having defined this essentially limited goal as the abiding purpose of the representation of labor envisaged by the Wagner Act, Millis and Leiserson used their majority to ensure that the self-activity of workers became focused fully on its realization by entrenching bargaining structures wherever they were established and functioning. This offered incumbents a considerable degree of relief from the insecurities engendered by the unit policies of the Madden Board, and with CIO as well as AFL unions increasingly interested in establishing institutional stability through permanent bargaining relationships with employers, the triumph of an industrial relations paradigm based on entrenched contractual relations was assured.[57]

Commentators writing in the pluralist tradition have, unsurprisingly, denied that any sort of "thermidor" in employee rights accompanied the transition from the Madden Board to the Millis Board. Millis himself represented the changes he helped to institute as little more than a logical and largely complementary extension of the Madden Board's policies. The Madden Board, he wrote, has established "the major outlines of the application of the law." Its successor's task had been to tidy up the loose ends: "to improve administration, in the interest of prompt, efficient and economical handling of cases, and to increase the emphasis upon good and workable industrial relations practices, which had to some degree been lost sight of in the tendency to legalistic emphasis in the first five years."[58]

Subsequent writers have followed the same track, ignoring the differences within the original reform coalition and minimizing the ideological conflicts over the implementation of federal policy that dominated the Board's first five years. This is typified in Philip Selznick's insistence that the Wagner Act was a "celebration of voluntarism and bargaining," which was "in spirit akin to traditional contract law in that its chief aim was to facilitate private transactions and arrangements." According to Selznick, the act's contribution began and ended at "creat[ing] the *conditions* for bargaining and formalized agreement."[59]

Pluralist writers like Millis and Selznick correctly describe what has *become* the role of American labor relations law. As we have seen, however, it is questionable whether their description proceeds from assumptions about the function and goals of labor relations law consistent with those embraced by the Wagner Act's mentors and early administrators. The ideology of industrial pluralism, I would argue, was not inscribed in the Wagner Act from the outset, nor was its hegemony necessarily what the act's architects intended. Rather, pluralist hegemony came about only after bitter conflicts over labor relations policy had undermined "debate in terms of legal and natural rights: in favor of "recognition of the necessity of 'give and take'" in industrial relations.[60] Only then did labor relations law begin to proliferate administrative innovations safeguarding incumbents and circumscribing collective activity.

Only then did it become apparent that in the service of that "give and take" the values of free choice and self-determination—values that it had once been claimed, would make the Wagner Act the symbol of a new age—would, where necessary, be allowed to fall by the wayside.

NOTES

1. See Katherine Stone, "The Post-War Paradigm in American Labor Law," *Yale Law Journal*, Vol. 90, No. 7 (June 1981), pp. 1509–80.

2. Karl E. Klare, "Labor Law as Ideology: Toward a New Historiography of Collective Bargaining Law," *Industrial Relations Law Journal*, Vol. 4, No. 3 (1981), p. 452.

3. Ibid. See also Karl E. Klare, "Critical Theory and Labor Relations Law," in David Kairys, ed., *The Politics of Law: A Progressive Critique* (New York: Pantheon, 1982), pp. 65–88; James B. Atleson, *Values and Assumptions in American Labor Law* (Amherst: University of Massachusetts Press, 1983).

4. Karl E. Klare, "Judicial Deradicalization of the Wagner Act and the Origins of Modern Legal Consciousness, 1937–1941," *Minnesota Law Review*, Vol. 62, No. 3 (1978), p. 291.

5. Melvyn Dubofsky, "Legal Theory and Workers' Rights: A Historian's Critique," *Industrial Relations Law Journal*, Vol. 4, No. 3 (1981), p. 498.

6. Matthew W. Finkin, "Revisionism in Labor Law," *Maryland Law Review*, Vol. 43 (1984), pp. 23–92; Howell J. Harris, "The Snares of Liberalism?" in Steven Tolliday and Jonathan Zeitlin, eds., *Shop-Floor Bargaining and the State: Historical and Comparative Perspectives* (Cambridge: Cambridge University Press, 1985).

7. Klare, "Judicial Deradicalization of the Wagner Act," p. 265.

8. See, generally, Lloyd Ulman, *The Rise of the National Trade Union* (Cambridge: Harvard University Press, 1955), pp. 190–200, 519–35.

9. John R. Commons, ed., *Trade Unionism and Labor Problems* (Boston: Ginn and Co., 1905), Vol. 1, p. vii.

10. William M. Leiserson, "Constitutional Government in American Industries," *American Economic Review*, Vol. 12 (Supp.), No. 1 (1922), p. 61. See also Paul J. NcNulty, *The Origins and Development of Labor Economics: A Chapter in the History of Social Thought* (Cambridge: MIT Press, 1980), pp. 127–51.

11. John R. Commons, "Trade Agreements," in Commons, ed., *Trade Unionism and Labor Problems*, pp. 1–12.

12. Ibid., p. 12; William M. Leiserson, "Labor Relations" (unpublished book manuscript), pp. ii–v, and Part I, pp. 1–14, 57–68, 88–90, in Leiserson Papers (State Historical Society of Wisconsin,

Madison), Box 52. See also John R. Commons, *Legal Foundations of Capitalism* (New York: Macmillan, 1924), pp. 143–53.

13. William Green, Speech to National Civic Federation Round Table (April 11, 1925) in *The American Federation of Labor Records: The Samuel Gompers Era* (Microfilm edition, Microfilming Corporation of America, 1979), reel 57; "Industry's Manifest Duty," in *Proceedings of the 43rd Annual Convention of the American Federation of Labor* (Washington, D.C.: AFL, 1923), p. 31.

14. Robert D. Cuff, *The War Industries Board: Business-Government Relations During World War One* (Baltimore: Johns Hopkins University Press, 1973). See, generally, Robert H. Wiebe, *The Search for Order, 1877–1920* (New York: Hill & Wang, 1967).

15. Robert H. Zieger, "Herbert Hoover, The Wage-Earner, and the 'New Economic System,' 1919–29," *Business History Review*, Vol. 51, No. 2 (Summer 1977), p. 168.

16. Steve Fraser, "Dress Rehearsal for the New Deal: Shop-Floor Insurgents, Political Elites, and Industrial Democracy in the Amalgamated Clothing Workers," in Michael H. Frisch and Daniel J. Walkowitz, eds., *Working Class America* (Urbana: University of Illinois Press, 1983), p. 241.

17. On the maturation of this consensus, see David Brody, "On the Failure of U.S. Radical Politics: A Farmer-Labor Analysis," *Industrial Relations*, Vol. 22, No. 3 (Spring 1983), pp. 152–57. However, see also Steve Fraser, "From the New Unionism to the New Deal," *Labor History*, Vol. 25, No. 3 (Summer 1984), pp. 405–30, describing the partial displacement of the AFL's voluntarism from the center of the liberal-labor trajectory by a newer proto-Keynesian impulse centered on the Amalgamated Clothing Workers. It is not unlikely that further exploration will reveal considerable symmetry in the relationship between Fraser's proto-Keynesians and the pluralist impulse in labor relations law. On this topic in the postwar period, see Stone, "Post-War Paradigm," pp. 1509–80.

18. Leiserson, "Labor Relations," Part I, pp. 66–67.

19. Charles O. Gregory, *Labor and the Law*, 2d ed. (New York: Norton, 1961), p. 192.

20. "Administrative Principles of the American Federation of Labor in Dealings Under the National Industrial Recovery Act" (June 8, 1933), in *AFL Records*, reel 57.

21. Peter H. Irons, *The New Deal Lawyers* (Princeton: Princeton University Press, 1982), pp. 205–11.

22. National Labor Relations Board, *Legislative History of the National Labor Relations Act* (Washington, D.C.: NLRB, 1949), p. 15.

23. Leiserson to Wagner (March 8, 1934) in *Leiserson Papers*, Box 33.

24. Leon H. Keyserling, "The Wagner Act: Its Origin and Current Significance," *George Washington Law Review*, Vol. 29 (1960), pp. 199–233, notes that Wagner's "was no simple doctrine of countervailing power." Rather, Wagner viewed collective bargain-

ing as "an integral part of an ever larger cooperative process guided by intelligence which would animate the whole economy, including the governmental sector." Pp. 220–21.

25. U.S. Congress, Senate, "S 2926, A Bill to equalize the bargaining power of employers and employees, to encourage the amicable settlement of disputes between employers and employees, to create a National Labor Board, and for other purposes," 73d Cong., 2d sess., February 28, 1934, p. 4 (emphasis added). The draft also made it an unfair labor practice "for an employer, or anyone acting in his interest, directly or indirectly, to attempt, by interference, influence, restraint, favor, coercion, or lockout, or by any other means, to impair the right of employees guaranteed in section 4." P. 5.

It is worth noting, if only to point up the contrast that a copy of the bill marked, apparently, by William Leiserson, recommends that section 4's general statement of employee rights be deleted (by reason, in part, of its "tautology and verbal confusion") and that the language of the subsequent unfair labor practice provision be amended so as to prohibit an employer or his agent from attempting "to impair the right of employees to engage in concerted activities for the purpose of bargaining collectively through representatives of their own choice." S 2926 "Marked Copy," in Leiserson Papers, Box 28.

26. U.S. Congress, Senate Committee on Education and Labor, *Hearings on S 2926*, 73d Cong., 2d sess., March 15, 1934, p. 115.

27. The phrase is Leiserson's. See *Hearings on S 2926*, March 16, 1934, p. 232.

28. Keyserling, "The Wagner Act," p. 217, quoting remarks made by Senator Wagner during a radio debate with James A. Emery, counsel for the National Association of Manufacturers. Wagner concluded, "Peace rests upon freedom, not restraint; upon equality, not subservience; upon cooperation, not domination."

29. This agency, the first to bear the title "National Labor Relations Board," was created by the Roosevelt administration at the end of June 1934 following passage of Public Resolution 44 by Congress. Chaired initially by Lloyd K. Garrison, and subsequently by Francis Biddle, the board had no more power than the old National Labor Board which it replaced. It could investigate 7(a) disputes and conduct elections but lacked any authority to enforce its decisions.

30. James A. Gross, *The Making of the National Labor Relations Board: A Study in Economics, Politics and the Law* (Albany: State University of New York Press, 1974), p. 130.

31. Special Committee on the Role of Government in Labor Relations, Twentieth Century Fund, Minutes of the Third Meeting (January 18, 1935), in *Leiserson Papers*, Boxes 40–41.

32. Ibid. Provisions to this effect were included in the committee's final report. See Twentieth Century Fund Committee, "Memorandum of Findings and Recommendations" (March 20, 1935), in U.S. Congress, Senate Committee on Education and Labor, *Hearings on S 1958*, 74th Cong., 1st sess., April 1, 1935, p. 723.

Robert S. Lynd was the only member of the committee to question the emphasis upon "modest and practical" measures that Slichter and Leiserson argued should characterize the committee's report. Lynd took the position that it was the committee's responsibility "to open up wide, at this time of national re-appraisal, the question as to how modern democratic government may best function in relation to a realistic conception of labor as a part of a socially guided economy." He was critical of his colleagues for failing, at a time when "the present psychology of Washington is so heavily that of dealing with immediate troublesome issues on a liberal basis that will pacify contending factions and break new ground only to the extent of rectifying a few of the more glaring discrepancies," to set their sights any higher than "simply augmenting the volume of suggestions for immediate action by Congress." Lynd proposed that the committee instead adopt as its point of departure the proposition that "equality of bargaining power [is] not possible, even with complete organization of labor," as long as "one party to the bargain owns and controls the necessary tools for work for private gain and the other party is in the position of the outsider forced to . . . win the opportunity to work." Robert S. Lynd, "Memorandum on Work of Twentieth Century Fund's Committee on the Relation of Government to Labor" (December 15, 1934), in Leiserson Papers, Boxes 40–41. In response to Lynd's suggestions, Slichter retorted that "in many industries labor had so much power that it could 'ruin the industry,'" and urged the committee to reject Lynd's proffered approach. (Twentieth Century Fund Committee, Minutes of the Second Meeting [December 14, 1934], in ibid.) Three weeks later, Lynd resigned.

33. Twentieth Century Fund Committee, Minutes of the Fifth Meeting (February 16, 1935), in Leiserson Papers, Boxes 40–41. "Dr. Slichter said he thought the big thing would be for the President himself to get the credit for bringing the two sides together. Nothing, he said, could do more to improve business sentiment and to help the general process of recovery. . . . [He] suggested that nothing be done until after the introduction and discussion of the Wagner bill, that the committee then approach the President and suggest the possibility of his getting the two sides together and getting the credit for it."

34. Twentieth Century Fund Committee, "Recommendations" (February 22, 1935), in Leiserson Papers, Boxes 40–41.

35. Twentieth Century Fund Committee, "Memorandum of Findings and Recommendations" (March 20, 1935), In Leiserson Papers, Boxes 40–41.

36. Ibid. Describing the committee's recommendations to the Senate Committee on Education and Labor, William H. Davis went to some lengths to emphasize that the "Federal Labor Commission," although otherwise modeled on the Federal Trade Commission, would not enjoy any of the initiating or investigatory powers claimed by the latter, but would be confined to rulings on matters brought before it by the parties. *Hearings on S 1958*, pp. 707–9.

37. The Wagner bill reads: "Employees shall have the right to self-organization, to form, join, or assist labor organizations, to bargain collectively through representatives of their own choosing, and to engage in concerted activities, for the purpose of collective bargaining or other mutual aid or protection." In contrast, the Twentieth Century Fund Committee defined employee rights as follows. "The right of the employees to full freedom of association, self-organization, and designation of representatives of their own choosing for collective bargaining with their employers is hereby recognized and affirmed. It shall be the duty of the Commission to foster that right and to encourage collective bargaining."

38. Section 10(a) of the Wagner Act reads: "The Board is empowered, as hereinafter provided, to prevent any person from engaging in any unfair labor practice (listed in section 8) affecting commerce. This power shall be exclusive, and shall not be affected by any other means of adjustment or prevention that has been or may be established by agreement, code, law, or otherwise." Compare the Twentieth Century Fund Committee's section 10(a): "The Commission is empowered, as hereinafter provided, to issue a cease and desist order to prevent any person from engaging in any unfair labor practice (listed in section 8) affecting commerce. The power to issue such cease and desist orders shall be vested exclusively in the Commission: *Provided,* That nothing in this section shall limit the jurisdiction of the several district courts of the United States, as provided in section 11."

    The committee's version would thus have allowed courts to adjudicate unfair labor practice disputes. As we have seen, among the passages on unfair labor practices in the committee's amendments were provisions restraining "anyone" from interfering with an employee's exercise of section 7 rights, and "either party" from "violat[ing] or fail[ing] to observe any condition" of a collective bargaining agreement registered with the Commission.

39. Leiserson to Stanley Mathewson (September 27, 1935), in Leiserson Papers, Boxes 40–41.

40. In 1960, however, Leon Keyserling revealed that "the head of one powerful union" pressed William Connery, the chairman of the House Committee on Labor, to withhold support from the bill, and further that "some of the older types of craft unions, fearful of the effect of some of the provisions of the bill upon the structure of their organizations, did not lend it their support and may even have worked against it." Keyserling, "The Wagner Act," p. 207.

41. Irving Bernstein, *The New Deal Collective Bargaining Policy* (Berkeley: University of California Press, 1950), p. 126.

42. 7 NLRB 1002 (1938).

43. Informal File R-638, *Shipowners' Association of the Pacific Coast,* in Record Group 25, *Records of the National Labor Relations Board* (National Archives and Records Service, Washington, D.C.).

44. Ibid.

45. *Legislative History of the NLRA*, p. 2311.

46. National Labor Relations Board Memorandum, "Invalidation of Contracts," in Wagner Papers (Georgetown University, Washington, D.C.), Labor Files 706–19.

47. Ibid. For examples of the impact of this policy, see *National Electric Products Corporation*, 3 NLRB 475 (1937); *Consolidated Edison Company*, 4 NLRB 71 (1937).

48. Testimony of Joseph A. Padway, in U.S. Congress, House Committee on Labor, *Hearings on Proposed Amendments to the Nation Labor Relations Act*, 76th Cong., 1st sess., June 14, 1939, pp. 753–81, *passim*.

49. James A. Gross, *The Reshaping of the National Labor Relations Board: National Labor Policy in Transition, 1937–47* (Albany: State University of New York Press, 1981), p. 89.

50. Leiserson to John R. Commons (September 9, 1939), in Leiserson Papers, Box 9.

51. See, for example, Leiserson's opinions in *American Can Company*, 13 NLRB 1252 (1939), and *Milton Bradley Company*, 15 NLRB 938 (1939).

52. *American Can Company*, 13 NLRB 1252 (1939), p. 1258.

53. Ibid., p. 1260.

54. The difference, stated in the broadest possible terms, was between a position that took seriously the act's commitment to the achievement of an equality of bargaining *power* and saw section 9 as the key to that commitment, and a position that held, as William H. Davis put it in his testimony before the Senate Committee on Education and Labor in 1935, that the equality mooted in the act was not an equality of power between employees and employers but an equality of opportunity to be represented in collective bargaining. "You cannot get strong, outright, friendly cooperation, unless you have equal parties on the two sides of the table. *By that we mean equally free to represent the people they are there to talk for.*" *Hearings on S 1958*, p. 713 (emphasis added). Davis also here expresses the pluralist view that the union is the party principal on the labor side, and that the significance of section 9 resides primarily in its provision of a channel through which employee consent to union decisions might be obtained.

55. See, for example, Edwin Smith's comments on the course of Board policy since Leiserson's appointment contained in his dissent to the majority decision in *Libbey-Owens-Ford Glass Company*, 31 NLRB 243 (1941).

56. Leiserson to John R. Commons (November 22, 1940), in Leiserson Papers, Box 9.

57. Gross, *The Reshaping of the National Labor Relations Board*, pp. 232–40; Nelson Lichtenstein, *Labor's War at Home: The CIO in World War Two* (Cambridge: Cambridge University Press, 1982), pp. 8–25.

58. Harry A. Millis and Emily Clark Brown, *From the Wagner Act to Taft-Hartley: A Study of National Labor Policy and Labor Relations* (Chicago: University of Chicago Press, 1950), p. 52.

59. Philip Selznick, *Law, Society and Industrial Justice* (New York: Transaction Books, 1969), p. 139.

60. Millis and Brown, *From the Wagner Act to Taft-Hartley*, p. 673. And see pp. 669–77, *passim*. The contribution historical analysis might make to a critique of the pluralist paradigm in industrial relations theory and practice is canvassed by Robert H. Zieger in a short but suggestive essay, "Industrial Relations and Labor History in the 1980s," *Industrial Relations*, Vol. 22, No. 1 (Winter 1983), pp. 58–70. My own attempt at such a critique has received its fullest development in *The State and the Unions: Labor Relations, Law, and the Organized Labor Movement in America, 1880–1960* (Cambridge: Cambridge University Press, 1985).

INDEX